To Leonard W. Blake

with appreciation for your many years of loyal support and hard work for the Missouri Archaeological Society and for the preservation of Missouri's past.

Carl H. Chapman
Eleanor F. Chapman

October 5, 1975

The Archaeology of Missouri, I

University of Missouri Studies LXII

The Archaeology of Missouri, I

By Carl H. Chapman

Illustrations by Eleanor F. Chapman

University of Missouri Press
Columbia, Missouri
1975

ISBN 0–8262–0160–1

Copyright © 1975 by The Curators of the University of Missouri

University of Missouri Press, Columbia, Missouri 65201

Library of Congress Catalog Number 73–92242

Printed and bound in the United States of America

Preface

It is not really possible to acknowledge individually all those who have aided in one form or another the compilation of the information on the archaeology of Missouri. The assistance and cooperation of hundreds of students and Missouri Archaeological Society members have furnished much of the basis for the book and is greatly appreciated.

The University of Missouri Research Council made it possible through a Summer Research Fellowship to get a start on the project by furnishing the financing for travel and equipment necessary to obtain many of the photographs that have been used as illustrations.

My wife Eleanor has prepared most of the drawings and some of the photographs included as illustrations. Furthermore, without her proofreading, helpful criticisms, and pertinent questions the text would have been much less readable.

David R. Evans, Director of the Archaeological Survey of Missouri, shares equally in the development of the locality divisions that have been used in the book. The locality-region approach is now being used in the Archaeological Survey of Missouri by the University of Missouri and the Missouri Archaeological Society.

The fine work of the Technical Education Services at the University of Missouri—Columbia on the preparation of some of the photographic prints used in the illustrations, and especially the advice of Harvey Rathert, Russ Nall, Paul Dunard, and Ron Marquette are appreciated.

Thanks are especially due the following who furnished collections for study and illustration or who furnished photographs and data for illustration: Leo Anderson, Kenneth Barrow, Robert Benson, Leonard W. Blake, Richard S. Brownlee, Harryette Campbell, Mr. and Mrs. Harry L. Collins, S. P. Dalton, Mr. and Mrs. W. L. Davidson, J. Allen Eichenberger, Mr. and Mrs. Henry W. Hamilton, Jean Hon, Lyle Jeffries, Sam G. Jones, Paul Corbin, Mr. and Mrs. Clarence Kelley, Clair Kucera, J. J. McKinny, Merle N. Millard, Jean Moodie, George W. Nichols, Charles Orr, John Rinaldo, Ralph Roberts, Garrison E. Rose, Edward A. Scheib, Paul V. Sellers, J. Mett Shippee, John W. Taylor, Floyd Vavak, Jeanette White, J. R. Williams, Fred Winfrey, Carl Woolfolf, and Edward Zimmerman.

Richard Turner supplied the drawing for one of the illustrations. W. Raymond Wood read the manuscript and offered helpful suggestions. R. Bruce McMillan read a portion of the manuscript, furnished one of the illustrations and specimens to be used in others. The task of typing the manuscript has been an arduous one accomplished primarily by Dele Doke but shared by Sherry Brown and Loretta Welch.

Others who have been helpful in furnishing information and aid are: James Baker, Robert T. Bray, Mr. and Mrs. T. M. Hamilton, Dale R. Henning, Charles M. Keller, Walter E. Klippel, W. L. Logan, Kerry McGrath, Richard A. Marshall, Rolland E. Pangborn, Clarence Scrivner, Robert Seelen, George U. Shelby, and Tom Witty.

C. H. C.
Columbia, Missouri
December 1973

Contents

Illustrations

The Archaeology of Missouri, I

1. An Introduction

Thousands of pages have been written on the archaeology of Missouri, but there is no one place where this information is readily available. Although a general description of the lifeways of Indians that lived in the state from the time they first discovered it until the arrival of Europeans has been given in the handbook, *Indians and Archaeology of Missouri* (Chapman and Chapman 1964), it necessarily did not include the detailed information and references ordinarily a part of archaeological reports. This study presents that information. It is proposed as a foundation for continued studies, to be expanded, changed, or updated as new data occur or as different interpretations are imposed on the old data. It concerns the inhabitants of Missouri and adjacent related regions from the earliest settlers until approximately 1000 B.C. It is organized along the general lines of the broad interpretations of archaeology of the Eastern United States.

Physical Environment of Missouri

In any study of mankind, it is important to consider the environment in which a society exists. The natural environment provides the basic materials and the alternatives for furnishing food, clothing, and shelter. Rocks, minerals, soils, animals, plants, weather, climate, and topography are all important factors in cultural development. The environment affects both the physiological and psychological aspects of life. Therefore it is important to know the characteristics of the physiographic provinces in Missouri in order to study the archaeology of the state.

There is no absolute agreement on the manner in which Missouri should be divided physiographically, but the state is generally included in the following divisions: the northern and west-ern part in Central Lowland or Interior Plain, the southern central part in the Ozark Plateau, and the southeastern corner in the Coastal Plain. Subdivisions are the Till Prairies and dissected Loess Covered Till Prairies of northern Missouri, the Springfield-Salem Plateau and the Boston Mountains in the south-central area, the Mississippi Alluvial Basin in the southeast, and the Cherokee Plains overlapping with the Springfield Plateau along the western edge of the state (Atwood 1940; Branson 1944; Fenneman 1938; Raiz 1957) (Figure 1–1). In general the respective physiographic subdivisions might be expected to have somewhat different cultural growths within them.

In an earlier compilation of the archaeology of Missouri (Chapman 1946: 8–14), the state was divided into the physiographic subareas of Northern Prairie, Western Prairie, Ozark Highland, and Southeast Lowland. Although there was cognizance of variation in cultural developments in different parts of the state and certain areas tended to be relatively distinct, there was much overlapping of cultural chronologies and a general interpretation was made on the basis of three main geographical areas, the Northern, Southwestern, and Southeastern (Chapman 1948b: 146–55).

On the basis of archaeological work during the past twenty-five years, archaeological description and interpretation have been organized in six general physiographic subdivisions designated as regions: (1) Southwest Drainage; (2) Western Prairie; (3) Ozark Highland; (4) Northwest Prairie; (5) Northeast Prairie; (6) Southeast Riverine (Figure 1–2).

A new approach to the study of patterns of prehistoric settlement has been employed in conducting the Archaeological Survey of Missouri.

Each of the regions was subdivided into stream drainages, which have been designated as localities. The regions and their localities do not have in reality the clearly defined borders shown on the accompanying maps (Figures 1–2, 1–3). They are perhaps more precise in that divides between

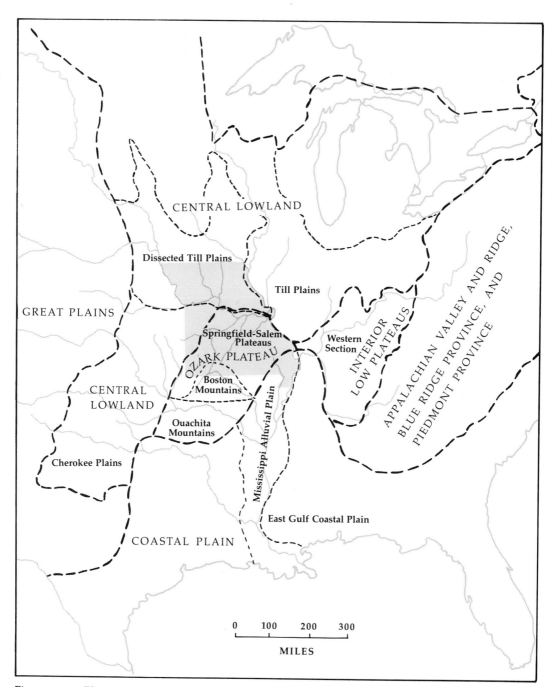

Figure 1–1. Physiographic provinces in the lower Missouri–central Mississippi Valley

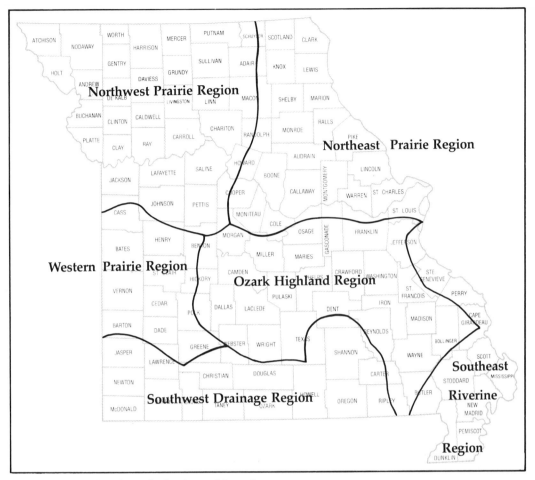

Figure 1–2. Archaeological–physiographic regions.

the different drainages have been used to separate one locality from another. Where major streams join, the basin of the larger stream has been used to define the borders of a locality. For example, the Lower Missouri Valley II Locality includes within its borders the lower reaches of the Osage and Gasconade rivers. It also encompasses the full length of such streams as the Moniteau, Moreau, Bonne Femme, Perche, Cedar, Auxvasse, and Loutre. The regions as they are used here are geographical units that have in common certain physical, biotic, and archaeological characteristics that make them relatively distinct from other regions surrounding them.

Physical characteristics deemed of greatest significance for defining the regions are spatial (geographical location—latitude and longitude), climatic, topographical, and geological. The most important biotic traits are the flora and fauna that existed prior to the introduction of Old World species. Settlement patterns and cultural developments were considered to be important criteria for defining the regions. The practicality of this approach was based on the assumption that cultural adaptation would reflect the selection of available physical and biotic resources in a region. Cultures similar in subsistence level and adapting to a particular environment would tend

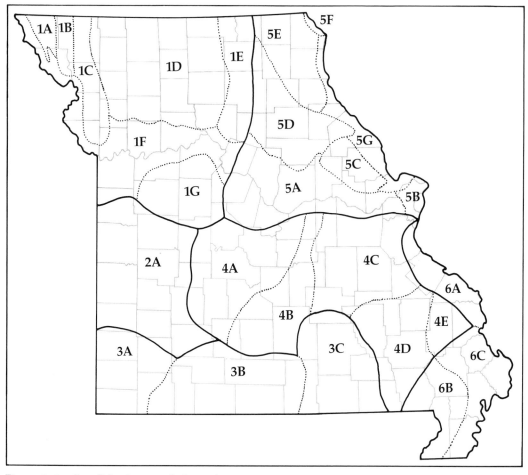

Figure 1–3. Localities (stream drainages).

Northwest Prairie Region: 1A Tarkio, 1B Nodaway, 1C Platte, 1D Grand, 1E Chariton, 1F Lower Missouri Valley I, 1G Lamine.

Western Prairie Region: 2A Upper Osage.

Southwest Drainage Region: 3A Neosho, 3B White, 3C Current–Eleven Point.

Ozark Highland Region: 4A Lower Osage, 4B Gasconade, 4C Meramec, 4D Upper Black–St. Francis, 4E Castor–Whitewater.

Northeast Prairie Region: 5A Lower Missouri Valley II, 5B Greater St. Louis, 5C Cuivre, 5D Salt, 5E Wyaconda–Fabius, 5F Des Moines, 5G Mississippi Valley North.

Southeast Riverine Region: 6A Mississippi Valley Central, 6B St. Francis Riverine, 6C Bootheel Riverine.

to have similar settlement systems. Furthermore the cultures within a specific environment would be likely to develop somewhat differently from those in a different environment. Therefore, the spatial distribution of the combination of physical, biotic, and archaeological (human) characteristics over the landscape within a relatively cohesive area is the basis for the definition of regions. The borders of the regions proposed in this work are in no sense absolute. They are open to redefinition as more complete information becomes available.

Extremes of temperature, amounts and times of precipitation, topography, and soils are variables that potentially affect the character, establishment, and movement of biotic communities. Biotic communities consist not only of plants but also of animals and the interrelationship of both. The floral-faunal symbiotic relationship or interaction of the physical habitat and the biotic community forms the *ecosystem* (Shelford 1963: 1–3), which in turn interacts with the cultural system in the region. Ideally the interaction of physical, biotic, and cultural systems reaches adjustment. The cultural adjustment to the ecosystem, or *cultural adaptation,* is of special interest both from the standpoint of the limitations imposed on the cultural system by the natural environment and the changes made in the ecosystem by the culture (Odum 1971: 511). Ecological-archaeological studies are in a sense basic to most archaeological work and are a necessary means of understanding past cultural developments. Ecological-archaeological studies in localities and regions should form the base for all archaeological interpretations in the future and are absolutely necessary if boundaries of localities and regions are to be determined with any precision.

The physical features of geographical location, geological formations, topography, soils, and climate have always been the basic factors dictating the use of Missouri's resources and were important criteria for defining regions and localities. In ecological terms an area of surface with its physical features could be defined as a *habitat.* Perhaps a more important consideration in regard to human use of Missouri in the past is the distribution of biota (plants and animals) in the state.

Plant distributions will be emphasized in describing the biota for the state and for each region because vegetation appears to be a prime factor in establishing the nature of the association of plants and animals, or the *biotic community* (Odum 1971: 140–41). All criteria used in defining the regions have been described briefly and summarized in maps (Figures 1–1 through 1–10).

The geographical position of Missouri in relation to the North American continental mass and to the central major stream drainages is considered to be important in relation to climate, geological resources, soil, vegetation, animal life, human settlement systems, and potential routes of travel and contact by early inhabitants (Figure 1–1).

Collier (1955a: 379–80) considered both physical and modern cultural features when he divided Missouri into four geographic provinces, Western Old Plains, Ozark Highland, Northern Glaciated Plains, and Southeastern Lowlands. In order to emphasize the smaller units or subregions, he (Collier 1955a: 381) referred to the larger units as provinces and the smaller as regions. His regions (Collier 1955a: Figure 12) in some instances compare favorably with localities and in others with the regions that are used here.

In a later publication Collier (1959) changed the names of his regions to Northern Plains, Western Plains, Ozark Highland, and Southeast Lowland "areas," which were divided into 17 subdivisions (Figure 1–4). Although his areas and subdivisions were based on the manner in which they are used in the twentieth century, there are striking correspondences with usage in past archaeological periods in the same general regions.

The geology of Missouri has had its effect on topography, soil formations, water, mineral resources, and availability of natural shelter such as caves and overhanging rocks (Figure 1–5). Glaciation of the northern half of the state resulted in the relatively level plains and the north to south pattern of stream drainage. A great variety of stones and minerals not native to the area, carried from the far north, was available in the glacial moraine deposits. The Ozark uplift in the south-central part of the state has provided a

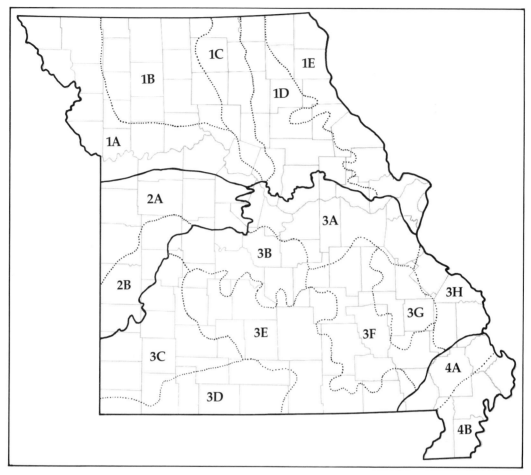

Figure 1–4.   Geographic areas.

Northern Plains: 1A Loess Hills, 1B Grand River Hills, 1C Chariton River Hills, 1D Audrain Prairies, 1E Mississippi River Hills.

Western Plains: 2A Osage Plains, 2B Cherokee Plains.

Ozark Highland: 3A Northern Ozark Border, 3B Osage–Gasconade Hills, 3C Springfield Plain, 3D White River Hills, 3E Central Ozark Plateau, 3F Courtois Hills, 3G St. Francois Knob and Basin Area, 3H Eastern Ozark Border.

Southeast Lowland: 4A Southeastern Ridges and Basins, 4B Southeastern Alluvial Lowlands.

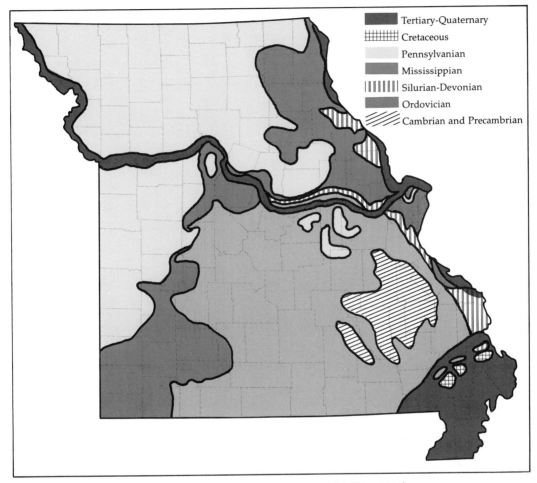

Figure 1–5. Geological formations (after Scrivner, Baker, and Miller 1966).

variety of igneous rocks such as granite and por-phyry in the heartland of the St. Francois Mountains. Surrounding this igneous core, old sedmimentary rock formations of dolomite and limestone containing large amounts of chert have made readily available cryptocrystalline hard stone, which could be fashioned easily into sharp tools and weapons. Throughout the Ozark Highland such stone is in every streambed, and outcrops are within easy walking distance. The Burlington limestone at the borders of the Ozark Highland contained chert or flint, which was in such demand by the Indians that a great deal of quarrying was carried on to obtain the stone, where it was near the surface. Extensive mining occurred in the old sink holes in the Ozark High-

land during aboriginal times for the red and yellow pigment in hematite and limonite, and red and yellow ochre that had formed there. Sandstone was used for milling stones and whetstones.

The leaching of limestone and dolomite by ground water caused solution cavities to develop into extensive caverns containing large underground streams, which surfaced in the Ozark Highland and produced some of the largest springs in the world. These caverns, where exposed by erosion, furnished shelter and thus became important storehouses of cultural records. Solution channels in St. Peters sandstone in central Missouri have produced similar shelters, for example Graham Cave. The western part of the

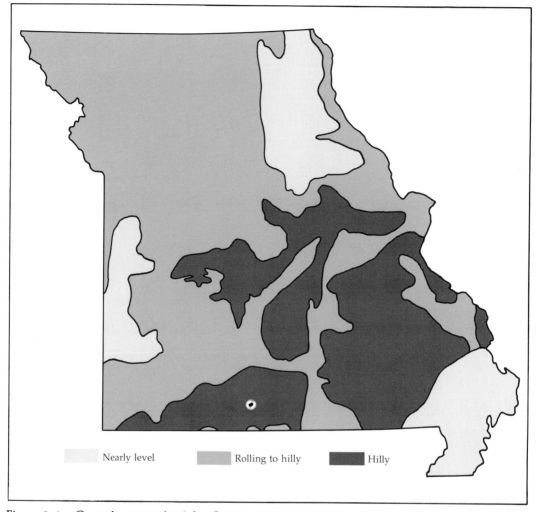

Figure 1–6.   General topography (after Scrivner, Baker, and Miller 1966).

state is set apart topographically from the rest of Missouri by an erosional feature called a peneplain, a flat plain with numerous isolated moundlike hills or erosional remnants. Rock formations include coal outcroppings on the surface. In the southeastern alluvial lowland of the Bootheel of Missouri, high ridges, like Crowley's Ridge, are capped with Mesozoic and Cenozoic deposits. Pleistocene glacial outwash and subsequent erosion were responsible for the various low ridges such as Sikeston Ridge. Glacial drift covers the northern half of the state (Figure 1–5).

The topography of the state aids in its separation into regions (Figure 1–6). Cozzens (1939:

Figure 1) shows Missouri divided into dissected till plains in the north, Osage plains on the west, Ozark plateaus in the south central to southwest, and Mississippi alluvial plain in the southeast. Although these general topographic regions are agreed upon by other authors (Branson 1944; Collier 1955b), subdivisions differ. A generalized relief map shows that elevation ranges from 200 to 400 feet in the southeast, and from 1600 to 1800 feet in the highland portion of the Ozark Plateau (Figure 1–6).

Soils in general differ with the topographic and geological areas of Missouri. They are dependent on the effects of elevation, slope, climate, rain-

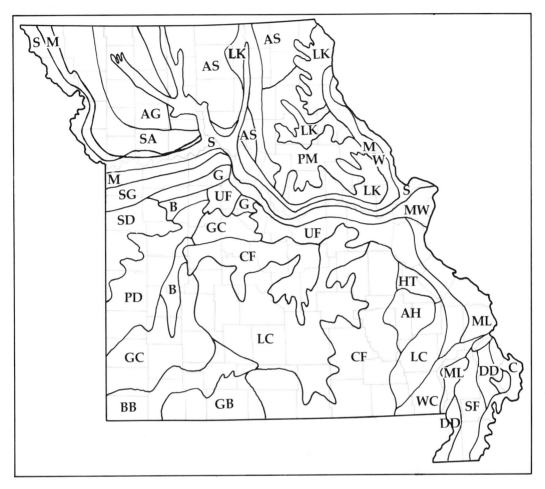

Figure 1–7.   Major soil areas (after Scrivner, Baker, and Miller 1966).

Northern Missouri Loess and Loess-till Landscapes
Prairie and Prairie-forest Transition Natural Vegetation: M, Marshall–Knox; SA, Sharpsburg–Grundy–Adair–
Shelby; SG, Sharpsburg–Grundy–Ladoga–Pershing; G, Grundy–Pershing; AG, Adair–Shelby–Grundy–
Lagonda; AS, Adair–Shelby–Seymour–Edina and Armstrong–Gara–Pershing; PM, Putnam–Mexico
Forest Natural Vegetation: MW, Menfro–Winfield–Weldon; LK, Lindley–Keswick–Hatton

Southern Missouri Residual and Loess-residual Landscapes
Prairie and Prairie-forest Transition Natural Vegetation: SD, Summit–Newtonia–Parson–Dennis; PD, Parsons–
Dennis–Bates; GC, Gerald–Craig–Eldon and Newtonia–Baxter
Forest Natural Vegetation: B, Bolivar–Mandeville; BB, Baxter–Bodine; GB, Gasconade–Bodine–Clarksville;
LC, Lebanon–Nixa–Clarksville and Hobson–Clarksville; CF, Clarksville–Fullerton–Talbott; AH,
Ashe–Tilsit–Hagerstown; HT, Hagerstown–Tilsit; UF, Union–Fullerton–McGirk; ML, Memphis–Loring

Alluvial Valley Landscapes
Missouri and Upper Mississippi Rivers: S, Sarpy–Haynie–Onawa–Wabash
Southeastern Missouri: C, Commerce–Hayti–Caruthersville; DD, Dexter–Dubbs–Dundee–Boskett; SF,
Sharkey–Alligator–Forrestdale; WC, Waverly–Calhoun

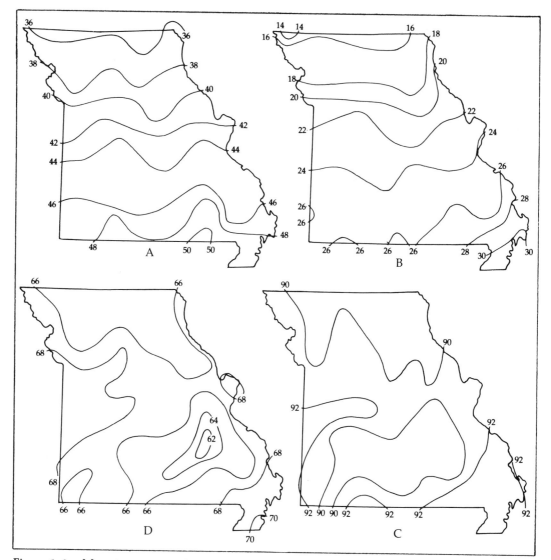

Figure 1–8.   Mean temperatures in winter and summer, 1931–1952.
A, Mean maximum temperature (°F) in January; B, mean minimum temperature (°F) in January; C, mean maximum temperature (°F) in July; D, mean minimum temperature (°F) in July.

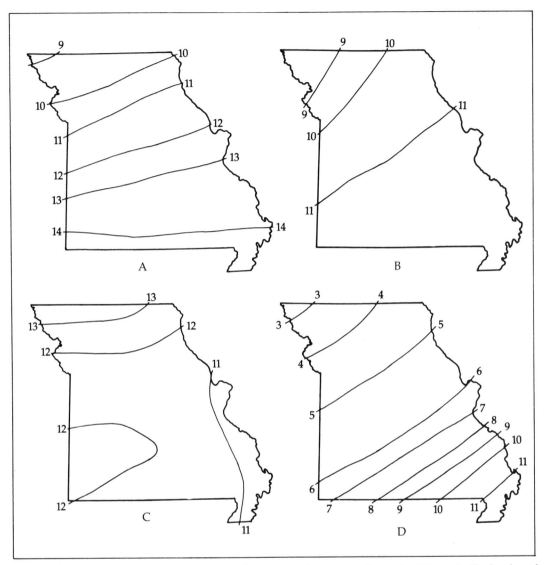

Figure 1–9.   Average precipitation (after Collier 1955b, from maps drawn by Wayne L. Decker based upon U.S. Weather Bureau data).
A, Spring; B, Autumn; C, Summer; D, Winter.

fall, and vegetative cover on the basic soil-forming materials. The northern part of Missouri has predominantly windblown, glacial till, and alluvial soils. The southeast has alluvial soils of great variety. The Ozark Plateau has soils formed on limestone and dolomite, most of which are cherty and low in fertility. The map shows the general distribution of major soil series and their associations in the state (Figure 1–7).

The climate of Missouri is midcontinental; the differences between extremes in temperature in winter and summer, respectively, range from 40 to 54 degrees. The map (Figure 1–8) shows the extremes in temperature in January and July (McQuigg 1959). The killing freezes begin between October 10 and 20 and end between April 15 and 20 throughout most of Missouri. These dates are quite different from those in the Southeast Lowland where the first freezes occur between October 25 and November 24 and the last between March 26 and April 10. The average frost-free period varies from 178 days in the north to 220 days in the extreme southeast (Collier 1955b: 26). Mean annual precipitation ranges from 34 inches in the extreme northwestern corner of the state to 47 inches in the extreme southeastern corner. The four maps (Figure 1–9) show the precipitation during the different seasons.

The vegetative cover of Missouri is as varied as the physical characteristics. Different physical habitats tend to support different biotic communities. Thus prairie vegetation occurs in the northern and western plains, hardwood forest in the bottomlands, and oak–hickory and oak–pine forest in the Ozark Highland. The map (Figure 1–10) shows the distribution of the general forest types and prairies (Collier 1955b: 16; Kucera 1961: 225–28; Scrivner, Baker, and Miller 1966). The northern and western parts of Missouri are a portion of the Prairie Peninsula as it has been defined by Transeau (1935). The shortleaf pine occurs in what were known as pineries in the Ozark Highland, and remnants of these forests are still there. Flatwoods and swamp vegetation are distinctive of the Southeast Riverine Region (Kucera 1961: 226–27).

Missouri lies primarily within the temperate deciduous forest or oak–deer–maple *biome,* a bi-

ome being the largest community including both plants and animals. Only a small part of the state is within the needle-grass–antelope or temperate-grass biome (Shelford 1963: 14) (Figure 1–10). The white oak, white-tailed deer, and turkey are important constituents of the oak–deer–maple biome. The wolf, mountain lion, elk (wapiti), and black bear were other important constituents that are gone now. Bison were once present but never in large numbers. Other important animals were and are the bobcat, gray fox, raccoon, fox squirrel, gray squirrel, eastern chipmunk, beaver, muskrat, white-footed mouse, pine vole, short-tailed shrew, blue jay, white-breasted nuthatch, owls, hawks, red-bellied, hairy, and downy woodpeckers, numerous song birds, lizards, box turtle, common garter snake, timber rattlesnake, and northern black racer.

The biome in Missouri can be divided into three deciduous forest regions: (1) oak–hickory, (2) mixed mesic tulip–oak, and (3) stream-skirting forest. Grassland occupies the remainder of the northern and western parts of the state.

Oak–hickory forests consist of white-oak-post-oak–hickory forests. An oak–shortleaf-pine combination occurs in the Ozark Highland. The largest population of turkeys existed in the oak–hickory forest, due to the edibility of post oak and blackjack oak acorns. The density of the turkey population is estimated to have been 22 per square mile. The opossum, striped skunk, ruffed grouse, copperhead snake, rat snake, and king snake were other animals important in the forests (Shelford 1963: 56–59).

Floodplain forest biotic communities in the Southeast Riverine of Missouri, the tulip–oak region, include several varieties of willows, cottonwoods, the scrub American elder, trumpet vine, grapevine, pepper vine, honey vine, and morning-glory vine. Mammals in the community include the swamp rabbit, opossum, raccoon, white-footed mouse, gray squirrel, deer, wapiti, and bison. There is a great variety of resident and migrant birds (Shelford 1963: 89–114).

The transition from grassland to deciduous forest is abrupt in moist regions. In this stream-skirting forest region, the assemblages of plants

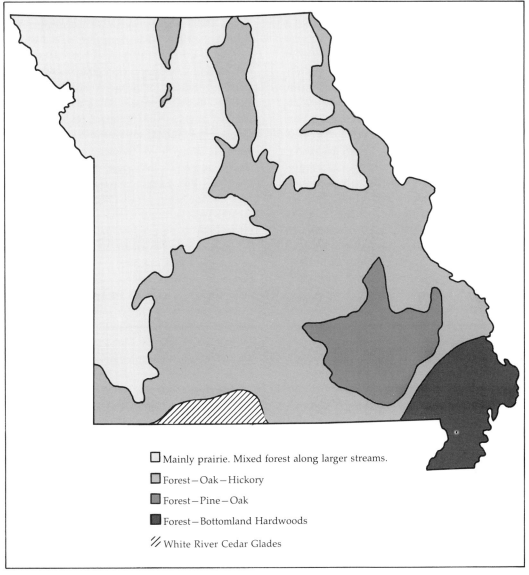

Figure 1–10.   Distribution of vegetation (after Kucera 1961).

and animals are different from those of either grassland or forest. The forest-edge communities are in a state of constant flux, concomitant with changes in climate. In general, trees consist of burr oak, pin oak, red oak, other oaks, butternut, hickories, black walnut, hackberry, slippery elm, ironwood, basswood, and maples. The pecan, though not a dominant species, may have been important to past cultural economies. Undergrowth includes honeysuckle, black raspberry, Virginia creeper, grape, and wild rose. Other important trees and shrubs are dogwood, persimmon, hawthorn, plum, crab apple, redbud, cherry, hazel, elder, pawpaw, and sumac. A few common plants, such as sunflower, goldenrod, wolfberry, and coralberry, are commonly found at the prairie-forest edge (Little 1971: Maps 99–E, 101–E, 114–E, 133–E; Shelford 1963: 306–17).

Forest-edge animals were black bear, turkey, white-tailed deer, gray fox, gray squirrel, cottontail, bobwhite, bison, wapiti, raccoon, red fox, coyote, striped and spotted skunks, ground squirrels, meadow jumping mouse, salamanders, lizards, crayfish, and a great variety of birds and insects (Shelford 1963: 313–17).

Tall grasses grow in the Northern Temperate Grassland where it extends into the northern and western sections of Missouri. The grasses are bluestem, Indian grass, wild rye, switchgrass, sloughgrass, bluepoint, porcupine grass, preupine grass, Junegrass, western wheatgrass, blue grama, buffalo grass, prairie dropseed, sideoats grama, plains mulky, hairy grama, and panic grass. Associated species are scurfy pea, common reed, broomweed, goldenrod, sunflower, ragweed, and soapweed (Kucera 1961: 226; Shelford 1963: 328–34). Mammals, birds, and reptiles of importance were bison, pronghorn, badger, white-tailed and black-tailed jack rabbits, cottontail, wapiti, deer, gray wolf, coyote, ground squirrels, meadow voles, hawks, prairie chicken, meadow lark, dickcissel, horned lark, and bull snake (Shelford 1963: 334–36).

Bones of mammals are often present in archaeological sites, and various types of habitats and plant communities can be identified by determining the type of mammal that lived in an area. Mammals that are distributed throughout the state are opossum, short-tailed shrew, least shrew, eastern mole, little brown bat, Keen's bat, silver-haired bat, eastern pipistrelle, big brown bat, red bat, hairy bat, evening bat, eastern cottontail rabbit, eastern chipmunk, eastern gray squirrel, eastern fox squirrel, southern flying squirrel, beaver, prairie white-footed mouse, woodland white-footed mouse, prairie meadow mouse, pine mouse, muskrat, red fox, gray fox, raccoon, long-tailed weasel, mink, spotted skunk, striped skunk, river otter, white-tailed deer, elk, and bison (Schwartz and Schwartz 1959). Those mammals that occur only in specific regions will be listed under the description of that region.

The preceding information has been of a general nature about the major regions of the temperate forest and northern temperate grassland biomes that encompass the state of Missouri. Another general biotic classification of North America by Dice (1943) should be mentioned. He defined *biotic province* as a broad geographical area over which the environmental complex was sufficiently uniform to permit the development of characteristic types of ecologic associations. Dice (1943: 4–23) noted three biotic provinces extending into Missouri: Illinoian, Carolinian, and Austroriparian.

In the Illinoian province the prairie and deciduous forest alternate and the dominant plants are moderately tall grasses. The upland prairie forest is dominated by oaks and hickories, and the flood plains and moist hillsides contain a richer forest of deciduous trees. The fauna includes many prairie animals that are completely independent of woody vegetation, but many animals in the deciduous forest follow the strips of timber along the valleys across the province bringing about a mixture of prairie and forest species. The Northeast Prairie, Northwest Prairie, and Western Prairie regions of Missouri lie within the province.

The Carolinean province takes in the Ozark Highland and the Southwest Drainage regions. Richly diversified hardwood forests are characteristic. Oak–hickory is the climax association in most of the part of the province that lies in Missouri, and pines are a subclimax.

The Austroriparian province encompasses the Southeast Riverine Region of Missouri. It contains many swamps and marshes and the forests are hardwoods differing from those of the Carolinian province. Gums and cypresses are dominant in the swamps; oaks, magnolias, and hickories are dominant in the uplands. No animals in the province hibernate in the winter, and many birds that breed in northern provinces winter there.

The foregoing has been a generalized description of some of the important physical and biotic data that should be considered in any regional classification. A brief description and discussion of the general characteristics of each region follows.

Summary Descriptions of Regions

The Southwest Drainage Region includes all of the White River drainage in Missouri and Arkansas to the junction of the White and Black rivers; on the west it encompasses the Neosho River drainage in Missouri, Arkansas, and Oklahoma. It is subdivided into the White, Current–Eleven Point, and Neosho localities. Branson (1944: 351–53) did not differentiate the White River drainage from the Ozark region topographically, but earlier Sauer (1920: Figure 18) placed all of the White River drainage except the upper reaches of James River and that of Eleven Point and Current rivers in a geographic subdivision he called White River Hills. Cozzens (1939: Figure 6) designated the same area as White River Hills Mixed Forest natural area and included the White River basin to the junction of Black River within it. He placed the Eleven Point–Current–Black River basins in a separate division that he called Pomme de Terre–Gasconade–White River Upland. It encompassed the headwaters of all of the streams mentioned in the name of the area. He described the central part of the White River Hills, designated *Southwest Drainage Region* here, as an area of "steep-sided hills carved from strata of high differential resistance by the White and James rivers." Relief was noted as mostly 500–600 feet (Cozzens 1939: 56–57). Valleys are deep, narrow, and closely spaced. Stream mean-

ders are entrenched. Slopes are steep and the soil is thin and stony (Collier 1959: 9). Slopes exceed 14 per cent over half the region, and 75 per cent of the area has slopes steeper than 5 per cent.

Forestland is predominant (Collier 1955a: 387), and the forest types are oak–shortleaf pine and oak–hickory (Collier 1955b: 16). Kucera (1961: 226), on a map showing vegetation in the state, designated the heart of the Southwest Drainage Region as White River Cedar Glades. He described this area as having distinctive glade prairies on dolomitic outcrops that have the usual prairie complement of grasses and herbs as well as arborescent species of scrubby form including Eastern red cedar, *Juniperus virginiana*.

Mammals possibly distinctive of the region are gray bat, Indiana bat, western and eastern lump-nosed bat, swamp rabbit, woodchuck, fulvous harvest mouse, brush mouse, golden mouse, common cotton rat, eastern wood rat, meadow jumping mouse, coyote, red wolf, black bear, badger, bobcat, puma, and possibly the nine-banded armadillo (Schwartz and Schwartz 1959).

The Western Prairie Region includes the Cherokee Plains west into Kansas and on to and including the drainage of the headwaters of the Neosho River, south to the junction of the Spring River, northeast following the divide between the Osage and Spring river drainages, north along the west side of the Pomme de Terre River, north along the east edge of the drainage of the Marais des Cygnes and west to encompass the headwaters of the Neosho River. In Missouri, it is made up of a single locality, the Upper Osage (Figure 1–3). Branson (1944: 352–55) called the region Old Plains because the only remnants of an older surface remain as moundlike or linear hills; the region as a whole is a relatively flat plain. Rock outcrops of shale, limestone, sandstone, coal, and fire clay, in that order, are Pennsylvanian in age (Branson 1944: 270). Cozzens (1939: 48) placed the region primarily within his Pennsylvanian–Permian geologic region and excluded it from his Ozark province. Sauer (1920: Figure 2) also excluded it from the Ozark Highland and placed the region mostly within the Coal Measures, consisting principally of shales and limestones. Soils are primarily silt loam (Oswego) and the fertility is generally lower than the glacial and loessial soils of the glaciated till plains of the Northeast Prairie and Northwest Prairie regions and of higher quality than those in the Ozark Highland (Collier 1955a: Figure 6; 1955b: 18–19). Collier divided the region into Osage Plains and Cherokee Plains, the former overlapping into the Ozark Highland Region. Part of Collier's Springfield Plain is also included in the Western Prairie Region (Collier 1955a: 385–87, Figure 12). The region has low relief and gentle slopes, and valleys are wide and shallow. Hills rise 100–200 feet above the usual level and are linear erosional remnants of some of the drainage divides or isolated conical hills. The northern part of the region is hillier than that of the south (Collier 1959: 20). Vegetative cover is tall-grass prairie with bottomland hardwoods in stream valleys (Collier 1955b: 16; Kucera 1961: 226).

Mammals with a restricted distribution in Missouri that occur in the region are the least bat, black-tailed jack rabbit, woodchuck, thirteen-lined ground squirrel, Franklin's ground squirrel, plains pocket gopher, western harvest mouse, common cotton rat, eastern wood rat, meadow jumping mouse, coyote, badger, and the southern lemming mouse in the northern and western part of the region. The black bear at one time lived in the wooded areas, and the pronghorn and possibly the nine-banded armadillo also had inhabited the area (Schwartz and Schwartz 1959).

The Ozark Highland Region starting south of the Missouri River on the north, includes the major stream drainages into the Mississippi on the east and into the Missouri River on the west and north. It is made up of the Castor–Whitewater, Upper Black–St. Francis, Lower Osage, Gasconade, and Meramec localities. The southeastern edge is bordered by the St. Francis River to the mouth of Black River where it empties into White River. A line drawn north and west from that point following the divide between the White River drainage, then north between the Lamine River and Osage River drainage to the Missouri River, forms the western boundary (Figure 1–2). More has been written on the Ozark Highland than any other region of Missouri

(Branson 1944; Collier 1953; 1955a; 1955b; Cozzens 1939; Sauer 1920). The region as it is defined here excludes the greater part of the Northern Ozark Border Region as defined by Collier (1953), the White River Hills, and all of the White River drainage including the Eleven Point and Current rivers, which are in effect tributaries of the White River, and the Spring River–Neosho River drainage system in the southwestern corner of Missouri. I have excluded these areas mainly on the basis of archaeological rather than physiographical considerations. As more information becomes available some revisions may be in order. Branson (1944: 351) noted that the "boundaries of the Ozark Region have not been agreed upon and before definite boundaries can be drawn it will be necessary to decide what constitutes the boundaries, and even after deciding what constitutes each boundary, all of them will be indefinite." Underlying rock formations have greatly influenced the character of the Ozark Highland as has the fact that it is an area that has continued to be uplifted but unevenly for millions of years, making it one of the oldest land surfaces in North America. The topography of the region is complex. The highest distinct hills in the Ozark Highland are in the southeastern part of the region in a unique area known as the St. Francois Mountains. This is the only part of the state where igneous rocks outcrop. This area has the highest elevation in the state. Hills have medium slopes and valleys are narrow at the bottom (Branson 1944: 351–53). Cozzens (1939: Figure 3) called this subdivision St. Francis Knob and Basin Region. Sauer (1920: 8–12) noted that the hills or knobs of igneous rock are elevated 500–843 feet above the surrounding plain, which is underlain with sedimentary rocks. The hills are mainly symmetrical cones with small summits. Soil is clay base, thin, and infertile. Streams cutting through the igneous rocks have very narrow channels. Whole valleys are sometimes not much wider than the stream channels and thus could be called gorges. The sedimentary rocks surrounding the St. Francois Mountains are predominantly cherty dolomitic limestone with limestone, sandstone, and shale well represented.

Surface chert is abundant. It is derived from massive formations or from nodules occurring in the dolomite or limestone deposits on which the soils formed. The divides between the streams may be sharp and narrow or broad and flat, making possible the development of prairies.

Sauer (1920: 5–6) characterized the Ozark Highland as (1) elevation generally higher than that of the surrounding regions; (2) greater relief; and (3) general accordance of summit levels. He pointed out that it was "an elevated peneplain, developed upon domed rocks, which are for the most part highly resistant to erosion."

The principal forms of vegetation in the Ozark Highland are upland forests and pine woods. There are small prairie areas between stream drainages where there are relatively flat divides. Some are sizeable areas in the northern and northwestern part of the region. Oak–hickory is the principal upland forest type, next being pine woods made up of shortleaf pine and mixed oak and pine stands (Kucera 1961: 226-27).

Native fauna of much interest to early settlers and the Indians before them consisted of bison, elk (wapiti), deer, bear, mountain lion (panther), wolf, bobcat, beaver, otter, muskrat, mink, raccoon, opossum, skunk, fox, gray squirrel, fox squirrel, cottontail, chipmunk, turkey, quail, and passenger pigeon (Sauer 1920: 59–60).

Mammals occurring but not restricted to the region were the gray bat, Indian bat, least bat, western lump-nosed bat, woodchuck, western harvest mouse, southern lemming mouse, meadow jumping mouse, coyote, black bear, badger, bobcat, and puma. The plains pocket gopher lived in the northern part and the golden mouse, common cotton rat, and eastern wood rat in the southern part of the region (Schwartz and Schwartz 1959).

Fish in the clear streams of the region were bass, walleyed pike, sunfish, stone cat, suckers, channel cat, bullhead cat, mud cat, buffalo, crappie, short-nosed gar, eel, and minnows (Sauer 1920: 60).

The Northwest Prairie Region includes all the drainage of the Nishnabotna, Tarkio, Nodaway, Platte, Fishing, Chariton, and north Grand rivers and the drainage of the Missouri River from Lincoln, Nebraska, to Topeka, Kansas, and east including the drainage of the Lamine River to the narrowing of the valley near Boonville, Missouri. The eastern divide of the Chariton River separates it from the Northwest Prairie Region. It has been subdivided into the following localities: Tarkio, Nodaway, Platte, Grand, Chariton, Lamine, and Lower Misouri Valley I.

The Northeast Prairie Region includes the Missouri River east of the Chariton and Lamine rivers and encompasses the drainage of the Mississippi River south of the Des Moines River to the junction of the Missouri River; major streams are the Des Moines, Wyaconda, Fabius, Salt, and Cuivre in Missouri, the Mississippi and the Illinois River in Illinois. Localities are the Lower Missouri Valley II, Greater St. Louis, Des Moines, Wyaconda-Fabius, Salt, Cuivre, Mississippi Valley North. The method of defining the borders of the Greater St. Louis Locality is not consistent with the other divisions but was made on the basis of the uniqueness of the locality at the junction of the Missouri and Mississippi rivers and the unusually fertile soils and wide valley at the American Bottoms.

The boundaries of the Northeast Prairie and Northwest Prairie regions were determined more by location than topography, climate, geology, or vegetation. The Northeast Prairie Region seems to tie more closely with the Mississippi River drainage and to the cultural developments to the northeast whereas the Northwest Prairie Region relates more closely with the Missouri River basin and the cultural developments to the northwest. Topographically, geologically, and biotically, both are defined as a single region by geographers, geologists, and botanists. Collier (1955a: 380; 1959) referred to it as the Northern Plains; Branson (1944: 355, Figure 45) as the Old Plains modified by glaciation; and Steyermark (1963: xxii) as the Glaciated Prairie or Dissected Till Plains.

The major physical differences between the Northeast Prairie and Northwest Prairie regions are the drainage patterns and the types of soil and vegetation. In the Northeast Prairie, Putnam–Mexico and Lindley–Keswick–Hatton soil series are predominant, followed by Menfro–Winfield–Weldon, Adair–Shelby–Seymour–Edina and Armstrong–Gara–Pershing. The latter soil associations are more prominently in the Northwest Prairie Region where their distribution is nearly equalled by Adair–Shelby–Grundy–Lagonda to the west and farther west by Sharpsburg–Grundy–Adair–Shelby followed by Marshall–Knox (Scrivner, Baker, and Miller 1966: 6, 9, 11–18). There are also differences in the vegetation as reported by King, Roberts, and Winters (1949: 11). The prairie predominated over forest land in the Northwest Prairie Region, and the forest types were bottomland hardwood and prairie oak–hickory. In the Northeast Prairie Region the oak–hickory forest type, which is similar to the one in the Ozark Highland, predominates over bottomland hardwoods and almost equals the prairie in distribution. The forest distribution along Chariton River coincides with that in the Northeast Prairie Region, and this fact should be taken into consideration in any revision of the northern prairie regions in the future. Another consideration is that it might be possible to extend the Ozark Highland Region farther north to encompass the southern border of the Northeast Prairie Region. Collier (1953) combined the two areas and called them the Northern Ozark Border Region. Steyermark (1963: xix) included this area in the Ozark Highland because the growth of Ozark flora extends north of the Missouri River and up the Mississippi halfway to the Iowa border and as far southwest as Howard County. Sauer (1920: Figure 1) also drew the northern limits of the Ozark Highland to encompass the Lower Missouri Valley II Locality, which is included here in the Northeast Prairie Region. No matter with which region this locality is placed, the Northeast Prairie or with the Ozark Highland, it is significant that there is a great deal of agreement that the topography, soils, and vegetation of the locality make it relatively distinct and that it can be separated from other adjoining localities. Collier (1953) pointed out that the locality was not typical of the upland as a whole and was of intermediate character between the more rugged interior of the Ozark

Highland and the dissected till plains to the north.

Mammals that occur in both the Northeast Prairie and Northwest Prairie regions in wooded areas are the least bat, woodchuck, thirteen-lined ground squirrel, Franklin's ground squirrel, plains pocket gopher, western harvest mouse, southern lemming mouse, meadow jumping mouse, coyote, badger, and black bear. White-tailed jack rabbit and pronghorn were found in the Northwest Prairie only (Schwartz and Schwartz 1959).

The Southeast Riverine Region includes the alluvial valley of the St. Francis to Black River on the west and from the mouth of Black River to the mouth of the St. Francis on the south. Its eastern border extends north beyond Memphis and follows the drainage of the Mississippi to the mouth of the Missouri River. The highlands of the Ozark Plateau form the northern and western border. It is subdivided into the Mississippi Valley Central Locality, which extends from the mouth of the Missouri River to Cape Girardeau, Missouri, and encompasses the drainage of the Mississippi River between those two points. The region south of Cape Girardeau is divided into the St. Francis Riverine and Bootheel Riverine localities. The divide between the St. Francis and the Mississippi river drainages separates the localities.

There appears to be close agreement by various scholars that the Southeast Riverine Region is quite distinct topographically, geologically, and in other physical characteristics. The Southeast Riverine Region is the only place in Missouri where there are Cretaceous (of Mesozoic age) and Tertiary (of Cenozoic age) outcrops (Branson 1944: 329–36). The soils differ in the three localities making up the region with the greatest variety in the Bootheel Riverine Locality. Those soils in the other localities are similar in part; the loessial Memphis–Loring association is dominant (Scrivner, Baker, and Miller 1966: 4, 29). Topographically the region is low and nearly flat except for a few ridges running northeast-southwest that divide the lowlands into several parallel areas approximately east to west. An example is Crowley's Ridge. In the past much of the lowland was so low that it was swamp, and a great deal of it was annually subject to overflow from the Mississippi and St. Francis rivers.

The heights of the ridges range from 50 to 200 feet, and the width is as great as 20 miles, but there are also low sand ridges only 10–20 feet higher than the surrounding lowland. Sikeston Ridge is an example and is approximately 3 miles wide and 28 miles long (Collier 1959: 22–26).

The type of vegetation in the Southeast Riverine Region is distinctive and, although classed in general as bottomland hardwoods (Collier 1955b: 16), was noted as flatwoods swamp with some upland forest on the higher ridges by Kucera (1961: 226–27). The flatwoods and swamp vegetation that are dominant here but not elsewhere are bald cypress, tupelo, sweet gum, and overcup oak. The American beech and holly grow on Crowley's Ridge. The swamps and ridges of the region provided habitats for a great variety of animals and plants and vast quantities of fish and waterfowl.

Mammals of the region that have restricted distribution in the rest of the state are the gray bat, Indiana bat, eastern lump-nosed bat, swamp rabbit, western harvest mouse, golden mouse, common cotton rat, southern lemming mouse, red wolf, bobcat, puma, black bear, and possibly the southeastern shrew (Schwartz and Schwartz 1959).

The preceding brief summaries of regions were included to point out major congruences and differences in physical and biotic resources of regions in the state. The information is not sufficiently detailed to be used for locality studies except as a guide to general sources. There is a need for compilation of basic data on the physical, biotic, and archaeological information on any locality before archaeological investigations are conducted within it. In most instances it will be necessary to obtain the information from state and local archival materials, such as the original land survey records in the Department of State Archives in Jefferson City, the Western Historical Manuscripts Collection of the State Historical Society and University of Missouri and their libraries at Columbia, and the Missouri Historical Society Archives in St. Louis.

There is evidence of a certain amount of cultural homogeneity in each region, but full information on the cultural history in each is not as yet available. The regions should be useful units for broad comparative purposes. They are in no sense final and should be reviewed when more information has been compiled. The locality must be the subdivision used for specific studies.

Ethnography, Archaeology, and Environment

Ethnographically and archaeologically, Missouri has always been difficult to categorize. Mason (1896; 1912: 428) divided the state into two major environmental or ethnic areas. They were the Plains and the Mississippi Valley, and their boundaries were defined by the manner in which plants and animals were distributed as well as by the Indian tribes that lived there. Wissler (1938) placed the state in the Bison area and the Eastern Maize area, a division similar to that of Mason. On the basis of the distribution of Indian tribes and their cultures he further divided the state into Plains, Eastern Woodland, and Southeastern areas. Kroeber (1939) on the basis of physiographic and cultural characteristics, divided the Plains area of North America into four parts archaeologically and two areas ethnographically. His Plains area did not extend as far east as Missouri. Much of the state was included in a Southern Prairie or Central Siouan subarea in which the Missouri Indian tribe was placed.

The Illinois tribes were included in Kroeber's Ohio Valley subarea, and the Illinois lived west of the Mississippi in Missouri part of the time, so there is an overlap of the Ohio Valley subarea into the state. The Southeast area overlaps into southeastern Missouri physiographically, and if the Quapaw Indians were to be included in that area, it would substantiate the inclusion of the Bootheel of Missouri in Kroeber's Southeast subarea. Finally, the placing of the Osage tribe primarily in the Red River subarea suggests the overlapping of the Caddoan culture into southwestern Missouri. Kroeber then noted the possibility of dividing Missouri into four subareas, Red River, Southern Prairie, Ohio Valley, and

Southeast, on the basis of ethnographic and physiographic data. He pointed out that in this over-all area, there is much uncertainty in the placement of several of the ethnographic cultures such as the Osage and Quapaw-Arkansas.

Driver (1961: 16, Map 2) placed the Missouri Indian tribe wholly within his Prairies area. He distinguished them as follows:

> These Indians were very much like those of the Plains except that they farmed and lived in permanent villages near their farms part of the year. Most of them also hunted the buffalo as well as other animals.

Driver and Massey (1957: 173) defined the Prairies area as follows:

> This area is located in the Middle West from about the hundredth meridian to the Appalachians in a west-east direction, and from northern Minnesota to southern Texas on a north-south axis. Although all of these tribes farmed, most of them depended more on hunting. They resided in villages during the farming season but roamed in hunting bands the greater part of the year. Their culture is probably more similar to that of the Plains than to any other culture area, because much of Plains culture stemmed directly from that of the Prairies. Nevertheless, the Prairie area also shows many ties with the East and appears to be culturally transitional between the two.

Ethnographical and archaeological data are not always comparable. The ethnologist tends to deal with the symbolism of language and needs the living, participating members of the society as his informants. He deals with symbols and ideas synthesized by individuals taking part in the culture.

The archaeologist often must deal with artifacts and their interrelationships with other artifacts and physical remains more nearly related to the natural environment than to the ideas and institutions that sponsored them. Artifacts may reflect only broad categories of culture and the means by which the environment was used in providing sustenance and protection and in maintaining social and philosophical institutions. The greatest emphasis in cultural development is not always reflected in the nonperishable artifacts, even in the realm of technology. Items

such as feather robes, baskets, wooden bowls, and bows might have had few if any solid clues residual in a village site that would be available for excavation by the archaeologist. Ceremonies may have been an important part of society in a hunting–gathering economy, yet leave no artifactual remains of a nonperishable nature as evidence. Even the efficiency or the effectiveness of the tools that were used is not always reflected in the artifacts themselves.

Archaeologists must necessarily emphasize artifacts in their research because they are the prominent residues of past cultures. This fact need not detract from the basic purpose of archaeology, which is the reconstruction of past culture, society or history; the study of mankind's development of culture in relation to natural and cultural environment; the explanation of cultural change and process. In the past the classification and manipulation of the objects in series, statistically or in other ways, to show their relationships to each other and to groups of objects preceding them or following them has been put ostensibly on a scientific plane. Likenesses have been interpreted as cultural or historical relationships and for example, the history of cultural developments extending over several centuries has been predicated on the basis of changes in the techniques and decoration of pottery vessels. Artifacts have been used to interpret social relationships, division of labor, status, and ceremonial activities. Cultural change and process have been interpreted on the basis of artifacts. These interpretations should be considered as hypotheses or assumptions and should be tested fully by the use of the best available historical sources and comparable artifacts.

Archaeological Investigations

Few archaeological investigations have been conducted with the planning and intent of the complete reconstruction of the culture or way of life of the people who left the remains at the site. Research strategies have been aimed at a description of the distribution of archaeological remains and the answers to certain fundamental questions: Who were the people who produced the remains in terms of complexes of artifacts or measurements of human bones? When did they live? Where did they live? What was their pattern of settlement? Who preceded and who followed them? How did their artifacts relate to those of other people? How did their culture change? What caused them to maintain the status quo or to change? How did they adjust to their environment? What was the full extent and range of their activities throughout the year? What was the population density? What was the total population in each village and community? What was their social structure and how did they relate to other people occupying the same general area? Seldom are there more than a few of the questions asked in the research project and the answers have been fewer yet. In fact, seldom does the archaeologist have the financing, time, or trained personnel to conduct an investigation that will answer all the questions that should be asked. Yet, only through investigations that produce information on all aspects of particular cultures will it ever be possible to interpret past culture with any certainty and to check the postulates derived from "pottery studies" and "projectile point studies" and other classification studies so prominent in the past. The goal of the new archaeology (Bayard 1969; Binford 1962; 1965; Binford and Binford (eds) 1968; Dunnell 1971; King 1971; Kushner 1970; Martin 1971; Struever 1968; 1971; Watson, LeBlanc, and Redman 1971; Woodall 1972) is to apply explicitly scientific approaches to archaeological investigations. This approach has promise but is in its beginning stages and thus far has produced minimal explanations.

There are huge gaps in our information concerning the cultural past of Missouri; no single site has yet yielded its potential to the archaeologist's study. Few sites in the United States have been excavated with the avowed purpose of extracting a rounded view of the lifeways of the people who lived at the site, how many individuals lived there, and how they related to and interacted with each other and their neighbors. The total size of the village at any certain time, the size of the population, the arrangements of the village, and the use of all structures in the village

are important considerations, yet they are seldom more than touched upon in the reports on most archaeological excavations because the type of investigations necessary to produce such information was considered too time consuming and expensive. Relationships and interaction between villages, campsites, and other areas of activity are not usually explored except in terms of types of artifacts, the meanings of which are often obscure. The relationship between cultural and environmental systems is only beginning to be researched. The full information on the cultural, historical, and environmental potential of our archaeological sites is basic to understanding past culture. Students in the future are dependent on us to obtain it while it is still possible to do so.

What can be done? Teamwork of experts from numerous sciences is needed for even the smallest excavations. No one individual can live long enough to become expert in all the subjects necessary to conduct an excavation that would recover all the data essential to obtain a clear picture of what happened on a site. A knowledge of techniques of obtaining and recording data about soils, including chemical tests that can be conducted during the excavations, techniques for recovery of palynological and other data on vegetation, tests for obtaining samples for dates through radiocarbon, archaeomagnetic, and thermoluminescence, techniques to obtain samples that are statistically reliable and replicable, and techniques for determining size and density of populations are some of the requirements for retrieving and recording the data for the interpretation of the cultural activities at any site. A complete team of scientists would include a soils expert, botanist, palynologist, dendrochronologist, climatologist, zooarchaeologist, physical anthropologist, dietician, astronomer, nuclear physicist, computer programmer, and technicians who can operate sophisiticated equipment such as electron microscopes. Knowledge of what should be done to collect the data, the knowledge that should be possessed by the archaeologist, is only the beginning in the process of interpreting the happenings of the past. Teamwork and a great deal of time, effort, and funds are needed if the full potential in any of the archaeological sites is to be realized. Furthermore, intensive archaeological investigations of single localities and entire sites are needed in order to gain an understanding of the relationships of the sites and settlement in localities to cultural developments.

At this point we do not have the information available from archaeological studies to do more than suggest a cultural history for any one region in Missouri, much less give explanations for cultural developments that have taken place. In most instances we must deal almost entirely with the artifacts from archaeological sites for our inferences concerning the lifeways of the people who lived in the villages, towns, or natural rock shelters or who built structures for ceremonial or burial purposes. There have been a few ecological studies, but cultural interrelationships with the ecosystem and descriptions and explanations of cultural systems and cultural processes are challenges for the future.

Review of Earlier Interpretations

Several schemes of classification have been applied to the archaeological data from Missouri and surrounding states. Holmes (1886: 369, 427) was one of the first to designate archaeological provinces in the Mississippi Valley, using pottery as the basis. Two main provinces were noted to be represented in Missouri, the Middle Mississippi Valley and the Upper Mississippi Valley. He later designated *culture characterization areas* (Holmes 1914: 424–28, 430–32), and the state of Missouri was placed within his Middle and Central Mississippi Valley Region and the Plains and Rocky Mountains. Wissler (1938: 271–76) called the three archaeological areas the Mississippi–Ohio Area, the Great Lakes and Upper Mississippi Area, and the Plains. They are essentially the same as the divisions Holmes devised. Another compilation by Martin, Quimby, and Collier (1947: map inside cover) showed four archaeological areas within the boundaries of Missouri: Plains, Illinois, Ozark Plateau, and Middle Southern areas. Although the authors did not give their reasons for such a division, it appeared that the materials available to them were easier to handle as separate entities, perhaps due to the actual separateness of the areas both physiographically and culturally.

In an earlier review of the archaeology of Missouri, I (Chapman 1946; 1947; 1948a; 1948b) divided the state into four physiographic subdivisions and interpreted the archaeology in each, using the terminology of the Midwestern Taxonomic System (McKern 1939). The physiographic divisions were the Ozark Highland, Western Prairie, Northern Prairie, and Southeast Lowland. Time–cultural periods proposed were Archaic, Early Woodland, Middle Woodland, Late Prehistoric, Proto-Historic, and European Contact. This sequence was proposed for only three areas: North Missouri, Southwest Missouri, and Southeast Missouri.

Perhaps the most thorough coverage was a broad interpretation of the archaeology of the Eastern United States edited by Griffin (1952a); it, however, did not consider the archaeology of the entire state. Missouri archaeology was discussed in two different chapters. One was on the Central Mississippi Valley (Griffin 1952b) and the other on the Lower Missouri Valley (Chapman 1952b). Willey (1966: 248) did not subdivide the whole of the Eastern United States but placed a bit of the northwestern part of Missouri in the Plains and then put the rest of the state into three subareas, the Ozarks, Central Mississippi Valley, and Upper Mississippi Valley.

A general coverage of Missouri archaeology (Chapman and Chapman 1964) provided a sequence from early to late as follows: the Earliest Americans; Missouri's First Explorers, Early Hunter period; the Foragers, Hunter–Gatherers of the Archaic period; the First Potters, Early Woodland period; the Traders, Middle Woodland period; the Regional Isolationists, Late Woodland period; the Townspeople, Mississippi period; the Prairie Dwellers, Protohistoric period. The work was a broad introduction to Missouri archaeology in handbook form. The scheme of classification was not supported with detailed analyses.

Terminological Framework

The terminology in this work has been adopted from other writings. This approach should facilitate relating the findings in Missouri to those of adjacent areas and in the whole of the Eastern United States.

Major cultural traditions (Willey 1966) are comparable to the cultural periods used earlier by Griffin (1952b: 352–64), but time periods may or may not be coterminous with the tradition. They often appear in many localities and regions in a cultural area and may extend through more than one period. Major cultural traditions are identified by the manifestation of broad cultural trends in a locality or a region.

Region may be defined as the space correlating with a physiographic–archaeological subdivision. Regions are thus an important aspect of studying archaeology, for human culture adjusts to environment and human beings have always been selective in all customs associated with their mode of living. Regardless of how poor or rich the environment, or how limited or varied as a rule the selection might have been, a society maintains itself primarily by use of the materials available to it in the local environment.

The term *culture* may be defined as the means by which human societies have adapted to their natural and cultural environments. Cultures include the habits, customs, and artifacts associated with societies for gaining their living, organizing their social and political activities, and practicing their religious rituals and ceremonies. *Archaeological culture* is an arbitrary unit of cultural form placed in definite categories of space and time by reference to its preserved content and whatever of the common social and philosophical tradition that can be inferred therefrom. As culture is not inherent in artifacts, an archaeological culture is the pattern of cultural significance manifested in the artifacts, rather than the artifacts themselves. *Tradition* is the socially transmitted cultural form that persists in time; thus we may speak of artifact tradition, religious tradition, local cultural tradition, regional cultural tradition, technological tradition, or a major cultural tradition. The latter describes the general over-all cultural developments that occurred in the Eastern United States and are reflected in regional sequences in Missouri archaeology.

If a *technological tradition* is used it should be labeled for what it is and not called a culture or cultural tradition. A technological tradition is a manufacturing technique resulting in a class of material objects with definable attributes that extend through space and time. For example Bryan (1965: 25) divided leaf-shaped points into a large leaf-shaped and smaller leaf-shaped bipoints and suggested that each could be traced through space and time as a technological tradition. Using the same terminology, fluted forms, if used alone, should be referred to as the fluted technological tradition.

A *regional chronology* as used here is the sequence of cultural units within one of the regions proposed for Missouri.

Phase is substituted for *focus* as it was used by McKern to fit with the more general usage of the term as it is applied to the archaeology of the Eastern United States (Willey and Phillips 1952: 22). McKern (1939: 308) defined *focus* "as that class of culture exhibiting characteristic peculiarities in the finest analysis of cultural detail, and may in instances correspond closely to the local tribe in ethnology." McKern thought it would be dangerous to define focus in any ethnological terms. Willey and Phillips (1958: 49–51) also pointed out the problems of equating the archaeological unit or phase with society. However it is considered to be reasonable that distinctive phases can be defined on the basis of the discrete cultural units or the organizational evidences of the people who occupied various sites. Eventually strategies of archaeological approaches may be devised that will make it possible to identify social units with precision.

In ethnological terms the villages of the Big Osage Indians would be a tribe. In archaeological terms they would be a phase. *Phase* is the manifestation of a basic cultural unit that could be comparable to social units in ethnography, such as a tribe or interrelated bands or any unit that has relatively definite boundaries spatially and chronologically and is relatively uniform culturally. The latter might be made up of more than one social unit. It is important that the phase be limited to the evidences in a specific space, such as a region or a subdivision of a physiographic area, and in a brief time interval as has been suggested by Willey and Phillips (1958: 22). Only hypothetically can phase be treated as though it were a social unit.

Although excavation procedures have not been developed that provide complete or nearly complete cultural information concerning discrete cultural units or components of a phase, the partial information available can be used in the definition of specific phases. The concept of phase by Kidder, Jennings, and Shook (1946: 9) was probably used by most archaeologists in deriving phases:

> A cultural complex possessing traits sufficiently characteristic to distinguish it, for purposes of preliminary archaeological classification, from earlier and later manifestations of the cultural development of which it formed a part, and from other contemporaneous complexes.

The term *complex* is preferable to phase in many instances where data are incomplete. *Complex* is defined (Wood 1961: 5) as "a series of assemblages or of components which might be defined as a focus (phase), but where there is enough uncertainty as to their associations to refrain from so grouping them."

The term *component* will be used as defined by McKern (1939: 308), "the manifestation of any given focus (phase) at a specific site." Willey and Phillips (1958: 49) suggest that the social equivalent of component is the community and that the band, neighborhood, or village could be represented by it. Caution should be used in the equivalence of component and community, for the component may be representative of only a small part of the whole of a cultural entity, for example a burial mound or a temporary campsite. The component is often a partial unit, and seldom are the components that are used for comparative purposes wholly comparable in representational value to the whole discrete cultural units they purportedly represent. In practical application, the component is a selection or abstraction of traits, whether through circumstance, accident, or intent, that in combination with other similar components comprise a complex or phase. The information should be complete enough that it forms a discrete cultural unit. There is also the danger that the cultural manifestation at a particular site or in the sequence at a site may not be a component, or representative of a single phase, but may instead be an aggregate of two or more components. This is particularly true in cave or shelter sites that were used intermittently by different cultural entities during the same time period or at quite different time periods. Each occupation may have been of such short duration that the evidences left by different cultures occur in a single level of a site and provide a complete integration of traits left by the two different groups of occupants. Until there is certain evidence that components are part of distinct and discrete cultural units, it is probably best to consider that the component is a localized and usually incomplete manifestation at a single site. It could be treated as part of a discrete cultural unit that may be found at the site or in a particular spatial position on the site, and which may be shown to be related to a larger cultural class, the complex or phase by an analysis of the traits present in the component.

Probably most of the archaeological units with which the archaeologist works are *assemblages,* groups of artifacts that appear to belong to single discrete cultural units, or *aggregates,* the sum total of artifacts occurring on an archaeological site or in a stratum. The term *aggregate* is particularly apt when artifacts alone are used in the description of the site or its component traits. A *trait* is the smallest unit of a cultural manifestation. It is an item that is considered to be a part of, or representative of a part of, a discrete cultural unit. It may be an artifact, a pit, a house structure, or a burial position. An *attribute* is a specific characteristic of a trait such as the elements of flaking, form, or material that make up the characteristics of a flaked-stone tool.

The basic terms I have used to describe the cultural units and units of space are relatively widely accepted by archaeologists. The chrono-

logical position of the cultural units and terminology relating the units to regional and areal
chronologies need more detailed definition because the anthropological profession, which spe-
cializes in American archaeology, has not yet
standardized these terms. Nor has there been a
concerted effort to develop this means of communication. It is a crucial problem.

It is unfortunate that there is no absolute
agreement by archaeologists working in the Eastern United States on terminology for traditions
and periods. There has been the tendency to
equate or use interchangeably the terms *cultural
tradition, evolutionary stage, cultural complex,* and *time
period* and to establish a name that covers both the
cultural content and the time period within
which it occurs. This type of approach might
work very well when cultural complexes have
similar form and tradition that extend through
only one period of time. Too often cultural
traditions do not coincide with time periods,
and it is not possible to juggle either the traditions or the time periods to make them fit consistently, nor is this a systematic or scientific approach.

In general the terminology in use in the Eastern
United States has been followed here except that
the concept of cultural stage has not been used
(Jennings 1968; Krieger 1953a; Willey and Phillips 1958). The framework selected is one that
attempts to separate cultural designations from
units of time. Major cultural traditions are not
always bound within the same time period in all
of the physiographic divisions of the *Eastern
United States Cultural Area.* Thus it is not feasible
to construct a neat framework of time periods
that corresponds exactly with certain major cultural traditions only and that can be used for all
regional chronologies. The basic chronological
framework selected is as follows: Early Man,
(?)–12,000 B.C.; Paleo-Indian, 12,000–8000 B.C.;
Dalton, 8000–7000 B.C.; Archaic, 7000–1000 B.C.;
Woodland 1000 B.C.–A.D. 900; and Mississippian,
A.D. 900–1700. The names of major cultural traditions in Missouri roughly equate with the time
periods, respectively: Unspecialized Hunter–
Gatherer, Early Hunter, Hunter–Forager, Forager, Prairie-Forest Potter, and Village Farmer.

Time Periods

Cultural stability and cultural change are major realms for study by the anthropologist, and
a vast store of cultural data for such studies lies
in the archaeological record in Missouri. A
chronological framework onto which major cultural traditions and regional developments can be
attached could be useful in making such studies.
Physical environment must also be considered,
and the approach here (Chapman and Evans
1972) has been to select coherent physiographic
regions and localities in which to study the cultural manifestations. Physical environment may
change through time, and there is the probability
that cultural change occurs to adjust to major
environmental change. Hurt (1953), for example,
has pointed up the usefulness of taking climatic
changes into consideration in the interpretations
of cultural developments during the Paleo-
Indian and Archaic periods. Evidences of periods
of change as well as stability in the environment
were sought as guidelines in delimiting time periods.

The proposed chronological framework is not
an attempt to depict the exact timing of environmental events, for the knowledge available concerning them is still very limited. Periods have
been rounded to even numbers in hundreds of
years, for even if it were possible to date these
periods absolutely, local and regional chronologies would probably need to be adjusted according to their respective positions in regard to areas
of criticial change, such as the border between
the Western Prairie and Central Ozark Highland
regions. For example, people living in the Western Prairie Region would be affected by a sus-
tained drought sooner than those in the Central
Ozark Highland with its many springs or the
Southeast Riverine with its bayous and swamps;
thus, their culture might adapt to the environmental change at a different time period. The
critical points in time selected for separating
chronological periods are in general those at
which change in climate occurs after which it is
stabilized for reasonably long time spans.

Specific information on the climate in Missouri
during the late Pleistocene and for most of the

post-Pleistocene periods was not really available. Radiocarbon dates and paleontological and paleobotanical data from the Lower Osage Locality were specific for the period 14,500–11,500 B.C. (Mehringer, King, and Lindsay 1970), and radiocarbon dates from Rodgers shelter (McMillan 1971) provided chronological information on climatic changes in the same locality. However, it did not seem advisable to set up a statewide chronology on the basis of this locality alone. Instead the proposed framework is similar to that used by Willey (1966: 73, 456) but differs in details based upon past climatic episodes (Bryson, Barreis, and Wendland 1970; Bryson and Wendland 1967). For example, Willey (1966) proposed a Big Game Hunting Tradition beginning about 12,000 B.C. in the Eastern Woodland, which included Clovis Fluted and extended approximately until 8000 B.C. It overlapped the time of the Big Game Hunting Tradition and was followed by Graham Cave 1 and Modoc 1. Dalton was then shown to begin about 8500–7000 B.C. in the Archaic Tradition. Next at about 5500 B.C. Grove was followed at 5100 B.C. by Eva, then Three Mile and ended with Big Sandy shortly before 1000 B.C. Here the periods have been named and given specific time values. The earliest period, that preceding 12,000 B.C., ended at the approximate time of the maximum of the Cary glaciation (Wright and Ruhe 1965: 41) and the end of loess deposition in Iowa. To the north in northeastern Minnesota there was tundra vegetation (Wright 1968: 82) and in southwestern Missouri in the Lower Osage Locality a spruce forest may have lasted until about 12,000 B.C. (Mehringer, King, and Lindsay 1970) when it began to be replaced by prairie vegetation.

Bryson, Baerreis, and Wendland (1970: Table 2, 3) provided a terminology and tentative chronology for climatic episodes prior to 550 B.C., and Bryson and Wendland (1967: Table 23) did the same for the period A.D. 550–1960. These findings have been combined in the following chart and are shown in relation to periods that will be used as the chronological framework in this book. Radiocarbon dates indicated as B.P. (Before Present) have been changed to B.C. by subtracting 1950.

They have not been adjusted further. Most dates are given in absolute time units B.C. and A.D.

Early Man Period

The term *Early Man period* may draw a certain amount of criticism because the proposed evidence for man having inhabited Missouri during the time period is controversial. Nevertheless there is evidence that people lived in North America prior to 12,000 B.C. (Gruhn 1965: 57), the date at which the beginning of the Paleo-Indian period is usually set. Therefore, in order to discuss the cultural evidences of man in the North American continent prior to 12,000 B.C. and to avoid disregarding the potential information about the appearance of man in Missouri prior to 12,000 B.C., the designation *Early Man period* has been used.

Old accounts of evidences purported to be very ancient in the Americas often used the term *Early Man* (cf. Antevs 1937; Barbour and Schultz 1936; Cressman 1946; Cresson 1890a; Eisley 1945; Fischel 1941; Gidley 1926b; 1929; Holmes 1893a; Howard 1935; Hrdlicka 1907; 1937b; Sauer 1944; and Walter, Cathoud, and Mattos 1937). The term was so generally used that an entire book was devoted to the subject and entitled *Early Man* (MacCurdy and Merriam 1937). The term was being used so widely and included so many different evidences that Johnson (1951) questioned whether or not *Early Man* should be used any more as a heading for the assembly of references to ancient occupations in America. The term has continued in use by numerous authors to the present (Bryan 1964; 1969; Butler 1964; 1965; Crook and Harris 1957; Giddings 1954; Greenman 1960; Honea 1965; Irwin-Williams, 1967; Jelinek 1957; 1965; Lanning and Patterson 1967; Lindig 1970; MacGowan and Hester 1962; Mason 1960; Mayer-Oakes 1963; Sellards 1952; Stalker 1969; Wendorf 1966; Wilmsen 1965).

Early Man was by no means the only term used nor did it always pertain to similar time periods. In discussing finds that were purportedly evidences of ancient people who had arrived in America prior to or during the last major glaciation, various writers used different terms to de-

Climatic Episodes and Proposed Chronological Periods

Climatic Episodes	Rough Date	Period	Absolute Date
Recent	A.D. 1970		1970
	A.D. 1850 ———	Historic	
Neo-Boreal			1700 ———
	A.D. 1550 ———	Late Mississippi	
Pacific II			
	A.D. 1450 ———		1450 ———
Pacific I		Middle Mississippi	
	A.D. 1200 ———		1200 ———
Neo-Atlantic		Early Mississippi	
	A.D. 900 ———		900 ———
Scandic		Late Woodland	
	A.D. 400 ———		400 ———
			A.D. 1
			1 B.C.
		Middle Woodland	
Sub-Atlantic			
			500 ———
		Early Woodland	
	940 B.C. ———		1000 ———
Sub-Boreal		Late Archaic	
	2730 B.C. ———		3000 ———
Atlantic IV		Middle Archaic	
	4030 B.C. ———		5000 ———
Atlantic III			
	5100 B.C. ———		
Atlantic II		Early Archaic	
	5780 B.C. ———		
Atlantic I			
	6500 B.C. ———		7000 ———
Boreal II		Dalton	
	7190 B.C. ———		
Boreal I			
	7700 B.C. ———		8000 ———
		Paleo-Indian	
Pre-Boreal			
			12,000 ———
		Early Man	

scribe the period and the culture supposedly represented by the finds. Some of the more commonly used terms were *glacial man* (Babbitt 1884b; Gidley 1929; Holmes 1893b; Leverett 1893; and Wright 1893; 1895), *Pleistocene man* (Birdsell 1957; Carter 1957; 1959; Harrington and Simpson 1961; Jenks 1936), *paleolithic man* or *paleolithic implements* (Babbitt 1884a; McGee 1889; Owen 1909; Putnam 1888; Wilson 1895; 1889), and *ancient man* (Heizer 1948; Hrdlicka 1920; Ray 1934, Wormington 1957).

The concept of stages as steps in cultural evolution has been adopted by many archaeologists, and this approach to the ordering of and interpretation of archaeological data is discussed fully by Krieger (1964), Willey and Phillips (1958), and others. Jennings (1968) has used stages as a major means of interpreting the archaeology of North America. One of the difficulties in using stages to explain cultural developments is that of the identification of the technological stages by the cultural remains. Another is that a particular stage of culture may persist through long periods of time allowing no good means for studies of cultural change to be conducted. Furthermore, the characteristics of stages are often very general in nature. The best examples of stages proposed for the earliest evidences of people in America have been called *Lithic* by Willey and Phillips (1958: 79–103); and *Pre-Projectile Point* by Krieger (1964: 42–51).

The term used most frequently and most consistently to refer to the very earliest potential evidence of man in America is *Early Man*. Therefore it was selected as the name for the earliest period of possible human occupancy, in Missouri, prior to 12,000 B.C.

Paleo-Indian Period

Roberts (1940) apparently was the first to use the term *Paleo-Indian* but did not define it except in general terms and in association with certain types and complexes of artifacts. Wormington (1957: 3) used the term

> to refer to people who hunted animals which are now extinct, to the people who occupied the western United States prior to about 6,000 years ago, and to the makers of the fluted

points found in the eastern United States. . . . There are no firm dates for the latter, but there is reason to believe that some, at least are quite old.

Griffin (1952a: 352–53) used the term to refer to a period of simple hunting–gathering, "with very few individuals living in small bands with temporary, easily built shelters, regularly on the move following game and taking advantage of the food supply available in localized areas." He tentatively equated the eastern Paleo-Indian evidences with those from the southwestern United States. In another chapter of the same book Griffin (1952b: 365–68) cited radiocarbon dates for western sites, which established the Paleo-Indian period as approximately 10,000 to 6,000 years ago. Later, Griffin (1964: 223–25) no longer referred to Paleo-Indian but introduced a different terminology, *The Fluted Point Hunters,* and postulated the time as 12,000–10,000–8000 B.C. In his summary of Eastern North American archaeology Griffin (1967: 176) suggested that the distribution of the Fluted Point Hunter resulted from the northern spread of vegetation and animal life after 13,000 or 12,000 B.C. There was a further suggestion that the fluted point developed in the Southeast rather than the Southwest or Southern Plains. He wrote of a "Fluted Point" hunting complex, an "early hunting tradition" that could be divided into "an early Llano complex which has Clovis-type projectile points, and a later phase identified most clearly with the Folsom-type point."

Rouse (1964: 392) referred to a Paleo-Indian epoch and equated it in general with the "Early Lithic Stage" of Willey and Phillips (1958), but then stated that the epoch was primarily a unit of time rather than degree of cultural evolution.

Mason (1962: 227–29) noted a Paleo-Indian stage and in discussing "The Paleo-Indian in Western North America" stated:

> Clearly, a single life-way is represented, one homogeneous in its big-game hunting orientation . . . a single culture type whose unity and cohesiveness through time can be documented by reference to artifact typology, subsistence and shared traits, both positive and negative. This continuum, tradition, culture stage, or

culture type, however it may be viewed, is what American archaeologists usually call Paleo-Indian.

In his discussion of "The Paleo-Indian in Eastern North America," Mason (1962: 232–33) included within it: fluted points; the lanceolate points in the west called Plano; and eastern point complexes identified by Suwanee, Quad, Dalton, and similar forms. He used the modifiers "early" for fluted point assemblages proper, and "late" for "the usually non-fluted lanceolate forms and other artifacts with which they were associated." Krieger (1962b: 256–59) in commenting on Mason's paper pointed up the inconsistency in usage of terms such as *culture, patterns, stage, tradition, complex, period, horizon*, etc., and then used the term *Paleo-Indian stage* in his further discussion. He disagreed with Mason's interpretation that either the material culture or economy of the Plains peoples was "closer to that of the fluted-point horizon than to the full Archaic. The opposite appears to be true!"

Earlier, Mason (1959: 1–3) wrote about the "Paleo-Indian Period" and the fluted points that were "index points" of the period. He equated the Paleo-Indian period with the earliest evidences of people in the Americas. In yet another article Mason (1958: 1) spoke of a Paleo-Indian cultural horizon "comparable to the High Plains fluted-blade industries."

Schwartz (1967: 75–80) proposed the term *Early Hunter* as a descriptive unit for the Paleo-Indian of Kentucky in view of the fact that W. S. Webb had referred to evidence of Kentucky's earliest occupation with that term. The term has been used here in a similar manner but is limited to the broad cultural tradition that is most prominent in the Paleo-Indian period.

Willey (1966: 89) in his discussion of the "Precursors and Foundations of the Meso-American Cultural Tradition" segmented it into major periods, one of which he called "the Paleo-Indian Period." He noted that a period was to be considered "as strictly horizontal time division, adhering to absolute dating insofar as this is possible." He explained further that periods were not stages and that the "cultural characteristics of the periods do not always coincide with strictly horizon-

tal time division." This concept has been adhered to here. Willey's (1966: 89) brief description of the Paleo-Indian period follows: "This period [before 7000 B.C.] pertains to those early complexes of the late Pleistocene which were characterized by hunting subsistence patterns." In his use of the term *Paleo-Indian* for eastern North America he again emphasized that it was used as a period and pointed out that: "It is important to bear in mind the distinction between the concepts of traditions and periods. The former are cultural patterns persisting through time. The latter are intended as horizontal time bands." This concept also has been followed here.

The term *Paleo-Indian* appears to have been used to designate a stage of evolutionary cultural development, a culture, a cultural tradition, a stone technology, and a time period by different writers, and sometimes by the same writers. In spite of the employment of the term in different ways, its meaning has often been clear due to the context in which it has been found, and it has been used here to designate the period 12,000–8000 B.C.

Dalton Period

A Dalton period, 8000–7000 B.C., is proposed to encompass the time of change from major emphasis on hunting to foraging, a transitional period between the Paleo-Indian and the Archaic. Willey (1966: 63) noted that cultures of the Archaic type came into existence between 8000 and 7000 B.C., two or three thousand years before the characteristic Archaic ground-polished stone artifacts became common. Dalton Serrated is often associated with Hunter–Forager complexes occurring during the period.

Archaic Period

A good discussion of the history of the term *Archaic* can be found in Jennings (1968: 109–11). Jennings used it to designate a stage of cultural level "a fundamental lifeway, not geared to any one ecosystem." He said,

> In considering the Archaic, the problem of keeping chronology . . . separate from *stage* becomes acute. Then, too, if the Archaic is defined as above, problems are automatically en-

gendered through the inclusion of several sites which others included in the Protoarchaic, or even label as Paleo-Indian.

In his summary he noted that the Archaic stage lasted until European contact in many parts of North America and commented (Jennings 1968: 334–35) "that the Archaic at an essentially Meso or early Neolithic level of technology is perhaps the most adaptable lifeway ever developed by man." In short, there is little or no climatic control on an Archaic population, in that the Archaic subsistence stage was inclusive rather than exclusive.

Willey (1966: 60–63) used the term *Archaic Tradition,* "to refer to those cultures of the eastern North American Woodland river valleys in which the subsistence was based on small game hunting, fishing, and wild plant collecting."

Another discussion of the Archaic concept can be found in Rolingson and Schwartz (1966: 3–5). They used the term to refer to a "stage of cultural adaptation which used a wide variety of local flora and fauna. In the eastern United States it involved increasing specialization in a forest environment with refinement of food-collecting methods and tools, resulting eventually in seasonal cycles of foraging." All of the authors tended to agree that foraging was the most important means of subsistence and thus characterized the economy of the people. There was also general agreement that the complexes that had been identified as Archaic were within the period 8000–1000 B.C. Since a transitional Dalton period has been proposed, 8000–7000 B.C., the term *Archaic* as it is used here refers to that period of time from 7000–1000 B.C. The Archaic has been divided into three subperiods: Early, 7000–5000 B.C. ; Middle, 5000–3000 B.C; and Late, 3000–1000 B.C.

Traditions

With the view that in describing a terminology the cultural tradition should reflect a cultural criterion of the tradition, the major cultural tradi-

tions in the Lower Missouri-Central Mississippi river valley have been called Unspecialized Hunter–Gatherer, Early Hunter, Hunter–Forager, Forager, Prairie-Forest Potter, and Village Farmer. Each tradition will be discussed in the text preceding the discussion of its occurrence in Missouri. The general placement of the cultural tradition in relation to time periods follows (Chapman 1972):

TRADITION	PERIOD
Village Farmer	Late Mississippi A.D. 1450–1700 Early Mississippi A.D. 900–1450
Prairie-Forest Potter	Late Woodland A.D. 400–900 Middle Woodland 500 B.C.–A.D. 400 Early Woodland 1000–500 B.C.
Forager	Late Archaic 3000–1000 B.C. Middle Archaic 5000–3000 B.C. Early Archaic 7000–5000 B.C.
Hunter–Forager	Dalton 8000–7000 B.C.
Early Hunter	Paleo-Indian 12,000–8000 B.C.
Unspecialized Hunter–Gatherer	Early Man (?)–12,000 B.C.

The names of periods that are used in the chart are comparable to the broad divisions and periods in general use in the Eastern United States (Chapman and Chapman 1964; Griffin 1952a; 1964; 1967; 1968; Willey 1966) so that they can be conveniently compared with published materials elsewhere.

2. The Coming of Man to America

A great deal of research has been conducted on and much study and discussion have been devoted to the first Americans. Many hypotheses have been proposed about the earliest Americans, but only a few of them will be discussed here. In spite of the general acceptance of certain theories concerning the first Americans, there are still uncertainties and many unanswered questions. The few questions of special interest that seem to have been answered concern their physical type and origin. There is a concensus that the earliest Americans were modern Homo sapiens (Birdsell 1951; Hrdlicka 1907; 1918; Neumann 1952: 13–14; Stewart 1960). It is fairly well established that they originated in eastern Asia (Chard 1963).

Some of the subject areas that are in need of further study are (1) the time or times that migrations occurred, (2) the route or routes followed by the emigrants, (3) their mode of transportation, (4) the technological tradition or traditions brought with the first migrants, and (5) certain evidence of the existence of man in the North American Continent prior to 12,000 B.C. We know much more now about Early Man in America than we did 30 years ago, but even the broadest questions concerning that period are still controversial subjects, and answers are clouded with uncertainties. In this chapter, the preceding five subject areas will be discussed.

The time that people first entered the Americas is not at all certain; the estimates range from 100,000 to 12,500 years ago. There is no full agreement by students of the American Indian on how many different migrations might have occurred, and if there were several, no one knows just when they took place. Wormington (1964b: 141) wrote, "I am inclined to believe that there was some occupation of the New World between 30,000 and 40,000 years ago, although I realize that no sites of comparable age are now known in eastern Siberia." Krieger (1964: 68) suggested a similar time of 35,000 to 40,000 years ago.

Hopkins (1967: 461–62) noted that an episode of high sea level during the Wisconsin stage, the Woronzofian transgression, took place within the interval from 35,000 to 25,000 years ago; therefore it seems likely that there could have been a migration after that interval. Campbell (1963) suggested that the time would coincide with the Mousterian culture of Europe. Wendorf (1966: 267–68) noted that the most probable time for migration was between 25,000 and 18,000 B.C., when the Bering platform was exposed but the ice barrier did not exist. Bryan (1969) proposed the hypotheses that (1) the corridor in the ice in northern Canada was closed by 25,000 years ago and (2) Beringia was submerged between 35,000 and 25,000 years ago, and for the Hunter–Gatherers to have been present south of the coalescent ice sheets 11,500 years ago they must have entered Alaska prior to that time. Chard (1963: 120) proposed that the American Indians may have derived from a movement of people into North America from the Far East along the Pacific shore, which brought an industrial tradition illustrated by chipped bifaces, amorphous flakes, and probably the Levalloiso-Mousterian technique, perhaps in Würm I time about 40,000 years ago. Chard (1963: 120–21) noted further that it is conceivable that there was a secondary movement from interior Siberia during the Classic Wisconsin glaciation via the Lena-Arctic coastal route about 25,000 years ago but said, "I think it more likely, however, that any secondary movement at this time again came from the Far East along the Pacific Coast, bringing an embryonic blade technique well established by then in East Asia."

There may be merit to Haynes's (Bryan 1969: 354) argument that there was a separate Clovis migration after 12,000 B.C. with a technology and skill in mammoth hunting, for mammoth hunting was a well-established technique in the Old World at that time. On the other hand, mammoth hunting had been developed several thousand years earlier in the Old World, and, even though the migrants came by sea, they could well have retained a verbal tradition of big-game hunting that was converted to use when the situation warranted it at a much later time. Migrants along the coast by boat probably brought with them a tradition of big-game sea-mammal hunting.

Muller-Beck (Bryan 1969: 358) stated, "There are enough data available to claim an origin for the Clovis-Llano tradition in the Mousteroid technology of northeastern Eurasia." Thus, if this technology were the one introduced to America earlier than 12,000 B.C., there would be no need to have a separate migration bringing it across Beringia and through Canada at a later period.

It is not unreasonable to hypothesize that Hunter–Gatherers came to America a few thousand years prior to the Early Hunter Tradition development of fluted projectile points, which were in full production and use 11,500–11,000 years ago (Haynes 1966). It is difficult to accept Haynes's assumption that the fully developed fluted-point tradition of the Paleo-Indian period was introduced to America by mammoth hunters from Asia only 500 years earlier. It seems more likely that the first migrants came to America at least as early as the period 20,000–14,000 B.C. and probably 40,000–35,000 B.C.

It is generally presumed that climate was an important factor dictating the time that migrations to America took place. Climate might have affected the route of migration as well. Scientists have not yet been able to determine fully the nature of the climate during the Wisconsin stage in the southern regions of North America (Miller 1958). No attempt will be made here to compile all the available information concerning the subject, but some of the important factors will be discussed. It is quite clear that the time interval 20,000–12,000 B.C. is encompassed by the Wood-

fordian substage of the Wisconsin stage of glaciation (Frye and others 1968: E18). During this substage the climate was cold and land temperatures were very low in North America as far south as the Mexican border (Deevey 1949). The temperate biota of eastern North America appears to have been forced into refuges in Florida and Mexico (Hubbs 1958: 473). Temperatures were 5°–12.6° F below those in modern times (Reeves 1965: 48). Periglacial phenomena occurred in northern Illinois, Indiana, and Ohio (Wayne 1967). Spruce and pine extended from present locations in the mountain area at least 300 miles into the Great Plains (Daugherty 1968: 66), and boreal forest covered most of the central United States (Martin 1958: 383). Although there may have been some differences in the effects of the glaciation on various parts of North America, in general glacial influence extended well beyond the margin of the ice (Wendorf 1961a). Sears (1948: 326) reported that recent sediments in the Gulf of Mexico are underlain by a subarctic faunal layer and that evidences of Canadian conifers have been found in Florida, South Carolina, North Carolina, Louisiana, and Texas. Although these evidences were not dated, it is presumed that some are records of the cold climate of the Woodfordian substage. Deevey (1949) pointed out that there were relict flora in the Northeast and Southeast that probably related to past extreme variations in the climate, but there is no way to determine which pluvial glaciation or interstade produced the relict populations or if in fact they did so. In any instance, the evidence is certain that the Woodfordian substage produced important changes in the climate that in turn affected the types of dominant vegetation in most of the southern part of North America.

The ice reached its maximum advance between 18,000 and 17,000 B.C. (Flint 1957: 1963: 404), at which time it covered most of the northeastern part of Illinois. It was during the retreat of the Woodfordian glaciers, after they had reached the headwaters draining into the Mississippi and Illinois river valleys, that the greatest deposits of loess in the continent were laid down. The deposits beyond the Woodfordian glaciation are called Peoria loess and extend from eastern

Colorado to Ohio and from Wisconsin to Missis-sippi (Frye, Willman, and Black 1965: 56). In western Nebraska the Peorian loess is 200 feet thick (MacClintock 1937: 122). Furthermore, ex-tensive floods occurred in the tributaries and the main stem of the Mississippi River, which ag-graded the major valleys 50 feet or more and formed extensive terraces, many of which in the Mississippi Valley proper have been washed away by later floods (Frye, Willman, and Black 1965: 56). In southern Missouri, spruce (*Picea* sp.) and larch *(Larix laricina)* were the forest cover dur-ing the late Pleistocene, and indication of cold, wet climate. The nearest place to Missouri that these species occur together today is northwest-ern Minnesota (Mehringer and others 1968: 567). In general the climate during the Woodfordian in central North America was not an inducement to migration there.

In the southern High Plains, pollen analysis and radiocarbon dates have shown that the period 20,500–12,000 B.C. was cold and wet and that there were open boreal woodlands of pine and spruce (Hagsten 1961: 90). The fauna that occurred there until about 13,000 B.C. (Tahoka Pluvial stage) were mammoth, mastodon, horse, sloth, camel, Capromeryx, bison, tapir, peccary, deer, jack rabbit, and turtle in the Monahans dune area but was limited to bison in the Llano Estacado (Wendorf 1961b: 130). The fauna could have supported big-game hunters and might have attracted them to the area.

The effects of the Woodfordian substage must have reached as far south as Panama, which may have been a savannah during the glacial max-imum. Beginning about 16,000 B.C. the glaciers began a retreat, the story of which is not yet clear (Kerby 1964: 30). Floods and dust storms may have discouraged occupation of much of the southern half of the United States, but extensive grasslands and concomitant herds of large game animals along the Gulf of Mexico and in the southwestern United States could have en-couraged a northward move of land hunters from Mexico. Coastal areas were probably influenced by a maritime climate, which made travel by foot or boat easier and settlement more desirable there (Davis 1965: 398).

The route of migration is usually considered to be across the Bering land bridge, through Alaska into northern Canada, and then south to the northern plains. Creager and McManus (1967: 23) supplied evidence that the Bering land bridge was open to foot travel from 20,000 to 12,000 B.C. It would have been possible for mi-grants to travel across a wide land bridge on foot on its southern margin or by boat if the sea level were 20–25 fathoms lower than today. It is sug-gested that the route from Cape Chaplina, Si-beria, north of St. Lawrence Island and then to Norton Sound was more favorable than that from Cape Dezhneva to Cape Prince of Wales (Byers 1957: 21). Byers (1957: 22, 25–26) noted that when this area was exposed, it must have been gently rolling land, perhaps dotted with several lakes and small streams, and he pointed out that evidence was available that the Bering Strait area was already submerged more than 20 fathoms, its approximate depth today, by 11,000 years ago. Thus, hunters following big game on foot would have had to migrate earlier than that time. Haag (1962: 116) wrote that the sea level was lowered at least 50 fathoms (300 feet) at the optimum glaciation in the Wisconsin stage and that migrants most likely moved along the coastal margins.

An alternative to the theory of migration to America from west to east via the Bering land bridge is the proposal that very early migrants came from Europe via the Arctic (Farmer 1964; Greenman 1960; 1963; Lee 1961; 1968; Ridley 1960). The evidences were the similarity of cul-tural items and art forms in Europe and North America and the circumpolar distribution of plants and animals. People may have reached America from Europe by a land connection, the frozen Arctic Ocean, ice floes, and by boat.

Greenman (1963) proposed that Upper Paleo-lithic inhabitants of Europe used the skin boat, citing the paleolithic cave paintings of boats (Fig-ure 2–2A–B). The paintings are similar to rock carvings of Norse boats (Figure 2–2C). Although unsupported by absolute evidence, this hypothe-sis is very important and should be given full consideration in discussions of the origin of Early Man in America, for if boats were in use during the Paleolithic, the inhabitants during the Upper Paleolithic in eastern Asia could have been the boat- or float-using progenitors of the American Indian.

Farmer (1964) thoroughly reviewed the possible Arctic routes of migration in the North Atlantic and cited as evidence a site dated geologically at 30,000 years ago at Sheguiandah, Ontario (Lee 1955; 1956), which reportedly had several stages of pre-projectile-point quartzite tools similar to Old World Paleolithic assemblages. Radiocarbon dates of deposits overlying the evidences of a stone technological tradition are about 7000 B.C. The discussions of this alternative route of migration to America via the Arctic are stimulating, and any solid evidences of such a possibility should always be given a hearing. However, the weight of the evidence for the movement of early immigrants from Asia to North America in the vicinity of the Bering area is almost overwhelming (Chard 1958; Hopkins 1967; Solecki 1951).

Campbell (1963) also proposed that there were early connections between Europe and the New World but considered that people came to America via a northern route across Asia and the Bering land bridge shortly after the Wisconsin maximum. He suggested that this migration occurred during the Mousterian of Europe. This explanation of European traits in North American complexes is more feasible than a circumpolar route or one across the Atlantic Ocean.

If the first migrants to America during the height of the Wisconsin glaciation walked across the Bering land bridge along the southern edge of the bridge to the Alaska Peninsula, they would have encountered a glacier at Unmak Island (Hopkins 1967: 462, Figure 3). Perhaps it was possible for a few people to find their way on foot along the coast to California at a very early time, as early as 40,000 years ago, but without some form of water transportation it does not seem probable (Bryan 1969: 339). Geologic movements of land could have affected the contour of the shoreline, allowing travel by foot along the shore, but this possibility seems unlikely (Daly 1929; 1934). It is possible that much more of the west coast was also exposed than has

been generally thought, for it is now known that most of the continental shelf was exposed along the east coast prior to 11,000 years ago (Emery and Edwards 1966).

MacGintie (1968: 73) noted that during pluvial glacial stages the effects on life were "greatest along the southern extension of the glacial fronts, but these effects are found far to the south (in the mountains of Mexico, for instance)." The areas with the most favorable climate were along the Pacific Coast and the southern Atlantic seaboard. This contention would support the hypothesis that Early Man came to the Americas via the Pacific Coast and would not negate the hypotheses about a route along the coast of the Arctic Sea to the eastern coast of North America.

Exceptions might be those areas of North America adversely affected by the Wisconsin glaciation. Cold climate and boreal forest must have covered much of the southern half of North America and extended perhaps into northern Mexico (Cushing and Wright 1967; Dillon 1956). Glaciers were in the Rocky Mountains during much of the Woodfordian substage in the mid-continent region, in the approximate period 22,000–10,500 B.C. Richmond (1965: 227) noted an interstade about 18,000–16,000 B.C. in the Rocky Mountains that could denote that there had been acceleration of warm climate in the southern half of North America at that time. This condition would have allowed a population that might have lived along the coastal areas to expand into the interior. In any instance the Rocky Mountains were glaciated during most of the period 20,000–12,000 B.C. and thus would have effectively sealed off or greatly limited migrations from the coastal areas across the mountains during that time. It would be probable if earlier migrants were living along the west coast 20,000 B.C. or earlier that the first major penetrations of the continental mass by migrants from the west coast would have begun at the coast of California or the Gulf of California. The major adaptations and settlement inland may have occurred even farther south, where the climate was mild and the biota abundant and varied.

It seems likely that the early migrants to North America followed the coastline as long as food

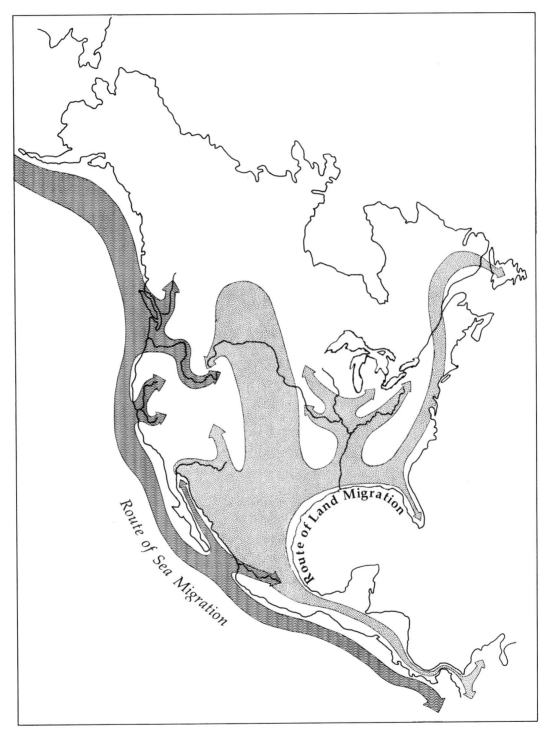

Figure 2–1. Proposed routes of migration to and through North America.

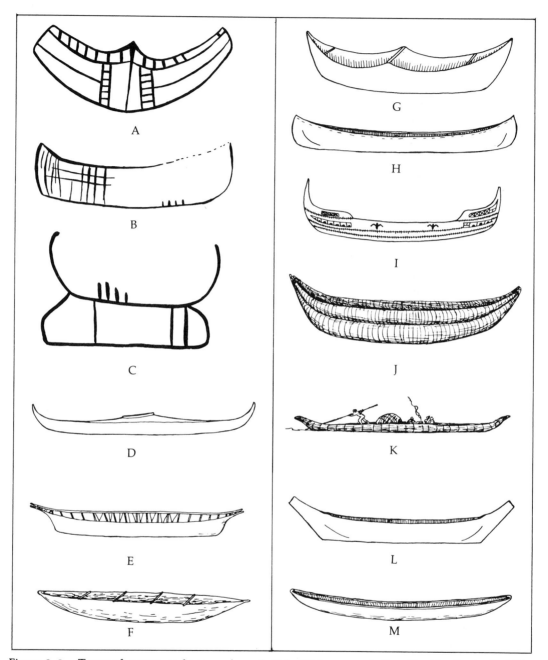

Figure 2–2. Types of canoes, early to modern. A, Paleolithic cave painting, Castillo, Spain (Del Rio, Breuil, and Sierra 1911: Figure 183, Plate LXXVI); B, paleolithic cave painting, Castillo, Spain (Del Rio, Breuil, and Sierra 1911: Figure 187); C, petroglyph near Nourköping depicting a Norse boat (Brown 1963: 472); D, Eskimo kayak (Wissler 1938: Figure 11b); E, Eskimo woman's boat (Wissler 1938: Figure 11c); F, Fuegian bark canoe (Wissler 1938: Figure 11f); G, Beotuk canoe (Whitby 1967: Figure 3D); H, birchbark canoe (Wissler 1938: Figure 11e); I, sewn-plank boat (Durham 1960: 94); J, balsa (made of bundled bullrushes) from Lake Titicaca, Peru (Villiers 1963: 499); K, Choimini Yokuts balsa barge (Durham 1960: 98); L, North Pacific Coast dugout (Wissler 1938: Figure 11g); M, Amazon dugout (Wissler 1938: Figure 11h).

was available. Some probably did walk and settled in what is now Alaska. If they were using
boats, the exploration and settlement would
have been on the coast; only gradual exploration
and exploitation of resources would have been
conducted where water courses allowed passage
into the interior, for example, the Strait of
Georgia and the Fraser River in British Columbia,
Canada, and the Columbia River valley as far
south as the Dalles in Oregon and Washington.
Continuing south along the coast, the Gulf of
California might have funneled the migrants into
the interior. Given time, those coast-living, sea-
oriented people could have adapted to living off
the land and may have moved into the interior
of the continent from the gulf's eastern shores
(Figure 2–1).

If, as Greenman (1960) and Hrdlicka (1932)
have suggested, the first migrants had knowledge
of water transport, such as the frame boat covered with skin or bark, the sewn-bark canoe, the
log raft, the reed bundle float, or skin float, and
if they had some skill in hunting and fishing, the
coastal migration route would have been easy.
The sewn-bark, sewn-plank, skin-covered,
framed-and-waterproofed, and dugout canoes,
reed bundle floats (balsas), log rafts, and hide
floats all have counterparts in the Old World
(Durham 1960; Edwards 1965; Greenman 1960;
Hodge 1912; Mason and Hill 1901; Mitman 1923;
Sollas 1924: 268–71). Boats, canoes, or floats were
probably one of mankind's very early technological accomplishments (Figure 2–2).

Hrdlicka (1932: 398–99) proposed that early
parties of migrants to America must have been
well acquainted with coastal navigation as a
means for subsistence and movement. The hypothesis was submitted that they had small skin
boats for individuals and large ones, probably
with sails, for groups. Their movement along the
west coast of North America was toward the sun
to Cook's Inlet and on to the Northwest Coast.
Thus the oldest evidences of habitation of the
New World should be found in spots in southern
British Columbia, Washington, Oregon, and
California. "The lower Columbia River basin and
parts of California would seem especially propi-
tious" (Hrdlicka 1932: 399).

Wissler (1938: 38) pointed out that watercraft
were in use in the Americas wherever they were
advantageous and "from this point of view may
be considered universal." They were distributed
throughout North and South America (Figure
2–2). Watercraft are undoubtedly an old cultural
trait and probably were a part of the cultural
technology of the first migrants to America. It is
postulated that the earliest American explorers
and settlers were "canoe nomads" dependent
primarily upon ocean resources for their subsistence. They might have been people with a limited culture, with a technology and economy
similar to that of the Yahgan of Tierra del Fuego
(Bridges 1948).

Edwards (1965: 112–13) wrote that there is
really no basis for denying ancient men "the abil-
ity to make limited open water crossings and to
travel by water along coast lines on such craft as
reed floats or simple rafts." He then posed the
corollary thesis that early immigrants were
"shore-line people capable of gaining their livelihood from the sea and its edge, and moving along
it at times when inland ice may have imposed
severe limits on exclusively land-based subsistence." Game and fish were plentiful along the
coast to the tip of South America. The migration
of the earliest Americans to the North American
Continent by canoe, raft, or float is certainly a
reasonable and acceptable hypothesis.

If the canoe–nomad hypothesis is to have any
validity, it is vital to consider evidence that early
Hunter–Gatherers in America had water transportation, however simple it might have been.
Remnants of the sewn-bark strip canoe, skin
float, reed bundle float, or log raft would be difficult to find in early sites. Sewn-bark strip boats
were in use by the Alacaluf and Yahgan when
they were first encountered by Europeans (Figure
2–2F). A crescent or gondola shape characterized
other craft built by inhabitants of the west coast
of South America as far north as Peru (Bird 1946:
67; Cooper 1946: 88). Double-ended floats were
in Lake Titicaca (Figure 2–2J) and were probably
of coastal derivation (Edwards 1965: 102). Simple
bark canoes, instead of dugout canoes (Figure
2–2M), were used in the upper branches of the
Amazon by the more isolated or nomadic people

(Steward and Faron 1959: 298). The presence of the bark boat in this marginal area suggests that it was an early trait. Although bark or skin boats have not been found between Peru and Alaska, the general structure and appearance, if not construction materials, of balsas may be related to the bark boats of Tierra del Fuego and the skin boats of the Arctic; they appear in California (Figure 2–2K) and again along the South American coast. Durham (1960: 96) wrote, "Its use was substantially continuous from the Columbia River to Patagonia." In later times sewn-plank boats (Figure 2–2I) and dugouts replaced the sewn-bark boat of the Yahgan and Alacaluf, and the same may have been true along the Northwest Coast (Figure 2–2L). Hide floats, which were made of skins from sea lions, were still being used on the Chilean coast in modern times and seem to have been remnants of an ancient form of water transportation. They were double-pontoon floats of animal hide and apparently made a very seaworthy craft that was especially useful along rocky shores (Edwards 1965: 17–20). A similar type of craft could have been used by very early sea-oriented nomads.

The Kutenai bark canoe had extensive north-south distribution in the northwest but reached its highest development in the upper Columbia and Kutenai rivers. It may represent a survival of an old cultural trait; it resembles closely the Goldi Asian Bark canoe (Durham 1960: 35–36).

Ekholm (1955: 106–7) noted that the potentialities of small craft traveling long distances at sea and the hardiness of early mariners have been underestimated. It has also been pointed out by Cole (1946: 2–4) and others that in the recent past natives using skin boats (Figure 2–2D–E) crossed from Asia to St. Lawrence Island or the Diomedes and then to American shores carrying with them household goods, trade goods, and dogs. No doubt similar sea trips took place in prehistoric times.

Ethnographical evidences other than canoes and floats tend to support the hypothesis about migration to and on the west coast. Bryan (1965: 82–83) noted that the evidence in general indicated that most modern Indian populations have remained in their present geographic loca-

tions for long periods of time. These settlers would be especially likely to stay in a particular area after there had been cultural adaptation to the natural resources there. Furthermore, if there were no major climatic changes to provoke adjustments, the cultural changes might instead have resulted after adventurous splinter groups separated from the main group and filled in different ecological regions or after increased population forced an overflow from the original settlement into adjacent, less desirable regions where there was adaptation to different resources. The great variety of languages along the Pacific Coast from British Columbia to Mexico might well be explained by its being the primary route or first route of migration. The population may have gradually increased and spread down the coast, each splinter group or overflow pool isolating itself to the point that it diverged linguistically. A counterhypothesis is that the western coast of North America continued to be the major route for migrants from Asia, as well as a reverse migration route of expanding populations in the south, perhaps as far as the Mexican coast.

The type and degree of technological achievements by the first migrants to America are just as debatable as the means and the time of migration. Krieger (1953b: 241) pointed out that cultural material is already on hand that is "older than any of the projectile points popularly thought to mark the oldest American occupation." He also suggested the possibility that there was a bone industry, which preceded the manufacture of projectile points but may have been concurrent with an early stone technology. The lack of distinctiveness of types of tools or even their recognition as tools by the lay public may have prevented the discovery of evidence of these people. If artifacts from the "Pre-Projectile Point stage" that were made by a method similar to Old World Paleolithic Levalloiso-Mousterian flaking technique (Bordaz 1959) were found in the Americas, most observers would not notice or report them unless they were associated with remains of large animals. Krieger (1964: 42–48; 1965: 270–72) proposed and made a strong case for the occurrence of this stage but did not succeed in producing irrefutable evidence. Some of the claims he presented have been doubted because of the lack of sufficient data (Bird 1965; Heizer 1964: 119–22; Wormington 1957: 221–22). Jennings (1968: 65–70) pointed out that evidence on sites of the chopper–scraper complexes do not indicate that there had been any migrations before the "Big Game Hunters" and concluded that "neither the age nor the cultural significance of this complex can be settled."

Migrants to America during the period 40,-000–12,000 B.C. could have availed themselves of the advanced technological developments of their time, which were of greater variety than generally thought (Figure 2–3). For example, Valoch (1968) indicated that the Middle Paleolithic in Europe had leaf-shaped biface forms associated with it (Figure 2–3A), perhaps as early as Early Würm, more than 40,000 years ago. He said that the "hole stick" or "baton de commandement" occurred at Moldova on the Dniester as early as 22,050 B.C. (Figure 2–3J), and Haynes and Hemmings (1968) have reported a similar artifact from North America. Ivanova (1968: 375), commenting on Valoch, noted that radiocarbon dates from Moldova ranged from 22,050 to 27,050 B.C. and confirmed that there was interstadial rise in temperature during that period. Judging from the evidence, then, it would have been possible for the so-called Middle Paleolithic hunters with a varied stone technology as well as bone technology to travel across northern Eurasia to Beringia during the interstade. A possible example of evidence of such travelers was found by Bader and Geresimov (Anon. 1965); a mammoth hunter's grave about 130 miles northeast of Moscow that contained a flint knife, a massive scraper, ivory beads, a pierced-stone pendant, arctic-fox teeth ornaments, and red pigment. The grave tentatively was dated about the same time as the early dates on the Moldova site (27,000+ B.C.). The hunter was wearing tailored fur clothing. This find lends credence to Campbell's (1963) premise that there was a movement of European hunters from west to east at an early period.

There were perhaps earlier migrations that brought a less technologically developed stone industry between 70,000 and 40,000 B.C., but of greater importance in understanding cultural developments in the Americas are the carriers, or originators, of the leaf-shaped bifacial form that has been identified as a projectile point (Figure 2–3A). The form could have developed independently in the Americas, as Bryan (1965: 89; 1969: 342) has proposed, but because it appeared in the Middle Paleolithic of Europe (Valoch 1968), the Upper Paleolithic at Kamchatka (Dikov 1968; Rudenko 1964: 275–76), northern Russia, and the Trans-Baikal (Okladnikov 1959; 1961), the islands of Hokkaido, and Honshu, Japan (Befu and Chard 1960; Kotani 1969; Morlan 1967), Central Asia (Chard 1959), and the Paleolithic of Siberia (Bushnell and McBurney 1959), this possiblity is irrelevant. Often-cited evidence from Asia indicating that early migrants to the New World could have come well equipped is the Ust-Kanskaia paleolithic cave site, which yielded bipointed, leaf-shaped bifaces, typical Mousterian points, perforators, core tools, crude oval or almond-shaped chopping tools, and blades (Rudenko 1961) (Figure 2–3).

It seems very logical to suppose that the first migrants brought with them the knowledge of stone technologies, including the production of the bifacial leaf-shaped point, of laurel-leaf or bipoint shape or both. They are the general preform shapes that are the logical precursors of fluted projectile points made during the Early Hunter Tradition (Roosa 1956; Wormington 1962). Wendorf (1966: 267–68) indicated that the basic stone technology was available in Stage I of the Siberian Paleolithic, 18,000 B.C. The early emigrants probably used simple log rafts, skin floats, reed bundle floats, or canoes made of strips of bark or skin sewn together and reinforced with bone or wood (Figure 2–2). Their stone technology was advanced enough to manufacture bifacial, bipointed leaf-shaped and laurel-leaf shaped points or knives, snubbed-end flake scrapers, perforators, blades, burins, side scrapers, and choppers (Figure 2–3). They had a bone-working industry, slings, spear throwers, bolas, and cordage and knew how to construct stone hearths (Figure 2–3).

Sites in continental North America, which have possibilities of being earlier than 12,000

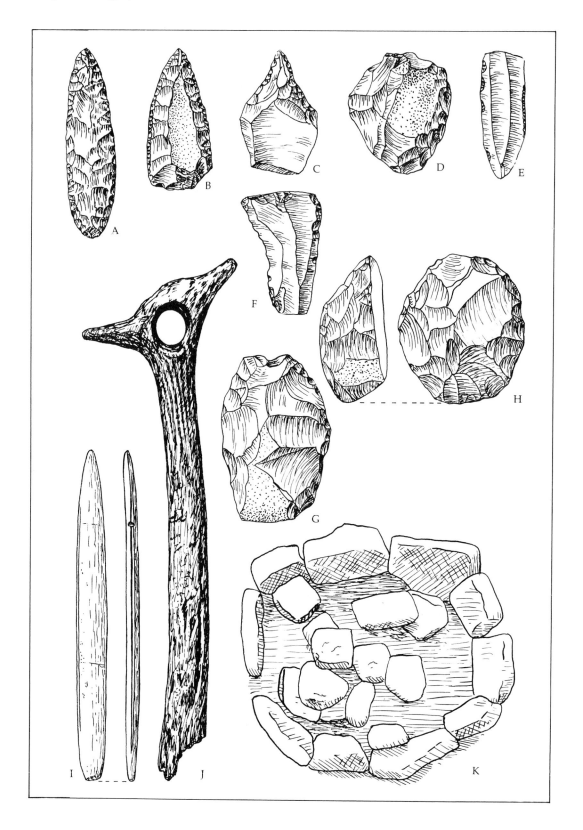

B.C.; prior to the Paleo-Indian big-game hunting tradition, have a distribution that appears to be very revealing. The distribution seems to bear out the hypothesis that the first migrants to North America came by way of the Pacific Coast. The most northerly sites of probable great antiquity, other than those in Alaska proper, appear inland 100 miles from the Gulf of Georgia at the mouth of the Fraser River and in the intermontane area via the Columbia River access (Borden 1960; 1961; 1968; Cressman 1946; 1960; 1966; Daugherty 1956b; Gruhn 1965; Rogers 1966). The hypothesis is proposed that these intrusions were originated at the coast and were not made by the first migrants down the coast, but by their progeny toward the end of the glacial maximum (Figure 2–1).

Not all the possible sites have been specified, and some that have been shown on the map (Figure 2–4) may prove to be later or more culturally diverse. The sites have been selected from the following compilations and site reports: American Heritage 1966: 18–19; Aveleyra 1956; 1964; Borden 1962; Bryan 1962; 1965; 1969; Butler 1961; 1965; Crook and Harris 1957; 1958; Harrington and Simpson 1961; Haury 1950: 174–76; Hibben 1937; 1941; 1942; 1943; 1945; Irwin-Williams 1967: 345; 1968: 40; Jennings 1968: 61–108; Johnson 1951: 265; Krieger 1964: 43–44; McGee 1889; MacNeish 1963; 1964b; 1964c; Rogers 1966: 114–17; Sellards 1940; 1952; Wormington 1957.

If the migrants to America came by float or boat during the height of the Wisconsin stage, 22,000–12,000 B.C., most of the places they would have beached would now be at least 20 fathoms (120 feet) under water and could be as deep as 50 fathoms (300 feet) (Hopkins 1967: 464). Therefore, most of the evidence of America's first emigrants would have been destroyed. The archaeological sites of the early migrants that might now be available might not be along the seacoast but at desirable places inland on streams

such as the Columbia. The Dalles on the Columbia could have been an attractive spot to Early Man at certain periods of the year, during the salmon runs (Borden 1962; Bryan 1962). Boaters would have to have been lured by some special means of subsistence, such as the salmon runs, to travel inland. The early migrants along the Pacific Coast may have had a way station as far north as the location of the Olcott site (Figure 2–4). Olcott, with Fraser Canyon and Haller Lake, are inland areas that probably could have been penetrated during or toward the end of the Woodfordian substage of the Wisconsin stage. A Haller Lake projectile point (Butler 1961: Figure 2b) is comparable to Olcott points in size and shape. Still farther north in the Frazer River Canyon, British Columbia, the lowest level in the Yale site (Figure 2–4) has yielded "several leaf-shaped bipoints, two of which have bilateral shouldering and convergent bases" similar to Sandia points (Bryan 1965: 176). Although this level of the Yale site is dated only about 7000 B.C., it is the earliest occupation in the area. The bipoint forms, along with the percussion flaking industry indicated by cobble choppers, scrapers, and hammerstones, compose the type of complex that hypothetically would have been the tool kits of the first people to penetrate the interior toward the end of the glacial period. The people at these sites could have been the descendants of the first migrants down the Pacific Coast who had with them the knowledge of producing large, leaf-shaped bifacial points or bipointed forms. They were probably Unspecialized Hunter–Gatherers who fished, collected, hunted small game, and occasionally hunted the larger sea mammals. It is likely that they knew how to use spears or harpoons and may have tipped them with the leaf-shaped bipoints.

An important site is at Five-Mile Rapids, Oregon (Figure 2–4), where Cressman (1960: 59) found that the early phase was based primarily on the exploitation of salmon, although elk ant-

Figure 2–3. Cultural equipment available in the Old World, 40,000–12,500 B.C. Scale, A–J, 1:2. A, Bipointed, leaf-shaped biface form; B, typical Mousterian point; C, perforator; D, core tool; E–F, blades; G, crude oval chopping tool; H, core tool; I, bone point; J, baton de commandement or hole stick; K, stone-lined hearth (actual size, approximately six feet in diameter).

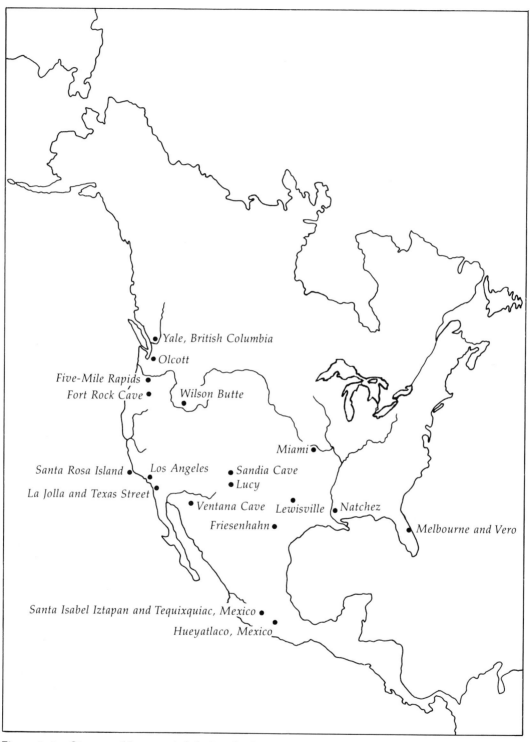

Figure 2–4. Sites possibly occupied during the Early Man period.

lers and bones of large scavenging birds were in the deposits. The people there used bolas, heavy chopping tools, burins, unifacial and bifacial percussion flaked knives or points, and some pressure-flaked tools until about 7,500 years ago. This inland spot would have logically attracted Unspecialized Hunter–Gatherers as they moved into North America along the west coast, as Cressman noted, because of the availability of fish, sea animals, and land animals. Cressman (1960: 7, 68) proposed the hypothesis that the people who adapted to the ecological resources of the region had earlier occupied the interior. This is opposite to the proposal I have made that the people came from the coast. Another site is Fort Rock Cave (Figure 2–4) in eastern Oregon dated 11,250± 720 B.C. in occupation levels below fluted points (Bryan 1969: 340).

At the Wilson Butte Cave site, Snake River, in Idaho (Figure 2–4) a stratum in which there were a leaf-shaped, bifacially flaked implement of basalt, a chalcedony blade, a utilized flake, and a modified animal bone (Figure 2–5) was radiocarbon dated 14,450±500 B.C. Another date of 13,050±800 B.C. was thought to have inconclusive supporting evidence of the association of man with the stratum. The site is located near Snake River, a tributary of the Columbia River, the first probable entrance to the interior by migrants following the coast in small boats during the height of the Wisconsin stage.

On the California coast the Texas Street site (Figure 2–4) has a radiocarbon date that shows it to be more than 35,000 years old, but mankind was not necessarily associated with it at that time. Simpson supported the idea that the date is an Early Man association, but Krieger (1958: 974–78) suggested that the artifacts and charcoal were of natural origin. The Texas Street hearths have been questioned as being man made by Cruxent (1962) because of their lack of phosphorus content. The Scripps Institution site at La Jolla, California, also called the La Jolla site (Figure 2–4) but not to be confused with the La Jolla complex, has produced what have been termed hearths that have been dated at 21,500 years by the radiocarbon method. The Santa Rosa Island finds (Figure 2–4) have been dated at 29,650±

2500 B.C.; these dates have been obtained from the fire areas with burnt dwarf mammoth bones, but no items that are definite artifacts have been found in association. Los Angeles Man (Wormington 1957: 230–31), a human skull found in pleistocene deposits, appears to be definite evidence of the occupation of California at a very early period (Figure 2–4).

As the midcontinental glaciers began to dissipate, there was a long period allowing adaptation to, and some specialization of, the hunting of big game. Some groups could have become experts at hunting the mammoth, as is perhaps illustrated by the second find at Santa Isabel Iztapan, Mexico (Figure 2–4) (Aveleyra 1956; 1964; Wormington 1957: 91–99). The mammoth in this instance has been identified as a different species from those associated with the Early Hunter (Llano) Tradition. Furthermore, estimated dates from similar formations range from 16,000 to 11,000 years ago, and if the older dates were accepted, the site could have been a way station for hunters preceding the fluted-point tradition of the Early Hunter. The projectile points are of the general leaf-shaped type that are proposed here as the equipment of migrants to the Americas during the Early Man period (Aveleyra 1956; 1964; Aveleyra and Maldunado-Koerdell 1953). Another bifacial bipointed form was found in a stratum containing horse, camel, mammoth, and mastodon bones at Hueyatlaco, Valsequillo, Mexico (Irwin-Williams 1967: 340–45) (Figures 2–4, 2–6). The artifact was recovered in direct association with the partially articulated bones of a horse. According to Irwin-Williams (1967: 345), "The artifact was made by soft-hammer percussion with terminal pressure retouch" (Figure 2-6C). It is possible evidence of very early big-game hunters in south-central and southwestern Mexico perhaps 20,000 years ago (Irwin-Williams 1968: 40).

To the north, at Ventana Cave, Arizona (Figure 2–4), an artifact complex in the lowest level was associated with a pleistocene fauna consisting of horse, ground sloth, tapir, jaguar, and wolf. The artifacts were different from those associated with Clovis Fluted. The projectile point in Ventana Cave, which was said to resemble Clovis

Fluted was leaf shaped but with a concave base. Choppers, scrapers, planes, and knives accompanied the bifacial leaf-shaped point (Rogers 1966: 117). Haury (1950: 174–76) noted that there were two possible tools, a basalt flake suggesting a scraping tool and a discoidal basaltic hammerstone in a conglomerate layer that also contained charcoal underneath the layer in

which the projectile point and other tools were found. The earliest level was possibly occupied during the Early Man period.

Still farther north, early deposits in Sandia Cave (Figure 2–4) (Hibben 1937; 1941; 1942; 1943; 1955) could be evidences of a way station. Although there are no definite radiocarbon dates on Sandia points (Agogino 1968: 2), one type is

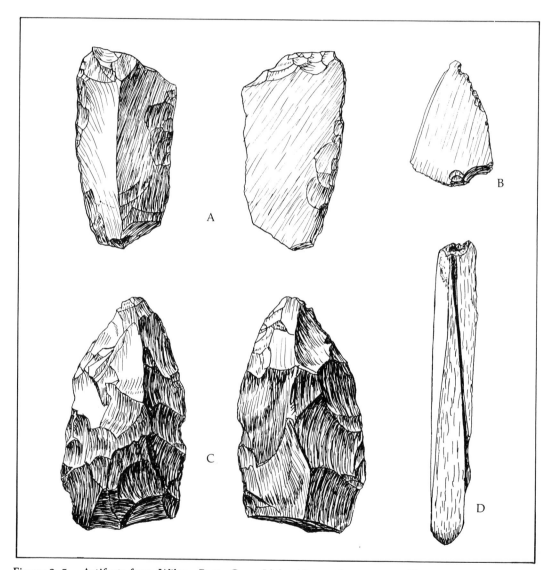

Figure 2–5. Artifacts from Wilson Butte Cave, Idaho (drawn from casts at University of Missouri—Columbia, Museum of Anthropology). Scale 1:1.
A, Chalcedony blade (both faces); B, utilized flake; C, basalt biface (both faces); D, modified animal bone.

basically a leaf-shaped bipoint and thus theoreti-
cally could be earlier than Clovis. The Lucy site,
New Mexico (Figure 2–4), contained fluted
Sandia points, which may indicate that Clovis
Fluted was derived from Sandia (Roosa 1956:
310).

To the east and south in the West Gulf Section
of the Atlantic Coastal and Gulf Coastal plains
is Freisenhahn Cave (Figure 2–4), which has the
association of Pleistocene animals and flake
scrapers. Farther east and to the north in the
southern plains is the Lewisville site (Figure 2–4),
where the time is estimated by radiocarbon dating as 35,000 B.C., and where simple flaked tools
were associated with hearths and various extinct
animals from the Pleistocene. The associations
and hearths have been questioned, but the evidence cannot be discounted completely at this
time (Crook and Harris 1957; 1958; Heizer and
Brooks 1965).

If Hunter–Gatherers from the Early Man
period moved due east after crossing Texas, the
next way station could have been the site near
Natchez, Mississippi (Figure 2–4), where human
bones were reported as occurring in the same
deposit with mastodon and other remains of
Pleistocene animals (Quimby 1956). Then in
Florida, the Melbourne and Vero (Figure 2–4) associations of man with extinct animal forms need
reconsideration with the evidence from chemical
content that the human bones were probably
from the same deposit as the animal bones (Sellards 1952: 127; Wilson 1895: 724–25). At an undisturbed level of another site in Florida, New
Smyrna, artifacts were present with the remains
of extinct animals.

In Iowa, Indiana, and Ohio there are some uncertain evidences of men from an early period
who could have migrated from Florida or Texas;
one of these evidences was the possible associa-

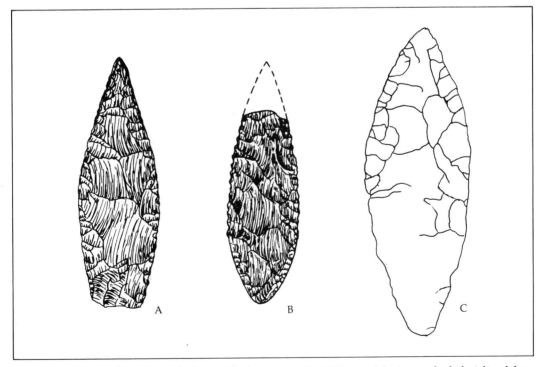

Figure 2–6.   Projectile points or knives with the mammoth at Iztapan, Mexico, and a bifacial tool from
Hueyatlaco, Mexico (after Aveleyra-Arroyo de Anda 1956; Irwin-Williams 1967). Scale 5:6.
A–B, Points found with the mammoth at Santa Isabel Iztapan, Mexico; C, bipointed leaf-shaped point
found in early levels at Valsequillo, Mexico.

tion of an artifact with mastodon bones (Sellards 1952: 139). A recent find, the Miami, Missouri, mastodon site (Figure 2–4) is good evidence of association of a chert-flake tool with the mastodon bones.

In general the pattern is the same in all the studies when the Llano and Plano complexes are not included. The distribution of possible Early Man sites starts to the north at the Frazer River and Columbia River passageways, the latter an inland route to the Intermontane–Great Basin areas. The sites are distributed along the coast to southern California and Mexico and then northward inland to Arizona, New Mexico, and Texas. Finally the distribution extends across the lower part of the southern United States to Florida, then north to Missouri and the Ohio River drainage. A few possible evidences are from Kansas, east to Ohio, south of the boreal forest during the Valders readvance about 8700 B.C. (Martin 1958: 385, Figure 3).

Enough evidence has been accumulated to suggest a revision in the theory about the major route of migration of the Indians from Asia to America. The hypothesis is proposed that the first migrations to America were by boat down the west coast, perhaps as early as 40,000 years ago during the Altonian substage, and definitely prior to 12,000 B.C. The proposed route and the possible penetrations into the interior at a later time are shown on the map (Figure 2–1), and possible evidences are shown in Figure 2–4.

The northern Asiatic coast has no evidences of early culture and in this regard is similar to the Northwest Coast of North America. Chard (1959) said that the earlier evidences of human occupation along the Asiatic coast were covered by advancing seas. The same situation probably prevailed along the west coast of North America; only those penetrations to the interior in later time are evident. The proposition that the migrants to America brought only chopping tools with them and developed other technologies later can probably be discarded. Byers (1959), for example, noted that a late Levalloiso-Mousterian order of stoneworking technology must have been known to the ancestors of the makers of

Clovis points, and it seems likely that it was known to the first migrants.

There was penetration of the Pacific Mountain System, Pacific Border province in the Puget Trough physiographic section, as indicated by the Yale site (Figure 2–4) at the mouth of the Fraser River (Borden 1961), and throughout the Columbia River valley into the Intermontane Plateaus, Columbia Plateaus province, and on south into the Basin and Range physiographic province, as indicated by the Wilson Butte site (Figure 2–4) (Crabtree 1969; Fenneman 1938: 34; Gruhn 1961; 1965).

The penetrations into the southern Basin and Range province probably originated from the coast of southern California and the coast of the Gulf of California. The movement inland into central Mexico must have been very rapid because of the milder climate and the great variety of plant and animal life that might have encouraged a population explosion. People could have quickly exploited the ecological potential in the area and expanded both north and south. The northern expansion into the interior of North America appears to have taken place while glaciers were still spreading cold far to the south while boreal forest covered most, if not all, of southern North America and part of northern Mexico (Sears 1948: 326). Pleistocene fauna in the northern Mexico area included the mammoth, camelids, and horses that were prairie-grass-eating animals. These herd animals probably furnished food for some of the Early Hunters. It is possible that during the cold period of the Woodfordian substage the Hunter–Gatherers penetrated as far north as the Missouri–Mississippi–Ohio drainage or in the states of Kansas, Missouri, Illinois, Indiana, and Ohio (Figures 2–1, 2–4). It is probable that any permanent occupation of this central part of the North American Continent took place at a later date, after 12,000 B.C.

Some of the hypotheses and speculations of interest about Early Man can be found in the following references: Antevs (1935; 1937); Bank (1962); Barth (1950); Beals (1957); Bryan (1968); Bushnell and McBurney (1959); Chard (1958;

1960; 1969); Colbert (1942); Dikov (1968); Harrington (1933: 190); Hester (1966); Howard (1936); Hrdlicka (1942); Jelinek (1965; 1971); Kerby (1965); Krogman (1941a); Mather (1954); Solecki (1951); and Wright (1912). Good summaries and bibliographies can be found in works not previously mentioned as follows: Agogino and Rovner (1964); Agogino, Rovner, and Irwin-Williams (1964); Bryan (1965; 1969); Byers (1957); Campbell (1963); Daugherty (1956a); Graham and Heizer (1967); Haynes (1889); Haynes (1971); Heizer (1964); Howard (1935); Irving (1963; 1971); Irwin (1971); Irwin-Williams (1968); MacDonald (1971); MacGowan and Hester (1962); Martin (1967a); Mayer-Oakes (1963); Meighan (1965); Rogers (1966); Sellards (1947; 1952; 1960); Shutler (1971); Wendorf (1966); Wheat (1971); Wilmsen (1965); Winsor (1889); and Wormington (1957; 1962; 1971).

It appears that the answers to questions of the time of migration, the route, the manner by which the emigrants came, and the equipment they brought with them, are thus far hypothetical. The generally accepted hypotheses concerning the path of migration to America of the first Indian ancestors, the time of migration, and their cultural equipment are in need of reevaluation. Evidence has continued to build in support of the viewpoint that there was an occupation of the west coast, Mexico, and the southern United States at a time preceding the height of the Woodfordian glacial substage, probably 40,000–30,000 B.C. The hypothesis that people who spread into the North American Continent along the western shore were nomads who came by float, canoe, or boat is proposed as probable in view of the evidence available. The further hypothesis has been submitted that the emigrants brought with them a technology of stoneworking that included the production of bifacial, laurel-leaf shaped, and bipointed projectile points or knives and that those were the basic forms from which other American-innovated forms were derived.

3. Hunter–Gatherer Tradition, Early Man Period

In the past a fair number of artifacts were found in the Eastern United States that were assumed to be of Early Man period or produced by Hunter–Gatherers. The age of the finds had been determined on the basis of typology of artifacts, geological evidence, and association with Pleistocene animals. So much controversy developed concerning all Early Man discoveries that the findings were generally discredited regardless of the apparent veracity of the evidence. Hrdlicka (1903; 1907; 1912; 1918; 1920; 1925; 1928; 1932; 1937a; 1937b; 1942) was one of the leaders in discounting the great age of human remains regardless of their geological context or paleontological associations on the basis that modern man was represented in every instance and thus the finds could not be ancient. Holmes (1890; 1893a; 1893b; 1901; 1903b; 1910; 1919) cast doubt on discoveries that were reportedly Early Man, or he presented other hypotheses and interpretations of the evidence to refute them. His antipathy toward great antiquity of human remains and artifacts in America culminated in two articles, one in 1925 entitled "The Antiquity Phantom in American Archaeology," in which he discounted the evidence he had not seen or had a chance to evaluate fully concerning the discovery in Melbourne, Florida, and the second in 1928 "Pitfalls of the Paleolithic Theory in America" where he stated (Holmes 1928: 175):

> In closing I venture to make the assertion that there has not been collected either in North, Middle or South America, a single archaeological object attributed to great antiquity that can stand the test of the scientific requirements made plain; and the same is true of any skeletal finds as had well been shown by Dr. Hrdlicka, however confidently announced as very ancient and by whatsoever authority.

Hrdlicka and Holmes were giants in their respective fields of physical anthropology and archaeology, and because they took such a stand, the field was temporarily closed to further serious exploration of the idea of ancient man in America.

After the discovery of Folsom, research on ancient man in America was resumed, and old sites and evidence were reexamined in some instances. For the most part, finds once discredited were disregarded, and the incompleteness of evidence for their antiquity probably justified this attitude.

What evidences do we have in the Missouri–Mississippi Valley that the first settlers may have arrived in the area 20,000–12,000 B.C. or earlier? Krieger (1964:42–48) in his discussion of the Pre-Projectile Point stage, equated with the Early Man period here, does not list any complexes or sites in the Missouri–Mississippi Valley proper. His "defining characteristics" of the stage are a low level of stoneworking technique similar to the Lower Paleolithic of the Old World. Stone tools were made by percussion and consisted of core and flake types and pebble tools but lack thin biface forms. Bone tools, tubes, and splinters are the other characteristics. He says that no hearths lined with stone have been found associated with the stage. He notes (Krieger 1964: 52) that the same is true for the Llano culture of the Paleo-Indian stage.

Rock-lined prepared hearths are paleolithic in the Old World. A rock-lined hearth was found at the Makarovo site in the Lena River basin (Figure 2–3K), and similar hearths have been found on the Genisay, at Kokorevo village, Russia (Okladnikov 1964: 42–43). The people of the Early Man period in the New World could easily have known how to prepare and use them. Furthermore, examples of such hearths may already have been found and reported upon. In New Mexico, Hibben (1941: 27) described a hearth in the Sandia level of Sandia Cave that was partially enclosed by small limestone boulders. Hibben wrote, "These small boulders roughly outlined the charcoal area. A Sandia point of Type I was touching one of the boulders, and the hearth was assigned to the early phase of Sandia occupation."

In northwestern Missouri at the Beverly site, a deeply buried hearth was discovered that could have been built quite early. The hearth was buried 15 feet in loess, and it was noted that a few cobbles were imbedded in the loess at the level of the hearth but were found nowhere else in the windblown deposit.

> The hearth itself consisted of angular limestone blocks 100 to 200 mm. in diameter arranged in a circle which has a diameter of about 3 feet. Small fragments of charcoal were scattered through the loess within the circle of limestone blocks, and the blocks were reddish brown on the side facing the center of the circle and gray on the side facing away from the center of the circle. Within 4 feet of the hearth and at the same level as the hearth were found a bone fragment, part of a deer's *(Odocoileus?)* jaw, one complete valve of a fresh water clam and 3 small fragments of clam shells, one small bone fragment, and one flint chip. . . . These were evidently washed out of the loess and probably came from the horizon of the hearth (Davis 1955: 135–37).

On the basis of fossil shells found in the loess above the hearth, it was suggested that the date of the site might be the same as that of the Lime Creek site, Nebraska (Davis 1962). However, no fossils were found in the lower stratum of loess that encompassed the hearth. It would seem, then, that the prepared rock-lined hearth of the Beverly site might be earlier than the Lime Creek site, but is probably later than the Early Man period in Missouri. It is interesting, though, that a somewhat similar hearth was found in Ohio at the Tomilson Well site (Gilbert 1889; Holmes 1919: 79). The hearth was 15–18 feet beneath the surface and consisted of three boulders about a foot in diameter lying close together and sur-

rounded by ashes and charcoal. Charred sticks were in the center of the hearth. The hearth was thought to be covered by glacial deposits.

Two other hearths were reported at Portsmouth, Ohio, at a depth of 15 feet (Foster 1881: 77–78). They were described as places where fires had been built "on a circular collection of small stones, a part of which were embedded in the bank." The stones were red from heat, and charcoal lay among them.

Certainly hearths alone, even when found in ancient geological contexts are not sufficient evidence to denote an Early Man period, but they are traits that could have been associated with the period. Furthermore the dates of their use can now be determined through radiocarbon, archaeomagnetic or thermoluminescent methods.

In collections of surface material, a primitive level of stoneworking technique is apparent at many sites in Missouri and the Eastern United States. In most instances with them are associations of bifacial projectile points or knives and other tools supposedly characteristic of later periods. The full evaluation of the evidences has not been made, but an indefatigable group of students has emphasized the collection and study of tools other than projectile points and bifacial blades in the lower Mississippi Valley (Josselyn 1965a; 1965b; 1966; Lively 1965; Lively and Josselyn 1965). At the very least there is now a search for and an interest in the less spectacular tools that might indicate occupation of the Missouri–Mississippi Valley during an Early Man period prior to 12,000 B.C.

Several evidences have been reported in Missouri that are perhaps pertinent to the Early Man problem. For example, a crude implement made of yellow jasper, possibly a scraper, was found in a glacial deposit below the windblown loess in northwestern Missouri. It was reported as "Another Paleolithic Implement" (Owen 1909: 110–11).

The first accounts that might be considered evidence of an Early Man period in Missouri were Koch's (1839; 1841; 1843; 1860) reports on finds of artifacts in association with mastodons (Figure 3–1A–E). These finds have been discussed by numerous writers (Andrews 1875;

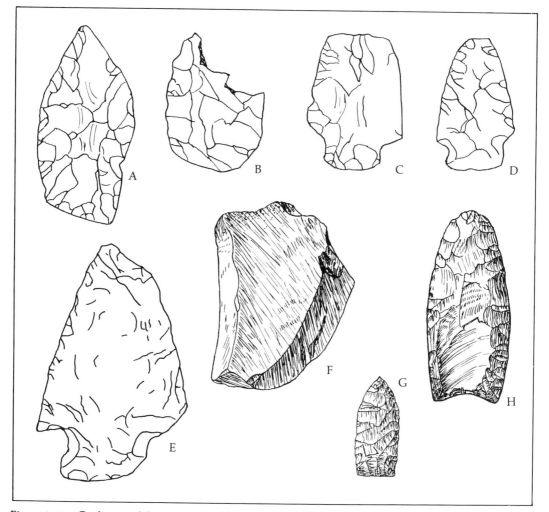

Figure 3–1.   Outlines and drawings of artifacts reportedly found in deposits with mastodon bones. Scale A–D, 3:5, E–H, 1:1.

A–D, Artifacts possibly associated with Koch's mastodons in Missouri (after Gross 1951); E, artifact possibly found with Koch mastodon (after Rau 1873); F, flake knife–scraper found with the Miami, Missouri, mastodon; G, very small lanceolate biface from Trolinger Bog (J. A. Eichenberger, cast, UMC); H, Clovis Fluted from Kimmswick mastodon site (from photo, courtesy John Rinaldo, Chicago Museum of Natural History).

Dana 1875; Eiseley 1946; Foster 1881: 62–66; Fowke 1928; Gross 1951; Johnson 1952; Mehl 1962; Montagu 1942; Montagu and Peterson 1944; Simpson 1943; Wislizenus 1860). Several artifacts found in deposits in which mastodon bones have also been found are shown in Figure 3–1. Most are considered to be fortuitous associations of artifacts that were produced after

12,000 B.C., probably later than 8000 B.C., long after the mastodon was extinct in Missouri.

Information about the possible association of a fluted point with the Koch mastodon in the Kimmswick bone bed is inconclusive, but it may help explain Montagu's reference to a letter from M. W. Stirling (Montagu 1942; Montagu and Peterson 1944: 419). Stirling stated that W. H.

Holmes had said in the winter of 1927–1928 that on an earlier visit to the Missouri Historical Society, St. Louis, he had been shown a projectile point, which was said to have been found with the Koch mastodon remains. Holmes said that the distinctive feature of the point was that it had a concave base, and a long flake had been struck from the base on either side passing longitudinally beyond the middle point, i.e., a fluted-point form. The visit was probably in 1901 (Holmes 1903b: 237) but may have been in 1903 or 1904 shortly before the Louisiana Purchase Exposition of 1904, because a picture of Holmes at the mastodon site, which was taken for publicity of the exposition, is in the photo files of the Missouri Historical Society, Jefferson Memorial Building, St. Louis.

The point described may have been the one that is now at the Field Museum of Natural History, Chicago, and that purportedly came from the Kimmswick mastodon site about 25 miles south of St. Louis in Jefferson County (John Rinaldo, personal communication, November 1, 1949) (Figure 3–1H). Holmes (1903b: 237) noted:

> The question of association of human remains with those of mammoth and mastodon has been raised at this place [Kimmswick bone bed], but up to the present time the evidence collected is not at all conclusive. It is believed that the bones found which so closely resemble the humerus of man may be portions of the fibulae of young mastodon, and that the flint implements reported as occurring with the fossil remains may have been recently introduced, since identical forms are plentiful on the surface of the site.

Knoblock (1939: 36–37) reported on the finding of what is probably the same fluted point that was discovered deep in the Kimmswick site deposits. It appears to be evidence of early use of the Mississippi Valley Central Locality in the Paleo-Indian period, if not associated with the remains of the mastodon at the site. Knoblock (1939: 36–37) quoted a letter from W. F. Parks dated October 1, 1931, which noted that the fluted point and another, a barbed point two and one-half inches long, were found "with the bones of mastodon, horse, *Equus complicatus,* and ground sloth, *Megalonyx,* and other bones of prehistoric animals."

A new look should be taken at the Koch mastodon finds since new information has become available concerning the climate and flora at the time mastodon lived in southwestern Missouri. Recently it was discovered that there was a late-Pleistocene boreal forest in southwestern Missouri at the time the mastodon lived there (Mehringer and others 1968). The evidence came from two spring bogs in the Pomme de Terre Valley near the original find made by Koch in 1840. One bog, Boney Spring, yielded spruce pollen, and spruce and larch macrofossils, denoting a late-Pleistocene boreal forest dating between 14,630±220 B.C. and 11,750±600 B.C. Associated fauna included ground sloth, giant beaver, and mastodon. The boreal spruce forest also had minor deciduous elements. Although a chert scraper and other chipped-stone tools were recovered with mastodon bones and other fossils in the spring conduit, the association was noted as spurious because of "the disparity in age between the mastodon and the artifacts" (Mehringer and others 1968).

At a similar spring bog, Trolinger Spring (Figure 3–2), an arrowhead or a very small lanceolate biface (Figure 3–1G) was recovered in 1967 in the spring conduit, which also contained bones of muskox, mastodon, and horse. The small lanceolate form was judged to be intrusive "since no archaeological data were recovered from the more extensive excavations in 1968 to corroborate the age implied by its presence in the bog deposits" (Mehringer and others 1968). Both of the spring sites are within three miles of the Koch Pomme de Terre mastodon find in Benton County.

The investigations at Boney Spring and Trolinger Spring (Figure 3–2) did not clear up the question left by Koch's (1841; 1843; 1860) controversial reports of finding evidences of man associated with mastodon in a spring in the Pomme de Terre River valley in 1840. It seems apparent from the new evidence that the associations of artifacts and mastodons were probably fortuitous, for the mastodon bones were dated earlier than any of the accepted radiocarbon dates associated with fluted forms or other chipped-stone bifaces in the Missouri–Mississippi Valley.

A

B

Figure 3–2.   Excavations at Trolinger Bog, Benton County.
A, Excavations in 1967; B, excavations in 1968.

Further evidence indicating that the American mastodon, *Mammut americanus,* existed at an early time was obtained at the Grundel site in northwestern Missouri. The scattered skeletal remains were in Farmdale loess and were dated by the radiocarbon method from associated charcoal at 23,150±200 B.C. The "stacking" of the bones and the green bone fracture of one tusk and other bones were postulated by one of the excavators as evidence of human activity (Mehl 1966). Although the mastodon bones and the surrounding area were thoroughly investigated, no human-made artifacts were discovered. I aided in the excavations and was not convinced that there was any evidence of the association of man with the mastodon, but the possibility should be left open.

Another mastodon skeleton was located in northeastern Missouri in Lincoln County during the construction of a bridge by the Missouri State Highway Department. The state geologist, William Hayes, and his assistant, Jerry Vineyard, were on the scene along with Walter Klippel and J. Allen Eichenberger, research associates in American Archaeology, Department of Anthropology, at the University of Missouri—Columbia. There was little time for meticulous excavation due to water seepage and urgency of continuing the construction of the bridge. There did not seem to be any direct association of human beings with the remains of the mastodon, but slightly above them in a gravel layer and a few feet distant, a large chipped piece of chert, possibly an artifact, was found *in situ* (Klippel and Eichenberger, personal communications 1971). It was suggested by the geologists that the gravel deposit in which the possible artifact was found could have been a gravel bar at the edge of the bog in which the mastodon had been trapped. The evidence here is nebulous, and the large, rough, chopperlike implement or core could have occurred at almost any period in Missouri archaeology.

Broadhead (1881) described the finding of a mastodon associated with artifacts in a spring south of Sedalia in Pettis County, Missouri. A funnel-shaped area about 15 feet in diameter contained mastodon bones *(Mastodon americanus cuvier)* and pieces of wood resembling cypress. "A few flint implements [spearheads] and one stone club were found with the bones" (Broadhead 1881: 520). The disposition of the bones and artifacts is not known, and no detailed description of them was made at the time of discovery. The site is located on a terrace, and as it is a spring still being used as a water source, Indian campsites were probably located near it from time to time in past periods, which could account for the artifacts in the spring.

Although there have been several finds of mastodon bones and possible association of artifacts, there is no conclusive evidence that early people in eastern North America hunted the mastodon. The evidences of artifacts that in several instances were associated with mastodon bones in the area have been reviewed by Williams (1957), and all are too vague to be accepted as indisputable proof. Some scholars proposed that the mastodon survived into the Archaic period (Mehl 1962: 54; Williams 1957: 367). This hypothesis is difficult to believe. Perhaps one reason that the late dates have been cited is that so many of the remains have been found in spring bogs, and the materials in such locations have been greatly mixed. Many of the radiocarbon dates have been taken from wood, charcoal, or other associated material that may not have been any more contemporaneous with the mastodon than the artifacts found with the bones. The dates from tusks seem to be particularly unreliable. Seemingly solid evidence to indicate that a mastodon was butchered was discovered at one site. The evidence was similar to that at the Grundel mastodon site; no artifacts were associated with the mastodon remains (Wittry 1965).

A recent find of a mastodon in a road cut at Miami, Missouri, produced in association with it a chert-flake tool, which had evidence of a great deal of wear on one surface (Figure 3–1F). The bones of the animal appeared to have been displaced and the bones and the flake were buried under an old soil horizon beneath 14 feet of undisturbed windblown soil. Flecks of wood charcoal were among and under the bones. This appears to be definite evidence of the association of man and mastodon.

Although there have been numerous excavations to bedrock in cave and shelter sites in southwestern Missouri, and to sterile deposits in the early sites in northern Missouri, such as Graham Cave and Arnold Research Cave, no evidences of an industry that occurred before the development of the chipped-stone bifacial form or bifacial bipoint have been reported. In every instance where an excavation has been conducted to sterile soil, flaked-stone bifaces usually considered to be projectile points or knives have been found. The lack of a pre-projectile-point complex in excavated sites is not necessarily conclusive evidence that people were not in the Missouri–Mississippi drainage prior to the well-known Paleo-Indian period, which is dated after 12,000 B.C., but it considerably diminishes the possibility.

There are alternative postulations to the assumption that Early Man did not appear in the central regions of the New World until after 12,-000 B.C. It can be speculated that during the Woodfordian substage of the last glaciation (Frye and others 1968), in the warmer part of the year the larger streams were choked with the outflow from the melting ice. Large mud flats must have resulted that stifled or smothered vegetation and in dry, windy periods provided the source of the dust carried by strong winds that made settlement in or even passage through the valleys undesirable. Both people and animals may have moved to higher ground overlooking the valleys or have gone a few miles away in order to avoid the dust storms and to seek out vegetation for food or fuel. The plant life in the valleys could have been destroyed by floods or may have been an impassable morass to such heavy-bodied animals as the mastodon. Those large animals may have starved due to the destruction of their natural food supplies. Any evidences of human beings prior to 12,000 B.C. could also have been covered or destroyed. In the period 20,000–12,-000 B.C. the climate north of a line drawn across Missouri from Kansas City to St. Louis must have been harsh indeed, for at that time the boreal forest extended throughout much of the southern half of the United States.

It is likely that if big game were sought at all, it was an occasional source of meat rather than a steady one. Furthermore, prior to the specialization of techniques and implements used for big-game hunting, the larger animals such as the mastodon and mammoth may not have been hunted at all but utilized opportunely when the animals were crippled or enmeshed in some natural trap so that they could be readily dispatched. Therefore, kill sites would be few and not readily found in east-central North America.

If people hunted the mastodon and mammoth in the Early Man period, it was only occasionally. If they did not have specialized hunting gear such as the fluted spear point of the Early Hunter Tradition, Paleo-Indian period, where would evidences of their existence likely be found? Land surfaces near streams, dating 20,000–12,000 B.C., would be potential sources. These ancient surfaces might now be encompassed in river terraces. Caves or shelters that could have protected small groups of wanderers, who depended for their existence on an unspecialized or generalized collecting–hunting, gathering, and fishing, might be other places to look. The most promising area for such finds in the Missouri–Mississippi drainage would be in the Ozark Highland, the area least affected by glacial outwash. Here also the deep valleys with entrenched meander streams and numerous terraces would aid the protection of vegetative cover, and there would be little reworking of old terraces by the streams because of meander entrenching. The places to look, then, are the terraces of river valleys of the Ozark Highland and in the many caverns and shelters formed in the limestone and dolomite rocks underlying much of the Ozark area.

If people arrived in the Missouri–Mississippi River area during the Woodfordian substage of the Wisconsin stage of the Pleistocene, approximately 20,000–12,000 B.C., the types of tools they would have been using should have been to some extent specialized, and the technology of stoneworking must have been fairly sophisticated. They probably would have known how to manufacture bifaces, blades, unifacial points, choppers, perforators, bone points, hole sticks, and how to build stone-lined hearths (Figure 2–3).

Although there is no dating available, the Old Quartz Industry in South Carolina and Georgia is a possible manifestation of the pre-Paleo-Indian period in the Eastern United States (Caldwell 1954). The artifacts in general were the roughly oval or leaf shapes that have been proposed as evidence of the early inhabitants of the far west. Caldwell (1954: 37) described the complex as follows: "Most frequent artifact types are ovate blades [bifaces], not core tools, but often small, well made, and finished with secondary chipping. Diminutive, oppositely beveled, so-called 'spinner points', together with side and end scrapers, form consistent minorities." Stemmed points were rare in the complex. In a later report Caldwell (1958: 8–9) noted that the stemmed forms that occurred in the complex had shoulders that projected only slightly, and the corner notches were scarcely indicated. Most sites were less than 150 feet in diameter and located on the tops and slopes of eroded hills. The complex was probably Archaic period.

Artifacts of the Lively complex are also possibly evidences of an Early Man period in the southeastern United States (Josselyn 1965a; 1965b; 1966; Lively 1965; Lively and Josselyn 1965). It has not yet been proven to be a distinctive Early Man period complex. The approach to the designation of the complex is very similar to that of the nineteenth-century search for paleolithic man based on the typology of stone implements or paleoliths.

Greenman (1943; 1948; Greenman and Stanley 1943) reported that the GL–1 site in Ontario had produced core choppers, bifacial scraper knives of semilunar outline, and tortoise-core implements of Levallois type, all of which were comparable to European specimens of early age. In a later article (Greenman 1960) it was noted that single-shouldered stemmed points similar to Sandia points had been found in the Great Lakes area and in paleolithic sites in France. Possible relationships of numerous traits in eastern North America and in Europe were also explored by Greenman (1963). The relationships of the ar-

tifacts were made on typological grounds. The sites in Michigan are probably Archaic period rather than Early Man or Paleo-Indian. Griffin (1965: 660) suggested that the sites dated after 9000 B.C.

Most of the findings of so-called paleolithic tools or pre-projectile-point sites in Missouri and the Eastern United States were reported from places that were possibly not glaciated in the period 20,000–12,000 B.C. One of the finds that evoked early interest was in the Trenton Gravels of New Jersey where Lewis (1881) reported evidence of paleoliths, and Abbott (1881: 484–85) noted an argillite implement.

Geological as well as typological evidence of paleolithic man was discovered in Little Falls, Minnesota (Babbitt 1884a; 1884b). Other finds were reported in stratified glacial till in Indiana (Cresson 1890b), Pennsylvania (Cresson 1890a), and the District of Columbia (Wilson 1889). The "paleolithic" finds did not receive much attention until Putnam (1888; 1890) and Wright (1888; 1890; 1892) took the lead and proposed strong arguments for the existence of glacial man in America. They cited typological and geological evidence at Trenton (New Jersey), Ohio, and elsewhere and compared implements from New Jersey, Minnesota, and Ohio with Mousterian and Acheulean tools of the Old World. McGee's (1889) convincing review of paleolithic finds promoted the popularity of the idea of glacial man, and Cresson (1890a) wrote a report substantiating the early geological occurrence of the finds of paleoliths in glacial gravels and in the bottom level of a shelter that held only paleoliths of argillite. The typological, geological, and archaeological evidence seemed convincing that paleolithic man had indeed inhabited the Eastern United States during the Pleistocene period.

Not everyone was convinced by the evidence that people lived in North America during the Ice Age. For example, Proudfit (1889: 245) concluded that the paleoliths at Trenton, New Jersey, were really wastage from an Indian quarry site of no great antiquity. Holmes (1890) reached a similar conclusion concerning the findings in the District of Columbia, and this opinion no doubt influenced his outlook concerning the possibility of paleolithic occupants throughout America. The pendulum began to swing from belief to disbelief in glacial man.

The attack against the evidence for the antiquity of mankind in America was just as zealous as the efforts to prove its existence. Holmes (1893a) stated dogmatically that there was no evidence of paleolithic man at Little Falls, Minnesota, and refuted the finds in Ohio at Newcomerstown and Loveland (Holmes 1893b). Powell (1893) joined Holmes in discrediting Wright (1892) and those who supported his view concerning the geological evidence for Early Man and succeeded in swinging many geologists to his side. Salisbury (1893) joined in the fray and in a review stated that Wright's book, *Glacial Man in America,* was sloppy and presented only one side of the question. Upham (1893) remained a major supporter of Wright and his ideas, but the trend in favor of proving the existence of paleoliths or paleolithic man in America had been reversed.

Only a few brave souls dared to report or publish purported evidence of glacial man. Leverett (1893) reported finding a chipped-stone ax 20–25 feet deep in the glacial gravels of Ohio, and Claypole (1896) described a ground-stone ax from the glacial drift in the same state. Wright (1893) replied to Holmes's criticism, furnishing still more evidence on old finds and presenting new evidence from the Ohio River (Wright 1895). Cope (1895) took exception to Holmes's views concerning the existence of evidence of paleolithic occupants of America and wrote, "It is well known that Messrs. Holmes and Maguire have endeavored to prove not only that there was no paleolithic man in North America, but that his existence in Europe is problematical." Cope also pointed out that paleolithic flints had been found at Little Falls, Minnesota, at Newcomerstown, Ohio, and near Trenton, New Jersey, in beds of Pleistocene age and that the evidence Holmes used to discredit them was not adequate. Thomas (1898: 366–69) was not fully convinced that the evidence for paleolithic man was not there, and in his report he illustrated and noted the similarity of the typology of implements from Texas, Wyoming, Virginia, and the District of Columbia to Acheulean and Chellean imple-

ments of Europe. Wright (1912) finally wrote another book in which he presented detailed evidence for the existence of glacial man and proposed a theory about the origin of man in America. However, among most archaeologists and geologists the subject was closed.

Carter (1951) stirred up some interest in Pleistocene dwellers in the Eastern United States. Norris (1953) followed up with a report on six artifacts that were bailed up from a well that had been drilled 82 feet into glacial till in Madison County, Ohio. The gravel was 10 feet thick, overlying a deposit of glacial till, which was overlain by alternating layers of till, sand, and gravel, a total of 72 feet. The projectile point or knife forms came from the depth of 72–82 feet, within the gravel layer that was judged to be an early subdivision of Cary (latter part of the Woodfordian) substage or possibly Tazewell-Cary (Twocreekan) interval. The two projectile points pictured from the well (the only ones that could be located) were an ovoid or leaf-shaped biface and a stemmed form with slight shoulders (Figure 3–3). Another ovoid, weathered biface (Figure 3–3C) was reported to have been found under 30 feet of gravel in Scioto County, Ohio. Although other "glacial drift artifacts" were reported in Ohio, their provenience in the drift was not recorded (Long 1953). The types were stemmed projectile points or knives.

Smith (1953) reported end scrapers, flaked tools, stemmed projectile points with small to no barbs, and some oval-shaped bifaces in the glacial gravels of northern Ohio. This evidence was questionable but could have been an indication of Early Man occupants. In the same general area, Smith (1954) found waterworn artifacts seemingly related to fossil glacial lake beaches.

Carter (1956; 1957; 1958; 1959) continued to argue that North America had been occupied by man early in the Pleistocene. He found few supporters of his views. Lending credence to Carter's hypothesis was the evidence recorded by Munson and Frye (1965) of an artifact in the deposits of Altonian substage (Wisconsin stage), which are considered to be 35,000–40,000 years old. The single artifact was concave based and seemingly related to tool types of the Early Hunter Tradition, Paleo-Indian period. It could, of course, have been a prototype.

Lee (1953; 1955; 1956) also reopened the possibility that there was occupation of northeastern North America at an early date. He reported that Early Man occupied the Sheguiandah site, which was considered to be a quarry by some investigators. Griffin (1965: 660–61) placed the site in his Early Archaic period and interpreted the "Valders glacial till" as a secondary deposit after the Valders advance.

The study of representative tools was only one of the approaches used by archaeologists in the latter half of the nineteenth century to research the problem of paleolithic or Pleistocene inhabitants of North America. Examining evidence of human remains was another method of investigating Early Man. Discoveries that led to claims of great antiquity of mankind in eastern North America were based on some combination of physical typological, geological, paleontological data, and associations with cultural materials. Major finds of human bones that have had a prominent place in the literature or that have had reasonable evidence for their authenticity or antiquity have already been mentioned in regard to their association with geological, paleontological, or cultural evidences.

The skeletal or physical evidence of Early Man has been written about extensively and will be briefly reviewed here. One of the early reports of human remains in the southeastern United States was by Professor Agassiz in 1853 (Haven 1856: 86–88). A fossilized skull and foot bone were found in a bluff on the shore of Lake Munroe, Florida. The skull, though fossilized,

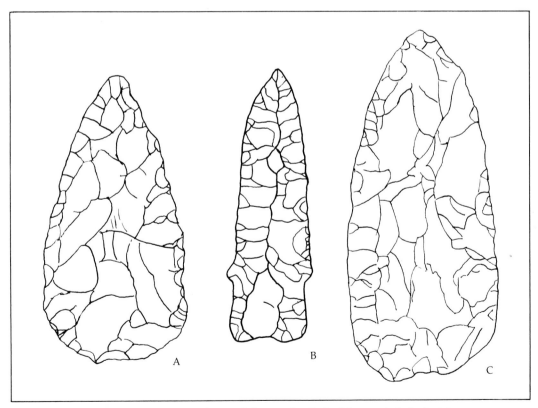

Figure 3–3. Artifacts possibly manufactured during the Early Man period. Scale 1:1.
A, Ovoid biface; B, stemmed projectile point or knife (from a well 72–82 feet deep); C, ovoid biface from 30 feet deep in Scioto County, Ohio. (After Norris 1953.)

was modern in type and was estimated to date at 10,000 years ago. Foster (1881: 76–77) claimed that the evidence was erroneous. This reporting and discounting seems to have been the general pattern concerning most early human remains.

The now-famous finds at Vero and Melbourne, Florida, have been discussed in detail by numerous writers (Gidley 1926b; 1929; 1930; 1931; Gidley and Loomis 1926; Hay 1918; Hrdlicka 1918; 1937b; Loomis 1924; MacCurdy 1917; Sellards 1916; 1917; 1937; 1947; 1952). Surprisingly, in spite of the working and reworking of the information available, the exact age of the finds is still open to some question (Cooke 1928; Rouse 1950; 1951; 1952; Stewart 1946; 1951; Wormington 1957: 226–30). Cooke (1928) thought he had valid geological evidence of the association of bones of man and extinct animals at Vero, Melbourne, and New Smyrna. Rouse (1950) argued that the human remains and artifacts at Vero and Melbourne were in the Melbourne–Van Valkenberg geological interval and that they were intruded into the Melbourne deposits by burial or digging of wells during a dry period. The following dates were given: Melbourne up to 2000 B.C. and Van Valkenberg 2000 B.C.–A.D. 1 (Rouse 1951). Rouse (1952) still maintained that the human bones at Vero and Melbourne had been intrusive and that the extinct animal forms were late survivals. It would appear that the dating and interpretation of finds at Vero and Melbourne should undergo further work and perhaps reevaluation.

Human bones associated with extinct animal bones were also found at Natchez, Mississippi (Dickenson 1846; Leidy 1889: 9–10). Hrdlicka (1907) questioned the association of the human bones with the extinct animal bones and decided that the human remains had to be modern Indian. For the most part the site was not accepted as evidence of Pleistocene human occupation (Foster 1881: 59–62). Wilson (1895: 724–25) ran fluorine tests on the human bones and associated mylodon bones and showed that they were of the same age. This fact seems to have been overlooked by most writers until Quimby (1956) re-opened the question about the Natchez site and supplied evidence that it was in a deposit estimated at 9,000–40,000 years old (Cotter 1966).

Farther north, human bones and those of giant ground sloth *(Megalonyx jeffersoni)* were found together at the Gillenwater site in Kentucky, but it was concluded that the human and extinct animal bones were not associated (Webb and Funkhouser 1934). Fluorine tests on the sloth and human bones would be appropriate to determine their possible contemporaneity.

The discovery of the Lansing skeleton in Kansas caused much controversy and met the fate of all other finds of the time. It was discounted as a record of an important find of human remains during the Pleistocene period (Chamberlin 1902; Fowke 1928; Hrdlicka 1903; Shimek 1917; Upham 1902; Williston 1897; 1902).

The Minnesota Man or Woman probably needs no discussion except that it appears certain that it was buried under deposits that were laid down in a lake formed during or shortly after the last glaciation of the Northeast (Bryan and MacClintock 1938; Jenks 1936; 1938). There has been the usual discussion of the find (Bennett 1952; Hrdlicka 1937a; 1937b). Another Minnesota find, Sauk Valley Man, received less attention but the same fate (Bryan and MacClintock 1938; Jenks 1937; Jenks and Wilford 1938).

Although a great deal has been written and rewritten concerning the possibilities and evidences of human beings in the Missouri–Mississippi Valley drainage and the eastern part of North America at an early time period, the Early Man period prior to 12,000 B.C., at present there is no conclusive evidence that any people were there. However, there are a few possibilities, and the search should continue.

It is proposed that the earliest people to reach Missouri came from the south up the Mississippi River valley or from the Southwest through the Gilmore Corridor (Krieger 1948: 168–78) and across the Cherokee Plains. Possible evidences of an Early Man period are from the Kimmswick, Pomme de Terre, Grundel, and Miami mastodon sites. If Early Man period migrants did reach central Missouri–Mississippi Valley, the time of their arrival is uncertain and may never be known.

The Early Hunters in the Paleo-Indian period may have been the first to penetrate the central United States. Specialized hunters of mammoth and other grass-eating animals in Mexico and the southwestern United States, if they expanded rapidly to the north, following the herds of game as the grasslands spread through the Great Plains and the boreal forest to the north receded, must also have traveled to the east. The east coast and the Mississippi drainage were then probable major routes for the spread of the fluted-point makers during the Early Hunter Tradition (Figure 2–1).

4. Early Hunter Tradition, Paleo-Indian Period

There appears to be general agreement among American archaeologists that there was a distinctive cultural tradition in eastern North America between 12,000 and 8000 B.C. (Bryan 1969; Byers 1965; 1966a; 1969; Griffin 1965; 1967; 1968; Haynes 1964; 1966; 1967; 1970; Jennings 1968; Stephenson 1965; Wendorf 1966; Willey 1966; Williams and Stoltman 1965). In this book I shall refer to this tradition as *Early Hunter* in the Paleo-Indian period. In Mexico, the southwestern, and western United States, the Paleo-Indian period is represented by an Early Hunter Tradition, which is defined by absolute dates, a relatively compact distribution of evidences, distinct tool kits, and the association of extinct fauna. It would appear that tradition and period were coterminous. In southeastern, central, and northeastern North America there are several complexes, aggregates of tools, and fluted forms that seem to be related to the western and southwestern complexes, and in some instances radiocarbon dates indicate that the aggregates are indeed from the Paleo-Indian period.

Data have accumulated to indicate that hunters using highly specialized spear points or knives and fluted forms were scattered throughout much of North America between 9500 and 9000 B.C. Haynes (1964; 1966; 1967) surmised from this dating and distribution that big-game hunters using fluted projectile points came from Asia about 10,000 B.C. following herds of game south and leaving their easily recognized fluted spear points with the remains of their victims. Haynes argued that 500 years was enough time for a single band of 30 people, consisting of 5 families, to produce between 2 million and 14 million fluted points and to multiply to a population of 800–12,000 individuals. He indicated that the migrants who produced Clovis Fluted brought their stoneworking technology with them. He later revised the hypothesis about the origin of the mammoth hunters because there was not sufficient evidence that they had forebears in the Old World (Haynes 1970).

Haynes (1966: 106–7) proposed that the manufacturers of Clovis Fluted followed a route from the north across Beringia, through northern Canada, and into the southwestern United States. Bryan (1969) and Wendorf (1966) noted the improbability of that route, and Haynes (1970) concluded that the hunters who used fluted forms developed their stone technology from earlier migrants.

If the progenitors of the Early Hunters migrated by boat or float along the western coast of North America to Mexico and then north on foot as I have proposed (Figure 2–1), their progeny could have left the concentration of campsites and kill sites that have been reported in the west-central part of North America. Some time as late as the period 18,000–16,000 B.C., the time of the interstade in the glaciation of the Rocky Mountains coinciding with Leighton's (1960) Gardena interglacial, Hunter–Gatherers could have migrated inland from the coast, adapted to hunting land-based big game, and moved into what is now northern Mexico and the southern United States. Big game was plentiful, and somewhere in this broad area from Mexico and southwestern United States to Florida, Clovis Fluted was invented. Perhaps it was an outgrowth from Sandia points as Wormington (1962: 235) has illustrated. Wormington's thesis—that the leaf-shaped bifacial form derived from the Old

World was the prototype to which the fluting technique was applied—is the logical answer. As the glaciers continued to retreat and temperatures became milder far to the south by 9500 B.C., the Clovis-Fluted-making big-game hunters in the southern part of the North American Continent moved north and east following their quarry, the mammoth, to the grass-covered Plains area.

The association of Clovis Fluted with extinct big-game animals, the limited range of radiocarbon dates on them, and the concentration of sites on which they have been found seem to indicate that the earliest fluted points are found in Arizona, Colorado, New Mexico, Texas, and Oklahoma. Thus, on the basis of faunal, chronological, and distributional evidence, this area might be considered to be the heart of development of Clovis Fluted in connection with big-game hunting and to have spread from there.

Although there has been the tacit assumption that Clovis Fluted indicated big-game hunting wherever they occurred, whether or not there was evidence of it, the assumption does not appear to be supportable. Many of the fluted-point sites did not have evidence of a big-game-hunting complex and may date at a much later time than the Clovis complex, 9500–9000 B.C. Big-game hunting may have been a restricted adaptation, especially the mammoth hunting that was so prominent in northern Mexico and the southwestern and Great Plains areas of the United States.

As far as distribution is concerned, if Clovis Fluted were used to show the spread of big-game hunters, and northern Mexico–southwestern United States were assumed to be the place where the fluting technology was developed, there is evidence for a southern route of migration to Ecuador as well as that to the north (Bell 1960b; Mayer-Oaks 1963) (Figure 2–1). Bryan (1965: 93) proposed that the technique of the "Fluted Point Tradition" diffused to Ecuador, "where it appears alongside the Willow-Leaf Bipoint Tradition"; this assumption is reasonable.

In the Eastern United States perhaps the best-known and most widely distributed type of projectile point or knife to be used as a diagnostic or index of the Early Hunter Tradition is the fluted form. In many instances the fluted form has been cited as the sole evidence of the earliest manifestations of an Early Hunter Tradition during the Paleo-Indian period. It has been further assumed that Early Hunters were dependent upon big game such as mammoth, giant ground sloth, horse, camel, and other extinct Pleistocene animals. This is speculation, for only two of the eastern campsites have yielded any bones of the big-game animals. A single toe bone identified as that of Barren Ground caribou (Cleveland 1965) was found at the Holcombe site (Fitting, Devisscher, and Wahla 1966). The Dutchess Quarry Cave site (Guilday 1967) yielded caribou *(Rangifer tarandus)* bones and a Cumberland, a variety of Clovis Fluted. Furthermore, certain evidence for big-game hunting is lacking in most of the sites identified as Big Game Hunting Tradition in the Eastern United States.

The Big Game Hunting Tradition in the West, where most of the known sites are kill sites with remains of mammoth or extinct bison, has been divided into earlier Llano and later Plano complexes (Jennings 1955; Sellards 1952; Spencer and Jennings and others 1965; Wormington 1957). The distinguishing item of Llano is the Clovis Fluted, the flutes of which were characteristically formed by the removal of flakes from opposite faces of the base to form a central channel or groove roughly parallel with the sides (Figure 4–1A–B). Folsom Fluted is considered to be a later development of the Clovis Fluted (Figure 4–1E). The distinctive features of Plano are long, slender projectile points or knives of unusually good workmanship that frequently resulted in collateral or ripple flaking (Figures 4–1H–J, 4–2C–D). Other Plano complex types are shown in Figures 4–1F–G, 4–2E, H. They were being made in the Paleo-Indian, Dalton, and Early Archaic periods and should then be representative of Early Hunter, Hunter–Forager, and Forager traditions in the Great Plains and Eastern United States cultural areas.

Some of the Plano types, Plainview for example (Figure 4–1G), were contemporaneous with the Folsom Fluted. Bryan's (1965: 94) assumption that the "Parallel-Flaked Point Tradition" (Plano

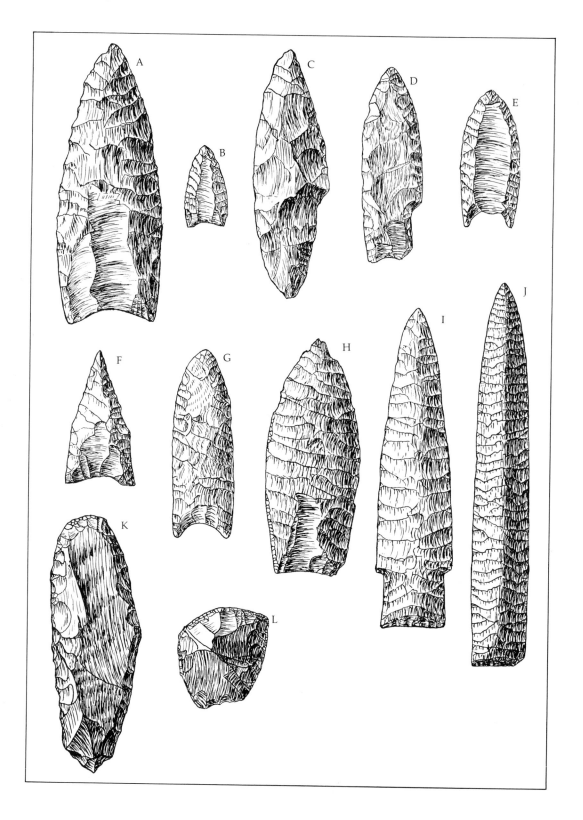

complex) moved north into northeast Asia may be a reversal of the direction of movement by the people manufacturing the parallel-flaked forms. The parallel-flaked technique may have come to North America before 8000 B.C., but, if so, may have been restricted to Alaska and ice-free areas north of the continental glaciers. It could then have been brought by hunters following game, perhaps bison, through the corridor in the ice that had opened after 8000 B.C. Since most of the big game would have been in the Plains area, the remainder of the hunters from the north would have been concentrated in that area, but would have spread east through the Prairie Peninsula which was beginning to form at that time and which also must have supported big-game herds (Wright 1968: 83). Mason (1962: 242, Figure 8) showed the distribution of Plano forms in the Mississippi Valley. This distribution may portray the eastward spread of the Plano types.

Many interpretations concerning the Paleo-Indian period in Eastern North America have been made solely on the basis of fluted forms, without supporting data as to age or cultural affiliation. However, there is some question as to whether or not the fluted forms found primarily east of the Mississippi River, such as at the Quad site (Soday 1954: 7–20), the Shoop site (Witthoft 1952: 464–95), the Bull Brook site (Byers 1954: 343–51), the Debert site (MacDonald 1966: 59–62; Byers 1966a), and the Parrish site (Webb 1951: 435–38) are all at the same time level as the Llano complex sites in the Plains and the Southwest cultural areas. Some scholars have assumed that the eastern sites were earlier (Witthoft 1952) and others that they were later (Byers 1955). Byers (1959) changed his opinion and submitted evidence that the Bull Brook site and the Debert site (Byers 1966b; 1969) were contemporaneous with Clovis (Llano complex). Fitting (Fitting, Devisscher, and Wahla 1966) decried the use of broad generalized forms such as Clovis Fluted to assume cultural relationships and called for bet-

ter-controlled typologies in specific regions. His suggestion should be heeded.

Griffin (1965: 655–60), in his review of Northeastern Woodlands cultural area, proposed that there was a gradual occupation of the Northeastern area by Paleo-Indian groups as the ice withdrew. To these "earliest primitive hunters recognized in the Northeast" he applied the name "Fluted Point Hunters," derived from the shape and manufacture of their most diagnostic artifact. The Paleo-Indian period was defined as beginning with the first occupation of North America and ending "with the passing out of style of fluted points," about 9000–8000 B.C. in the Northeast. Time period and cultural tradition were coterminous and a section entitled "The Paleo-Indian Fluted Point Occupation" (Griffin 1965: 658) seems to indicate that time period, technique of point manufacture, and cultural tradition were equated. Griffin noted that, although "The Fluted Point Cultural Complex" had been identified first in the Southwest and western Plains, "The earliest soundly established American cultural complex developed first in the Southeast, spread then to the Northeast, and westward into the Plains and Southwest." The southwestern manifestations were regarded as later than those in eastern North America. Griffin's hypothesis that the southeastern people of the Early Hunter Tradition were by inference the originators of the fluted points and the Early Hunter Tradition is of special interest. The greatest variety and number of fluted points are found in the Eastern United States, suggesting that they may have orginated there (Chapman 1935: 4; Chapman and Chapman 1964). Furthermore, the hypothesis supports rather than negates the proposition here that the earliest migration of Early Man to the southern United States came via Mexico.

Williams and Stoltman (1965: 669–79), in their article on the southeastern United States, used a different approach to the interpretation of the

---

Figure 4–1. Paleo-Indian artifacts from the Llano and Plano complexes (J. A. Eichenberger, casts, UMC). Scale 4:5.
A–B, Clovis Fluted; C–D, Sandia; E, Folsom Fluted; F, Meserve; G, Plainview; H, Brown's Valley; I, Scottsbluff; J, Eden; K–L, scrapers.

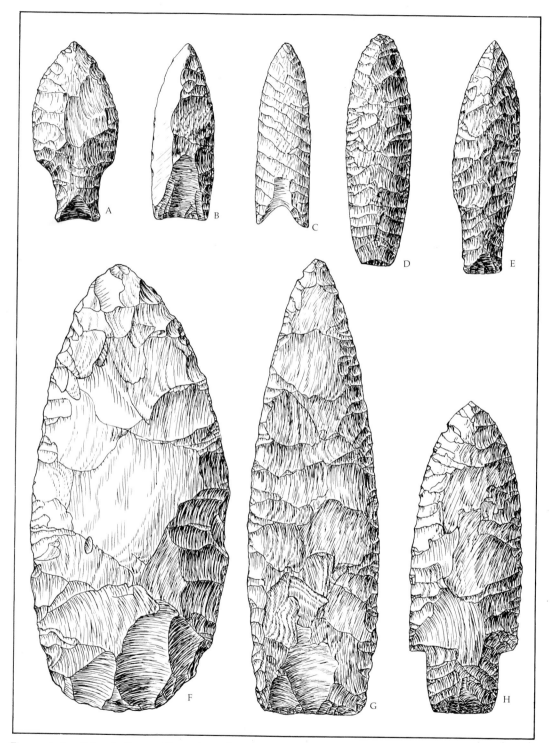

Figure 4–2. Paleo-Indian artifacts from South America and the southwestern United States (J. A. Eichenberger, casts, UMC). Scale 7:10.
A–B, Points from Fells Cave in South America; C, Jimmy Allen; D, Angostura; E, Hell Gap; F–G, preforms from the Simon site; H, Alberta.

earliest periods of occupation of the Southeast. They proposed a "Paleo-Indian Era" with four periods in the "Fluted Point Tradition." They concluded that the fluted points were the product of a single technological tradition, the base of which was Clovis Fluted. They accepted the idea that during the Paleo-Indian era big-game hunters who roamed the area made fluted forms of projectile points or knives. Evidence consisted of an overlapping of the distribution ranges of fluted forms and Pleistocene mastodons (Williams and Stoltman 1965: 677, Figure 6). They defined time periods as Period I, from 15,000 to 10,000 B.C. (with no data); Period II, "Clovis Points" centering between 10,000 and 9000 B.C., which they compared with finds in the Great Plains and Southwest; Period III, "Regional Variations of Fluted Points," from 9000 to 7500 B.C. (with no data); and Period IV, "Dalton and Suwanee Points," from 7500 to 6500 B.C.

Stephenson (1965: 685–96), in his discussion of the Quaternary human occupation of the Plains, proposed the term *Paleo-Indian stage;* it began when the first people entered the area and ended when big-game animals became extinct and small game became economically important, as evidenced by the disappearance of lanceolate projectile points in the Plains about 8,000 or 7,000 years ago. He suggested that the Paleo-Indian stage began perhaps as early as 40,000 years ago and included the Llano culture, the Lindenmeier culture, and the Plano culture, which he dated at 10,000–8,000 years ago.

The three articles in the compilation by Wright and Frey (1965) are summaries of areas that touch on and include parts of Missouri and have been used as examples to describe the Paleo-Indian period. There was reasonable consensus about the time period during which it occurred. All were agreed that at about 10,000 B.C. there was a hunting culture, complex, tradition, or stage present in the Plains and Eastern United States that was recognizable because fluted forms were part of it. The one thing that stood out in all the discussions was the lack of agreement on terminology; the names *Paleo-Indian period, era,* and *stage, Fluted Point Hunters, Clovis points,* and *Llano culture,* were applied to essentially the same time

period, cultural techniques or industries, cultural traditions or stages.

Griffin (1967: 176) divided the "Fluted Point Hunters" into a complex dating between 9500 and 8000 B.C. and a later phase lasting to 7000 B.C. The term *Fluted Point Hunters* certainly is a good one for those complexes that might be dominated by the fluted point or that have a fair percentage of fluted forms within them. His terminology may be especially pertinent in the sense that our knowledge comes primarily from the people who have been interested in hunting and collecting fluted points. Unfortunately some of them have neglected to record related ecological data or to collect the other very important items found on the same sites.

The term *Early Hunter Tradition* has been used here to describe the hunting tradition that comes within the Paleo-Indian period already defined, because thus far there is no conclusive evidence that the Early Hunters in Missouri and in most of the Eastern United States actually hunted big game. If they did, the big game may not have been particularly important to their over-all economy.

The study of fluted points alone can provide a great deal of information about people who lived on a site. Use–wear patterns can provide important information about their function, and the methods of manufacture can be clues to relationships between sites. Unfortunately on the basis of present information, there can be few comparisons between the techniques used to manufacture fluted forms in Missouri and elsewhere in the Eastern United States, except in very general terms. Until exact measurements of the length, width, and thickness of the forms, the grinding at the base and sides, the size of the flutes, and use–wear patterns are recorded, no precise typology , or description of technique of manufacture and function of the artifacts can be provided. Furthermore, without relationships to a more complete description of the cultural tradition that includes tools other than the fluted forms, there can be little more than a suggestion that a hunting tradition is represented by them, as the fluted forms do not seem to be enough in themselves to indicate that their presence is evidence of a fully developed Early Hunter complex or tradition. They do of course indicate a stone-working technique of producing fluted lanceolate-shaped implements. Too little data can be derived from this stoneworking technique alone. It is also necessary to collect additional information about the size of sites, their relationship to the terrain, and to resources of water, plants, and animals. It is the integration of these ecological factors with the cultural necessities of furnishing food, clothing, shelter, and companionship, organized around certain goals and principles to guide the endeavors of the group of people that form the way of life, the culture of the people. Cultural-ecological evidence is required before a people can be positively classified as hunters. Furthermore, there is still no absolute certainty as to the time that the stoneworking technique of fluting was initiated or when it was abandoned. Our knowledge is not really complete enough at this time to draw the broad conclusions, as a few writers have done, that only the Early Hunters or Big Game Hunters manufactured fluted projectile points and knives.

In spite of the paucity of evidence there seems to be the generally accepted assumption that the presence of fluted forms is indicative of an early hunting tradition and the hunting of big-game animals. Furthermore, it is assumed that the tradition continued only until the end of the Paleo-Indian period. Most of these speculations or extrapolations lack positive supporting information when they pertain to the Eastern United States. There is no doubt that some of the fluted forms were associated with the Early Hunter Tradition and Paleo-Indian period. There is the further probability that the fluting technique is distinctive and can be used as an identifying trait of the Early Hunter Tradition and of the complexes occurring in the Paleo-Indian period. Because this hypothesis has been accepted by most archaeologists, I have adopted it in this book but with the caution that the interpretation has not been proved in most instances by evidence from controlled excavations in the Eastern United States.

Many Clovis Fluted and Folsom Fluted and thus possible evidences of an occupation of Missouri by groups of the Early Hunter Tradition

during the Paleo-Indian period have been found. Several years ago a survey for fluted points was initiated through the *Newsletter* of the Missouri Archaeological Society. There was a good response, and the compilation resulting from the survey was published (Chapman 1967a; 1967b; 1973). Too often the exact location of sites was not given, but fortunately some reports were detailed. A comprehensive survey is now underway by the University of Missouri—Columbia Archaeological Survey and the Missouri Archaeological Society to obtain more exact information about as many of the fluted forms as is possible.

The map (Figure 4–3) shows the frequency of the occurrence of fluted forms in Missouri and thus the possible distribution of evidences of the Early Hunter Tradition. At the very least it shows the distribution of the technique of fluting of the lanceolate-shaped biface chipped-stone tools, which have generally been called fluted points. Differences in the fluted forms can be seen in the drawings and photographs (Figures 4–4, 4–5, 4–9, 4–10, 4–14 through 4–17, 4–20 through 4–23, 5–1, A5, A–6, A10), but no attempt has been made to establish a detailed typology for them, due to lack of sufficient data. Two main types, Clovis Fluted and Folsom Fluted, have been used. No doubt there can be a division of the Clovis into several varieties, which might be useful for cultural interpretations. More complete data concerning provenience, associated aggregates, or complexes are needed before it would be possible to establish a basis or a need for any such typology. Sufficient data were recorded for 300 of the fluted forms found in Missouri to plot them on a map by counties and in many instances by stream drainages or localities (Figure 4–3). The map was compiled primarily from information provided by members of the Missouri Archaeological Society and secondarily from publications (Bell 1960a; Bennett 1945; Central States Archaeological Journal 1967; 1968; 1970; Chapman 1967a; 1967b; 1973; Grimm 1953; Marshall 1957a; May 1959; MASN 1948; 1949; 1950; 1952c; 1954; 1957; 1958a; 1958b; 1959a; 1963; 1965; 1966; Sellers 1956; Shippee 1964; Smail 1951a; 1951b; Tuttle 1954). Several of the forms

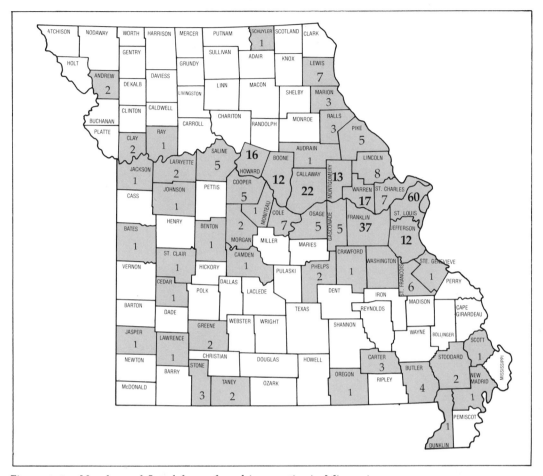

Figure 4–3. Numbers of fluted forms found in counties in Missouri.

that Smail (1951a: Figure 5, Numbers 8, 10, 14, 21, 27, 30, 35) identified as fluted have not been included because some seem to have more characteristics of the more recent Dalton Serrated and others do not appear to be fluted at all. Many other fluted forms from Missouri are known to be in private collections, but the sample used here is probably sufficient to show in a general way the pattern of distribution.

It is assumed that the people of the Early Hunter Tradition lived in small bands or family groups and were nomadic. Their campsites must have been small, and few evidences would be left on them. It is possible that the reason few campsites have been found in Missouri is because many of them were destroyed by flooding of

river valleys and deposition of silt and gravel after heavy rainfall during the Paleo-Indian period.

There is a concentration of Clovis Fluted along the main stems of both the Missouri and Mississippi rivers near their junction. Furthermore, where specific locations of sites that had Clovis Fluted or Folsom Fluted could be determined, they were on the hills and terraces adjacent to or within a few miles of the main streams. Significantly, finds have been scarce in the western, northwestern, and northern parts of the state and in those localities away from the major streams, and the concentrations were along the Missouri and Mississippi rivers. The distribution of fluted forms (Figure 4–3) compares favorably with the clustering and spread of fluted points shown by Mason (1962: 233, Figure 1).

It is premature to interpret the continuous, widespread occurrence of fluted points as a single complex. There is great variety in the shapes of the fluted forms that have been found in the area, and it is possible that the idiosyncracies in shape and other characteristics were due to local or regional styles and might be important in interpreting cultural-historical developments. For example, technique of manufacture may be a significant means of identifying cultural styles and the period of time of their manufacture. Many of the forms appeared to have been manufactured in the same manner as the Clovis Fluted of the Southwest and the Plains area; a few were manufactured in the same way as the Folsom Fluted of the Southwest; the technology of many of them seems to be the same as that of the Enterline Chert Industry in the Northeast (Witthoft 1952). One is a variety named Cumberland (Bell 1960a: 22–23).

No functional studies have been conducted to determine how the fluted forms were used. Definite manifestations left by the Early Hunters have as yet provided little information about their life style.

Snubbed-end flake scrapers, side scrapers, perforators, gravers, knives, prepared blades, modified flakes, and bifaces occurred in profusion in the Upper Paleolithic of Europe and Middle Paleolithic of Asia. They were the basic tool kit of the hunter in processing game animals and were just as important as the projectile point that was used in the initial procurement of game. Perhaps undue emphasis has been placed on so-called projectile points, because they were assumed to be associated with the masculine activity of hunting. As least as important to the life of the hunters was the women's task of preparing the meat and skins. The significance of their work is emphasized by the fact that the most numerous of any artifacts in the Early Hunter Tradition in the Paleo-Indian period are snubbed-end flake scrapers, gravers, side scrapers, and flake knives, or blades, which the women used in preparing the meat for food, the skin for clothing, containers, protection from the weather

in the form of shelter, and for the manufacture of tools from the bones to use in sewing, cooking, and weaving. Even in the Early Hunting Tradition, the preponderant types of tools were the ones used by the women. They were practical if unspectacular tools that were the very basis of the prime industries that supported the early society.

Griffin (1967: 176) noted that the small, snubbed-end flake scraper, often with spurs on each side of the beveled scraping edge, was the most common item in the Paleo-Indian period. It occurred with side scrapers, knives, drills, groovers, graving tools, and fluted points. He called this grouping or complex the "Fluted Point Hunters." Much earlier Witthoft (1952) made a detailed study on an early chert industry, including fluted forms, which he called the Enterline Chert Industry. It included fluted projectile point forms with triple channel flakes, side scrapers, end scrapers, some of which had spurs, and graver points probably used for punching sewing holes in skins. His interpretation that the Enterline Chert Industry was a blade-and-core industry has been questioned, for no cores were found, or at least none were illustrated, and there was further question as to the flakes having been blades. Byers (1966b: 6–8) noted that there was no evidence that the occupants of the Debert site, Nova Scotia, during the Paleo-Indian period, struck blades from a prepared core, "an ignorance that they shared in common with other eastern Paleo-Indians."

Witthoft (1957a: 19–20) defined blades as follows:

A blade, therefore, is a prism, or prismoid of flint, of trapezoidal cross section (sometimes triangular cross section because the blade from each ordinary core includes a few irregular examples), fairly massive and thick, rather than sheet-like, derived from a faceted core, which may be cylindrical, oval, a truncated pyramid, or a segment of any of these forms. Rarely, a blade was used as a tool without further modification, but most of them were chipped along the edges, particularly on the dorsal or convex face, to make more specialized tools. They were made into scrapers, skinning tools, knives, planes, burins and projectile points. They are too thick and massive to be included under certain other terms used in America, such as flake knife, lamellar flake, prismatic flake, lame, and sliver knife. . . . Another important thing about blades is that they generally make up a whole industry or set of tools, being modified into several different types of tools in every complex where they are found.

Under the title "Blades in the Enterline Chert Industry," Witthoft (1957b: 43–44) noted that:

> The vast majority of the tools found at the Shoop site, from which I described this industry, are very obviously based on blades, and are very different from any I know in normal American industries. . . . Blades at the Shoop site were struck from polyhedral cores of imperfect truncated pyramidal or conical form, with the apex of the pyramid rather than the base used as the striking platform in blade removal (the opposite to the Hopewell "haystack"). . . . Blades struck from these cores were drawn by resolved flaking, so that the bulbar end of the blade is small and deeply bruised, and the blade both widens and thickens from the bulbar end to the distal end. Most of the blades are straight, not curved, their longitudinal axis is nearly a straight line. . . . Side scrapers were made from long blades by secondary flaking of solidly supported bevels on one or both edges, and by chipping the bulbar end of the flake to an acute point. . . . End scrapers in this industry are made the other way around, the broad end is beveled and the narrower, thinner, bulbar end is the butt of the scraper. It would seem that blades for end scrapers were drawn from very short cores, rather than made of segments broken from longer blades, because practically every one preserves a bulbar area. . . . Probably the most distinctive and important features of the Enterline Industry pertain to these blade tools, they are tapered blades with bulbar end at the acute tip, drawn by resolved flaking, and they were beveled by resolved and flat flaking, re-edged by resolve flaking.
>
> Many of them are nearly indistinguishable from typical Upper Paleolithic blade tools of Europe, and are especially like the classic Middle Aurignacian.

Witthoft (1957c: 81–86) provided drawings illustrating various types of flaking, blade manufacturing, and flakes as well as a comparison of artifacts from various Paleo-Indian sites. Over-all he made a good case for his hypothesis that the flint knappers producing the Enterline In-

dustry had knowledge of the technique of producing blades.

Humphrey (1966: 588) stated that the blade tool assemblage associated with Clovis Fluted projectile points in the Driftwood Creek complex resembled the Aurignacian industry in the Old World more closely than any American collection. In comparing the complex with complexes in the United States he noted:

> The blades found in association with Clovis Fluted points at Blackwater Draw near Portales, New Mexico, U.S.A., . . . and blade tools of the Enterline Chert Industry of the eastern United States, also associated with fluted points . . . may reflect southern descendents of the Driftwood Creek complex from which certain highly specific blade implement types have been lost as the technique of fluting became culturally emphasized.

He drew the conclusion that the Paleo-Indian technique of fluting had a northern origin and that there were relationships with the Upper Paleolithic industry of European Russia and that the Utukok River area was a major and perhaps original route of prehistoric hunters from Siberia to the North American interior.

Although there has been little evidence other than similarity of form and fluting technique, it has been tentatively assumed that the occurrence of fluted forms in Missouri represents an Early Hunter Tradition complex comparable to the Llano in the west. In some few instances snubbed-end flake scrapers, gravers, and other tools have been found on sites in association with the fluted forms. The occurrence of these evidences does not seem to be restricted to any one of the localities or regions proposed for Missouri.

Southwest Drainage Region

In the White River Locality none of the sites dug in the Table Rock or Bull Shoals reservoir areas were interpreted as having an Early Hunter component. The base of a Clovis Fluted (Marshall 1963a: Figure 11, U2) and two other fluted forms were found at the junction of Aunts Creek and James River. A very wide range of projectile points was noted from the same site, which was judged to have been occupied intermittently

A

B

C

D

E

F

throughout the Archaic period. Two Clovis Fluted were found adjacent to White River in Taney County.

It is significant that the five fluted forms reported from the White River Locality in southwestern Missouri were adjacent to the main streams. At least three of the five recorded came from old, high terraces overlooking the present entrenched meanders of the river. One interpretation for their occurrence adjacent to the main streams is that people of the Early Hunter Tradition penetrated the area from the Mississippi alluvial valley by following the White River and its tributaries. This hypothesis is probable, for there are few other occurrences of fluted forms in the Southwest Drainage Region. Four Clovis Fluted have been found in the Current–Eleven Point Locality in Oregon and Carter counties. The one from Oregon County is small and very possibly was made during the Dalton period by Hunter–Foragers. The three fluted forms from the Leo Anderson Collection, Carter County (Figure 4–4A–C), appear to be quite different from each other in shape and technique of manufacture. The two in the upper row (Figure 4–4A–B) may be reworked, resulting in the stemmed appearance. The streams on which the forms were found drain into the White River in Arkansas and are therefore a part of the White–Mississippi River drainage. Furthermore, a classic Clovis Fluted has been reported downstream on the White River near Newport, Arkansas by T. J. Stephens (Personal Communication, December 14, 1967).

An intensive survey had been conducted in the Neosho Locality over a several-year period (Adams 1950; 1958), but no fluted forms were mentioned. One Folsom Fluted only 38 mm long was found near a small intermittent stream, approximately on the divide between the Spring–Neosho rivers and the Osage River (Marshall 1957a). Another fluted form was found in the upper drainage of the Sac River, again on or close

to the divide between the Upper Osage Locality and the Neosho Locality (MASN 1957). It was a large Clovis Fluted, 123 mm long, and had been resharpened.

Although Bell and Baerreis (1951) noted that a Paleo-Indian horizon occurred in Oklahoma, based on fluted and other early projectile point forms, their distribution in the state was not given. Perhaps they too were found along the main streams that drain into the Mississippi River. The fact that no fluted forms were reported from northeastern Oklahoma by Baerreis (1951) may be another indication that the southwestern prairies were not the major route by which the fluted forms were introduced to Missouri.

Western Prairie Region

Only six fluted forms have been recorded in the Upper Osage Locality, one each in Bates, Benton, Cedar (Smail 1951), and St. Clair counties, and two in Greene. The fluted form from Bates County was straight sided and narrow in relation to its length. It was narrowed at the base and could have been classified as stemmed if it were not for the deeply concave base. The specimen from Benton County was similar to the Folsom Fluted from the Neosho Locality and probably also can be classed as Folsom Fluted. One from Greene County, though fluted, is shaped more nearly like a Dalton Serrated. Only one of the six was a typical large Clovis Fluted. It was noted as coming from Cedar County, probably along the main stream of the Osage River (Smail 1951a: Figure 5, Number 19).

An unusual form of projectile point (Figure 4–5) found in Cass County near the western border of Missouri, but still in the Upper Osage Locality, appears to be more closely allied in the technique of its manufacture with Plano forms. It was included with the fluted forms because flakes had been removed from the base to thin

Figure 4–4.   Clovis Fluted from the Current–Eleven Point and Lower Missouri Valley I localities. Scale 5:6.
A–C, Current–Eleven Point Locality (Leo O. Anderson Collection); D–E, Lower Missouri Valley I Locality (M. N. Millard Collection); F, Lower Missouri Valley I Locality (Paul Sellers Collection).

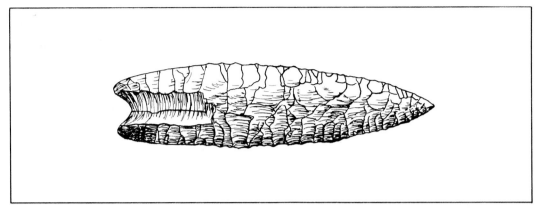

Figure 4–5.   Early type of projectile point from Cass County, Upper Osage Locality, which has features of both fluted and Plano forms (drawn from rubbings from the Edward J. Scheib Collection). Scale 1:1.

Figure 4–6.   Excavation beneath overhang at Rodgers shelter.

Figure 4–7.   Excavation in front of Rodgers shelter.

it, giving it the appearance of having been fluted. It is relatively straight sided, long in relation to its width, and has collateral flaking similar to Plano forms shown in Figures 4–1 and 4–2. Although the evidence is too limited to draw any conclusions, the occurrence of the Planolike form and the Folsom Fluted, both of which are later than the Clovis points in the Plains, may indicate that the Western Prairie Region, which was distant from the main streams, was settled later than those regions through which major streams flowed.

Ozark Highland Region

The part of the region represented by the Lower Osage and Gasconade localities is also lacking any great quantity of fluted forms. Only one fluted form has been reported in the Lower Osage Locality as an illustration of a Cumberland point (Bell 1960a: Plate 11). A somewhat similar

form in the sense that the fluting extended nearly its full length came from the Gasconade Locality and has been illustrated with Folsom Fluted. Since it came from Phelps County but without exact provenience, it is possible that it was within the Meramec rather than the Gasconade Locality.

One site, Rodgers shelter, in the Lower Osage Locality (Figures 4–6, 4–7), has yielded what may be an Early Hunter complex (Figure 5–1) in the bottom level but has been interpreted here as Hunter–Forager beginning in the latter part of the Paleo-Indian period and continuing into the Dalton period. A preliminary report (Wood and McMillan 1969: 2–5, Figure 2) noted that Dalton, Plainview and fluted points, scrapers, gravers, shaft shavers, bifacial tools, rubbed hematite, and abraders or anvilstones came from the bottom level of the site.

The occurrence of Dalton Serrated with Plainview and a fluted form (Figure 5–1E) in the earli-

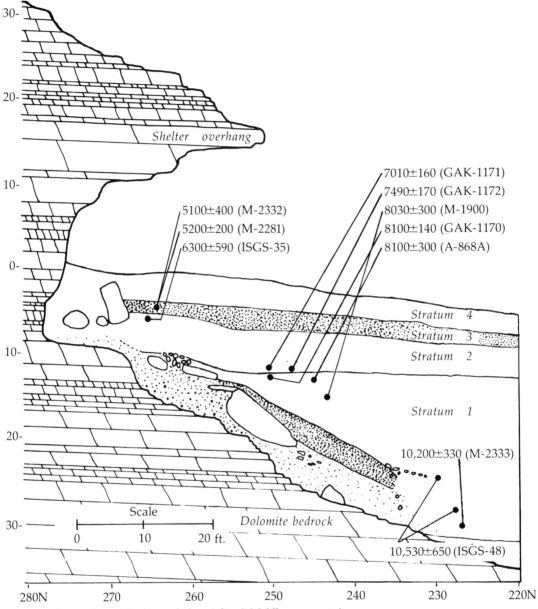

Figure 4–8. Profile of Rodgers shelter (after McMillan 1971: 81).

est component at the shelter could denote that the Dalton component was an aggregate of Early Hunter and Hunter–Forager Tradition, but in view of the fact that most of the forms can be classified as Dalton or related to Dalton Serrated in size and technology (McMillan 1971: Figure 46a–g), the evidences are considered to be from the Hunter–Forager Tradition. The radiocarbon dates obtained from the lowest levels were about 8500–8000 B.C. (Figure 4–8) and thus represent the very end of the Paleo-Indian period. The earliest dates are 8580±650 B.C. and 8250±330 B.C. (McMillan 1971: Figure 15).

Further analysis of the materials from Rodgers shelter has provided information on the function of tools, thus making it possible to interpret economic activities with more precision (Ahler 1970). McMillan (1971: 186) pointed out that tool kits of the Dalton component indicated that both hunting game and collecting vegetal foods were important subsistence activities. Deer, squirrel, and cottontail were part of their diet, and the evidence indicated that a small group of people occupied the shelter for a short period of time. These data are further support for assigning the earliest component in Rodgers shelter to the Hunter–Forager Tradition.

More Clovis Fluted have been found in the Meramec Locality than in any of the localities not along the main stream of the Missouri or Mississippi rivers. In fact, as many fluted forms were found there as in the Lower Missouri Valley I Locality. Perhaps the reason that a larger number of fluted forms has been reported from the Meramec Basin is that the lower Meramec River is close to St. Louis and has been thoroughly searched by collectors of artifacts. Another is that several of the Clovis Fluted have been found on two sites, both of which are on hills or hillsides high above the bottomland. Both have eroded surfaces that have exposed artifacts manufactured by the Early Hunters.

Northwest Prairie Region

In the far Northwest Prairie Region, which includes the Tarkio, Nodaway, Platte, and upper part of Lower Missouri I localities, only two

Clovis Fluted have been reported from Andrew County (Stubbs 1950: Figure 4, Numbers 11–12). Wedel (1959: 175, Plate 15f, h–j, Figure 96c) showed four fluted forms, both Clovis Fluted and Folsom Fluted from northeastern Kansas, thus presumably in the Northwest Prairie Region. All were found on the surface by local collectors.

A few Clovis Fluted have been found in the vicinity of Kansas City in the Lower Missouri Valley I Locality. Shippee (1964: 1–3) described and illustrated two Clovis Fluted from Clay County from sites 23CL13 and 23CL88. Both sites are on hilltops on which Nebo Hill aggregate material was collected. A Clovis Fluted was collected in Jackson County (B. W. Stephens, personal communication, January 1, 1953). The M. N. Millard Collection contained one from Cooper County near the Lamine River (Figure 4–4D), and two other fluted forms have been found in the same general location on high land between the Lamine and Missouri rivers. Five Clovis Fluted have been found in Saline County, two of which are shown in Figure 4–4E–F.

Northeast Prairie Region

The division between the Lower Missouri Valley I and II localities was made on the basis of what appears to be a major topographic change at a point above Boonville in Cooper and Howard counties. Sheer bluffs replace the more gently rounded hills of the Lower Missouri Valley I Locality, and woodland is more common than the prairie vegetation of the Lower Missouri Valley I. Why this change in topography and vegetation affected the spread of population of the Early Hunter Tradition is not known. Apparently they preferred the high bluffs and more rugged terrain of the Lower Missouri Valley II, because the number of fluted forms found in the locality increases tremendously as soon as the high bluffs are reached. Approximately 15 times as many fluted forms have been reported from the Lower Missouri Valley II and adjacent Greater St. Louis localities than from the Lower Missouri Valley I Locality.

Only one site in the Lower Missouri Valley II Locality thought to be Early Hunter Tradition has been sufficiently investigated to give an indication of the full complex. This is the Walter site. It had been collected upon for several years by George Nichols, a trustee of the Missouri Archaeological Society. He had been interested in fluted forms for many years and noticed that the material was similar to Folsom artifacts he had seen at Lindenmeier, Colorado. With the idea of finding out how the occupants of the Walter site had manufactured fluted forms and other tools, Nichols collected from the site intensively each time it was cultivated and kept a fair assortment of waste flakes and other debris as well as all of the artifacts that he could find (Biggs, Stoutamire, and Vehik 1970; Nichols 1970).

The site is located on a high ridge which is now at least one-half mile from the nearest regular water source. The area in which the evidences occur is no more than 300 feet long by 150 feet wide. It covers the highest point and south slope.

Clovis Fluted may not be the most distinctive item from the site (Figures 4–9, 4–10A). The most indicative tools of all may be the small, snubbed-end scrapers made from flakes, often with spurs or sharp points at one or both sides of the beveled edges (Figure 4–10D–G). Similarly, they were the most numerous in the Enterline Chert Industry and in the Folsom complex at the Lindenmeier site in Colorado. Other implements at the Walter site were flake knives produced from prepared cores, retouched on one or both sides of the flake and thus sometimes shaped, flakes with spurs or graver points (Figure 4–10B–C), Hardin Barbed, projectile points or knives similar to Dalton Serrated, trianguloid and bipointed knives, a large Planolike knife or spear point (Figure 4–11), and pieces of flint that may have been used as choppers, adzes, or digging tools (Figure 4–12).

One core showed that flakes were removed intentionally, perhaps for blades (Figure 4–13). The core demonstrates that the people inhabiting the site had the technology available to prepare blades. No true blades as such could be identified in the materials collected. Flakes were generally

thin and flat, but most were waste. Many were irregular in shape.

A study of wear patterns on the tools would give better insight into their function. Semenov (1964: 89) noted, "Tools can be very different in shape and yet have exactly the same function, and conversely, identical shapes may have had quite different funtions." Thus, actual traces of how a tool was used are the most important factors in the identification of their functions. Yet this criterion has not always been applied to the classification of artifacts.

Large hammerstones from the Walter site consisted of natural cobbles and pebbles used for battering flint. The edges are worn and roughened and show signs of being used to smooth the sharp edges on blades of projectile points and other tools in preparation for striking further blows or as platforms for pressure tools to produce proper flakes. Two are battered on all sides, three are pitted anvilstones, somewhat shaped, and another has a smooth surface, no doubt the result of its use in grinding or polishing.

The range of the items in the aggregate has been shown in Figures 4–9 through 4–13. The items called scrapers are not all alike, and it is probable that they were not all used for the same purpose. The ones with a beveled edge that were semicircular in shape usually had the edge worn smooth and were no doubt used as scrapers, probably in the preparation of hides or skins for clothing (Figure 4–10D–E). Those with sharp spurlike points at one or both sides of the steeply beveled scraping edge are most likely another type of tool, used primarily as a cutting instrument (Figure 4–10F–G).

The evidences from the Walter site are similar to those at the Shoop and Debert sites in many respects, but they are different. They should not be classed as a complex unless other similar components are found. A comparison of traits of the Walter site with those elsewhere that are believed to be Early Hunter Tradition (Big Game Hunting Tradition) and in the Paleo-Indian period led to the conclusion that the materials from the site on typological grounds were more

Figure 4–9.   Clovis Fluted and fragments from the Walter site (George Nichols Collection). Scale 4:5.

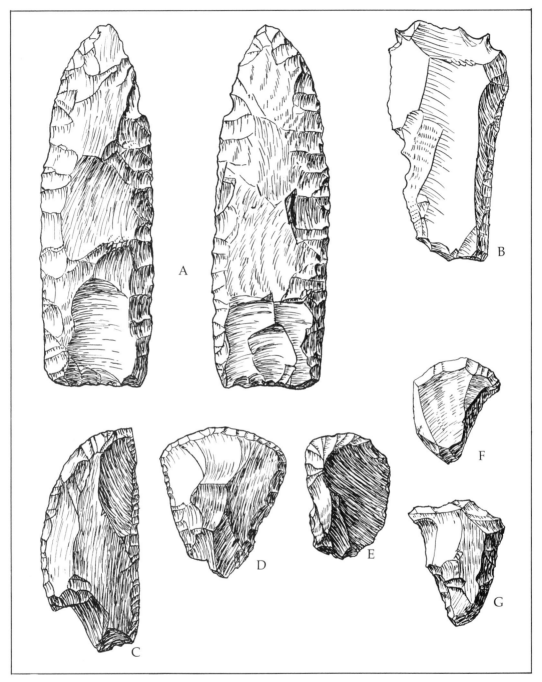

Figure 4–10. Artifacts from the Walter site characteristic of the Early Hunter Tradition (George Nichols Collection). Scale 1:1.

A, Clovis Fluted, both faces; B, beaked flake knife; C, scraper, cutting tool; D–E, snubbed-end flake scrapers; F–G, spurred, snubbed-end flake scrapers.

nearly Hunter-Forager Tradition, Dalton period, than Early Hunter Tradition, Paleo-Indian period (Biggs, Stoutamire, and Vehik 1970: 59–60).

The aggregate on the Walter site is basically Early Hunter Tradition in type, and the site was probably occupied in the transitional Dalton period. Another site in the vicinity on which Clovis Fluted have been found has lanceolate, notched, and stemmed projectile or knife forms, drills, adzes, digging tools, a chipped-stone ax, and ground-stone artifacts, including a three-quarter-grooved ax. This aggregate of tools seemed to signify that the site was occupied during the Archaic period, most intensively in the Late Archaic period.

In any instance, except for an early type drill, lanceolate forms with concave bases that were somewhat similar to Dalton Serrated and the fragments of Clovis Fluted (Figure 4–14), the stone technology is quite different from that at the Walter site. The Early Hunters probably used a number of campsites on their seasonal round of hunting, and the few Clovis Fluted found at this site, less than one mile away from the Walter site, could have been left there by an Early Hunter group that utilized both campsites.

Two very important fluted-point sites have been located in the Lower Missouri Valley II Locality by Richard S. Brownlee. His accurate recording of the site locations in Franklin County (Sites 23FR7 and 23FR8) and his collection from them have made it possible to obtain some interesting insights into the association of types of projectile points with other artifacts. Five excellent examples of Clovis Fluted came from one site (Figures 4–15, 4–16A). Associated with the fluted forms was another type that may be indicative of the change from Clovis Fluted to Dalton Serrated. It is of approximate pentagonal shape but is basically lanceolate (Figures 4–16B–D and 4–17D–E). Similar forms have been found at the adjacent Site 23FR8 (Figure 4–18B–D). They approach Quad in shape but not in other characteristics (Bell 1960a: 80, Plate 40). Some of the larger forms are fluted on one face of the base, and all have basal thinning. The cream-colored flint, similar weathering, and in some instances fluting of both the Clovis Fluted

and these lanceolate forms seem to indicate their contemporaneity. One of the lanceolates has been classed as Graham Cave Fluted (Figure 4–17F). Others have the appearance of an oversize Meserve point with beveling of the blade, probably from resharpening (Figure 4–17D–E). It can be speculated that this lanceolate form is one of the steps between Clovis Fluted and Dalton Serrated. If these forms were slimmed down, consistently beveled, and serrated, they would be classified as Dalton Serrated.

The beautifully made serrated forms from sites 23FR7 and 23FR8 in Franklin County (Figures 4–17A, 4–18A, 4–19B–C) are Dalton Serrated that had not been beveled by sharpening. They are much longer in proportion to their width than the resharpened Dalton Serrated. Furthermore, they do not have a pentagonal shape. They are very distinctive, and some of them are quite large. The Planolike lanceolate (Figure 4–19A) is perhaps the prototype or a large example of the Dalton Serrated. Though it is much longer than most Dalton Serrated and does not have basal grinding, it is basally thinned in much the same way. The proportions are much the same as those of Dalton Serrated, and it probably should be so classified.

Site 23FR8 has also yielded Clovis Fluted, Dalton Serrated, and lanceolate forms and early type drills (Figure 4–20). There is little question that there is a component of the Early Hunter Tradition at sites 23FR7 and 23FR8. The aggregates of artifacts from both sites are remarkably alike, and it is probable that much of the artifactual material from them is the handiwork of the same or closely related people.

A fair variety in size and shape of fluted forms occurs in the Lower Missouri Valley II and the Greater St. Louis localities. The greater variety of fluted forms here may indicate that the fluted-point makers had occupied this locality for a longer period of time than the other localities. However, the variety in size and outline of the fluted forms could signify that the tools were made to serve different functions (Figure 4–21).

Of particular interest is the finding of small, fluted forms that appear to be in the Folsom Fluted tradition of manufacture. It has already

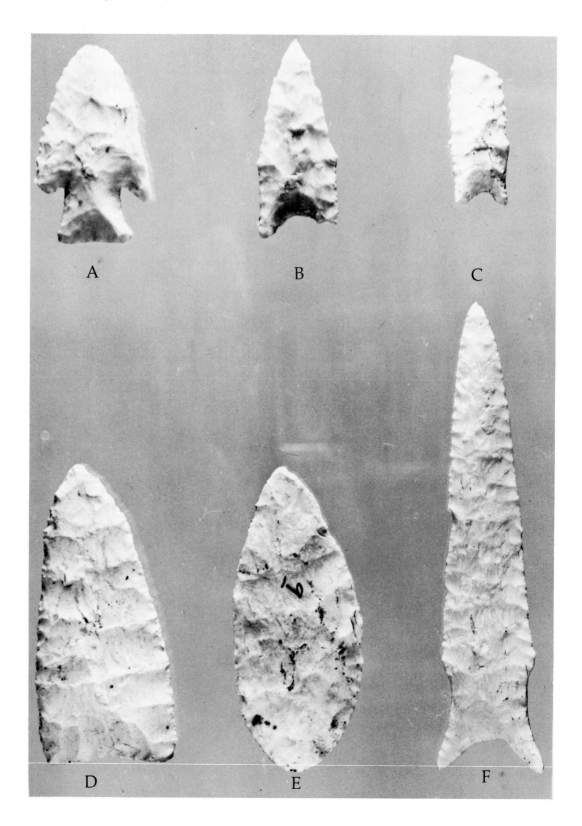

A   B   C

D   E   F

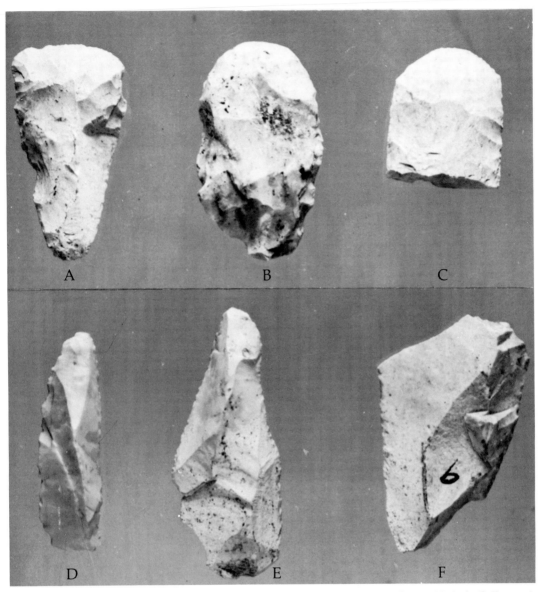

Figure 4–12.   Chopping, cutting, and scraping tools from the Walter site (George Nichols Collection). Scale 7:10.
A–C, Adzes, chopping, or digging tools; D–F, cutting and scraping tools.

Figure 4–11.   Projectile points and cutting tools from the Walter site (George Nichols Collection). Scale 7:10.
A, Hardin Barbed; B–C, Dalton Serrated; D, triangular biface; E, bipointed biface; F, Planolike stemmed form.

Figure 4–13.   Chert core from the Walter site (George Nichols Collection). Scale 1:1.

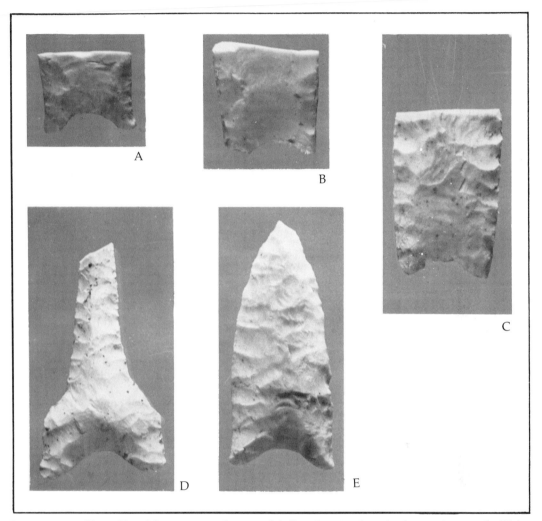

Figure 4–14.   Clovis Fluted fragments, early type of drill, and projectile point from a site near the Walter site (George Nichols Collection). Scale 1:1.
A–C, Bases of Clovis Fluted; D, drill; E, concave-based lanceolate form.

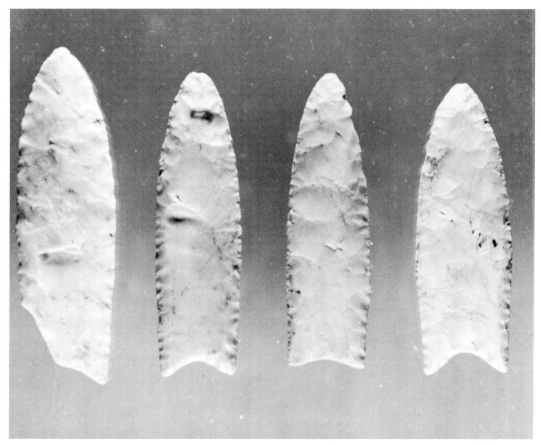

Figure 4–15.   Clovis Fluted from Site 23FR7 (Richard S. Brownlee Collection). Scale 7:8.

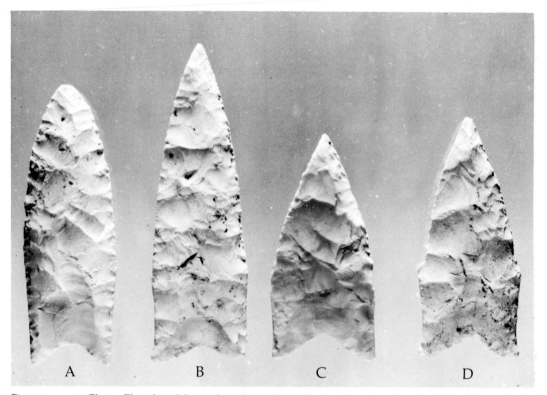

Figure 4–16.   Clovis Fluted and lanceolate forms from Site 23FR7 (Richard S. Brownlee Collection).
Scale 7:8.
A, Clovis Fluted; B–D, lanceolate forms.

Figure 4–17.   Artifacts from Site 23FR7 (Richard S. Brownlee Collection). Scale 7:8.
A, Dalton Serrated; B, drill; C–E, lanceolate; F, Graham Cave Fluted.

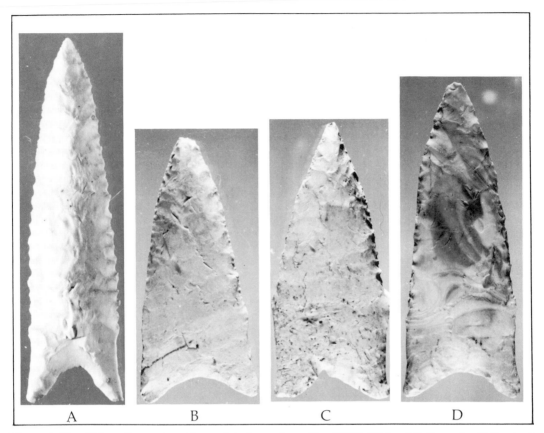

Figure 4–18.   Dalton Serrated and lanceolate forms from Site 23FR8 (Richard S. Brownlee Collection). Scale 1:1.
A, Dalton Serrated; B–D, lanceolate.

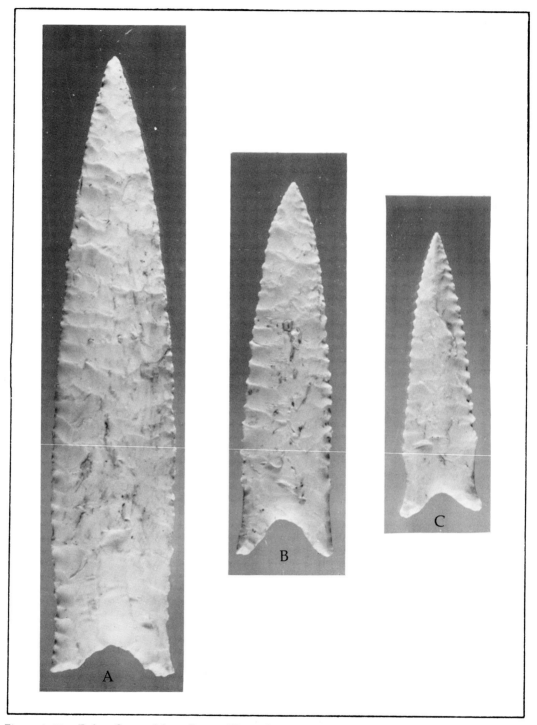

Figure 4–19.   Dalton Serrated from Sites 23FR7 and 23FR8 (Richard S. Brownlee Collection). Scale 1:1.

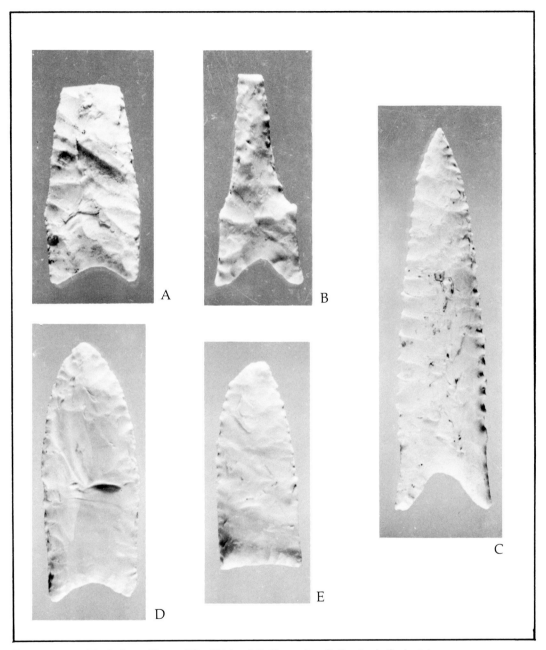

Figure 4–20.   Tools from Site 23FR8 (Richard S. Brownlee Collection). Scale 1:1.
A, Lanceolate form; B, drill; C, Dalton Serrated; D, Clovis Fluted; E, lanceolate form.

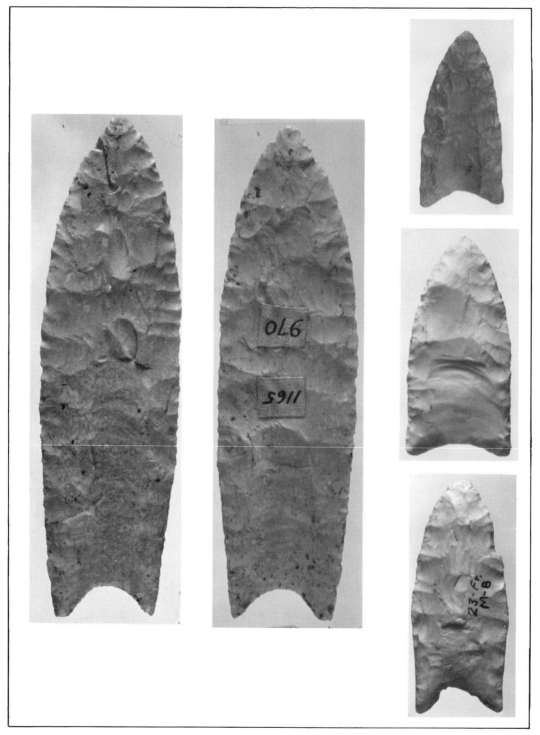

Figure 4–21. Clovis Fluted from the Lower Missouri Valley II and Greater St. Louis localities. Both faces of the large point are shown (J. A. Eichenberger, Paul V. Sellers, and Leo O. Anderson collections). Scale 1:1.

Figure 4–22.   Clovis Fluted from the Mississippi Valley North Locality. Both faces of the large form are shown (Paul V. Sellers Collection). Scale 1:1.

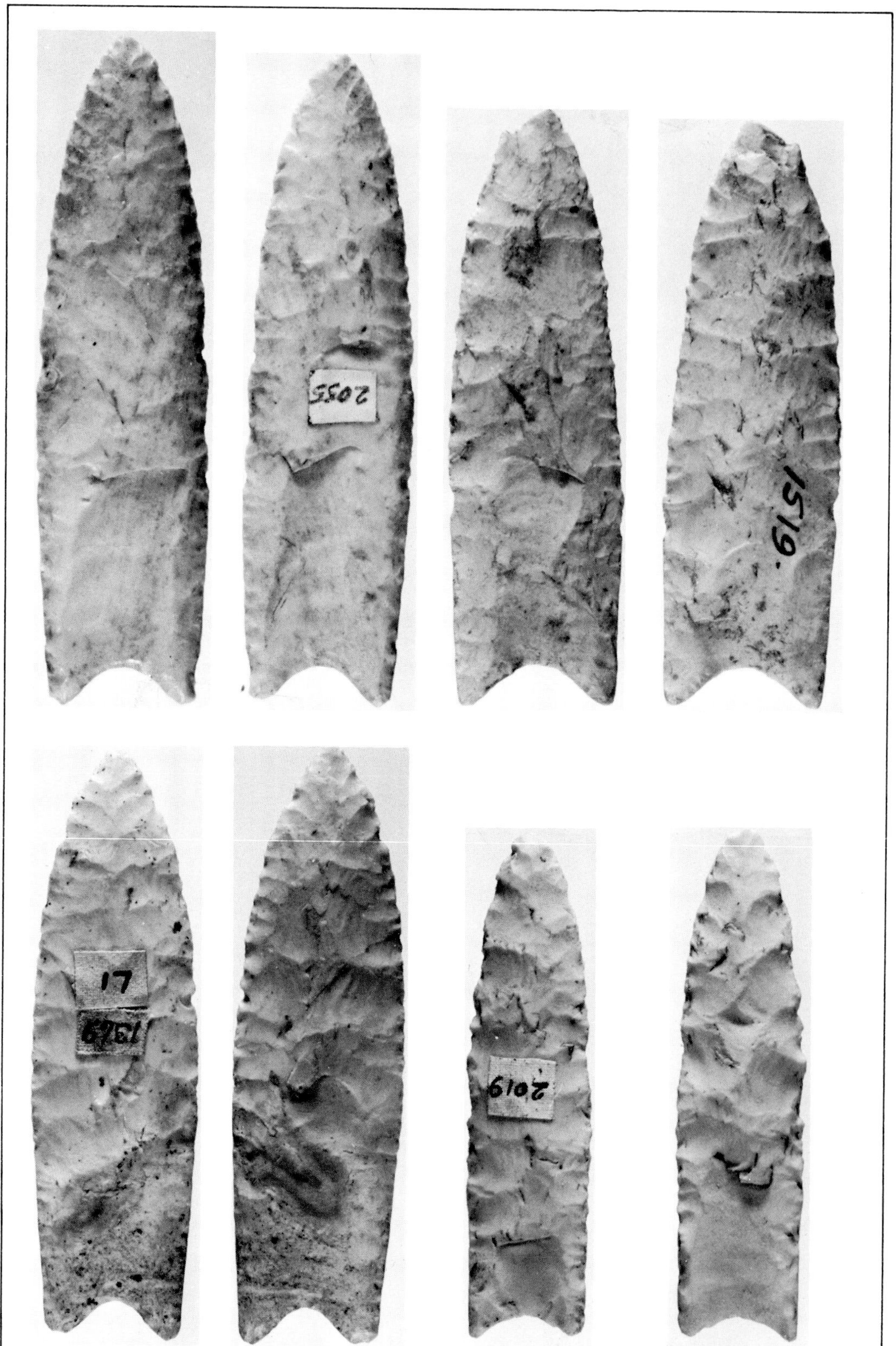

2055
1519
17
1369
2019

been pointed out that two Folsom Fluted were found near the western edge of the state and that they might indicate a later time period for the occupation of that region. Two others definitely identified as Folsom Fluted technological tradition were found in the Lower Missouri Valley II Locality, both in Boone County. They were found by Robert Benson (Appendix II) and Marilyn Powell Delling (1966: 235). The finding of Folsom Fluted in the locality should be no surprise, for Dalton period, Hunter–Forager Tradition aggregates are prevalent there, and the Dalton period in the Lower Missouri Valley includes the time that the Folsom stoneworking technology was in existence in the Plains cultural area.

Clovis Fluted have been discovered in the Northeast Prairie Region, north of the Missouri Valley, but in much smaller numbers. Furthermore, they seem to be restricted primarily to the bluffs and small valleys in the Mississippi Valley North Locality. There are several in the Paul Sellers Collection (Figure 4–22). Another group from the same locality in the J. Allen Eichenberger Collection is shown in Figure 4–23. The two collections must be a representative sample, for the Clovis Fluted illustrated have nearly as wide a range in size and shape as those in the Lower Missouri Valley II and Greater St. Louis localities, in spite of the fact that only 22 specimens are represented in the sample.

Only five fluted forms have been reported from the other localities making up the Northeast Prairie Region, north of the Lower Missouri Valley II. Two of them are from the Cuivre Locality; one is a large Clovis Fluted and the other a very small Folsom Fluted. Two Clovis Fluted are from the Salt Locality and one from the Wyaconda–Fabius Locality. The same situation seems to prevail here as it did in the Lower Missouri Valley localities. The distribution of the fluted points clusters close to the main stream, the Mississippi River.

Southeast Riverine Region

The records of discoveries of fluted forms diminish greatly in areas south of the Greater St. Louis and Meramec localities. Only nine Clovis Fluted have been recorded in the five-county area of the Mississippi Valley Central Locality, and all but one of them were found in the upper part, in Jefferson and St. Francois counties. There are only two Clovis Fluted reported from the Bootheel Riverine Locality and seven from the St. Francis Riverine Locality.

Regional Distributions of Evidences

The evidence from the distribution of fluted forms south of the mouth of Meramec River leads to the conclusion that the longest and most intensive occupation of Missouri and the central United States was in a band from Boonville on the Missouri River almost due east to the central Ohio River drainage, and south on past the mouth of the Missouri River to the state of Mississippi. The greatest clustering of evidence is along the main streams of the Mississippi, Missouri, Ohio, and Tennessee rivers (Mason 1962: 233).

Many evidences of the Early Hunter Tradition in Missouri appear to be representative of the latter part of the Paleo-Indian period, 8500–8000 B.C., as was demonstrated by radiocarbon dates in Rodgers shelter in the Lower Osage Locality and those at Modoc shelter in the Mississippi Valley Central Locality. The types of artifacts at the Walter site in the Lower Missouri Valley II Locality have been interpreted as late Paleo-Indian or Dalton period. There is also continuation of Early Hunter Tradition into the Dalton period or a continuation of the use of distinctive Early Hunter Tradition tools by Hunter–Foragers in the Dalton period. For example, there are overlapping dates on what could be near the end of the Early Hunter Tradition or a transitional

Figure 4–23. Clovis Fluted from the Mississippi Valley North Locality. Both faces of each specimen are shown (J. A. Eichenberger Collection). Scale 1:1.

Hunter–Forager component in Graham Cave (Chapman 1957: 47–49; Klippel 1971; Logan 1952), and at Rodgers shelter (McMillan 1971: Figure 15). Clovis Fluted and Folsom Fluted have been collected from a number of sites that may have been occupied in the Paleo-Indian period. Controlled surface collections and excavations are needed on such sites in Missouri before certain knowledge of the Early Hunter Tradition and the Paleo-Indian period can be made available.

In central Missouri, although excavations have been conducted at Graham Cave, Arnold Research Cave, and the Walter site, the results were not conclusive as to the complexes being Early Hunter Tradition and Paleo-Indian period (Biggs, Stoutamire, and Vehik 1970; Klippel 1971; Shippee 1966). There is also no certainty that the fluted forms found in Missouri were left during the Paleo-Indian period. There is the possibility that all the evidences thus far recovered were left by Hunter–Foragers in a transitional Dalton period.

There is a massive amount of literature about the Paleo-Indian period, so I have listed only a few of the pertinent studies here. Good compilations on the Paleo-Indian period, Early Hunter Tradition, in North America and those of particular interest to Eastern United States that were published after 1956 can be found in the following references: Agogino (1963); Agogino and Rovner (1964); Agogino, Rovner, and Irwin-Williams (1964); Bryan (1965; 1969); Butzer (1971: 485–515); Byers (1957); Davis, Brott and Weide (1969); Dorwin (1966); Fitting, Devisscher, and Wahla (1966); Graham and Heizer (1967); Griffin (1964; 1965; 1967; 1968); Guthe (1966); Haynes (1964; 1966; 1967; 1969; 1970; 1971); Haynes and Agogino (1960); Heizer (1964); Hester (1966); Hopkins (1967); Irving (1971); Irwin (1971); Irwin and Wormington (1970); Jelinek (1957; 1971); Jennings (1968); Jennings and Norbeck (1964); MacDonald (1971); MacGowan and Hester (1962); Martin and Wright (1967); Mason (1958; 1962; 1963); Muller-Beck (1966); Prufer (1960); Prufer and Baby (1963); Quimby (1958; 1960); Ritchie (1957; 1958; 1965); Rogers (1966); Rolingson (1964); Rolingson and Schwartz (1966); Shutler (1971); Spencer and Jennings (1965); Stephenson (1965); Wedel (1964); Wendorf (1966); Wendorf and Hester (1962); Wheat (1971); Willey (1966); Williams and Stoltman (1965); Wilmson (1968a; 1968b; 1970); Winters (1962); Wormington (1957; 1962; 1964a; 1964b; 1971).

5. Hunter–Forager Tradition, Dalton Period

Cultural homeostasis is the mechanism providing resistance to change. When old, proven methods fail to obtain the desired results, new formulae must be employed to cope with new situations. Culture, time, and environment interact to produce either stability or change. Stability occurs when homeostatic processes are stronger than cultural innovation. Cultural change occurs when the amount of innovation, contacts with other cultures, and changes in the environment are greater than the forces of stability and the cohesive *esprit de corps* of the society. Consequently, when the climatic changes of the Dalton period occurred, there was theoretically a transitional period as human beings adapted their culture to the altered environment.

Willey (1966: 62–64), in his discussion of the early Americans, pointed out that several archaeological sites in the Eastern United States, such as the Parrish site, Kentucky, Nuckolls site, Tennessee, Modoc rock shelter in Illinois, and Graham Cave in Missouri, showed mixtures of artifacts, principally projectile points, from the Early Hunter and Archaic traditions. He asked whether this seeming mixture of points was indicative of transition from Early Hunter to Archaic pattern, or due to contact between Archaic people in the east and fluted-point makers of the Plains cultural area. He concluded tentatively that Early Archaic people made contact with late-surviving Early Hunters at Modoc shelter and Graham Cave at a time after 8000 B.C. Willey (1966: 64) also proposed that there was a Big Game Hunting Tradition (Early Hunter) in eastern North America and that there was a local evolution or modification of the fluted projectile

points into Quad, Suwannee, and Dalton and then into large stemmed and notched forms entering the Eastern United States through the southern Plains area.

During the Paleo-Indian period the climate must have been cold in Missouri, particularly north of the Missouri River. It may have been similar to the present-day climate in Canada between 50° and 55° north latitude. If this were the case, hunting would probably have been the major subsistence activity, for Lee (1968: 42–43) demonstrated that in the recent past the primary source of subsistence for hunting–gathering people living in latitudes above 50° was fishing or hunting. Two of the groups Lee reported upon, the Chippewayan and Montagnais, were predominantly hunters who lived in regions that have a cold climate that was probably similar to that of Missouri in the late Pleistocene. He pointed out that in lower latitudes with climates like that of Missouri today, gathering was the dominant means of subsistence. Therefore, the people in a climate changing rapidly from intense cold to temperate, comparable to the difference between 50°–55° and 36°–41° north latitude, would predictably begin to shift their primary means of subsistence from hunting to foraging. It is proposed that the change in the climate, and a rescheduling of food-getting activities, rather than cultural contacts, brought about the mixed Early Hunter and Forager tool kits in Graham Cave and in other comparable sites in the Missouri–Mississippi Valley during the period 8000–7000 B.C. The reason that the tool kits changed little during the occupation of Graham Cave after 7000 B.C. (Klippel 1970a) is probably due to the fact that all of the activities being conducted in the cave were relatively uniform, owing to the location and nature of the site and its use as a hunting–gathering camp.

In general throughout the Eastern United States cultural area the Early Hunters adapted their cultures to a climate that was changing from glacial to post-glacial. Although it is possible that an increase in population resulted in a concomitant modification in societal environment, there seems to be no evidence to support the supposition.

Known campsites were all small and represented short-time utilization. According to findings, neither the size of camps nor the amounts of debris on them increased. Cultural difference was not even reflected markedly in the tool kits used in exploiting new ecological niches. Roots, fruits, nuts, and small seeds no doubt were collected. Small animals were trapped. Foraging probably became nearly equal to hunting as a means of obtaining food in some regions, whereas hunting continued as a major activity in others. Hypothetically it was a period of change from a nomadic, basically hunting economy, to a seminomadic foraging economy, but hunting camps such as Graham Cave provided little evidence of the change. Klippel (1971: 50) in a recent analysis said, "Even though there have been changes in the biophysical environment, accompanied by shifts in exploited vertebrate fauna, analyses of the distribution of stone tools from the cave suggest that many of the same kinds of activities were being conducted at the site throughout its prehistoric occupation." Klippel (1971: 52) continued by suggesting that the site "seems to have served as a camp for hunters and gatherers who utilized similar paraphernalia in their procurement and maintenance activities while frequenting the cave."

The transition from Early Hunter Tradition to Forager Tradition began some time in the Paleo-Indian period and ended some time before the Middle Archaic period. This transition for the most part took place in approximately one thousand years (8000–7000 B.C.). It has been designated the Dalton period, during which a Hunter–Forager Tradition has been proposed. Using this classification the complexes with strong elements of both Early Hunter and Forager traditions can be more easily identified in the developmental sequence in the Eastern United States.

Lifeways during the Hunter–Forager Tradition were not greatly altered from those of the Early Hunter Tradition. Hunting continued to be a major occupation. The tool kit of the Early Hunter was still in use. Fluted forms were manufactured, but the technique of producing long flutes was a thing of the past. Most of the projectile points and knives were only basally thinned or had relatively short flutes, and the unfluted lanceolate was the most common form. A specialized knife, Dalton Serrated, was diagnostic. It may have been a development from broad lanceolate forms, Graham Cave Fluted, or those with similar short flutes and a deep concave base. The small Dalton Serrated may have derived from the reworking of broken knives while still attached to the haft, for the Dalton Serrated was not beveled prior to resharpening, and was larger than the small form usually described as Dalton Serrated. In general, spear points or knives of the Hunter–Foragers were large, but they were beginning to produce smaller ones or reduce large ones by reworking, as evidenced by the prevalence of the small Dalton Serrated form (Figure 4–19C).

Adzes, spokeshaves, and steep-edged scraping and cutting tools indicated that woodworking played an important part in the activities of the Hunter–Foragers. Shafts for spears, spear throwers, handles for knives and scraping tools, containers, digging sticks, snares, and traps were probably made of wood.

The need for fitted or tailored clothing and the techniques of producing it were evidenced in the small, eyed, bone needles, splinter-bone awls, flint flakes with spurs (probably used for punching holes in skins for sewing), snubbed-end flake scrapers, and flake knives. The dependence upon small game such as the cottontail, raccoon, and squirrel indicated that hunting big game (deer) was only one of the skills of the Hunter–Forager. Sandstone mortars, pebble manos or pestles, grinding slabs, roller pestles, cupstones, and pebble hammerstones denoted that collecting nuts, berries, and seeds was an integral part of the subsistence activities of the Hunter–Forager.

The bands of Hunter–Foragers were small, but sufficient information is not available to make firm estimates of their size. Logan (1952: 18) recorded only nine fireplaces in clusters of five and four respectively, near the front center of Graham Cave. If one nuclear family used each fireplace, the location and clustering suggested that the cave was occupied by no more than an extended family or two (made up of four and five nuclear families) in the part of the cave excavated at that time. If an estimate of five per nuclear family were projected for the entire cave, there would be room for no more than 14 to 18 family units, or 60 to 90 individuals. There is, of course, no assurance that the fireplaces represent a single occupation, and it is possible that no more than one to five nuclear families ever occupied the cave at the same time. Klippel (1971: 15) suggested on the basis of size alone that 74 individuals could have used the cave, at about 8000 B.C.

The ceremonial life of the Hunter–Foragers is suggested by special structures and burial of the dead. A semicircle of stones was found on the west side of Graham Cave, east of a large rock, on the top of which a small fire had burned intermittently or continuously, long enough to discolor and crack the rock. The usual debris of split animal bones was not found in the hearth area, nor in any large quantities in the area enclosed by the circle of stones. One of the stones had been ground or polished on its upper face. The structure has been interpreted as being ceremonial in nature in view of the lack of evidence of its use for economic activities, the uniqueness of its construction, and the association with it of the hearth on the rock and the polished stone nearby. The burial had been interred under the natural floor of the cave. Only a representation of the bones was buried, less than one-half of the skeleton, but they had been placed in proper articulation to represent a flexed position. A small canine tooth with a hole drilled in it was associated with the burial. Care concerning the remains of the dead and placement of ornaments with the bones of the dead are marks of ceremonial activity and belief of life after death by the Hunter–Foragers in the Dalton period.

Nearly as many varieties of forms have been included under the term *Dalton* as have been included under the terms *Clovis* and *Folsom*. Dalton forms have a widespread distribution that is probably related in part to their derivation through technological tradition from the fluted forms that preceded them throughout the Eastern United States. Their broad distribution and their occurrence in association with fluted forms and lanceolate forms in the Dalton period suggest that the Dalton form was very early and developed from fluted and lanceolate forms. Dalton Serrated may have lasted for a relatively long period, overlapping with a variety of projectile point and knife types.

It is not good procedure to define a culture or cultural tradition on the basis of a single technological tradition. In spite of this, fluted forms and Dalton forms have been used as cultural tradition designates when little or nothing else was available for interpretation, and I have resorted to this procedure here when better information was not available. It should be kept in mind that chipped-stone technological traditions are represented by the projectile point or knife forms and that it is only hypothetical that those traits of major cultural traditions are indicative of the whole tradition.

Southwest Drainage Region

In the White River drainage, the White Locality, Dalton Serrated were reported from six different sites when the survey was made of the Table Rock Reservoir (Marshall 1960: 117–24, 157, 165). A great variety of points was found at the same sites indicating that these locations had been desirable as habitation or activity areas from the earliest time that people had occupied the locality. Unfortunately the association of Dalton Serrated with the other artifacts is possibly fortuitous, and at this time a Dalton complex cannot be extracted from the surface collections.

Two Dalton Serrated from Stone County, one from James River and one from a White River site, were examined in the R. B. Hatcher Collection. Dalton Serrated knives have also been reported from the Bull Shoals Reservoir area

(*MASN* 1958c). These occurrences of Dalton Serrated throughout the White Locality suggest that many parts of the locality were occupied during the Dalton period.

Two Dalton Serrated were recorded from the lowest levels of the Standlee shelter, 30–42 inches deep (Bray 1960: 487). Occurring in the same levels were types of projectile points from the Forager Tradition, Early Archaic period, as well as plano-convex, snubbed-end flake scrapers, oval and triangular bifaces, utilized flakes, trimmed flakes, rubbed hematite, unshaped pebble manos, pitted anvilstones, flat mealing stones, and core hammerstones. All but the projectile points and the core hammerstones usually associated with the Early Archaic period could be representative of Hunter–Forager Tradition in the Dalton period.

Bray (1960: 502) noted that two Dalton Serrated were found in the clay–gravel subsoil in Standlee shelter and were the oldest tools present. Unfortunately no clear-cut division could be made in the deposits or the cultural materials. White River Archaic (Graham Cave Notched) and Rice Lanceolate, anvilstones, flat mealing stones, pebble hammerstones, pebble manos, and oval and triangular bifaces were found in the same levels with Dalton Serrated. Bray (1960: 531–32) suggested that traits characteristic of the Dalton period were carryovers into the Archaic period rather than evidence of an earlier occupation at Standlee shelter.

The excavations at the Rice site (Bray 1956a: 55–61) produced evidences of three different aggregates, the earliest of which were nonceramic and not completely separable by artifact content. The earliest levels at the site contained an aggregate of tools as follows: Rice Lobed, Rice Contracting Stemmed, Rice Lanceolate, Dalton Serrated, Table Rock Stemmed, Breckenridge form (Wood 1962: 80, Figure 5g–m), and Stone Square Stemmed cutting tools, snubbed-end flake scrapers, stemmed scrapers, ovoid bifaces, pitted anvilstones, and an expanding-based drill. Mussel shell and split animal bone in the deposits indicated that both hunting and foraging were important activities.

Bray (1956a: 61) concluded that the earliest inhabitants were small groups of nomadic people who occupied the shelter intermittently. The Dalton Serrated, snubbed-end flake scrapers, and pitted anvilstones might represent a component from the Dalton period, but this interpretation is conjectural. Further excavation at the Rice shelter was conducted to aid in interpreting earlier excavations (Marshall and Chapman 1960). Four levels of occupation were isolated in the profile on the slope in front of the shelter, but the cultural materials recovered from the excavation were not correspondingly distinct. Another trait, a pebble chopper, was found in the lowest level and can be added to the earlier aggregate in the Rice site. No pitted pebble anvilstones occurred in the lowest deposits, and those projectile points or knives definitely identifiable and *in situ* were similar to Rice Contracting Stemmed and Rice Lanceolate. A pit, the outlines of which could not be defined absolutely, had been intruded into the deposits, disturbing them and mixing some of the later artifacts with the earlier. The presence of arrowheads and pottery fragments in the upper part of the lowest deposits can be explained by the pit disturbance.

A more helpful sequence of artifacts was discovered in the drip area, though natural levels were not as discernible. A Dalton Serrated, a Rice Contracting Stemmed, a Rice Lanceolate, a Rice Lanceolate made into a scraper, and possibly a Jakie Stemmed were the distinctive items found in the lowest levels. A small snubbed-end flake scraper, an ovoid biface, a side scraper, a triangular biface, and pitted pebble anvilstones were other artifacts in the lowest deposits. The aggregate appeared to correlate rather closely with that proposed as Early Archaic by Bray (1956a).

Evidence from the six sites located in the survey where aggregates of artifacts were found, from the early levels at Standlee I and Rice shelters and from three other locations where Dalton Serrated were found, indicated that Hunter–Foragers occupied the White Locality during the Dalton period. Representative artifacts making up the aggregate from the White Locality during the Dalton period cannot be separated from those of the Forager Tradition, Early Archaic period, with any certainty. Dalton Serrated, oval and triangular bifaces, snubbed-end flake scrapers, utilized flake knives, pebble choppers, pebble manos and pebble anvilstones made up the Hunter–Forager Tradition aggregate.

The archaeological investigations in the Current–Eleven Point Locality have been primarily surface surveys by amateur archaeologists. A brief reconnaissance and a compilation of previous information was conducted for the National Park Service at the time the locality was being considered for status as a national monument. The archaeological potential of the area was then evaluated (Chapman 1960a). Now that much of the Current River part of the locality is included in the Ozark Scenic Riverways National Park, more intensive archaeological investigations are underway in those areas being developed by the National Park Service (Born and Chapman 1972; Williams 1968).

Dalton Serrated collected on the surface of sites in Shannon County along Current River, in the Anderson Museum, Van Buren, Missouri, are the only basis for assuming that the locality was occupied by Hunter–Foragers during the Dalton period. The finding of an unsharpened Dalton Serrated (23CT3, Leo Anderson Collection) is somewhat more reliable evidence because similar forms have been found on sites in association with sharpened Dalton Serrated in the Lower Missouri Valley II Locality. Other associations are broad lanceolate forms and Clovis Fluted. The former may have been manufactured during the same time period as Dalton Serrated, for they occur with Dalton Serrated rather consistently on sites in the Lower Missouri Valley II.

A few Dalton Serrated have been reported from the Neosho Locality, probably indicating occupation during the Dalton period. Adams (1958: 50, Figure 24, Numbers 27, 28, 33) illustrated two Dalton Serrated and what appears to be a related form that is neither beveled nor serrated. Three other forms (Adams 1958: 50, Figure 24, Numbers 29–31) appear to be within the range of variation of Dalton Serrated. He (Adams 1958: 48) did not identify the sites where they

were found but said that the artifacts had been found only on a few of the larger sites.

Western Prairie Region

Intensive surveys and numerous excavations have been conducted in the Upper Osage Locality due to the proposed building of the Truman (Kaysinger Bluff), Stockton, Hackleman Corners, Butler, Freeman, and Nevada dams on the Osage River and its tributaries. Surveys financed with grants from the National Park Service have been conducted in each of the areas by the University of Missouri. A single Dalton Serrated fragment was found. It was on the surface in a small cave (Keller 1965: Figure 47c). On the basis of the find the cave was excavated. The upper 18 inches of the floor had indications of an occupation during the Mississippian period. The lower deposits, which were 4½–5½ feet deep, contained split and burned animal bone and wood charcoal and only one nondiagnostic artifact, the tip of a bone awl 3½ feet beneath the surface (Keller 1965: 208–10). It would appear that there was very little use if any of the Upper Osage Locality by Hunter–Foragers during the Dalton period.

Ozark Highland Region

The information available concerning the Dalton period in Rodgers shelter in the Lower Osage Locality is limited because deposits were accumulating from the Pomme de Terre River during much of the period (Figure 4–8). Furthermore, the radiocarbon dates near the top of Stratum 1 and the lower part of Stratum 2 are from the Early Archaic period, and it is probable that most of the cultural bearing deposits in Stratum 2 (McMillan 1971) were Early Archaic period rather than Dalton period (Figure 4–8). The aggregate in Rodgers shelter that was possibly representative of the Dalton period but that may have included items of the Paleo-Indian period is shown in Figure 5–1. The artifacts are representative of the earliest occupation of the shelter.

It looks as though there were few Hunter–Foragers in the Gasconade Locality during the Dalton period, for, although Dalton Serrated knives have been noted in the locality, they were not plentiful. McMillan (1965b: 54–56) did not include the Dalton Serrated in the Tick Creek complex, the earliest identifiable complex in the Gasconade Locality, nor did Roberts (1965) show Dalton Serrated from Tick Creek Cave.

There was a distribution of Dalton Serrated in the Meramec Locality similar to that in the Missouri Valley II Locality. Lying between the two localities, but within the Meramec River drainage, is a highland location covering several square miles in which Planolike lanceolate and Dalton Serrated were discovered. The Planolike forms (Figure 5–2) are of special interest because elsewhere they have been found in association

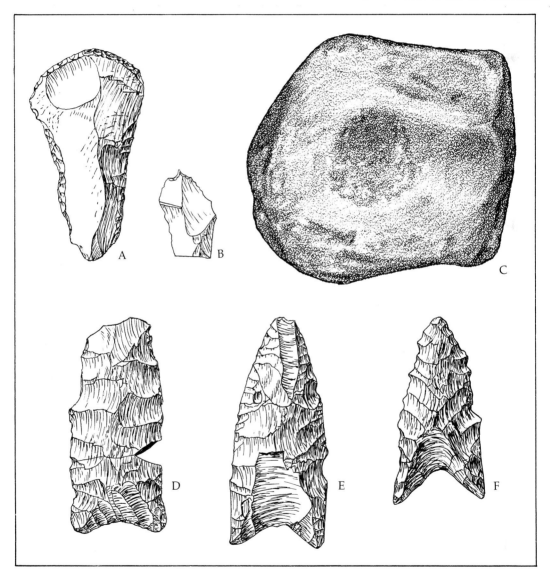

Figure 5–1.   The earliest evidences of occupation in Rodgers shelter. Scale 1:1.
A, Snubbed-end flake scraper; B, beaked flake; C, pitted anvilstone; D, Plainview; E, Clovis Fluted; F, Dalton Serrated.

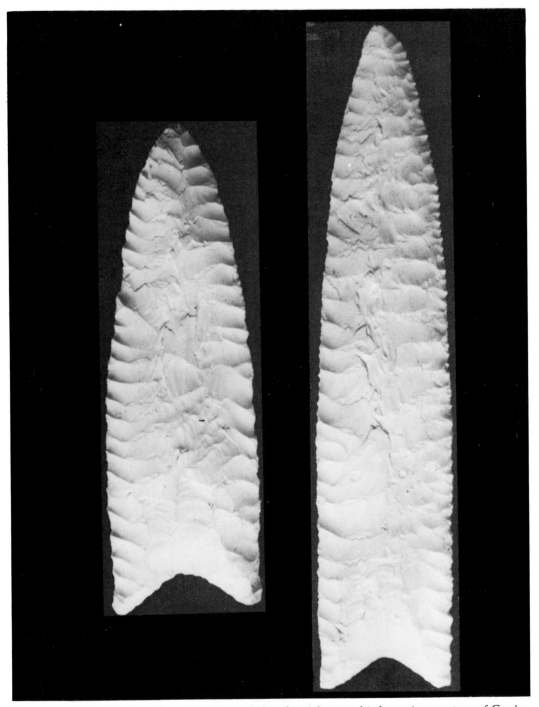

Figure 5–2. Planolike forms from the Meramec Locality (photo and information courtesy of Garrison E. Rose). Scale 1:1.

with types thought to be from the Paleo-Indian or Dalton periods. They are substantial evidence that the Plano technological tradition of the Plains penetrated as far east as the Mississippi River.

Sixteen Dalton Serrated, three Graham Cave Fluted, and a broad lanceolate form, as well as the two Planolike lanceolates mentioned, have been reported from the Meramec Locality (UMC, ASM, files: G. E. Rose, May 21, 1954; D. P. Dale, April 21, 1953; E. W. Zimmerman, April 26, 1953; L. W. Blake, n.d.). McMillan (1965b: 55) noted that Dalton Serrated were not found in the Gasconade Locality but appeared in the next drainage to the east, the Meramec. According to the report, the Dalton Serrated was from the lower deposits of an uncontrolled excavation in Shelf Cave, Crawford County.

One Dalton Serrated and a cache of Dalton Serrated came from the Upper Black–St. Francis Locality (Figure 5–3). They were Dalton Serrated forms that had not been resharpened.

Northwest Prairie Region

In the Lamine Locality, Dalton Serrated and forms that are possibly related to the Hunter–Forager Tradition have been found on the surface by local collectors (UMC, ASM, files: W. T. Christopher, November 12, 1967), but no cultural components have been isolated by excavations.

A collateral flaked form discovered by Richard Turner in the Western Prairie Region is a Scottsbluff (Suhm, Krieger, and Jelks 1954: 478, Plate 118), a Plano type (Figure 5–4A), and another identified as Scottsbluff was found by Jean Hon (Figure 5–4B). A similar collaterally flaked Scottsbluff (Figure 5–5A) and two concave-based lanceolate forms (Figure 5–5B–C) came from a

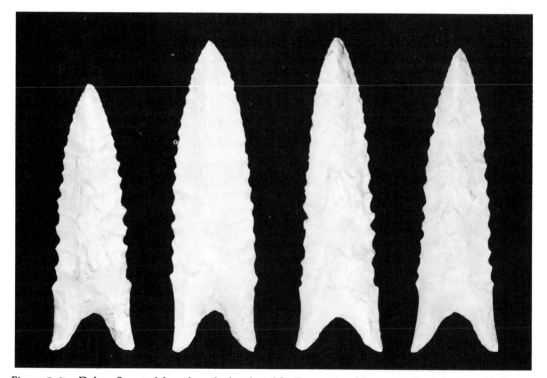

Figure 5–3. Dalton Serrated found on the border of St. Francois and Iron counties (photo and information courtesy of Leonard W. Blake). Scale 1:1.

single site near Sedalia and are in the Harry and Florence Collins Collection. They may be evidence of a Paleo-Indian occupation, but it is also possible that the Plano and Planolike forms occurring in the western part of the state represent occupations there during the Dalton period.

No absolute evidences of the Hunter–Forager Tradition in the Dalton period were noted in the Northwest Prairie Region away from the main stream of the Missouri River. In the northern part of the Lower Missouri Valley I Locality close to the Missouri River there is the record of only one Dalton Serrated (Stubbs 1950: 25, Figure 4, Number 15). It did not come from a site but was found in a gully near a small hilltop site.

The Lower Missouri Valley I Locality in the vicinity of Kansas City must have been particularly desirable to Hunter–Foragers in the Northwest Prairie Region during the Dalton period. No site has yielded a complex of materials that can be related definitely to the period, but several finds of Dalton Serrated and related varieties have been made. Two forms from Clay County are much like Scottsbluff (Shippee 1964: 33–34, Figure 15H). One of them is similar to Scottsbluff I type. Shippee (1950: 164; 1964: 4–5) reported an oblique parallel-flaked form that he identified as an unusually finely chipped Plainview. It was

found on eroded high ground, 2½ miles from the Missouri River. The location of the site was similar to those from which Nebo Hill aggregates have come. Shippee (1948: 30, Plate 11Da) showed a resharpened Dalton Serrated from Site 23CL14 as a part of the Nebo Hill complex. The Dalton Serrated and perhaps some of the concave-based lanceolate points illustrated may have been produced by people occupying the site at an earlier time than that indicated by the Nebo Hill Lanceolate, manos, grooved axes, celts, and digging tools at Nebo Hill. Another Dalton Serrated was later reported from the same site (Shippee 1964: 4–5). The base of what appears to be a Dalton Serrated was found on the Hopewellian Renner site by Waldo R. Wedel (Potter 1970: 3–5). Again it could indicate an earlier occupation, or it could have been picked up by people from the Woodland period who occupied the site. Shippee (1964: 2, Figure 1 C–D) showed three forms that were noted as similar to Dalton Serrated but not beveled. They appear to be newly made Dalton Serrated.

Dalton Serrated have been found more frequently downstream from the Kansas City area. Five good examples of Dalton Serrated, along with two stemmed Planolike forms similar to Scottsbluff I and II (Wormington 1957), were

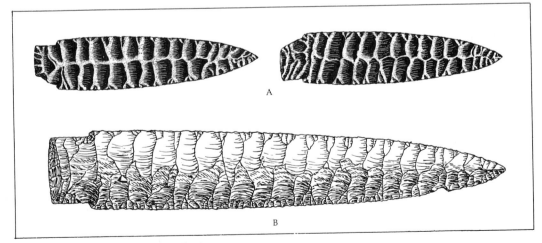

Figure 5–4. Scottsbluff points. Scale 4:5.
A, From the Lamine Locality (drawn by Richard Turner from his collection); B, from the Lower Missouri Valley I Locality (Mrs. Jean Hon Collection).

shown in a photograph of points from Lafayette County furnished by Mr. Charles Pevestorff (UMC, ASM, files: November 19, 1949). Seven Dalton Serrated from Lafayette and Saline counties were collected by Mr. and Mrs. J. M. Crick (UMC, ASM, files: December 26, 1967), who also reported two large collaterally flaked specimens that appear to be in the Plano technological tradition. They are concave based and have basal thinning. One of them came from the site in Saline County on which a Dalton Serrated was dis-

covered. Three other Dalton Serrated, a lanceolate form with concave base, three Sedalia Lanceolates, an Afton Corner Notched, and a piece of a bannerstone were reported from a small hillside site in Saline County (Bray 1962b: 3–7). The Dalton Serrated probably had no cultural relationship to the Sedalia Lanceolate, Afton Corner Notched, or the bannerstone.

Although the information concerning Dalton Serrated and the possible distribution of the Dalton complex in the Northwest Prairie Region is

Figure 5–5. Plano and Planolike forms from the Lamine Locality (Mr. and Mrs. Harry L. Collins Collection). Scale 1:1.
A, Scottsbluff; B–C, concave-based lanceolate forms.

Figure 5–6.   View of Graham Cave.

limited, the fact that the distribution parallels that of the fluted forms may be significant. The settlement pattern of the Early Hunters and the Hunter–Foragers may have been similar.

Northeast Prairie Region

Graham Cave (Figure 5–6) in the lowest level of occupation (Figure 5–7) contained the best-known Hunter–Forager component of the Dalton period in the Lower Missouri Valley II Locality. The transitional nature of the materials recovered from Paleo-Indian to Archaic has been discussed by Logan (1952). Radiocarbon dates on the early component or assemblage in Graham Cave range from 7850 to 6800 B.C. and thus are very defi-

nitely in the Dalton period. The assemblage is representative of the Hunter–Forager Tradition and in conjunction with the components at Rodgers shelter, Arnold Research Cave, and aggregates on campsites in the Lower Missouri Valley II Locality has been given the name Dalton complex. The following artifacts are in the assemblage and seem to be representative of the complex: Graham Cave Fluted, Dalton Serrated, Agate Basin Lanceolate, straight-sided lanceolate bifaces, plano-convex snubbed-end flake scrapers, concave-based drills, rubbed hematite, antler-tip tools, bone splinter awls, small, eyed bone needles, sandstone cupstones and mortars, roller pestles, flat mealing stones, rough bifaces, adzes, and pitted anvilstones. Other items in the com-

plex are a ceremonial fire area outlined by a ring of stones and a secondary burial (Chapman 1952a; 1957; Klippel 1971; Logan 1952) (Figures 5–8 through 5–14).

Arnold Research Cave in Callaway County is another sandstone cave even closer to the top of a hill than Graham Cave (Figures 5–15 and 5–16). The Dalton complex component by Hunter–Foragers was also found in Arnold Research Cave but was not as well defined. The series found there of lanceolate bifaces, Dalton Serrated, Graham Cave Fluted (Shippee 1957; 1966: 68–69), concave-based drills, plano-convex snubbed-end flake scrapers, oval bifaces, and eyed, bone needles are part of the complex (Figures 5–17, 5–18, and 5–19). The animals hunted most intensively by the earliest users of the cave were deer, squirrel, raccoon, and cottontail (Falk 1970: Appendix) and thus correspond to the type of game hunted by the Hunter–Foragers who left the artifacts of the Dalton complex in Graham Cave (Klippel 1970a: 124–30).

Dalton Serrated and lanceolate forms have been reported from bluff sites bordering the Missouri River and on ridges flanking it from Boonville to St. Louis. Some of the forms that were similar in shape and size to Dalton Serrated were not beveled or serrated, and others had no grinding on the sides of the base. Since the Dalton Serrated appears to be a specialized knife (Morse n.d.) and may often be the result of the resharpening of a larger form, some of the larger forms such as Graham Cave Fluted or the large, well-made Planolike lanceolates may actually have been the initial form, which were then reduced to the small, beveled Dalton Serrated when they had been sufficiently resharpened. The small, pentagonal Dalton Serrated with very little blade may in fact be worn-out knives that were discarded. Yet there are larger, unbeveled Dalton Serrated knives, which seem to have been the result of a specific method of manufacture.

The White-Sims site, two miles north of the

Missouri River toward Ashland, is worth mentioning because a collection from it contained fragments of ten concave-based forms that might be classified as Dalton Serrated and Graham Cave Fluted (Figure 5–20). Another site, 23BO851, also had yielded a Graham Cave Fluted, Dalton Serrated, and lanceolate forms (Figure 5–21). A nearby site, 23BO850, produced Dalton Serrated, lanceolates, and a concave-based drill (Figure 5–22). A great variety of lanceolate forms occurred on the same site with Dalton Serrated in this locality, some further variations being illustrated from Site 23BO835 (Figure 5–23).

Planolike projectile points or knives have also been found in the area (Figure 5–24). Similar Planolike, Graham Cave Fluted, and Dalton Serrated have been reported by Bill Vogel from the south side of the river at Site 23MU45 in Moniteau County (*MASN* 1959c).

No intensive archaeological survey has ever been conducted in the Lower Missouri Valley II Locality downstream from the mouth of the Gasconade River to the mouth of the Missouri, and few excavations have been made on sites in the locality. Judging from the reports obtained from amateur archaeologists who have made collections there, it is an extremely rich and important archaeological locality that may hold answers to many questions concerning the earliest occupations of Missouri. Reports (UMC, ASM, files: L. Herberger, October 16, 1967; W. W. Wanner, December 13, 1967; E. W. Zimmerman, April 26, 1953; and Disser 1965) noted Dalton Serrated knives, and L. W. Blake (n.d.) reported a Graham Cave Fluted in the Greater St. Louis Locality close to the mouth of the Missouri River, extending the distribution of the type to the Mississippi River Valley.

Actually, the Dalton site near the mouth of the Osage River, from which Dalton Serrated was named, contained relatively few of the Dalton Serrated knives in proportion to the full Dalton site aggregate. The aggregate at the Dalton site

Figure 5–7.   Deposits in Graham Cave (the lowest occupation level is visible as a lighter color below the place being pointed to by W. D. Logan; J. Wilson is standing).

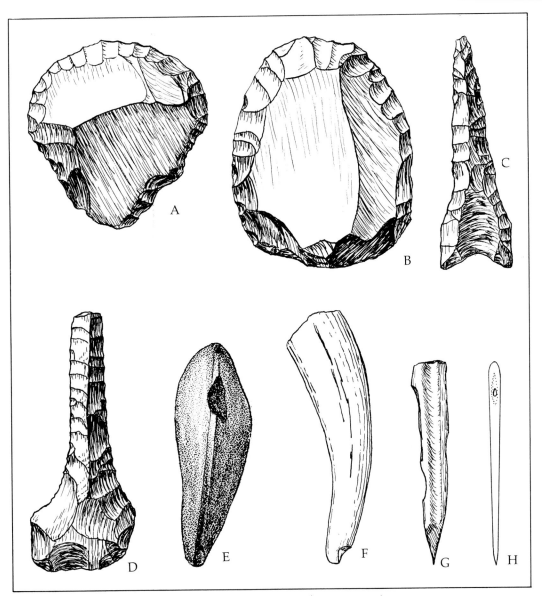

Figure 5–9. Tools from the Dalton complex in Graham Cave. Scale 1:1.
A–B, Snubbed-end flake scrapers; C–D, drills; E, rubbed hematite; F, antler-tip tool; G, bone awl; H, eyed bone needle.

Figure 5–8. Artifacts from the Dalton complex in Graham Cave. Scale 1:1.
A, Graham Cave Fluted; B–C, reworked lanceolate forms; D, drill; E–F, concave-based lanceolate bifaces; G–H, triangular bifaces.

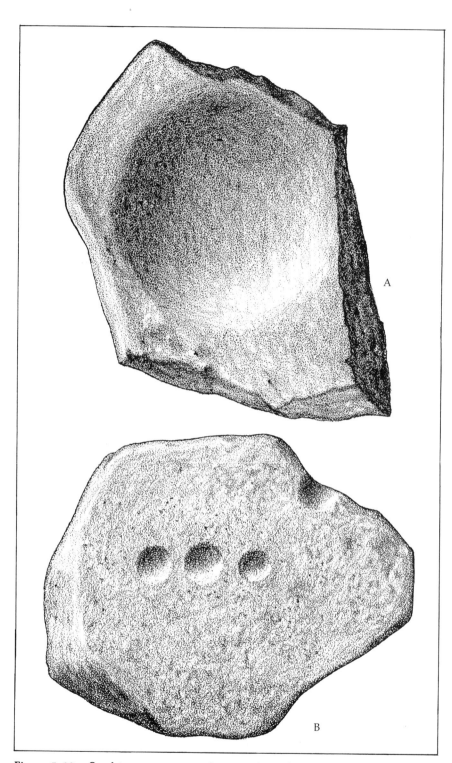

Figure 5–10. Sandstone cupstone and mortar from the Dalton complex in Graham Cave. Scale 1:2.

Figure 5–11. Roller pestle and flat mealing stones *in situ* from the Dalton complex in Graham Cave.

has been identified as Forager Tradition, Early Archaic period and will be discussed in the following chapter. Dalton Serrated or forms that are classed as Dalton Serrated because of their similarity in stoneworking techniques were found on two sites along the Moreau River in Cole County (Upp 1953: 23–24, 26, Figures 17, 24). Associated artifacts were too varied to determine whether or not the forms were the result of occupation of the sites by Dalton or by later Archaic components.

It was a real surprise to find that there was so little evidence of the distribution of Dalton Serrated into the Northeast Prairie Region north of the Lower Missouri Valley II and Greater St. Louis localities. Eichenberger (1956: 9) showed outline drawings of forms that could perhaps be classed as Dalton Serrated from two sites. One specimen, provisionally identified as Dalton Serrated, is shown by Eichenberger (1944: 11, Plate II) in a collection of points from the Northeast Prairie Region. At least one other Dalton Serrated has been found in the area (UMC, ASM, files: Garrison E. Rose, February 16, 1952), but the general lack of information on Dalton Serrated or related types from the region suggests that the distribution there of Hunter–Foragers was extremely limited. During a period of several years an intensive survey of the Salt Locality was conducted by the University of Missouri—Columbia, supported by grants from the National Park Service, River Basin Surveys in the proposed Cannon (Joanna) Reservoir area, and no Dalton Serrated were found.

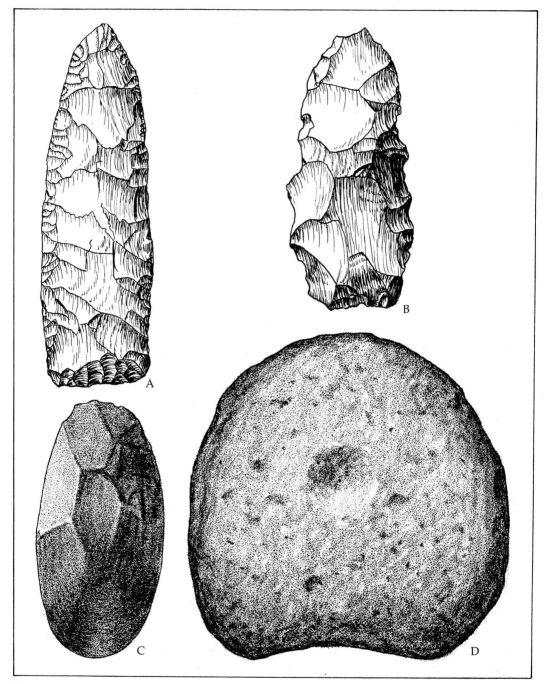

Figure 5–12.   Tools from the Dalton complex in Graham Cave. Scale 5:6.
A–B, Rough bifaces; C, hematite adz; D, pitted anvilstone.

Figure 5–13. Ceremonial fire area outlined by circle of stones from the Dalton complex in Graham Cave.

Figure 5–14. Secondary burial from the Dalton complex in Graham Cave.

Figure 5–15. Aerial view of Arnold Research Cave.

Figure 5–16. View of the entrance to Arnold Research Cave.

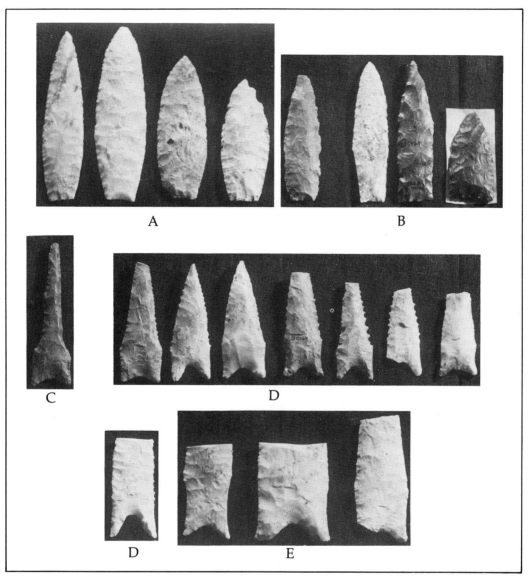

Figure 5–17.   Various chipped-stone artifacts from the Dalton complex in Arnold Research Cave. Scale 5:9.
A, Agate Basin Lanceolate; B, lanceolate forms; C, drill; D, Dalton Serrated; E, concave-based lanceolate.

Figure 5–18.   Chipped-stone artifacts from Arnold Research Cave (Clarence Kelly Collection). Scale 1:1.
A, Reworked lanceolate drill; B–C, Dalton Serrated.

Figure 5–19.   Snubbed-end scrapers from the Dalton complex in Arnold Research Cave. Scale 1:2.

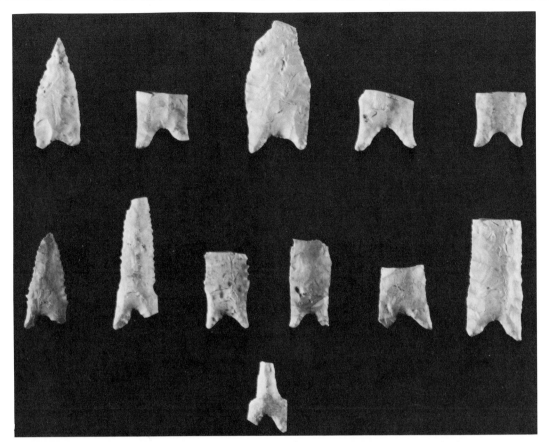

Figure 5–20. Early projectile points, knives, and drill from the White-Sims site. Scale 1:2.

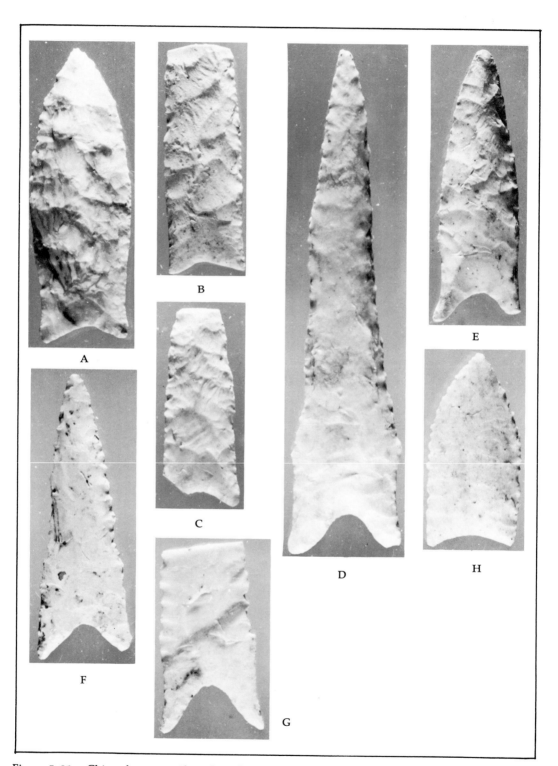

Figure 5–21.   Chipped-stone artifacts from Site 23BO851 (Richard S. Brownlee Collection). Scale 1:1.
A–C, Concave-based lanceolate bifaces; D–E, Graham Cave Fluted; F–G, Dalton Serrated; H, concave-based lanceolate biface.

Figure 5–22.   Artifacts from Site 23BO850 (Richard S. Brownlee Collection). Scale 1:1.
A–B, Dalton Serrated; C, concave-based lanceolate biface; D, drill; E–G, concave-based lanceolate bifaces.

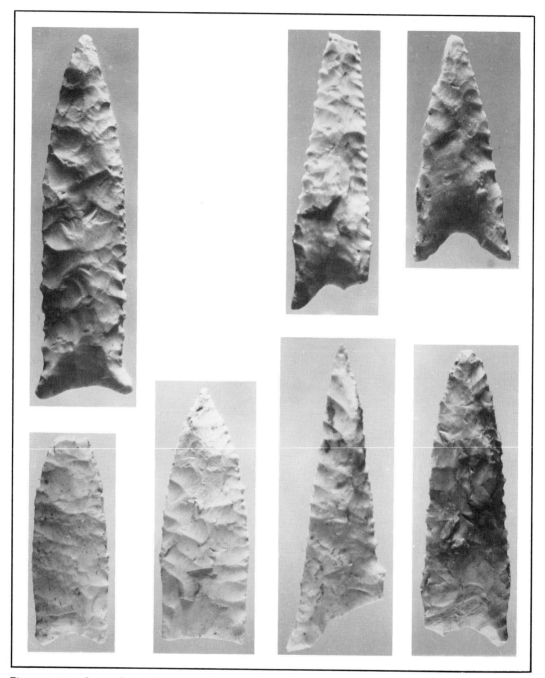

Figure 5–23. Lanceolate bifaces from Site 23BO835 (Richard S. Brownlee Collection). Scale 1:1.

Figure 5–24. Planolike lanceolate forms from Site 23BO426 (Richard S. Brownlee Collection). Scale 1:1.

Figure 5–25.   Early types of chipped-stone artifacts from the northern Bootheel Locality (Paul Corbin Collection). Scale 1:1.
A–C, Forms intermediate between Clovis Fluted and Dalton Serrated; D–F, Dalton Serrated.

Southeast Riverine Region

The Southeast Riverine Region seems to have a concentration of Dalton Serrated similar to that in the Lower Missouri Valley II Locality. Two Dalton Serrated and one Graham Cave Fluted were reported from the Mississippi Valley Central Locality (UMC, ASM, files: D. P. Dale, April 27, 1953). Twenty-five Dalton Serrated have been tallied from the St. Francis Riverine Locality by Edward Zimmerman (Personal Communication, April 26, 1953) and T. J. Stephens (Personal Communication, December 14, 1967). In at least two instances Hardin Barbed were reported in association with Dalton Serrated (Orr 1963).

The association of Hardin Barbed may have been fortuitous, but it could be evidence that a component from the Forager Tradition during the Early Archaic period was indicated. Hardin Barbed were in the complex at the Dalton site in central Missouri.

A sequence of large-bladed cutting tools has been identified at the Modoc shelter, Illinois (Deuel 1957; Fowler 1957; 1959a; 1959b; Fowler and Winters 1956), and two of the forms, Hidden Valley Stemmed and Graham Cave Notched, were found in levels of occupation during the Dalton period. It is also possible that the earliest occupation of the Hidden Valley shelter was during the Dalton period, but I have interpreted it to be Early Archaic in time and it will be discussed with the Early Archaic period.

In the Bootheel Locality the distribution of Dalton Serrated is much the same as that in the St. Francis Riverine. The latter and the Mississippi alluvial valley downstream were surveyed intensively by Dr. James A. Ford and collaborators for sites on which Dalton Serrated occurred. Dalton Serrated were found, but the greatest concentration of sites and points was in northeastern Arkansas (Redfield and Moselage 1970).

Dalton Serrated were reported from two sites in the Bootheel Locality by Donald P. Dale (UMC, ASM, files, April 27, 1953). The most interesting specimens were in the collection of Paul Corbin. They were from the northern part of the locality. They consisted of Dalton Serrated, forms which appear to be intermediate between Clovis Fluted and Dalton Serrated (Figure 5–25), and a Planolike lanceolate (Figure 5–26). The Planolike form is so similar to those from the Lower Missouri Valley II and Meramec localities (Figure 5–2) that it is considered to be still further evidence of the penetration of the Plano technological stoneworking tradition into the Mississippi River valley. It is again suggested that Planolike lanceolates may have been manufactured in the Mississippi Valley during the Dalton period. The same or a similar chipped stone technology was known to Hunter–Foragers of the Dalton period.

Regional Distribution of Evidences

The Dalton complex, as it has been described from Graham and Arnold Research caves, differs from the complex in Rodgers shelter in the Lower Osage Locality, and the information on this com-

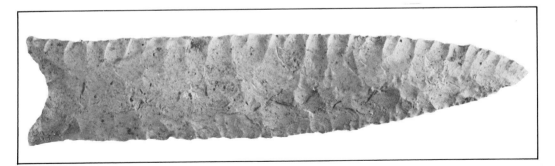

Figure 5–26.   Planolike lanceolate form from the Bootheel Locality (Paul Corbin Collection). Scale 6:7.

plex is very incomplete for all other sites in the state. When more evidences have been discovered and analyzed from the Dalton sites located in the Southeast Riverine Region and other regions, local differences will probably be represented in the Dalton complex. Unfortunately, so little information was at hand concerning the Dalton complexes in each locality, other than the Lower Missouri Valley II and Lower Osage, that the Dalton Serrated were resorted to as evidence of Hunter–Forager Tradition occupation and distribution of the Dalton complexes. As it was pointed out in discussing the Paleo-Indian period, it is not a good procedure to use a single type of tool to assume that members of a particular cultural tradition were present at a specific time. The justification for the procedure in this case is that there is strong evidence that Dalton Serrated was manufactured primarily during the period 8000–7000 B.C. and is a very specialized knife or cutting tool that must have been important in cultural adaptation to the environment during that period in certain portions of the central United States. The data concerning the distribution of Dalton Serrated and their concentration in specific localities are at the very least as valid evidence as the use of fluted forms. Furthermore, the consistent association of Dalton Serrated with Graham Cave Fluted, Clovis Fluted, and Planolike forms may be further evidence that the Dalton Serrated was invented during the latter part of the Paleo-Indian period,

became very popular during the Dalton period, and continued to be used during the Early Archaic period. Associations with Hardin Barbed, Rice Lanceolate, St. Charles Notched, Rice Lobed, Agate Basin Lanceolate, and other Early Archaic types suggest that Dalton Serrated continued to be used through Early Archaic times or possibly until 5000 B.C. If this were the case the distribution of the Dalton Serrated could be an indication of the areas occupied or avoided during the important time span when there was evidently a climatic shifting from cold and wet with forest vegetation to warm and dry with prairie vegetation dominant in the Prairie Peninsula and nearby physiographic provinces.

In order to set the record straight, it will be necessary to undertake intensive archaeological surveys in the Lower Missouri Valley II, Mississippi Valley Central, and St. Francis Riverine localities where the distribution of Dalton Serrated indicates that sites occupied during the Dalton period are most likely to be concentrated in Missouri. Cooperation of amateur archaeologists and local collectors in making controlled surface collections from sites on which Clovis Fluted, Dalton Serrated, and Planolike forms occur would be of tremendous aid to such an endeavor. Intensive problem-oriented excavations of a selection of the sites located by the survey will be needed to provide the answers to the questions concerning the occupation of the state during the Paleo-Indian and Dalton periods.

6. Forager Tradition, Early Archaic Period

During the Dalton period the Hunter–Foragers shifted their attention from big-game hunting to more diversified ways of gaining a living, including trapping of small game animals with nets and snares and collecting nuts, berries, seeds, and fruits. Means of subsistence always had been varied, but because the colder climate probably limited their supply of vegetal foods the Early Hunters were primarily concerned with procuring large to moderately large game animals. Small game was also a part of the subsistence of Early Hunters, but during the Dalton period it made up a much larger proportion of the diet. This shift in emphasis has been assumed to be adaptation to the changes in the makeup of the flora and fauna brought about by climatic fluctuation. From information available it appears that very little change in subsistence activities took place during the Dalton period.

The Forager Tradition began with the broadening of subsistence activities to exploit a greater variety of the ecological niches in the environment. Hunting and collecting on land during the Archaic period continued as a major economic activity, but more emphasis began to be placed on collecting shellfish and fishing with weirs, traps, nets, and spears. Vegetal foods assumed an important place in the economy. Nomadism and seminomadism began to be modified; Foragers began to use base camps as a point to which they returned at the end of hunting-gathering excursions. Early in the Archaic period numbers of people living and working together were small like those in the Paleo-Indian and Dalton periods, perhaps fewer than 100 in a group, and during much of the year may have been divided into extended families made up of 10–25 members.

An extended family or two (10–50 people) might hunt or collect together utilizing the same camping place as a base of operations for their particular activities.

The artifacts that appear on sites occupied during the Forager Tradition indicate the diversification of activities that was connected with obtaining food. Most of the tools and utensils remaining at the sites today were made of stone by means of percussion or pressure flaking techniques. Spear points and knives similar to those of the Hunter–Foragers were still being made, but different forms became popular when early Foragers began to experiment with manufacturing techniques. Fluting was no longer practiced, but the lanceolate shape of Clovis Fluted continued, and basal thinning was a step in the manufacture of some knives and dart points. The base was usually deeply concave. The sides of the base were ground. Dalton Serrated and small lanceolate dart points were often notched deeper at the base than Clovis Fluted. The large lanceolate form may have been shaped by trimming the sides of the base or ground, narrowing the width near the base and giving the impression that the form was stemmed, which is illustrated by Rice Lanceolate and Rice Contracting Stemmed. Rice Lobed possibly developed out of experimentation with the notching of the ovoid blades that occur in the earliest aggregates. Ahler (1971: 119, Plates 2, 3) noted that Rice Lobed specimens (his Category 3) were "associated with specialized sawing or slicing activities for tools, bonded to broad, split wooden handles."

Large, contracting-stemmed projectile points, or similar forms with a straight stem, were manufactured by some of the earliest Foragers. It is suggested that the large, contracting-stemmed form originated in an early Plano stoneworking technique derived from the Early Hunter Tradition. Stemmed forms have been found at the Lime Creek site, dating more than 9,500 years ago, at the Finley, Scottsbluff, and many other sites with associated Plano complexes. It is possible that the contracting-stemmed form represented a further reduction in the size of the stems of the Plano forms. The large, stemmed forms such as Eden (Figure 4–1J), Scottsbluff (Figure 4–1I), and Alberta (Figure 4–2H) may have been knives rather than spear points. At any rate the study by Ahler (1971: 119, Plates 2–3, 7–9) showed that many of the stemmed forms that were large in size and with broad blades were used for heavy-duty cutting and cleaving, and others were sawing and slicing tools. In any instance specialized cutting tools were important in the early part of the Archaic period.

Other chipped-stone tools made by the Foragers of the Archaic period were a variety of forms of scrapers, including the continuation of plano-convex snubbed-end flake scrapers, round scrapers, and scrapers that were reworked from broken projectile points or knives. Large drills were also reworked from knives or spear points.

In general a variety of tool kits indicating the exploitation of plants and animals native to streams, lakes, swamps, forests, and prairies was a part of the Forager Tradition in the Archaic period. Collecting tool kits were added to the hunting kits and incipient foraging kits of the preceding Hunter–Forager Tradition of the Dalton period. In some instances the earlier tool kits were expanded upon or were adapted to foraging needs. Presumably nomadism and seminomadism were superceded by a regular hunting–gathering range with specific base camp sites that were returned to at regular intervals.

The Archaic people adjusted to the land by exploiting the various ecological niches it provided. This adaptation in its culmination was what Caldwell (1958: 6) called *primary forest efficiency* and it is assumed that a full cultural-ecological integration took place in some parts of Missouri by the end of the period. Theoretically, the method of adaptation varied with particular ecological niches in differing physiographic regions and basic materials available for tools, and these diverse methods are reflected in cultural remains. Thus, during the Late Archaic, it has been assumed that the cultural aggregates, assemblages, and complexes of a region were the results of cultural-environmental integration and selective adaptation to the physical environment. This was not true in all regions, for in some, in spite of the fact that styles of artifacts changed, the old patterns of living continued much the same.

The Forager Tradition in the Archaic period in Missouri was a part of the over-all early diversification of means of gaining a living that was taking place throughout the Missouri–Mississippi–Ohio drainage and the Eastern United States. It is not improbable that many of the changes made during the Forager Tradition in the Archaic period originated in the lower Missouri-central Mississippi valley. In any instance, the changes are reflected there even if they were not conceived there.

Cultural developments in the Forager Tradition during the Early Archaic period overlapped with those of the Hunter–Forager Tradition in the preceding Dalton period, making it difficult to determine just which ones were really representative of the Forager Tradition and which were a continuation of the Hunter–Forager Tradition.

Assemblages or aggregates from the Forager Tradition indicate that the site locations in the Early Archaic period were small camps, and the major tool kits found on them can be associated with hunting and collecting. Foragers using the camps were still placing a great deal of emphasis upon hunting as one of the means of gaining their livelihood. Although there is evidence of the Forager Tradition in the Early Archaic period in the eastern two-thirds of Missouri, in many localities scatterings of projectile points thought to be Early Archaic are the only indications.

The manifestation of the Forager Tradition in each locality or region will be discussed separately using the period subdivisions Early, Middle, and Late. Extensions of the cultural developments into states adjacent to Missouri that are pertinent will also be discussed at the end of each section.

Southwest Drainage Region

Extensive archaeological surveys and excavations in the Table Rock Reservoir area have provided information on the archaeological complexes making up the cultural-chronological sequence in the Southwest Drainage Region. The sequence was described generally in a preliminary report on the archaeological research conducted through grants from the National Park Service in the River Basin Survey Program (Chapman 1956). Several of the projectile points or knives that were placed originally in the Paleo-Indian period in the report (Chapman 1956; Chapman and Chapman 1964) would now be interpreted as belonging to the Early Archaic period. Two of these forms are Rice Contracting Stemmed, which is relatively straight based, and Rice Lanceolate, which has a concave base and a serrated, beveled blade (Chapman and Chapman 1964: 29). Rice Lobed (Bray 1956a: 128; Chapman 1956: Figure 2e, f; Chapman and Chapman 1964: 27) is Early Archaic but continued into the Middle Archaic period complexes.

Bray (1956a: 46–134) provided information on the Rice site, which indicated that there was an Early Archaic component there. Judging from Bray's (1956a: 80–101) report, the early component contained Stone Square Stemmed, Rice Contracting Stemmed, Rice Lanceolate, Rice Lobed, small broad-bladed, corner-notched forms with concave bases, ovoid bifaces, scrapers made by resharpening broken, stemmed projectile points, and irregularly shaped pebble anvilstones with pits on one or both flat surfaces.

In the 20-page summary of a lengthy manuscript presented to the National Park Service in fulfillment of the River Basin Archaeological Survey contracts, more detailed information on the Early Archaic period was presented (Chapman 1960d: 1150–70). The interpretation of an Early Archaic period (7000–5000 B.C.) occupation

in the White Locality was supported by a radiocarbon date, 5112 B.C.±450, taken from Arbitrary Level 10 and Natural Level 2 in Jakie shelter. Natural Level 1 was never completely uncovered because the water table was reached before the bottom of the level was discovered, but the date of 7000 B.C. seems a reasonable estimate for the beginning of the Early Archaic period in the region.

The components of the Forager Tradition complex occurring in the Early Archaic period in the Table Rock area were derived from Natural Level 1 and the lower part of 2 at Jakie shelter, the lowest levels in the drip area, the central, and lower slope areas of Rice site (Bray 1956a; Chapman 1960d: 1150–70; Marshall and Chapman 1960a: 988–1044) and the lowest level in Standlee shelter I (Bray 1960: 485–532). It has been called the Rice complex due to the fact that the first component that was isolated was found at the Rice site. The Rice complex is composed of the following representative projectile points and knives: Dalton Serrated, a carryover from the Dalton period, Rice Lobed, Rice Contracting Stemmed, Rice Lanceolate, Agate Basin Lanceolate, and Graham Cave Notched (Figure 6–1). Other associated chipped-stone artifacts were snubbed-end flake scrapers, ovoid scrapers, stemmed scrapers, usually made from broken lanceolate forms, preforms or choppers, and trianguloid adzes or rough adz-shaped items. Pebble choppers and pitted pebble anvilstones also seemed to be items in the complex.

Dalton Serrated, Rice Lanceolate, and a notched form similar to a point on which the notches at the base are beveled (Bray 1956a: 91, Figure 24), from the early levels at Rice site and called Rice Beveled Notch by Marshall (1958: 113–14) and Breckenridge by Wood (1962), were found on one site in the Little North Fork branch of White River in Ozark County (Tong 1955). A component of the Forager Tradition, Early Archaic period is probably represented by the artifacts on the site. No evidences of the Early Archaic period have been reported from the Current–Eleven Point or Neosho localities.

Western Prairie Region

No solid evidences of Forager occupation during the Early Archaic period could be found in the Upper Osage Locality in the western part of the state, even though several caves and shelters were excavated in the Kaysinger Bluff and Stockton Reservoir areas, and most of them were dug to what was considered to be sterile soil.

Ozark Highland Region

In the Lower Osage Locality, an aggregate or complex that was definitely in the Early Archaic period (7000–5000 B.C.) according to radiocarbon dates (Figure 4–8) was found in Rodgers shelter (McMillan 1971; Wood and McMillan 1967; 1969). This site had a still earlier Hunter–Forager component that was dated in part at the end of

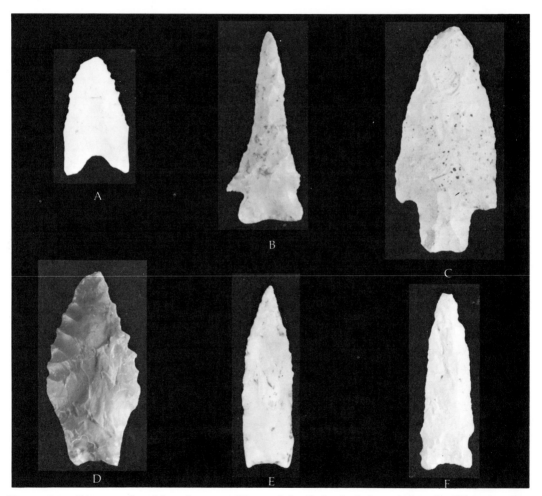

Figure 6–1. Rice complex chipped-stone artifacts of the Early Archaic period in the White Locality. Scale 2:3.
A, Dalton Serrated; B, Rice Lobed; C, Rice Contracting Stemmed; D, Rice Lanceolate; E, Agate Basin Lanceolate; F, Graham Cave Notched.

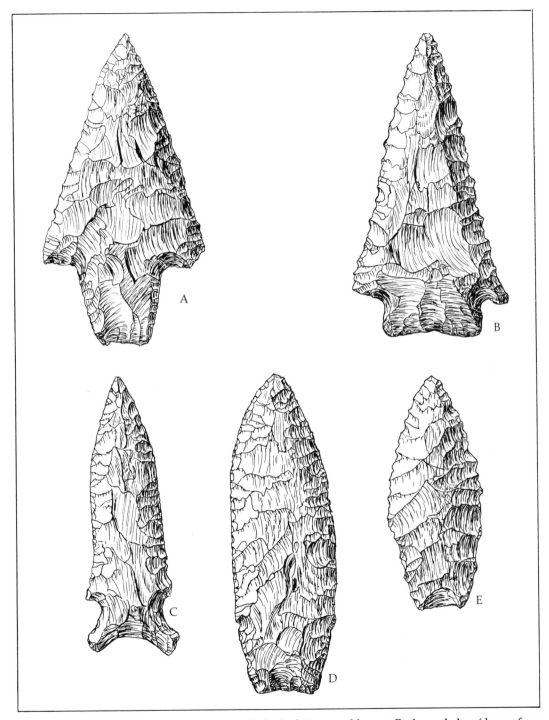

Figure 6–2. Chipped-stone artifacts in the Early Archaic assemblage at Rodgers shelter (drawn from specimens courtesy of R. Bruce McMillan, Illinois State Museum). Scale 1:1.
A, Hidden Valley Stemmed; B, Rice Lobed; C, Graham Cave Notched; D, Agate Basin Lanceolate; E, Rice Lanceolate.

the Paleo-Indian period but may have continued into the Dalton period (McMillan 1971: Figure 46).

The close of the Early Archaic period was marked by environmental change resulting in an erosional episode that produced an unconformity in the deposits, which set off Stratum 1 from Stratum 2 (McMillan 1971: Figures 15, 36) (Figure 4–8). In the upper part of Stratum 1 the diagnostic types of chipped-stone tools of the Early Archaic period assemblage were Hidden Valley Stemmed, Rice Lobed, Graham Cave Notched, Agate Basin Lanceolate, Rice Lanceolate (Figure 6–2), and Dalton Serrated (Figure 5–1F). The period of occupation represented by the types is probably after 7000 B.C. to about 5500 B.C. (Figure 4–8). The radiocarbon dates in the level above the erosional episode are approximately 5500–5000 B.C. or the end of the Early Archaic period.

The proposed Early Archaic as it is defined here overlaps into McMillan's (1971: 186) Middle Archaic, 6550–4050 B.C. McMillan (1971) noted that during the Middle Archaic period there was a gradual decline in deer hunting and in the use of plant foods prepared by milling, and greater reliance on rabbits, squirrels, and fish. Alternative procurement systems already available to them were used to adjust to an environmental change that reduced deciduous forest-edge habitats and increased grassland habitats. Evidences of grassland species of bison, pronghorn, and prairie chicken were present.

Another cave excavation that has produced information on what appears to be an aggregate containing Early Archaic period, Forager artifacts is Tick Creek (McMillan 1965b; Roberts 1965). McMillan defined a Tick Creek complex as the earliest cultural unit in the excavation and included in it the earliest component in Merrell Cave. Rice Lanceolate, Agate Basin Lanceolate, a corner-notched form with sharply beveled blade edges, which can be typed as Rice Lobed,

and Graham Cave Notched were Early Archaic period forms included in the complex (Figure 6–3). Expanding-based drills, snubbed-end flake scrapers, hafted scrapers, pebble manos, anvil-stones, rubbed hematite, bones smeared with hematite, split-bone awls, and a flexed burial were other traits listed for the Tick Creek complex (McMillan 1965b: 69). Two Middle Archaic types, a stemmed form with moderately to deeply concave base that can be equated with Jakie Stemmed and Stone Square Stemmed, were also noted in the complex. Therefore it is suggested that the Tick Creek complex is an aggregate containing tools made during the Early, Middle, and Late Archaic periods.

McMillan (1965b: 68) defined only two Archaic complexes at Tick Creek, an early and a late, so it is possible that he included some of the materials from the Early Archaic period in his Tick Creek complex. Also, the separation of materials at Tick Creek Cave was not always absolutely by cultural level, stratigraphy, or time period.

In the Meramec Locality, aside from the occasional finding of Dalton Serrated in sites with aggregates of later artifacts (Chapman 1948a: Figure 24, Number 14), the most clear-cut information on possible Early Archaic materials is in a manuscript by Marshall (1965: 30–118) on the Verkamp shelter. He proposed a tentative grouping of artifacts that he designated Verkamp Complex A to represent the earliest occupation of the shelter. The most important item used to define the complex was a single, complete lanceolate specimen. An ovoid biface, crude choppers, utilized flakes, rubbed hematite, and a hearth built next to a large rock were other associations. Marshall (1965: 114–15) noted that burned clay and mussel shells were in the hearth area, and split animal bones were in the level with the other artifacts. Although this is a limited inventory, the Verkamp Complex A has the po-

Figure 6–3. Early Archaic projectile points or knives in the Tick Creek complex. Scale 7:8. A–D, Rice Lanceolate; E–G, Rice Lobed; H, Graham Cave Notched; I–J, Agate Basin Lanceolate.

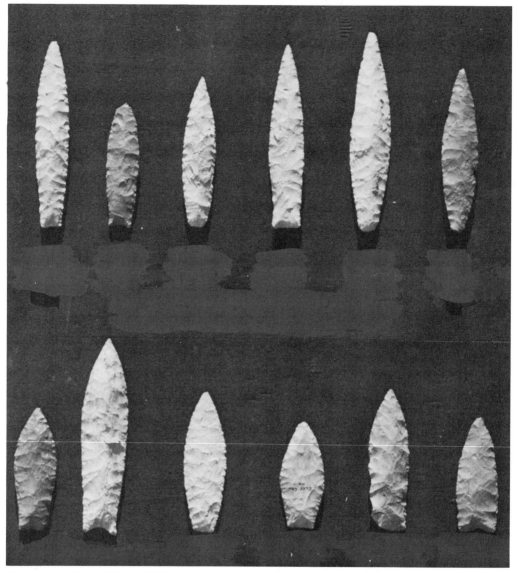

Figure 6–4. Typical Nebo Hill Lanceolate from the Kansas City area (after Shippee 1957b). Scale 1:2.

tential of being Forager Tradition and Early Archaic period.

In the Upper Black–St. Francis Locality a single Dalton Serrated and a Rice Lanceolate came from one site along with a wide variety of other chipped-stone artifacts (Williams 1959: Table II, 38). No other types of tools that could be associated with the Early Archaic period were noted in the extensive survey of the upper St. Francis River in the Wappapello Reservoir area (Wrench, Berry, and Chapman 1940).

Northwest Prairie Region

There appears to be no aggregate, assemblage, or complex described from the Northwest Prairie Region that can be considered as undeniably Early Archaic. Excavations conducted in the region have not isolated a single component of the Forager Tradition in the Early Archaic period. The existence of Hardin Barbed (Shippee 1964: Figure 16A–F) might be evidence of the Early Archaic period in the region. Part of the Nebo Hill aggregate could be identified as Early Archaic in the Lower Missouri Valley I Locality because it contained some elements of a Plano complex that, on the basis of types of projectile points, seem to have intruded into the Western Prairie and Northwest Prairie regions. One interpretation (Shippee 1948) is that the Nebo Hill materials were the result of a very early occupation of the locality by people from the west who were related to the Plano complex. This is a logical conclusion. It is suggested that the Nebo Hill Planolike elements in the Nebo Hill aggregate appeared toward the end of the Early Archaic period. The Nebo Hill Lanceolates that Shippee (1957b: 42–46) (Figure 6–4) considered typical, Dalton Serrated, and Hardin Barbed are possible evidence of an Early Archaic period, Forager Tradition complex in the locality. Shippee (1957b: 46) and Bray (1962a: 234) reported that the Nebo Hill complex was comparable in antiquity with the Long site at Angostura Reservoir, which is dated 5765±740 b.c., because of the similarity of projectile points at the two sites. Confirmation

or rejection of this dating will await a better definition of the Nebo Hill aggregate and the determination of its chronological position.

It is possible that the Nebo Hill aggregate (Shippee 1948; 1964: 6) was purely Early Archaic, but I have not interepreted it that way due to the occurrence in it of the three-quarter-grooved axes, rectanguloid celts of various sizes, and shaped manos either circular or rectanguloid in outline. Furthermore, no radiocarbon dates have been obtained on any Nebo Hill sites and the types of artifacts discovered at Nebo Hill are closely allied to the Sedalia complex, which is probably Late Archaic period. It seems likely that the aggregate at Nebo Hill is Forager Tradition during the Early to Late Archaic period.

Northeast Prairie Region

In the Lower Missouri Valley II Locality special attention has been given to the Dalton site because it is the type site from which Dalton Serrated was named. The site was discovered by Judge S. P. Dalton in a borrow pit alongside Highway 50–63, on the left bank of the Osage River on an old river terrace. It was approximately 8 feet beneath the surface. It was found long after the highway borrowing operations had removed the deposits above an old soil horizon, and erosion had exposed the cultural materials beneath it (Figure 6–5). The strata that contained the artifacts was immediately underneath a buckshot layer of Putnam silt loam in the buried soil horizon. One fireplace containing charcoal was found, but at a time before radiocarbon dating had been devised. The assemblage collected on the site has been interpreted as being Early Archaic, toward the end of the period at the time the Early Archaic Forager Tradition was merging into Middle Archaic and during which artifact types were changing rapidly.

It was quite evident that the site area was no more than 60 feet in diameter, which may be an indication that it had been occupied for a short duration. It is of course possible that it was a campsite used repeatedly for short periods of time and that the artifacts found on the site

Figure 6–5.   View of the Dalton site showing erosion.

represented a relatively long period of time, including the end of the Early and beginning of the Middle Archaic periods, but the small size of the area in which evidences were found makes that interpretation dubious.

The types of artifacts from the site were Dalton Serrated, Graham Cave Notched, Hardin Barbed, Rice Lobed, St. Charles Notched, stemmed forms, and corner-notched forms, Rice Lanceolate, Agate Basin Lanceolate, and unclassified forms. Other items in the assemblage were a bifacial knife, a bipointed and bifacial beveled knife, hafted scrapers, and concave-based drills. Ovoid bifacial tools, plano-convex snubbed-end flake scrapers, round scrapers, side scrapers, choppers, and cores were also part of the assemblage. Although Dalton Serrated was one of the most distinctive items, the most numerous forms were Rice Lanceolate and Agate Basin Lanceolate (Figures 6–6 through 6–13).

Two excavated sites, Graham Cave and Arnold Research Cave, contained aggregates in the lower levels that might be interpreted as Forager Tradition and Early Archaic period. The best-documented site is Graham Cave, the earliest occupation of which has been described as Hunter–Forager Tradition during the Dalton period. It is difficult, if not impossible, to separate the earliest Hunter–Forager complex from that of the Forager, Early Archaic period, on the basis of present information, for the two components overlap and in most instances it was not possible to distinguish a clear division between them.

What appears to be a Forager assemblage is denoted by Graham Cave Notched, which is quite long in proportion to its width, Hardin Barbed, Hidden Valley Stemmed (Logan 1952: Plates 5F–G, 6F–G), some of the Agate Basin Lanceolate or related forms (Klippel 1971: Figure 11B) and St. Charles Notched (Klippel 1971: Figure 13D). Snubbed-end flake scrapers and plano-convex scrapers seem to have been the predominant types in the earliest assemblage, which has been assigned to the Dalton period. The plano-convex scrapers were just as important as projectile points in the bottom level, Level 6, but became less important in Level 5 in comparison to the projectile points and knives. As scrapers were

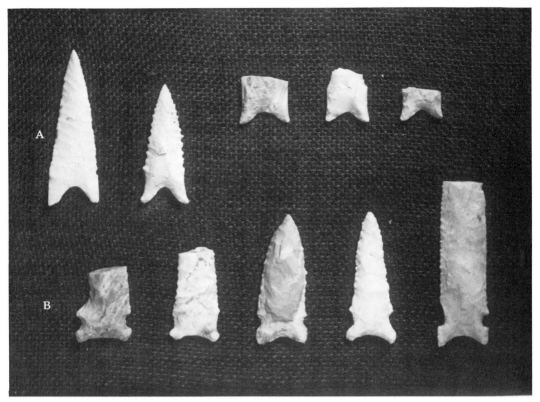

Figure 6–6.   Chipped-stone artifacts from the Dalton site (Judge S. P. Dalton Collection). Scale 1:2. Row A, Dalton Serrated; Row B, Graham Cave Notched.

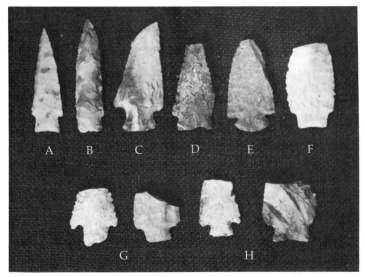

Figure 6–7.   Artifacts from the Dalton site (Judge S. P. Dalton Collection). Scale 1:3. A, Hardin Barbed; B–C, stemmed bifaces; D, Rice Lobed; E, St. Charles Notched; F, square-stemmed biface; G, stemmed bifaces; H, corner-notched bifaces.

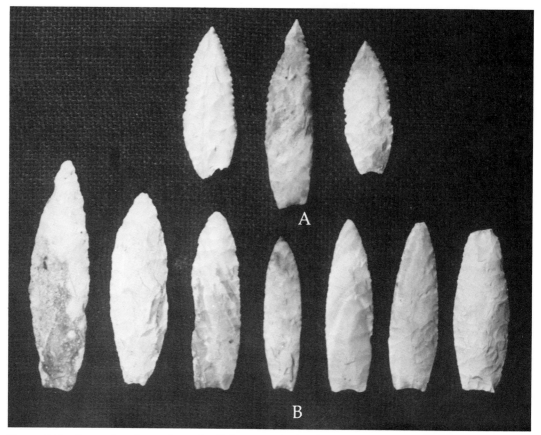

Figure 6–8.   Lanceolate forms from the Dalton site (Judge S. P. Dalton Collection). Scale 1:2. Row A, Rice Lanceolate; Row B, Agate Basin Lanceolate.

Figure 6–9. Lanceolates and other bifaces from the Dalton site (Judge S. P. Dalton Collection). Scale 1:2.

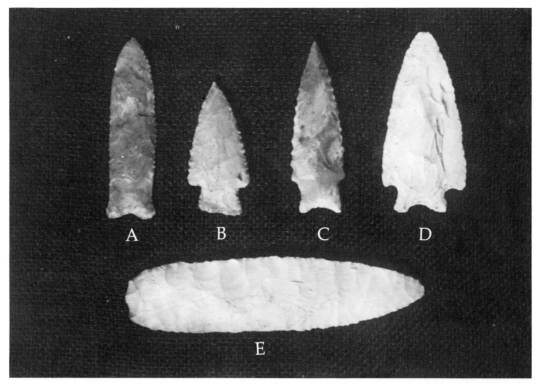

Figure 6–10. Chipped-stone artifacts from the Dalton site (Judge S. P. Dalton Collection). Scale 1:2. A, Lanceolate form; B–D, stemmed forms; E, lanceolate form.

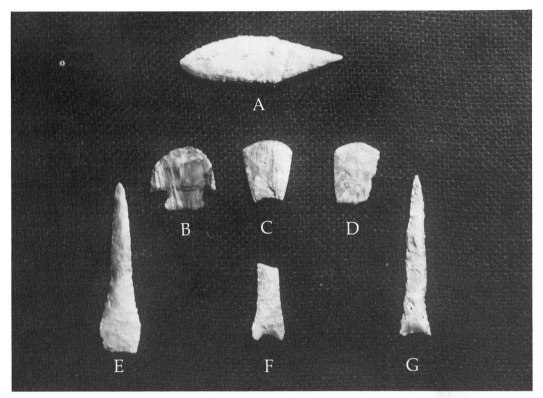

Figure 6–11.   Tools from the Dalton site (Judge S. P. Dalton Collection). Scale 1:2.
A, Beveled knife; B–D, hafted scrapers; E–G, concave-based drills.

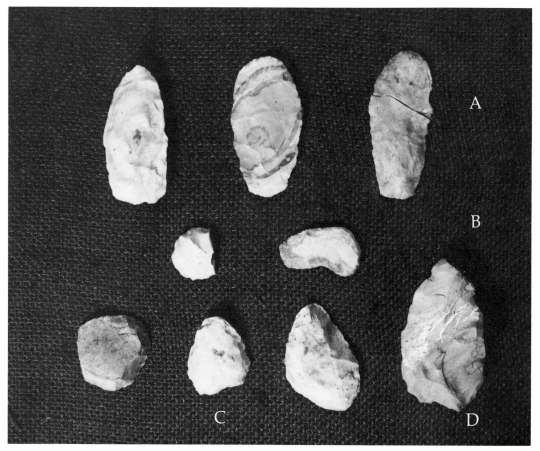

Figure 6–12.   Bifaces and scrapers from the Dalton site (Judge S. P. Dalton Collection). Scale 1:2.
Row A, Ovoid bifaces; Row B, plano-convex snubbed-end flake scrapers; C, round and side scrapers;
D, core or chopper.

Figure 6–13.   Choppers and cores from the Dalton site (Judge S. P. Dalton Collection). Scale 1:2.

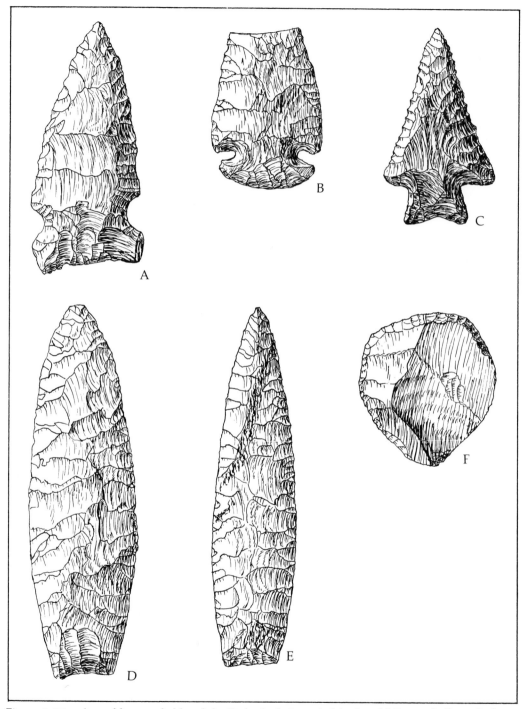

Figure 6–14.   Assemblage probably of the Early Archaic period in Arnold Research Cave. Scale 1:1. A, Graham Cave Notched; B, St. Charles Notched; C, Rice Lobed; D–E, Agate Basin Lanceolate; F, snubbed-end flake scraper.

the most abundant artifact in the Dalton period, their decrease in Level 5 in Graham Cave was probably a result of the change in emphasis from hunting deer to more diversified hunting and trapping of small game animals. The same type of scraper must have continued into the Early Archaic period. Expanding-based drills (Chapman 1952a: Figure 12 F, K, O, P), ovoid bifaces (Klippel 1971: Figure 15), choppers, antler-tip flakers, split-bone awls, flake knives, flat mealing stones, and mortars all seemed to be part of the

assemblage. Adzes, manos, pitted and unpitted hammerstones could also be included. Retouched and utilized flakes, hafted scrapers, rubbed hematite, cupstones, and mealing stones were other items in the assemblage.

An assemblage that is possibly Early Archaic in Arnold Research Cave includes Graham Cave Notched, St. Charles Notched, a small variety of Rice Lobed, Agate Basin Lanceolate, and plano-convex snubbed-end flake scrapers (Figure 6–14). One of the snubbed-end flake scrapers and three

Figure 6–15.   St. Charles Notched (Thebes) from the Mississippi Valley North Locality (J. A. Eichenberger Collection). Scale 8:9.

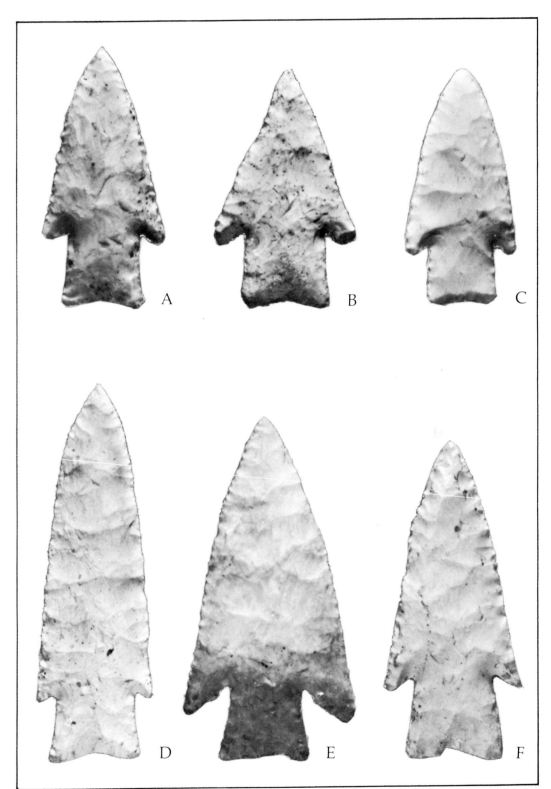

flake scrapers that Shippee (1966: 60–61) said were typical of the lower layers of occupation have been dated 4542±300 B.C. This date places them in the Middle Archaic period, but similar forms were in use during the Early Archaic, Dalton, and Paleo-Indian periods. Because it was an effective tool, it probably continued to be used during the Middle Archaic period when hunting was an important activity.

Klippel (1970a) worked through the full complement of excavated material from Graham Cave, reviewed some of the material from Arnold Research Cave, and conducted new excavations in both sites. He determined from an analysis of the sizes of the particles and from a study of the faunal remains in Graham Cave that the Early Archaic occupation followed a major climatic change from wet to dry. This interpretation accords with the cultural evidence, the earliest materials appearing to be Hunter–Forager in the Dalton period.

No early Forager aggregates or assemblages were noted in the surveys conducted in the Cuivre Locality (Chapman 1937). Henning (1961a: 173) suggested that the implements he discovered and identified as Nebo Hill might be indication of an Early Archaic occupation of the area, but the tools illustrated seem to be within the range of the Sedalia Lanceolate, which I have interpreted as Late Archaic. No other artifacts identified as Early Archaic period have been reported from the Cuivre or Salt localities, and it is possible that there was no Forager occupation there during the Early Archaic period.

Eichenberger (1956) included in the Hannibal complex Dalton Serrated, Agate Basin Lanceolate, St. Charles Notched, and Hardin Barbed (Figures 6–15, 6–16) from the Mississippi Valley North Locality. One site appeared to contain all three of the probable Early Archaic artifacts. A form similar to St. Charles Notched (Figure 6–17), called Thebes (Perino 1971; Winters 1963), is also probably an Early Archaic form. In an earlier publication, Eichenberger (1944: 34)

showed Agate Basin Lanceolate, St. Charles Notched, and Hardin Barbed from another site. Graham Cave Notched (Figure 6–18) has also been found in the locality. It is possible that an Early Archaic complex will eventually be isolated. There is, of course, an equally acceptable interpretation to explain the occurrence of the Early Archaic types of artifacts. Some of the artifacts representative of a particular time period and a cultural tradition often continue into the succeeding period or periods. Until comparable aggregates can be obtained by controlled surface collections and excavations from several sites that have provided artifact forms usually a part of a Forager Tradition assemblage in the Early Archaic period, the interpretation that the Foragers were in the Mississippi Valley North Locality prior to 5000 B.C. is very tenuous.

Southeast Riverine Region

In Jefferson County, Missouri, in Hidden Valley shelter, the earliest occupation, designated *Hidden Valley Shelter One* (Chapman 1948b: 140–42), is proposed as another complex from the Forager Tradition in the Early Archaic period. Hidden Valley shelter may have been used as a hunting camp, for the deposits appeared to be made up of a series of temporary occupations. There were fire pits on the original floor of the shelter, and several of the tools were associated with hunting, such as choppers, scrapers, knives, and spear or dart points. There were few projectile points or knives but several types were represented (Adams 1949: Figure 17). One of the types found in Hidden Valley Shelter I is a Rice Lobed (Figure 6–19D). Another is Hidden Valley Stemmed, which is rather large in size and for the most part well made (Adams 1941; Chapman 1948b: 141, Figure 32A, Numbers 1, 2, 4). Griffin (1968: 133) placed Hidden Valley Stemmed in a period estimated to date 6000–4000 B.C. Similar forms have been found in early levels of Modoc shelter in Illinois (Fowler 1959a: 30, Figure 9E).

Figure 6–16. Hardin Barbed from the Mississippi Valley North Locality (J. A. Eichenberger Collection). Scale 1:1.

Figure 6–17. St. Charles Notched from the Mississippi Valley North Locality (J. A. Eichenberger Collection). Scale 1:1.

Figure 6–18.   Graham Cave Notched and related forms from the Mississippi Valley North Locality (J. A. Eichenberger Collection). Scale 7:9.
A–B, Graham Cave Notched; C, side-notched scraper; D, side-notched form.

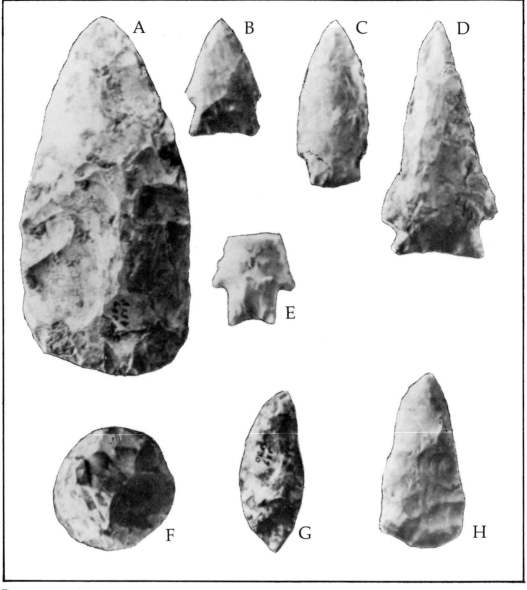

Figure 6–19.   Artifacts probably from the occupation of Hidden Valley shelter during the Early Archaic period (Adams 1949: Figure 17A). Scale 3:4.
A, Large adz or chopper; B, broad-stemmed, concave-based biface; C, stemmed cutting tool (thick); D, Rice Lobed; E, Rice Contracting Stemmed; F, round plano-convex scraper; G, bipointed leaf-shaped biface; H, preform or ovoid cutting tool.

Figure 6–20. Dalton Serrated from Site 23SO136 (Charles Orr Collection). Scale 1:1.

A smaller form of similar shape but classed as Rice Contracting Stemmed was found in the second excavation (Figure 6–19E). A large, straight-sided knife from the lowest level of Hidden Valley shelter (Chapman 1948b: 140, Figure 32A, Number 5) is similar to one found on the Dalton site in central Missouri (Figure 6–10E).

Adams (1949: 54–67) also reported a number of stemmed projectile points or knives (Adams 1949: Figure 18B, Numbers 3, 4, 6), a variety of other large stemmed forms (Adams 1949: 56, Figure 18A–B), a broad-stemmed concave-based form, a bipointed leaf-shaped knife, an ovoid cutting tool, a large adz or chopper, and a plano-convex round scraper with steep edges (Figure 6–19).

Three large and one small circular fireplaces were in proper stratigraphic position to be related to the component, but no artifacts that were identifiable were found in association. Deer, elk, and turtle bones and mussel shells were in the deposits containing artifacts. One of the corner-notched tools that Adams (1949: 59–60, Figure 20A, 2; 20B, left) considered to be diagnostic of the early and middle deposits

> was found in position under the small rocks against the back wall just west of the large rocks and appears to be diagnostic of the early and middle occupations. . . . It is similar to a projectile point found only forty centimeters above the tooth of extinct bison occidentalis and is on the same horizontal level as a mandible of a mastodon at the Kimmswick bone bed.

An ovoid projectile point or knife was also in the bottom level of the deposit (Adams 1949: 60–61, Figure 20A, 6).

There was some admixture of levels in the deposit because two potsherds and a fragment of a winged bannerstone (Adams 1949: 60, Figure 20, Numbers 8, 9) were in the same deposit with the early occupation material. The bannerstone or atlatl weight could have been a part of the early component.

Therefore the early level at Hidden Valley shelter can be considered to be an aggregate, Hidden Valley Aggregate I, that contains Rice Lobed, Rice Contracting Stemmed, bipointed leaf-shaped, ovoid leaf-shaped, a variety of large stemmed tools, round or ovoid scrapers, choppers, adzes or preforms, and a bannerstone, all of which could be part of an Early Archaic period, Forager Tradition, assemblage. Judging from the occurrence of pottery, it is probable that Archaic occupation evidences had been mixed mechanically with those from the Woodland period.

Dalton Serrated in the Southeast Riverine Region were associated with a different assortment of tools than those found at the Dalton site in central Missouri. Whether this difference is regional due to the adaptation to a different variety of ecological niches and thus a divergence in tool kits; whether it is due to the variation in the information available concerning the Dalton sites in the two regions; whether it is a difference in time; or whether it has some other explanation

Figure 6–21.   Hardin Barbed from Site 23SO136 (Charles Orr Collection). Scale 1:1.

remains to be determined. It is rather certain that the aggregate from the Dalton sites in southeastern Missouri differs from that found at the Dalton site.

In the St. Francis Riverine Locality, Site 23SO136 has yielded an aggregate of artifacts that may be representative of a component from the Early Archaic period. Dalton Serrated (Figure 6–20) and Hardin Barbed (Figure 6–21) were distinctive artifacts in the aggregate. Charles Orr found a cache of Hidden Valley Stemmed (Figure 6–22) in close association with a bannerstone and engraved gorget fragments on Site 23SO138 in the St. Francis Riverine Locality (Figure 6–23). The association of bannerstones and Hidden Valley Stemmed may indicate that they were contemporaneous in the Early Archaic, for a bannerstone was also found in association with Hidden Valley Stemmed in Hidden Valley shelter (Adams 1949: 60, Figure 20). It is also possible that the chronological range of bannerstones may span the entire Archaic period.

In general it appears that the Forager Tradition in the Early Archaic period is characterized by Forager Tradition complexes, assemblages, and aggregates that include Rice Lobed, Rice Lanceolate, Agate Basin Lanceolate, Rice Contracting Stemmed, Hidden Valley Stemmed, Graham Cave Notched, St. Charles Notched, Hardin Barbed, possibly Stone Square Stemmed, and ovoid leaf-shaped projectile points or knives. Snubbed-end flake scrapers, round scrapers, snubbed reworked projectile point scrapers, fairly large chipped-stone adzes or choppers, pitted anvilstones, pebble manos, and bipointed, bifacial, leaf-shaped knives are other items probably made and used by Foragers in the Early Archaic period.

Regional Distribution of Evidences

The intra- and inter-regional relationships of Forager Tradition aggregates, assemblages, and complexes of the Early Archaic period are dif-

Figure 6–22.   Cache of Hidden Valley Stemmed from Site 23SO138 (Charles Orr Collection). Scale 3:5.

Figure 6–23.   Bannerstone, bannerstone fragments, and engraved gorget fragments from Site 23SO138 (Charles Orr Collection). Scale, A, 6:5; B–D, 1:1.
A, Bannerstone; B, bannerstone fragment; C–D, engraved gorget fragments.

ficult to interpret. Only a few investigators have produced sufficient evidence to provide a solid basis for discussion of the Early Archaic period. In most Missouri localities there is no comparable information for interregional review.

Southwest Drainage Region

The extent of the distribution of the Rice complex is uncertain outside of the White Locality. There are artifacts from the excavation of the Breckenridge site in Arkansas (Wood 1963) that might be evidence for the Forager Tradition of the Early Archaic period in that area, but the complex represented could be later in the over-all sequence. The forms that were noted as unclassified beveled lanceolate (Wood 1963: Figure 5a–e) could be classified as Rice Contracting Stemmed and thus would be normally associated with the Early Archaic period. They occur above the Breckenridge points, which in the Table Rock Reservoir area were possibly from the Middle Archaic rather than Early Archaic period. Wood (1963: 79) identified an Agate Basin Lanceolate at the same site, the same type that was found in the deposits from the Middle Archaic period at Rice shelter and elsewhere in the Table Rock area. Rice Lobed was not reported from Breckenridge site, and it is one of the markers of the Early Archaic Rice complex in the Southwest Drainage Region.

There was very little evidence that the Foragers penetrated the rugged Current–Eleven Point Locality during the Early Archaic period.

To the west in northeastern Oklahoma, Period A in Site DIEvIII, Zones A to C (Baerreis 1951: 63–66), may be comparable to the Early Archaic in the Southwest Drainage Region. Baerreis (1959) called Zones A and B the Grove focus. It is possible that the Grove focus, Period A, is a mixture of the Forager Tradition from the Early and Middle Archaic periods because the full-grooved ax is one of the traits of the focus. The full-grooved ax is a trait of the Middle Archaic period in Rice shelter in the Southwest Drainage Region and in Graham Cave in the Northeast Prairie Region. A T-shaped drill and a distinct kind of roughly rounded based drill also in the early levels of the Oklahoma site (Zone A) may

indicate that Zone A is Middle Archaic rather than Early Archaic. The predominant type of projectile point or knife was straight stemmed or slightly contracting stemmed. According to the outline drawings, two forms (Baerreis 1951: 15, Figure 1G, J) appear to be Rice Contracting Stemmed and drawings of other tools in the same figure are square-stemmed forms, one of which is serrated and could be related to the Early Archaic Rice complex in Table Rock. Rice Lobed is illustrated by Baerreis (1951: 15, Figure IU), and other associations are scrapers made from broken square-stemmed forms, ovoid bifacial knife blades, drills (Baerreis 1951: 22, Figure 2A–C, G, I, L–M), snubbed-end flake scrapers (Baerreis 1951: 25, Figure 3 A–B, D, H–K), and choppers (Baerreis 1951: 27, Figure 4D–F). The assemblage or aggregate in Zone A at Site DIEvIII appears to relate to both Early and Middle Archaic complexes of the Table Rock area in the White River drainage. Differences may be the result of differences in localities. In any instance it is probable that the Forager Tradition in the Early Archaic period of the Southwestern Drainage Region extended westward into northeastern Oklahoma.

As so little information relating to the Early Archaic period is available in the Neosho Locality, it is possible that it was not permanently occupied during that time but was used only seasonally as hunting territory.

Western Prairie Region

The Western Prairie Region, which includes the Cherokee Plains, lacks any reliable evidences of occupation during the period 7000–5000 B.C. Perhaps the changing climatic conditions made it undesirable to the Foragers, and the region may have been unoccupied except for occasional hunting forays into it.

Ozark Highland Region

During the Early Archaic period the Ozark Highland Region was lightly settled by people with Forager tool kits that in the Lower Osage Locality were very similar to the ones in the White Locality. The evidences had been deeply buried in Rodgers shelter (McMillan 1971). In the Meramec, Upper Black–St. Francis, and Castor–Whitewater localities, manifestations during the Early Archaic period are scarce. This paucity of information is probably due to the lack of intensive archaeological work on deeply buried sites. Although many caves have been dug in the Ozark Highland Region, most were dug before the development of modern archaeological techniques (Fowke 1922) or were mined by relic collectors. Only a few excavations have attempted to penetrate the deepest cave deposits, and they yielded little definitive information on an Early Archaic period occupation (McMillan n.d.; 1965b; Marshall 1965; Roberts 1965). The earliest Foragers had occupied the Ozark Highland Region, but the utilization of it, the settlement pattern represented, the size of the population, and the duration of the occupation in the Early Archaic period are some of the problems yet to be solved.

Northwest Prairie Region

The Northwest Prairie Region may have been occupied by a people with tool kits and settlement patterns quite different from those in the Southwest Drainage and Central Ozark Highland regions. If the typical projectile points from the Nebo Hill aggregate actually were produced by Foragers in the Early Archaic period, these evidences are not found to the north and west except along the main valley of the Missouri River. Just how far east and south the Nebo Hill aggregate was distributed cannot be determined at this time. It is concentrated in the Lower Missouri Valley I Locality (Shippee 1964: 24, Figure 11).

The typical tools of the Nebo Hill aggregate, Nebo Hill Lanceolate and related lanceolate forms, may have been manufactured with a stoneworking technique of the Plano complex during the Dalton period. The Foragers who made them may have stopped using Clovis and Folsom Fluted during the Dalton and Early Archaic periods as they moved eastward. If it is assumed that the climate became still dryer and the prairies took over the woodland areas to the central part of Missouri, the plains and prairie-adapted Plano (Nebo Hill) people may have

made contact to the east, some penetrating beyond the Mississippi River, meeting and fraternizing with the woodland-dwelling natives who made stemmed and corner-notched projective points or knives (Paul Sellers Collection). The eastern distribution may encompass much of the prairie in northern Missouri. Nebo Hill-like lanceolates have been found as far east as the Wyaconda–Fabius Locality, Northeast Prairie Region (Paul Sellers Collection). Hardin Barbed occur consistently on Nebo Hill sites in the Kansas City area along with Scottsbluff and Plano-like lanceolate forms. Although there is no assurance that all of the forms were manufactured by the same people or during the same period, the possibility exists as evidence that the Nebo Hill aggregate was Early Archaic period.

Northeast Prairie Region

Evidences of habitation in the Northeast Prairie Region during the Early Archaic period are concentrated in the Lower Missouri Valley II Locality. The Early Archaic distribution eastward into Illinois is denoted by the Starved Rock Archaic, which includes forms somewhat similar to Graham Cave Notched (Mayer-Oakes 1951: Figure 100B), a Graham Cave Notched (Mayer-Oakes 1951: Figure 101, Number 2), Agate Basin Lanceolates (Mayer-Oakes 1951: Figures 100A, 101, Numbers 4–23, 31–36), plano-convex snubbed-end flake scrapers (Mayer-Oakes 1951: Figure 100D), and ovoid bifaces (Mayer-Oakes 1951: Figure 100K). Mayer-Oakes (1951: 322) noted that the similarities of the Starved Rock Archaic were primarily to the west.

In the center of the Lower Missouri Valley the contact of the western prairie-adapted (Plano) and eastern woodland-oriented cultures could have resulted in the complex and the great variety of artifact styles that has been discovered on the Dalton site and in Graham Cave and Arnold Research Cave.

One site in Hardin County, Illinois, the Godar site (Titterington 1950: 22), had a component from the Early Archaic period that included Hardin Barbed, Hidden Valley Stemmed, Agate Basin Lanceolate, concave-based expanding-based drills, and large convex-based knives similar to the one from the Dalton site (Figure 6–10E).

Southeast Riverine Region

Artifacts from the Early Archaic are distributed as far as the northern part of the Mississippi Valley Central Locality and are well represented at Modoc shelter in Illinois (Deuel 1957: 2; Fowler 1959a; 1959b; Fowler, Winters, and Parmalee 1956: Figures 4, 7). Fowler (1959a: 20, 23) stated that the levels in the shelter that were 19–24 feet deep had been occupied in 7000–4850 B.C. At that point he had uncovered Agate Basin Lanceolate, Hidden Valley Stemmed, Rice Lobed, plano-convex snubbed-end flake scrapers, ovoid bifaces, and expanding-based drills. A Graham Cave Notched is dated much earlier but may be part of the Forager Tradition complex from the lower level of Modoc shelter. In an interpretation of styles of projectile points in the central Mississippi Valley, Fowler (1957) proposed that the Graham Cave Notched, Agate Basin Lanceolate, basal-notched, straight-stemmed, contracting-stemmed, and corner-notched forms were present in the area from 7000 to 5000 B.C. This hypothesis was based on finds at sites in Kentucky, southern Illinois, and Missouri and represented the probable distribution of the Early Archaic Forager Tradition.

In the Mississippi Valley Central Locality and Southeastern Riverine Region, the settlement pattern of the Foragers may have been different from that to the north and west. Small camps or collecting stations were usually established on old river levees or high points in or at the edges on small streams. This pattern extends far into northeastern Arkansas in both the St. Francis Riverine and the Bootheel localities.

The Forager Tradition during the Early Archaic period has been much neglected, perhaps because sites often lie buried quite deeply beneath deposits laid down toward the end of the period. Shelters adjacent to the Mississippi River from St. Louis to Cape Girardeau and hilltops overlooking the Mississippi Valley might be the most potentially productive places to look for sites of the Early Archaic period, Forager Tradition. In the Southeast Riverine Region, old soil surfaces, particularly the old natural levees along small streams, would be the best places to look for sites occupied during the Early Archaic period.

7. Forager Tradition, Middle Archaic Period

The Middle Archaic period began with climatic fluctuations that led to the drying out of much of the central United States and ended at the height of a dry period. The cultural alterations that had begun during the Early Archaic as an adjustment to different physiographic regions and the changing natural environment continued, but most of the old cultural techniques and tool kits were retained. Hunting and trapping small animals and collecting vegetal foods, particularly nuts and seeds, continued to be very important. By the end of the period, there may have been complete economic adaptation from a wet to a moderately dry environment and a greater utilization of the expansive prairies that had formed in most of the central part of the northeastern United States.

Sites of Foragers continued to be small during the Middle Archaic period, and though there were changes in tool kits, indicating a greater diversity of activities, specialization or exceptional emphasis on any one exploitive subsistence activity was not evident. Hunting and associated activities continued to be very important. No one location, in relation to the topography, was indicative of the settlement pattern, which was not significantly different from that in the Early Archaic period.

The Forager Tradition in the Middle Archaic period had associated with it a chipped-stone technique that was used to produce a characteristic form of side-notched projectile point or knife of different proportions from that of Graham Cave Notched, an Early Archaic period type. This side-notched form has been given various designations, such as Raddatz, Black Sand, Big Sandy, White River Archaic, and has previously been considered to be a variety of Graham Cave Notched (Chapman and Chapman 1964). It is a distinctive type, and the basic form is similar to and may have been developed from Graham Cave Notched. It is smaller in size, and the technique of manufacture involved heat treating, which may be a distinctive characteristic of the Middle Archaic period. This medium-sized, heat-treated, side-notched form became prominent in Middle Archaic and continued into the Early Woodland period (Cole and Deuel 1937); an even smaller form of this type has been found on sites from a later period in the Plains cultural area (Kehoe 1966a; 1966b). The several varieties of the form can be separated typologically on the basis of size and heat-treating technique employed in their manufacture. I have selected the term *Big Sandy Notched* to designate the side-notched points from the Middle Archaic period sites in order to reduce the number of names for this particular form.

New types of tools appeared for the first time in the Forager Tradition of the Middle Archaic, and prominent among them were the full-grooved ground-stone ax and the celt, an ungrooved ax. Twined-fiber fabrics, probably bags, which may have been a part of the cultural baggage of Hunters and Foragers in earlier periods, were evidenced for the first time as impressions on clay at Graham Cave (Logan 1952) (Figure 7–1). Similar well-preserved twined fabrics, sandals, braided cordage, and twisted cordage of various plies and spins, were found in Arnold Research Cave (Henning 1966).

Many of the sandals, twined fabric, bags, and other perishable items were found in Arnold Research Cave. After Arnold sold it, most of the remaining deposits were removed for commercial purposes, but fortunately many items were sal-

Figure 7–1.   Impression of twined fabric on clay from the Middle Archaic level in Graham Cave. Scale 1:1.

vaged by Mrs. Clarence Kelly, one of the new owners. Though the nature of their association with cultural-chronological occupations in the cave is not certain, it is probable that some of them were associated with the Middle Archaic period. Similar twined fabric was definitely made in the Middle Archaic occupation zones at Graham Cave (Figure 7–1). The objects were highly unusual in the Missouri area and included woven-grass sandals, deerskin moccasins, as well as the twined-grass fabric bags (Figures 7–2, 7–3, 7–4).

The Forager Tradition became established as a broad cultural adaptation throughout most of Missouri during the Middle Archaic period. The Foragers utilized vegetal, animal, and mineral resources from woodlands, prairies, and river valleys. The manufacturing of ground-stone axes, the utilization of bone and shell for ornaments (Figure 7–5), the employment of bone and antler for a greater variety of tools, woodworking, and the use of fibers for making a variety of items

such as mats, clothing, and traps for small game were cultural trappings that were prominent in the period. Diversity rather than specialization marked the Forager Tradition in the Middle Archaic.

Southwest Drainage Region

Numerous sites have been excavated in the Table Rock Reservoir area, and a reconnaissance has been conducted of both the Bull Shoals and Table Rock Reservoir areas on White River in southwestern Missouri and northwestern Arkansas. Although the survey was by no means complete, it is possible to combine the assemblages of associated tools from the Forager Tradition on several excavated sites in the area and interpret them tentatively as a complex of the Middle Archaic period. Radiocarbon dates at Jakie shelter have indicated that the complex was present just prior to 5000 B.C. It has been given the name *White River complex* (Figures 7–6, 7–7,

Figure 7–2. Woven-grass sandal from Arnold Research Cave (top and bottom views) (Clarence Kelly Collection). Scale 1:2.

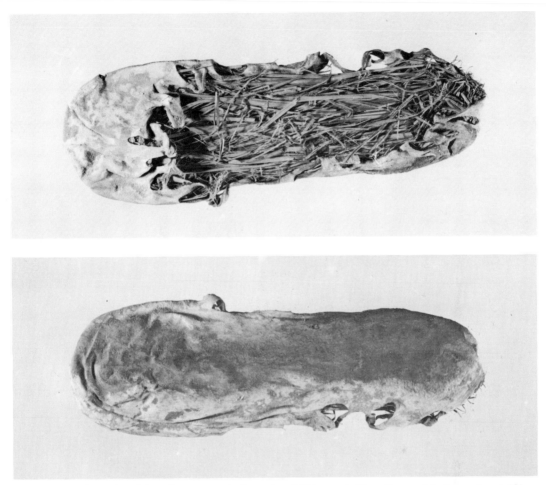

Figure 7–3. Grass-lined deerskin moccasin from Arnold Research Cave (top and bottom views) (Clarence Kelly Collection). Scale 4:7.

Figure 7–4A.   Twined-grass bag from Arnold Research Cave (Clarence Kelly Collection). Scale 1:2.

Figure 7–4B.   Twined fabric from Arnold Research Cave (Clarence Kelly Collection). Scale 4:9.

7–8, 7–9, 7–10, 7–11, 7–12). Components making up the White River complex were found in Natural Level 3 in Jakie shelter and in the earliest component at Crisp IV site, the middle components at Standlee Shelter I, Lander Shelters I and II, and the Rice site (Bray 1956a; 1957; 1960; Chapman 1960d; 1960e; Marshall 1958; 1960). Projectile-point and knife forms in the complex were large and predominantly stemmed and side notched. Big Sandy Notched, a Jakie Stemmed, Rice Lobed (Figures 7–6, 7–7), Stone Square Stemmed (Marshall 1958), and other stemmed varieties, and medium-to-large corner-notched forms are part of the complex. Other chipped-stone artifacts are notched, roughly flaked, double-bitted stone axes, pebble choppers, snubbed-end flake scrapers, and expanding-based drills. Pecked- and ground-stone items are full-grooved axes, celts, pitted pebble anvilstones, stone mor-

tars, and core hammerstones (Figures 7–6, 7–8 through 7–12).

Some of the chipped-stone forms from the Early Archaic period continued to be used in the Middle Archaic, such as Rice Lobed, Rice Contracting Stemmed, and Agate Basin Lanceolate. Most of the contracting-stemmed, flaring-stemmed, square-stemmed, and corner-notched forms were distributed from top to bottom in the deposits in the shelters, and though variations were apparent within the categories, there was so much overlapping of formal characteristics that it was not readily possible to segregate specific groupings by particular periods on the basis of form and manufacture alone. The analysis of functions and attributes might aid in determining the proper chronological order of these chipped-stone objects. Perhaps the reason all of the artifacts of similar form continued to be made dur-

Figure 7–5. Bone and shell ornaments from Arnold Research Cave (Clarence Kelly Collection). Scale 1:1.

Figure 7–6. Distinctive tools from the White River complex, Forager Tradition, Middle Archaic period, in the White River Locality. Scale 1:1.
A–B, Big Sandy Notched; C–D, Jakie Stemmed; E, full-grooved ax; F, celt.

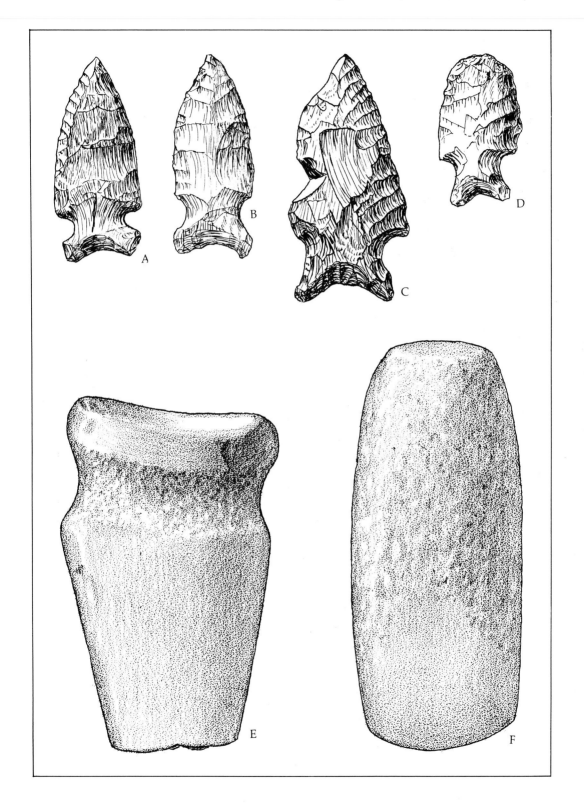

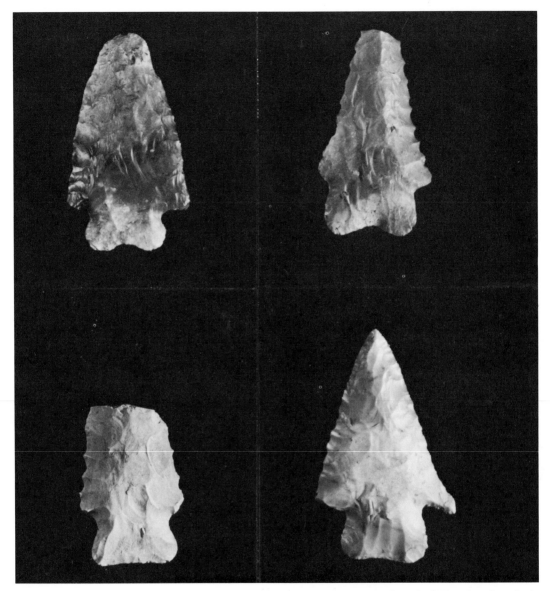

Figure 7–7. Rice Lobed from the Forager Tradition, Middle Archaic period, in the White Locality. Scale 1:1.

Figure 7–8. Axes from the White River complex, Forager Tradition, Middle Archaic period. Scale 1:1. A, Full-grooved ground-stone ax; B, double-bitted chipped-stone ax.

Figure 7–9.   Choppers from the White River complex, Forager Tradition, Middle Archaic period. Scale 1:2.

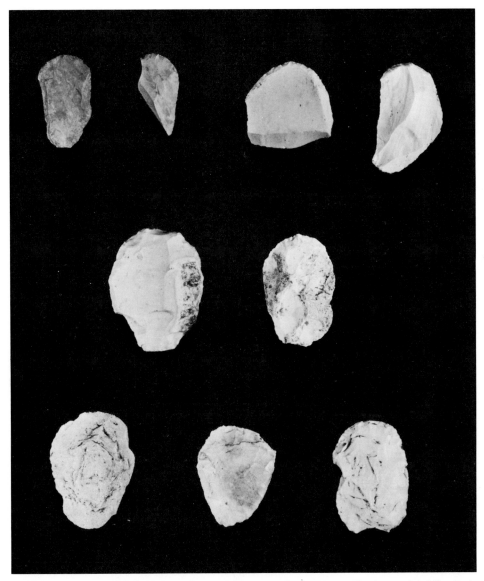

Figure 7–10. Scrapers from the White River complex, Forager Tradition, Middle Archaic period. Scale 5:9.

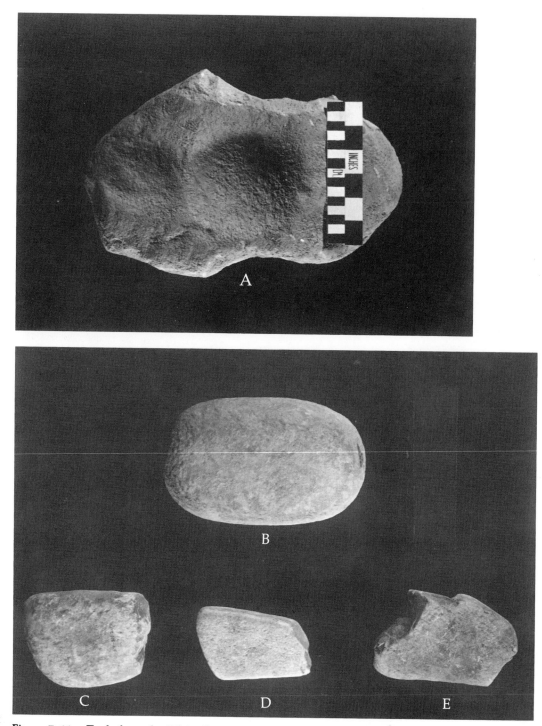

Figure 7–11.   Tools from the White River complex, Forager Tradition, Middle Archaic period. Scale, A, 1:4; B–E, 2:7.
A, Stone mortar; B, shaped mano; C–E, pitted anvilstones.

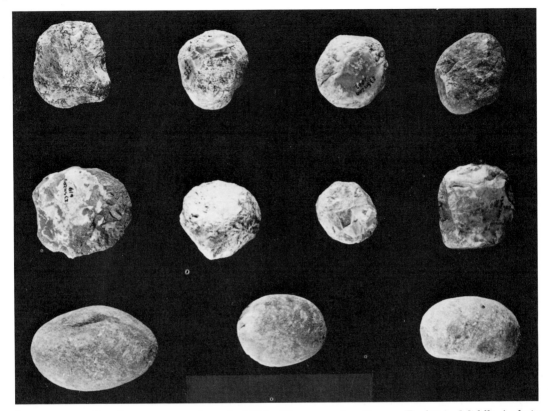

Figure 7–12.   Core hammerstones from the White River complex, Forager Tradition, Middle Archaic period. Scale 1:3.

ing the long period of occupation of the area is that the same use was made of specific forms for foraging activities throughout the entire Archaic period.

The Neosho Locality undoubtedly was occupied by Foragers during the Middle Archaic period but perhaps not continuously. Peabody and Moorehead (1904: Plate IX) illustrated a Jakie Stemmed from Jacobs Cavern in McDonald County, and Adams (1958: Figures 1, 2, 9, 14, 15) recorded core hammerstones, snubbed-end flake scrapers, celts, double-bitted chipped-stone axes, and full-grooved axes from various sites in the locality. Adams (1958: Figures 51, 81) also found Big Sandy Notched in Ash and Orwood Bluff caves, both of which he tested.

Western Prairie Region

The excavation of numerous sites in the Stockton and Kaysinger Bluff (Truman) reservoirs in the Upper Osage Locality has produced evidence of aggregates or assemblages that might be defined as Forager Tradition in the Middle Archaic period. Projectile points or knives similar to those distinctive of the Forager Tradition in the Middle Archaic period in the White Locality were found on two different sites in the Stockton Reservoir area (Powell 1962: 59, 60, 62–64). The distinctive items noted were Big Sandy Notched and chipped-stone axes.

The materials excavated from shelter sites in the Kaysinger Bluff Reservoir area were not easily compared from site to site due to the fact that occupation levels within them varied considerably. Sites judged to have components from the Middle Archaic period were the Brounlee shelter (Chapman and Pangborn 1965: 442–44), the lowest levels, D and E, in the Harrison shelter (Sudderth 1965: 505–10), and Level 8 in Woody shelter (Sudderth and Chapman 1965: 539–41). The main evidences indicating an occupation in the Middle Archaic period, Forager Tradition, were Big Sandy Notched, corner-notched and contracting-stemmed projectile points or knives, scrapers, pitted pebble anvilstones, and choppers. Admittedly the interpretation that Middle Archaic components were in the locality is very tenuous.

Ozark Highland Region

A Forager Tradition, Middle Archaic period, seems to have been isolated in Stratum 2 at Rodgers shelter, for there was an erosional cycle between 6000 and 5500 B.C. that aids in separating Stratum 1 from Stratum 2. Stratum 2 in turn is set apart from Stratum 4 by a deposit that resulted from a severe erosion of the hillside above the shelter beginning about the middle of the Middle Archaic period and ending at about the end of the period (Figure 4–8). Stratum 3 was derived from the erosion of the talus slope above the shelter. Big Sandy Notched, Jakie Stemmed, corner-notched forms, several full-grooved axes, and chert hammerstones (Figure 7–13) were found in the stratum that I have interpreted to be Middle Archaic period (McMillan 1971: Figure 58).

McMillan (1971: 186–88) described the Middle Archaic period (6530–4030 B.C.) as a time that appeared to represent a "series of adaptive responses to the shifting ecotone during the Atlantic episode." He noted that the environment continued to deteriorate until the locality was totally abandoned.

The Forager Tradition during the Middle Archaic period is very difficult to assess in the Gasconade Locality. McMillan (1965b), for example, equates the Tick Creek aggregate with the Early Archaic in the Southwestern Drainage and with Early to Middle Archaic in the Lower Osage Lo-

cality. Furthermore, a revision of the information from Fowke (1922) and personal observation at various sites in the Ozark Highland lead me to the conclusion that there is not substantial evidence that there was any intensive occupation of the Ozark Highland during the period. It is possible that cultural change was severely retarded in the narrow, isolated stream valleys in the Ozarks, much as it had been during the Early Archaic period. In any instance, the artifacts left by the Foragers during the Middle Archaic period are not readily separable from those evidences left by the Foragers of the Early and Late Archaic. The region could have been used primarily by Foragers whose base camps were farther east and who utilized the highland primarily for hunting and collecting trips. It is possible that a few bands continued to live in the region, but their population density must have been thin and their existence precarious.

Tick Creek Cave had an aggregate in Level 6 (Roberts 1965), which consisted of a full-grooved ax, Big Sandy Notched, Table Rock Stemmed, Smith Basal Notched, Agate Basin Lanceolate, and Rice Contracting Stemmed; it may have represented a mixture of components from Early to Late Archaic. There possibly was an occupation in the locality during the Middle Archaic because Big Sandy Notched and full-grooved axes, both of which have been distinctive of the period in other localities, were found in Tick Creek Cave and at other sites. A full-grooved ax was reported from Goat Bluff Cave (Fowke 1922: 40), and three full-grooved axes and a Big Sandy Notched were found in Miller's Cave (Fowke 1922: Plate 27, bottom row 2d from right, Figure 29 center). Seventy-three mortars and more than 100 pestles indicated that the cave was used by Foragers.

No solid evidence of a Middle Archaic occupation has come from the Meramec, Upper Black–St. Francis, or Castor–Whitewater localities unless the presence of full-grooved axes and a few chipped-stone forms associated with Middle Archaic period assemblages in other regions were accepted as evidence for such occupation.

One of the problems concerning the occupation of the Ozark Highland Region during the

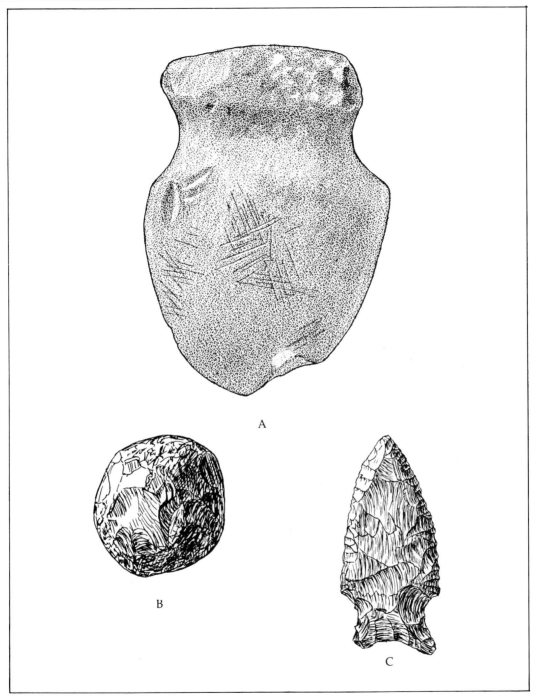

Figure 7–13.   Typical artifacts of the Forager Tradition, Middle Archaic period, in Rodgers shelter. Scale 1:1.
A, Full-grooved ax; B, core hammerstone; C, Jakie Stemmed.

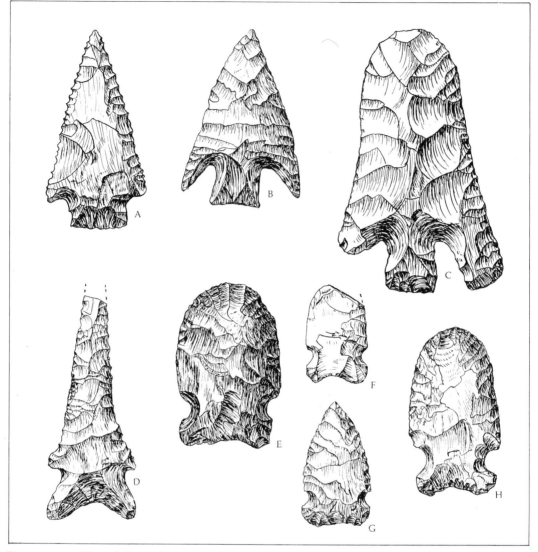

Figure 7–14. Typical chipped-stone artifacts of the Forager Tradition, Middle Archaic period assemblage in Graham Cave. Scale 7:9.
A, Rice Lobed (?); B–C, Basal Notched; D, Jakie Stemmed; E–H, Big Sandy Notched.

Archaic period is that too few investigations have been made on Archaic period sites. Another problem concerns the isolation of the region from the centers of cultural development in the Eastern United States. Cultural contacts in the region were probably limited as they have been in nearly every other period in the past. Studies of the full sequence of cultural development in this isolated region could be of special value in explaining the conditions and mechanisms bringing about cultural lag or the existence of culture in a steady state. We will not know very much about the Foragers of the Archaic period in the Ozark Highland Region until a concerted effort is directed toward obtaining data from the whole range of Archaic period sites in the region.

Northwest Prairie Region

No complexes, assemblages, or aggregates of the Forager Tradition of the Middle Archaic period have been identified in the Northwest Prairie Region. It has already been suggested that the people responsible for the tools in the Nebo Hill aggregate (Shippee 1948; 1957b; 1964) could have lived in the region during the Middle Archaic as well as the Early Archaic period.

Unfortunately the Nebo Hill collections are aggregates, and there is no assurance that the Nebo Hill Lanceolate, projectile points, knives, adzes or digging tools, ground-stone axes, celts, and manos were manufactured during the same time period or by the same people. It is clear that the characteristic Nebo Hill Lanceolate is similar in form to Plano complex types, but the cultural implications of the likeness are not clear. Until there are excavations of Nebo Hill sites to identify a true complex and determine the time of their occupation, little can be accomplished by further discussion. There appears to be a definite relationship of the Nebo Hill aggregate found in the Northwest Prairie Region and the materials of the Sedalia phase.

Unless new data place the Nebo Hill aggregate within the Middle Archaic period, the isolated finds of tools possibly from the Forager Tradition are the only other nebulous evidences of a Middle Archaic period occupation of the Northwest Prairie Region.

Northeast Prairie Region

The best-known assemblage of artifacts from the Forager Tradition of the Middle Archaic period in the Lower Missouri Valley II Locality is the middle assemblage in Graham Cave. The horizon markers are Big Sandy Notched, some of which were reworked into scrapers, full-grooved ground-stone axes, pitted anvilstones, choppers, engraved bone pins, and shell artifacts. Other items in the assemblage are a beveled form reminiscent of Rice Lobed, basal-notched forms, a drill reworked from a Jakie Stemmed, prepared cores, utilized flakes, and impressions of twined fabric (Figures 7–1, 7–14, 7–15). There was the continuation of the use of such tools as cupstones, mortars, pestles, bone awls, and antler hammers (Chapman 1952a: 97–101; 1957: 49; Klippel 1971; Logan 1952).

A similar assemblage was probably present in Arnold Research Cave, indicated by the prevalence of Big Sandy Notched (Shippee 1957a: Figure 22, top, bottom row) and Jakie Stemmed. An atlatl hook made of antler was a trait not found in Graham Cave. Shippee (1966: 33–35) noted that above the earliest level in the cave, which has been equated with the Early Archaic period zone in Graham Cave, there was a sterile area and then a general loose deposit of brown and gray fill in which there were very few artifacts. The artifacts included heavy side-notched forms as well as those with shoulders and straight stems (Shippee 1966: Figure 3 B, C). The types illustrated are very similar to those characteristic of the assemblage from Graham Cave of the Middle Archaic period; they are Big Sandy Notched, Jakie Stemmed, and a basal-notched form.

There is little doubt that there was an assemblage from the Forager Tradition, Middle Archaic period, in Arnold Research Cave, but a full definition of the assemblage could not be determined due to the disturbed nature of much of the deposit. Shippee (1966: 26) noted one full-grooved ax made of hematite and a small part of another in the cave. The ax was found at a depth of 50 inches in part of the dry deposit that was completely rotted, whereas the vegetal materials above it, 18–48 inches in depth, were not in a decayed condition. Another full-grooved ax was in Zone 3 in Arnold Research Cave (Heldman and Wyatt 1959). The antler atlatl hook and two Agate Basin Lanceolate found only 24 inches deep were dated at 5770±100 B.C., and another lanceolate form at a depth of 35 inches in the same type of deposit was dated at 4550±300 B.C. A Dalton Serrated at a depth of 37 inches was dated at 4330±350 B.C. (Shippee 1966: 18). The latter two dates fall within the Middle Archaic period.

The component in Arnold Research Cave that is representative of the Forager Tradition, Middle Archaic period is an aggregate rather than an assemblage. The radiocarbon dates below the ag-

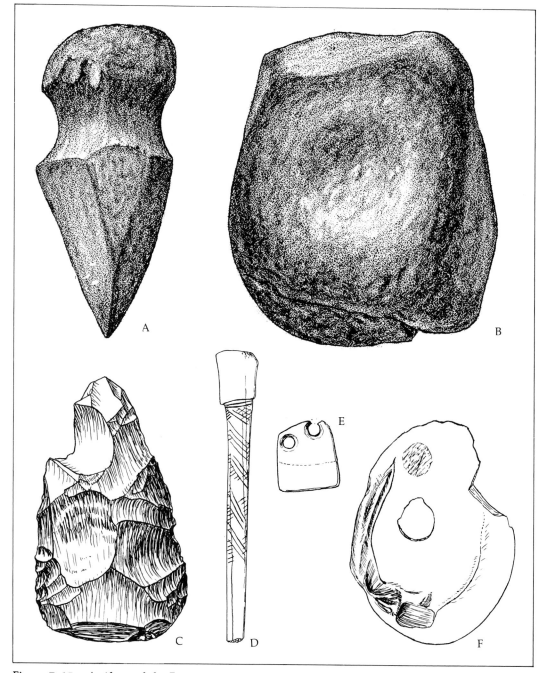

Figure 7–15.   Artifacts of the Forager Tradition, Middle Archaic period assemblage in Graham Cave. Scale 5:6.
A, Full-grooved ax; B, pitted anvilstone; C, chopper; D, decorated bone pin; E, shell pendant; F, shell scraper.

gregate come within the time span of the Middle Archaic period, but the Dalton Serrated associated at that level and one radiocarbon date of 7770 B.C. are indicators of the Forager Tradition of the Early Archaic period rather than Middle Archaic.

In the Salt Locality of the Northeast Prairie Region the occurrence of several Big Sandy Notched with a chipped-stone ax and snubbed-end flake scrapers on Site 23MN290 might be evidence of use of the locality during the Middle Archaic period. Big Sandy Notched also occurred on six other sites (Henning 1960a: Figures 14, 17, 20, 25, 37, 39, 80; 1961a: Figures 26, SN–4, 28C–D). Big Sandy Notched is not really diagnostic because it was used as late as Early Woodland period in the region. A full complex of artifacts of the Forager Tradition in the Middle Archaic period has not yet been discovered.

Southeast Riverine Region

The most important sites of the Forager Tradition in the Middle Archaic period in the Southeast Riverine Region are Hidden Valley shelter and Bonaker shelter in Missouri and Modoc shelter in Illinois (Adams 1941: 194; 1949: 60; Fowler 1959b). The Hidden Valley shelter contained an aggregate of implements, designated *Hidden Valley Shelter II.* Cord-marked, grit-tempered pottery sherds were found in the same level, but because the shelter fill at this point had been reworked by a stream that cut across the deposit, there was no certainty that the pottery sherds were a product of the same people who made the projectile points (Chapman 1948b: 140–42). The pottery and Big Sandy Notched came from channel B, about which Adams (1949: 59–61) said, "The objects from channel B were also obviously gathered from several different occupations. . . . Type five appeared to be diagnostic of the middle occupations but was also present in the early occupations." His type 5 (Adams 1949: Figure 20A) consisted of side-notched forms, two of which can be classified as Big Sandy Notched. Five Big Sandy Notched (Figure 7–16) were found in Gully B and were shown by Adams (1941: Plate XI–B). Other tools found with them were a cor-

ner-notched form, a fragment that is similar in treatment of the base to Jakie Stemmed, and a concave-based lanceolate with thinning of the base on both faces, the thinning extending from the base for one-third the length (Chapman 1948b: Figure 32B, Number 2). The latter may have been a type from the Early Archaic period. Two hafted drills were other chipped-stone items (Figure 7–16F). There were a few sherds with the other artifacts, but it was assumed that they had been in upper levels before the gulley was formed.

Adams (1949: 67, chart) placed the side-notched forms in a middle level above the Hidden Valley Stemmed, and this is another reason for suggesting that there is an aggregate from the Forager Tradition, Middle Archaic period in the shelter. The side-notched forms are comparable to those in the Faulkner site, Illinois, which is Archaic period (MacNeish 1948: 236–37). It would also be reasonable to assume that the Big Sandy Notched were from the Early Woodland period and that the pottery found with the type was contemporaneous because the side-notched forms are similar to those proposed to be a part of the Black Sand complex in Illinois, an Early Woodland period complex (Cole and Deuel 1937: 136–41, 226).

In the Bonacker shelter, in Layer II, one of the recognizable forms was side-notched, and Adams (1949: 71) described it as "similar to the Black Sand points from central Illinois and to those from the middle levels of the Hidden Valley Rock Shelter." Thus there is typological evidence from another shelter in the same locality for an occupation during the Middle Archaic period, for no pottery was found in association with Big Sandy Notched.

No systematic archaeological research has been conducted on sites occupied during the Archaic period in the St. Francis and Bootheel localities. Site 23SO138 in the St. Francis Riverine Locality may have contained a Middle Archaic period component. A wide range of artifacts probably from the Archaic period was collected from the site at the time it was being land leveled. Big Sandy Notched, one of which had been reworked into a scraper, snubbed-end

Figure 7–16.   Chipped-stone artifacts of the Forager Tradition, Middle Archaic period, in Hidden Valley shelter. Scale 1:1.
A–E, Big Sandy Notched; F, drill.

flake scrapers, stemmed projectile points or knives, expanding-based drills, and full-grooved axes (Figures 7–17, 7–18) collected on the site may be indicative of a Forager component from the Middle Archaic period. Dalton Serrated and the finding of a cache of Hidden Valley Stemmed (Figure 6–22) with a bannerstone (Figure 6–23) may denote that the site also contained a component of the preceding Early Archaic period. In any instance there is a good hint that the Foragers of the Middle Archaic period lived in the locality. Many Full-grooved axes and Big Sandy Notched have been found in the Bootheel Locality and are in the collections of Floyd Vavak and Paul Corbin.

Regional Distribution of Evidences

Southwest Drainage Region

Distribution of the White River complex is confined to the Southwest Drainage Region within the upper White River drainage from the Bull Shoals Dam to the upper end of the Beaver Reservoir area in Arkansas. It includes the Bull Shoals, Lake Taneycomo, and Table Rock reservoirs and extends into the northwestern corner of Arkansas and the northeastern part of Oklahoma (Adams 1950; 1958; Baerreis 1951; Chapman 1960d; Marshall 1958; Tong 1951a). The most northerly extension of the complex is on the James River near Springfield, Missouri, where a predominance of Big Sandy Notched, along with grooved axes were found on two sites in Greene County (Marshall 1955: 13–28).

Western Prairie Region

No aggregates, assemblages, or complexes of the Middle Archaic period have been found in the Western Prairie Region either in Missouri or Kansas. Perhaps the region was not a desirable place for Foragers during that period.

Ozark Highland Region

The stratum at Rodgers shelter that contained a Forager assemblage from the Middle Archaic period related more closely to the aggregate from the Middle Archaic period at Tick Creek Cave in the Ozark Highland Region than to the White River complex in the Southwest Drainage Region or the assemblage in Graham Cave in the Northeast Prairie Region. It is probably limited in its distribution to the Ozark Highland Region and may include more traits from the preceding period than other Middle Archaic complexes.

Northwest Prairie Region

The presence of extremely large side-notched, lanceolate, and straight-stemmed projectile points or knives (Shippee 1964: 27–34; Wedel 1943: Plate 43) in the Northwest Prairie Region may be evidence of occupation during the Middle Archaic period by people related culturally to those who occupied Rodgers shelter in the Ozark Highland Region and to the people in the Northeast Prairie Region who manufactured the large side-notched forms. Although the side-notched varieties are unusually large and cannot readily be related to Big Sandy Notched, they are similar in size and form to Osceola in Wisconsin (Bell 1958; Ritzenthaler 1957; Wittry and Ritzenthaler 1956). Titterington (1950: Figures 1, 5) illustrated similar specimens as one of the types in the nonpottery sites in the St. Louis area and in the Hemphill burial site, both of which are located in the Northeast Prairie Region and have been assigned to the Late Archaic period. The large side-notched points or knives were not found in the levels in Graham Cave or Arnold Research Cave in the Northeast Prairie area occupied during the Middle Archaic period. Perhaps they occurred late in time in the north, as they did in the St. Louis area. For example, the Osceola site of the Old Copper culture of Wisconsin, from which the Osceola type was named, has a radiocarbon date (1500±250 B.C.) that places it in the Late Archaic period (Ritzenthaler 1958). Furthermore, Mason and Mason (1961) questioned whether the Osceola type is actually a trait of the Old Copper culture, which occurred earlier. Wittry (1959a: 44; 1959b) gave the name Raddatz Side Notched to the medium-sized forms associated with the Middle Archaic zone at Raddatz shelter and the earliest level at the Durst rock shelter. Wittry (1959a: 65) suggested that the Middle Archaic at Raddatz shelter, in

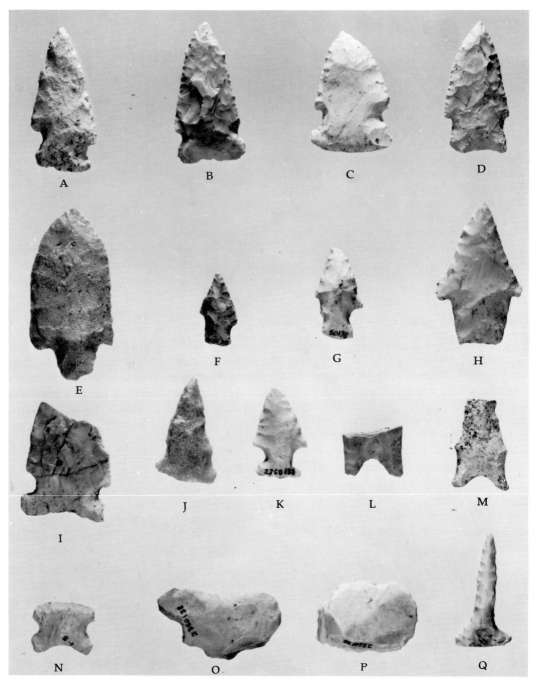

Figure 7–17.   Chipped-stone artifacts possibly of the Forager Tradition, Middle Archaic period, from Site 23SO138, St. Francis Riverine Locality (Charles Orr Collection). Scale 6:9.
A, Stemmed biface; B–C, side-notched forms; D–H, stemmed bifaces; I, Big Sandy Notched; J, side-notched form; K, stemmed biface; L–M, concave-based lanceolates; N, Big Sandy Notched; O–P, scrapers; Q, drill.

Figure 7–18. Full-grooved axes from the St. Francis Riverine Locality. Upper left is from Site 23SO138, upper right from Site 23SO164 (Charles Orr Collection). Scale 5:8.

which the Raddatz Side Notched occurred, is closely related to the Old Copper culture. Raddatz Side Notched appears to equate with Big Sandy Notched.

Side-notched forms appear during the Early Archaic period in western Iowa (Frankforter 1959; Frankforter and Agogino 1959). Similar side-notched forms have been found in the Logan Creek complex, Nebraska. This complex has been equated with the Pony Creek complex in Iowa (McKusick 1964: 56–58). The Hill site (McKusick 1964: 65), one of the components of the Logan Creek complex, was occupied toward the end of the Early Archaic or the beginning of the Middle Archaic. The Logan Creek site in Nebraska dates between 5300 and 4700 B.C. Small side-notched forms are distinctive members of the Logan Creek complex (McKusick 1964: 57), so it is possible that medium-sized side-notched forms were being made during the Early Archaic period. Larger side-notched varieties found at the Simonson site have been dated 6471 B.C. (Agogino and Frankforter 1960), and the large Graham Cave Notched is an Early Archaic type.

It appears that side notching of projectile point or knife forms is not a diagnostic trait for any segment of the Archaic period. Size, form, and method of manufacture of the artifacts are criteria that are helpful for identifying components associated with a specific division of the Archaic period.

To the west in Kansas and Nebraska, there are even fewer evidences of the Forager Tradition, Middle Archaic period. There are no identifiable Early or Middle Archaic complexes reported upon in the northeastern part of Kansas and the northwestern part of Missouri.

Northeast Prairie Region

The distribution of the Middle Archaic Graham Cave assemblage in the Northeast Prairie Region is not very evident to the east and north. A single fragment of a side-notched form identified as Graham Cave Notched but which could be Big Sandy Notched was in the 18–24-inch level at Starved Rock (Mayer-Oakes 1951: Figure 101) along with Agate Basin Lanceolate. The evidence was certainly not sufficient to suggest that

the site was used by Foragers in the Middle Archaic period.

It is possible that a horizon at the Koster site in the lower Illinois Valley was occupied during the Middle Archaic period (Houart 1971: 49, Figures 11, 12), but the artifacts found there are different from the Graham Cave assemblage and the suggested dating of 3500–2500 B.C. places it primarily in the Late Archaic period. Engraved bone pins, which are distinctive Middle Archaic period artifacts, were among the materials at the Koster site.

Farther east in the Wabash River valley at the edge of the Springfield Plains, near Vincennes, Indiana, Winters (1967: 18, 21) noted that "Faulkner side-notched" cluster in the valley and suggested that they were from the Early to Middle Archaic period. Farther south on the Patoka River branch of the Wabash in Indiana, the McCain site has yielded a complex of artifacts that are typologically Forager Tradition and Middle Archaic period (Miller 1941). The McCain site had Big Sandy Notched as the standard pattern and was further distinguished by the occurrence of full-grooved axes. Pitted manos, pebble manos, a cylindrical muller, expanding-based drills, reworked projectile point drills, and reworked projectile point scrapers were other items in the assemblage. There was a great deal of bone and antler work, including engraved bone pins. Straight-stemmed projectile point forms were next in importance to the standard side-notched and oval scrapers. There were large numbers of hammerstones. In general there were a greater number and variety of bone and antler artifacts at the McCain site than there were in Forager assemblages from the Middle Archaic period in Missouri. The basic stone assemblage was very much the same as the Graham Cave assemblage, and it appears that the distribution of the Middle Archaic period, Forager Tradition, should be extended as far east as Indiana.

It is not suggested that the assemblage from the McCain site is evidence of the distribution of a complex related to the Graham Cave Middle Archaic Forager assemblage to Indiana, but it is proposed that Foragers who adapted to a similar edge of the Prairie Peninsula environment were living along its southern extension from Missouri to Indiana and that their tool kits were similar.

Southeast Riverine Region

Much more is known about the Forager Tradition in the Middle Archaic period in Illinois than Missouri. The Modoc shelter in Illinois was occupied during the Middle Archaic period by Foragers who manufactured Big Sandy Notched, which were predominant in the period 5000–3500 B.C., although they appeared in quantity at 6000 B.C. and continued to 3000 B.C. They were associated with straight-based bifacial knives and corner-notched, stemmed, and lanceolate forms of projectile points (Fowler 1959a: 37).

Scrapers, perforators, flakers, abrading stones, milling stones, chopping tools, hammerstones, and full-grooved axes were part of the assemblage. Fowler (1959a: 57) interpreted the periods of occupation in the Modoc shelter as follows: "(1) the initial Archaic occupation, 8000–7000 B.C., (2) local adaptation 7000–3500 B.C., and (3) specialized adaptation, 3500–2000 B.C."

From the evidence at the Modoc site and at the Faulkner site in southern Illinois (Cole and others 1951; MacNeish 1948), it is clear that during the Middle Archaic period Foragers lived in the Mississippi drainage on the east side of the Mississippi River. The exact limits of this cultural manifestation beyond this locality are uncertain.

8. Forager Tradition, Late Archaic Period

The Late Archaic period was a time of intensive adaptation to ecological niches not exploited by earlier Foragers. At the beginning of the period the climate was probably very dry. Cleland (1966: 20–28) noted that the warmer period, called xerothermic by paleoclimatologists, began perhaps as early as 7000 B.C. and reached its maximum shortly before 2000 B.C. Prairies had shifted to the east, and the forest with its food supply of plants and animals had been diminished. The western part of Missouri and the related prairies may have been abandoned as a place of permanent abode during the preceding period; the cause is as yet unknown (McMillan 1971: 187). The climatic changes that had taken place may have brought about transfer of cultural phases from the western regions to those farther east. The tool kits of the Sedalia complex, assuming that they derived from the Nebo Hill aggregate, are evidence that Foragers as far east as the Northeast Prairie Region had adapted to a prairie–forest-edge environment.

Stone technology varied greatly from the preceding period; in some regions dart points were elaborated upon and reduced in size, and in others dart points were scarcely present. Special types of chipped-stone tools were manufactured. One of the tools was triangular, made from a large spall, flaked from one side only, had a straight or concave cutting edge, and has been called the *Clear Fork Gouge (2)* or *Planer Gouge* (Ray 1934; 1938; 1941; 1948). I have retained *Clear Fork Gouge* for this type of tool. The other, rectanguloid rather than triangular in shape, was flaked from both sides of the spall or core and often had a rounded cutting edge. Ray (1941: 153–54) named this type *Clear Fork Gouge (1)*. Here it is called *Sedalia Digger* to distinguish it from the Clear Fork Gouge. The Clear Fork Gouges often had polish from use on one or both sides, indicating that they were scraping, pulping, or woodworking tools. The Sedalia Diggers often had a high gloss from having been used for digging in the soil. Both types of tools were usually associated with foraging activities. Though present in the Early and Middle divisions of the Archaic period, the Clear Fork Gouge and related Sedalia Digger were not used in great numbers until the Late Archaic. During the Late Archaic they were the standard type of artifact on sites occupied by people of the Sedalia phase. This emphasis on artifacts associated with some type of collecting, gathering, and preparation of plant foods is indicative of a fully developed Forager Tradition.

In the Western Prairie, the northern part of the Ozark Highland, and Northeast Prairie regions, the tools suggesting adaptation to a subsistence on vegetal products, or movement of the cultural adaptation to the area, were the Clear Fork Gouges that were possibly used for pulping roots or cambium layers of trees; Sedalia Diggers with the characteristic corn gloss on their bits from digging roots in sod; and the many grinding tools such as manos, pestles, and hammerstones that could have been used for pounding and grinding seeds, roots, and pulpy plants. Other items of importance were the large knives or daggers, Etley Stemmed, Sedalia Lanceolate, and Stone Square Stemmed. They were almost certainly not a part of a hunting tool kit. The small flake scrapers and other flake tools, such as flake knives that are commonly associated with a hunting tradition were not well represented on the sites from the Forager Tradition, nor were there enough dart points to suggest that hunting was an important activity.

The dark-colored areas that have been observed on the open campsites were probably the result of decomposition of vegetal waste resulting from the preparation of roots or other plant foods. Just what this major food supply was remains a mystery. The prairie potato, which occurs in quantity in some dry prairie areas, might have been one of the foods, but there must have been others as well. Perhaps the cambium layer of elm was being processed for food. Yarnell (1964: 12) in describing the Late Archaic tools and subsistence noted that efficient woodworking tools would make tree sap and cambium more readily available during early spring when food sources would be hardest to find. It is relatively certain that important vegetable food plants were in the Prairie Peninsula and must have been concentrated at its edge in the Northwest Prairie, the northern Ozark Highland, and Northeast Prairie regions, extending at least as far as central Illinois.

The settlement pattern in the Late Archaic in the Northwest Prairie and Northeast Prairie had as one of its characteristics campsites encompassing one to four acres, arranged in a linear plan. Areas of intense activity were represented by elliptical or round humus concentrations about 25–50 feet across their long axes. The dark, humus-enriched areas contained numerous Clear Fork Gouges that were probably used for pulping the gathered food plants. The concentrations may have represented living areas because charcoal, burned soil, and burned rocks were found in them. It is possible that the areas were used for extraction of plant juices or for breaking down plant fibers so that they could be used for food, and the masses of collected material that built up in the occupation or food preparation areas formed a thick humus in the soil.

Klippel (1969) suggested that the food collecting on the Booth site occurred during the summer months. It is also possible that collecting was a spring or a fall activity, and it is further possible that the camps were established as a base of operations from spring to fall. Until it is known what foods were being selected and prepared or

other evidence can be obtained through archaeological investigations, there can be little more than speculation concerning the specific season or seasons the sites were used.

In most of the southern half of the state, in the Southwest Drainage, Ozark Highland, and the Southeast Riverine regions, there were differences in tool kits. Hunting was an important part of the Forager Tradition in the Southwest Drainage Region, and the general economy that developed during the Early Archaic period continued into the Late Archaic. In the Late Archaic period there were some inroads of a predominantly plant-foraging economy, again probably extending from the west and south into the Southwest Drainage Region from northeastern Oklahoma and northwestern Arkansas. A single component site near the mouth of James River in the Table Rock Reservoir area of Stone County, the James River site, is the best example of a typical plant-foraging assemblage of the Late Archaic period in the Southwest Drainage Region.

The assemblage differed considerably from the assemblages judged to be in the same time period in the shelters in the Table Rock Reservoir area. The latter were distinguished by a variety of small chipped-stone forms that were undoubtedly projectile points. It was speculated, on the basis of prevalence of dart points, that hunting continued to be emphasized. Hunting was also a prime occupation throughout most of the southern Ozark Highland Region, and it is possible that it extended into the Southeast Riverine Region as well. Specific information was not available from most sites, and the general impression that the Late Archaic development was oriented primarily toward hunting in the Southeast Riverine and Ozark Highland regions cannot be fully supported at present by excavated data.

The nature of phases during the period in the Ozark Highland and Southeast Riverine regions, the exact time of the period, and the full definition of the complexes that participated in the Forager Tradition as it adapted to the prairies cannot be determined at this time. They are major problems in midwestern archaeology and should be investigated. The Late Archaic is the critical period during which the framework was being laid for a change from foraging to a foraging incipient agricultural economy. A greater knowledge of cultural adaptations during the period should give some insight into the later development and perhaps some background on the domestication of plants that made possible the acceptance of the southern agricultural plants introduced to the region in a later period.

Southwest Drainage Region

The Forager Tradition in the Table Rock Reservoir area (Chapman 1960d: 1150–70) has been divided into two periods, 3000–1000 B.C. and 1000 B.C.–A.D.1. Only the former is Late Archaic period; the latter is Early Woodland in time. The Forager Tradition probably lasted relatively late in the region, due perhaps to physiographical and cultural isolation of the area.

The term *James River complex* is used for an important manifestation of the Forager Tradition during the Late Archaic period in the Southwest Drainage Region. Several components make up the complex. They are the aggregate in Level 4 at Jakie shelter, the entire assemblage at the James River site, and the middle level components at Long Creek A and B sites. Representative artifacts are Smith Basal Notched (Perino 1968: 90, Plate 45), similar to the Eva I point (Lewis and Lewis 1961: 40, Plates 10–11), Stone Square Stemmed, Table Rock Stemmed, and Afton Corner Notched. Other artifacts that were an integral part of the complex were trianguloid bifaces, chipped-stone notched axes, hafted and straight-sided drills, flake tools, flake knives and scrapers, chert core hammerstones, and pebble manos and anvilstones (Figures 8–1 through 8–8). A few contracting-stemmed and corner-notched projectile points also were present, but in small numbers.

The separation of the components of the James River complex from those of complexes before and after it in many instances was quite difficult, but the James River site appeared to have only a single component on it, and the assemblage of artifacts found on it are probably a good representation of the complex (Figures 8–1, 8–4, 8–6, 8–7, 8–8). The projectile points were few in relation to other chipped-stone tools. Table Rock Stemmed and the few small corner-notched and contracting-stemmed forms were the only types that were assumed to be used as dart points, and they made up less than 10 per cent of all the chipped-stone tools found. More than one-third of the chipped-stone tools was Smith Basal Notched, which was much too large to have been used as a projectile point. Henning (1960b: 806–9) noted that the basal-notched form was a wide, thick tool that could not have penetrated deeply into the flesh of most game animals, even with the force provided by a spear thrower. It was probably a cutting tool rather than a projectile point. Smith Basal Notched and Stone Square Stemmed made up most of the chipped-stone implements (Figures 8–1 through 8–5).

Judging from the occurrence of a variety of projectile points in nonceramic deposits in the shelters and caves in the locality, there is the good possibility that another complex of the Forager Tradition is present in the White Locality during the Late Archaic period. Since dates are lacking and there is not a clustering of distinctive types of artifacts in comparable levels from site to site, it has not been possible to derive another complex from the materials at hand. It is also possible, if not probable, that the latest nonceramic levels in the sites in the area may be later in time than the Late Archaic period, even though they appear to be Forager Tradition in character.

The Current–Eleven Point and Neosho localities have provided no sites with aggregates or assemblages that can be identified as Forager Tradition in Late Archaic time. Adams (1958: Figures 3, 17, 24, 25, 27–30, 37) depicted Smith Basal Notched and Afton Corner Notched found singly or in small numbers on several sites in southwestern Missouri, but in no instance was there a grouping of types shown that might be identified as Late Archaic Forager Tradition.

Western Prairie Region

The Harrison shelter (Sudderth 1965: 503–30) was divided tentatively into five natural levels on the basis of soil color and consistency, and these

A

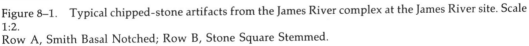

B

Figure 8–1.   Typical chipped-stone artifacts from the James River complex at the James River site. Scale 1:2.
Row A, Smith Basal Notched; Row B, Stone Square Stemmed.

levels had a general relationship to the cultural activity that took place in the shelter. Level 4 or D has already been mentioned as being associated with a Forager Tradition aggregate in the Middle Archaic period. The third level from the top, overlying the level containing evidences of the occupation during the Middle Archaic period, produced a series of chipped-stone forms and other items that typologically relate to the Forager Tradition of the Late Archaic period in the White Locality. For example, there were six Afton Corner Notched, five Table Rock Stemmed, and five stemmed forms that appeared to be closely related to Table Rock Stemmed. Both types have been identified in Late Archaic components elsewhere. A variety of other forms including Langtry (Bell 1958: 38) and Kings Corner Notched (Marshall 1958: 176) were in the

Figure 8–2. Smith Basal Notched from the James River complex at the Long Creek A site. Scale 3:5.

same level. Two were Scallorn (Bell 1960: 84), a Late Woodland period type arrowhead. Other artifacts were scrapers, spokeshaves, drills, adzes, ovoid bifaces, choppers, modified flake tools, metates, manos, cupstones, hammerstones, and antler tine flaking tools. Pottery was also in the same level. The association of pottery and Scallorn arrowheads may signify that there was admixture from a later period of occupation. In any instance, the Harrison shelter contained Afton Corner Notched and Table Rock Stemmed, possible evidences of a Forager Tradition aggregate,

and thus the shelter may have been occupied by a group of Foragers during the Late Archaic period.

Cat Hollow shelter (Chapman 1965c: 542–61), also located in the Kaysinger Bluff Reservoir area, was not stratified. The projectile points and other items within the shelter indicated that a clear sequence of cultural assemblages or components could not be determined easily. The pottery-making people who utilized the shelter had apparently stirred the deposits through digging activities until there was a mixture of materials

Figure 8–3. Chipped-stone artifacts from the James River complex at the Long Creek B site. Scale 1:1. A, Afton Corner Notched; B–D, Smith Basal Notched; E–F, Table Rock Stemmed.

Figure 8–4. Chipped-stone artifacts from the James River complex at the James River site. Scale 1:2. A, Stone Square Stemmed; B, Table Rock Stemmed; C–E, trianguloid bifaces.

from top to bottom. Table Rock Stemmed, Stone Square Stemmed, Smith Basal Notched, large corner-notched forms, expanding-based drills, pitted anvilstones, pebble manos, cupstones, and hammerstones found in Levels 3–9 were possible evidence of a Forager Tradition component of the Late Archaic period in the shelter. This possibility has to be in the realm of speculation because pottery was included in the aggregate along with a

wide range of tools that could have been associated with components of the Woodland period.

Two nonceramic sites in the Stockton Reservoir (Calabrese, Pangborn, and Young 1969; Pangborn, Ward, and Wood 1967), though appearing to be Forager Tradition, have not been described because they date in the Mississippi period. It is probable that the Forager Tradition lasted well into the Woodland period in the adja-

Figure 8–5.   Stone Square Stemmed from the James River complex at the Long Creek A site. Scale 1:1. A–B, Typical Stone Square Stemmed; C–D, variations of Stone Square Stemmed.

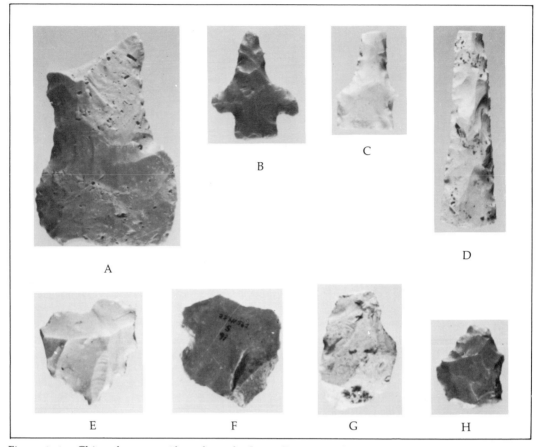

Figure 8–6. Chipped-stone artifacts from the James River complex at the James River site. Scale 2:3. A, Notched ax; B–C, reworked projectile point drills; D, straight-sided drill; E–H, flake tools.

cent Southwest Drainage and central Ozark Highland regions and that the Western Prairie was occupied by the Foragers from the south and east during the Woodland and Mississippi times.

There is definitely a Late Archaic Forager Tradition occupation in the Neosho River valley in Kansas, the Munkers Creek phase (Witty 1969) that may relate in general to the Sedalia phase because distinctive tools associated with both are adzes or gouges and digging tools. Other than these foraging tools the two phases differ greatly in artifact content.

Witty (1969) described the Munkers Creek phase as follows:

> The work in the Council Grove area located and identified a prehistoric Archaic culture of

which we were not previously aware. This group is termed taxonomically the Munkers Creek Phase. The particular site at which it was first noted was the William Young site which lies at the extreme north end of the Council Grove Reservoir. Here was located a buried campsite level from four to seven feet below the surface. Numerous chipped stone points, celts, blades and gouges were recovered along with two very unusual fired clay effigy heads. These small heads show detail of headdress or hairdo and indicate that the knowledge of firing clay into ceramics was known at least at this particular site. This is a very interesting discovery considering that the knowledge of making pottery vessels did not appear to any extent on the plains until a few hundred years after the time of Christ. Charcoal from the William Young site has dated the camp

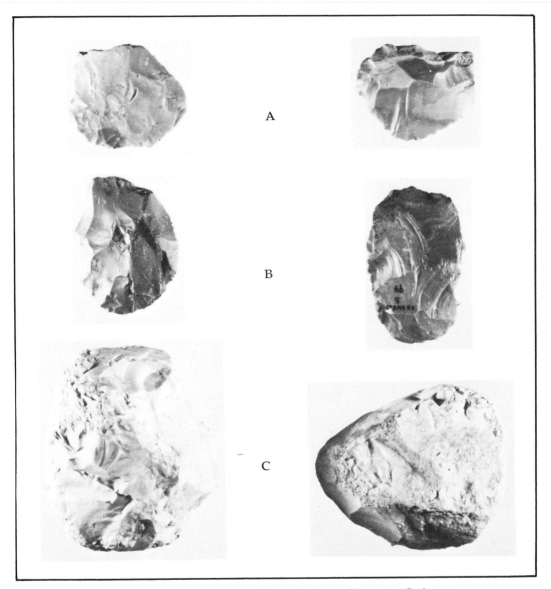

Figure 8–7.   Tools from the James River complex at the James River site. Scale 2:3.
Row A, Flake knives; Row B, scrapers; Row C, chert-core hammerstones.

level from 5,000 to 3,000 years ago. The projectile points are medium to large size specimens
indicating that the atlatl was still the principal
missile launcher of the period. The actual living level at this site was marked by hearths
made up of clusters of burned limestone fragments and levels of cultural detritus. On the
basis of similar artifacts at least four other sites
in the area between Junction City and Bazaar
have been identified as representing this Phase.

Witty (1969) also noted that in the John Redmond Reservoir another Late Archaic manifestation was found which differed from Munkers
Creek. An associated dart point was identified as
Table Rock Stemmed (T. A. Witty Jr., Personal
Communication, August 13, 1971). Piles of
burned lanceolate fragments, flexed human burials, and a dog burial were described from one

Figure 8–8.   Pebble manos and anvilstones from the James River complex at the James River site. Scale 2:3.
A–B, Pebble manos; C–D, anvilstones.

site. Witty (1969) noted, "The two radiocarbon dates from the site are 1550 and 1650 B.C."

Ozark Highland Region

It is not surprising that there is some confusion concerning the definition of the Forager Tradition assemblages and complexes in the Ozark Highland Region. It appears that the Late Archaic was a time of full adaptation to ecological niches, and the ecological niches in the localities in the region were varied due to overlapping with those in adjacent localities of different regions. The western part of the Ozark Highland Region is so situated between prairie and woodland that even minor fluctuation in climate could quickly be reflected in the movements of cultures adapted to prairie or to woodland ecozones. The western edge of the Upper Osage Locality is an ecotone bordering on the Western Prairie. The prairies may have moved into the woodlands of the Ozark Highland Region in times of drought, and the woodlands probably extended into prairies during long wet periods. The northern prairies also were adjacent to the woodland of the Ozark Highland and must have extended into the Ozark Highland Region during and following long dry periods. To the east and south, in the Southeast Riverine Region, riverine bottomland hardwoods and flatwoods, swamp vegetation, and fauna infiltrated the Ozark Highland through the many deep stream valleys whenever there was a wet, warm period. Although there appeared to be stabilization in the Prairie Peninsula and the Ozark Highland in general, fluctuations in the climate during the Late Archaic period in the Ozark Highland would probably have been reflected in a shifting of cultural complexes from one physiographic region to the other in accord with the movement of climatic zones east and west or north and south. Furthermore, cultural innovations in southeastern North America could be predicted to be found in the larger stream valleys draining to the south, and cultural ideas originating in the plains and prairies should be found in the stream valleys draining north and east. Hypothetically there should

be evidences of more than one phase or complex during the Late Archaic period in the region.

In Rodgers shelter the projectile point or knife forms occurring above and presumably later than the Middle Archaic types were as follows: a lanceolate form that possibly can be classified as a variety of Sedalia Lanceolate, Etley Stemmed, Smith Basal Notched, Table Rock Stemmed, other stemmed and corner-notched forms (Figure 8–9).

Adzes, pebble manos, pitted and unpitted anvilstones, a prismatic bannerstone, and an engraved stone plaque are other items that might be included in the aggregate. Identification of the Late Archaic aggregate as Forager Tradition wherein most major sources of food were being exploited is suggested by McMillan's (1971: 188–89) observation that deer hunting had again become important along with collecting plant foods. There was also a "new emphasis on collecting fresh-water mussels."

In the central part of the Ozark Highland Region in the Gasconade Locality two components were identified by McMillan (1965b: 57) as Middle to Late Archaic, one at Ramsey Cave and another at Tick Creek Cave. Some of the artifacts they had in common were two types of corner-notched and two types of side-notched forms, triangular and oval bifacial forms, bifacial-blade end scrapers, and unifacial-flake snubbed-end flake scrapers. Shaped-pebble manos, antler tine flakers, and deer bone awls were also in both components. A series of corner-notched stemmed, contracting-stemmed, and basal-notched forms in Tick Creek Cave was not present in Ramsey Cave. Other items in Tick Creek Cave that did not occur in Ramsey Cave were reworked projectile point scrapers, reworked projectile point drills, expanding-based drills, full-grooved axes, winged bannerstones, stone mortars, cupstones, rubbed hematite, deer ulna flakers, split and tubular bird-bone awls, deer ulna punches, terrapin-shell bowls and gorgets, bone pins, bone fishhooks, cut phalangeal bones, and mussel-shell spoons (McMillan 1965b: 58–59, Table 3). Traits that were definitely not in the earlier Middle Archaic period complex and that are probably distinctive of the

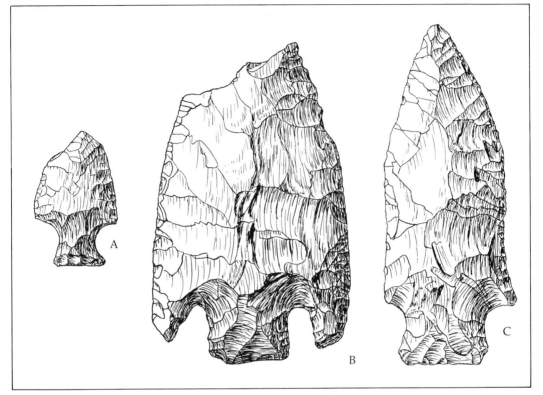

Figure 8–9.   Artifacts of the Late Archaic period in Rodgers shelter (courtesy of R. B. McMillan, Illinois State Museum). Scale 1:1.
A, Table Rock Stemmed; B, Smith Basal Notched; C, variant of Stone Square Stemmed.

Figure 8–10.   Bannerstones from the Upper Black–St. Francis Locality (Kenneth Barrow Collection). Scale 7:9.

A

B

C

D

E

F

G

H

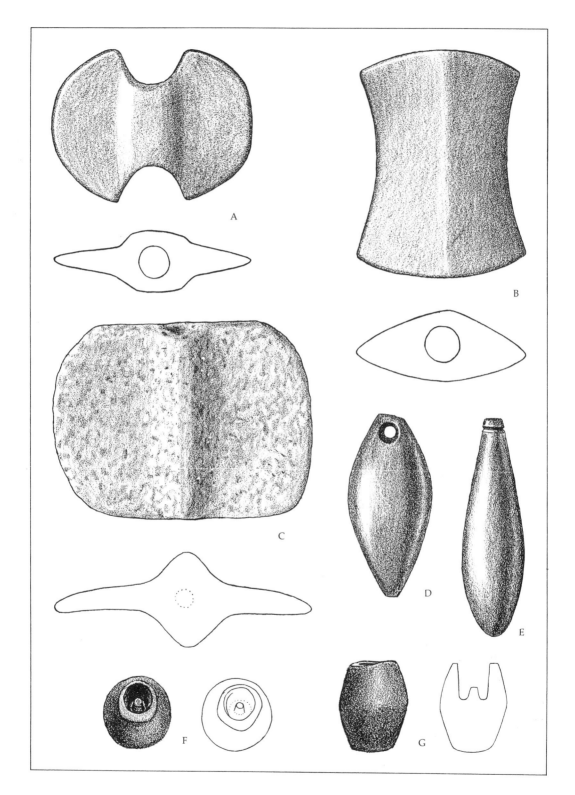

A

B

C

D

E

F

G

Late Archaic are Afton Corner Notched, Table Rock Stemmed, Smith Basal Notched, and Stone Square Stemmed. Other items that are integral parts of the complex are winged bannerstones, terrapin-shell bowls and gorgets, bone pins and bone fishhooks. Cut phalangeal bones and mussel shell spoons should be noted as questionably part of the Tick Creek complex. The separation of the aggregate into Late Archaic and Middle Archaic units in Tick Creek Cave is not at all certain; the deposit had been mixed a great deal, and the controls were not always absolute during the excavations.

The Verkamp shelter in the Meramec Locality contained indications of a Late Archaic component. Marshall (1959) noted a preceramic zone in which there were possibly several types of projectile points, one of which predominated and he named *Verkamp Stemmed.* It is a straight- to flaring-stemmed point. It was associated with pottery levels in the site as well as the levels containing no pottery. Verkamp Stemmed appears to be the same as Munkers Creek points, a Late Archaic period form in the Western Prairie Region in Kansas on the basis of descriptions and drawings provided by T. A. Witty, Jr. (Personal Communication, August 13, 1971).

In a preliminary report on the Verkamp shelter, McMillan (n.d.: 1–24) attributed the following artifacts to the Late Archaic occupation: a small, stemmed projectile point that could be classified as Table Rock Stemmed, a basal-notched form similar to Smith Basal Notched, and a snubbed-end flake scraper. The evidences of the Late Archaic period at Verkamp shelter are limited but may indicate that there was a temporary use of the shelter by Foragers during the Late Archaic period.

Although intensive surveys have been made in the Meramec River drainage and test excavations have been conducted, the information was not sufficient to define a Forager complex for the Meramec Basin (McMillan 1964: 92). Again it was suggested that the aggregates were from the Middle to Late Archaic period on the basis of excavations in two shelter sites, Component I at Tonky West Shelter II and Component I at Stuesse shelter and the surface collections on the Essman campsite. The collection from the Essman site had been selective of chipped-stone projectile points and knives. Since it contained arrowheads as well as dart points, spearheads, and knives, the only way to determine if the tools were from the Forager Tradition was typologically. McMillan (1962) described and counted each type of tool from the site. Converting McMillan's categories to type names, the following were obtained: Agate Basin Lanceolate, Smith Basal Notched, Rice Contracting Stemmed, Big Sandy Notched, and Table Rock Stemmed. They made up 28 per cent of all the forms that were collected. It is probable that a component of the Forager Tradition is included in the aggregate found on the site because most of the types are usually associated with Forager complexes. There is not enough evidence to place it in time, but it is possibly Late Archaic period. Earlier types could have continued into Late Archaic times, or the aggregate could contain elements of earlier Forager Tradition components.

A variety of bannerstones has come from the Upper Black–St. Francis Locality (Figure 8–10). Bannerstones of different shapes have been found in northern and central Missouri (Figure 8–11 A–C). Other ground-stone items such as plummets and stone beads drilled in the same manner as bannerstones may also have been produced during the Late Archaic period (Figure 8–11 D–G). For example, Houart (1971: 32) noted a plummet (bola stone) and a drilled red ochre bead from the Late Archaic Horizon IV in the

---

Figure 8–11. Tools and ornaments, probably of the Late Archaic period, from central and northern Missouri. Scale 3:4.
A, Winged bannerstone and end view showing drilled hole; B, hour-glass bannerstone and end view showing drilled hole; C, unfinished winged bannerstone and end view (Jean Moodie Collection); D–E, plummets or bola stones; F–G, unfinished stone bead (F, top view and sketch showing grinding line; G, side view and cross-section showing depth of drilling).

Koster site. Bannerstones may have been made in Early and Middle Archaic periods and are not necessarily distinctive traits of the Late Archaic period Forager Tradition. Furthermore different types of bannerstones could have been used at different time periods and in different localities at the same time period. Fowler (1959: 264) reported 4 bannerstones from the Modoc site in Illinois, 3 of which were in Zone IV in the Late Archaic period. The fourth was in Zone II and probably was made during the Early Archaic period. He stated that the latter was of a different shape from those found in the upper zone. In a few instances bannerstones have been associated with what appear to be Late Archaic period aggregates such as the components of the Titterington focus (Titterington 1950), and that is another reason for including them in the Late Archaic period. Until we have better data, we cannot make anything more than tentative statements concerning the placement of bannerstones in Early, Middle, or Late divisions of the Archaic period. One thing certain is that bannerstones, bola stones or plummets, and ground-stone beads are characteristic traits of the Forager Tradition (Figure 8–11).

Northwest Prairie Region

As has been pointed out in previous discussions of the Forager Tradition, during the Archaic period in the Northwest Prairie Region very few evidences of intensive occupation have been discovered. The only positive evidences were the sites of the Nebo Hill aggregate. It is possible that the Nebo Hill aggregate was much later than proposed by Shippee (1948; 1964). A Clear Fork Gouge was found on the Nebo Hill type site and a few of the lanceolate forms in the Nebo Hill aggregate can be identified as Sedalialike lanceolate (Shippee 1964: 4–5), but are much smaller (Figure 8–12C). Some characteristics of the Forager Tradition are the expanding-based drills

(Shippee 1964: Figure 5, G), digging tools, Sedalia Diggers (Shippee 1964: Figure 7 B–D), three-quarter-grooved axes (Shippee 1964: Figure 8, 9A), celts (Shippee 1964: Figure 9 B–E), shaped manos, pestles, and hammerstones (Shippee 1964: Figure 10)(Figure 8–12). Thus, the conclusion has been drawn that the Nebo Hill aggregate is closely related to the Sedalia complex, perhaps as its progenitor, and may have been contemporaneous with it during the early part of the Late Archaic period.

The most prominent and widespread Late Archaic occupation of the Northwest Prairie Region consisted of Foragers producing the Sedalia complex (Seelen 1961). The complex was proposed on the basis of collections from several sites within a 10–20 mile radius of Sedalia in Pettis County, Missouri. The largest collections came from Site 23PE1, and typical artifacts collected there by Harry L. and Florence Collins are illustrated in Figures 8–13 through 8–15. They are Sedalia Lanceolate, Smith Basal Notched, Stone Square Stemmed, Clear Fork Gouges, drills, and Sedalia Diggers. The complex was equated with the Nebo Hill aggregate in the Northwest Prairie Region by Seelen (1961), and Early Archaic period was suggested for its appearance. In an early compilation on Missouri archaeology the complex was called "Nebo Hill" (Chapman 1948b: 138–40), but the artifacts illustrated were from sites of the Sedalia complex.

Another site in the same general area has been collected on by one individual for many years and has yielded 3,406 items (Turner 1965: 1–10). In this instance the specimens were found on what appeared to be a definite occupation area described as two wide parallel strips on either side and around one end of a field. A greasy black substance ran through the strips. These strips were probably sites of houses or used for food preparation. Evidences of the people producing the Sedalia complex are often found just over the crown of the slope on high ridges. Characteristic

Figure 8–12. Tools similar to the Sedalia complex from the Nebo Hill site (J. M. Shippee Collection). Scale 2:3.
A–B, Nebo Hill Lanceolate; C, Nebo Hill Lanceolate similar to Sedalia Lanceolate in shape; D, shaped mano; E, chert hammerstone; F, digging tool; G, three-quarter-grooved ax; H, flat celt.

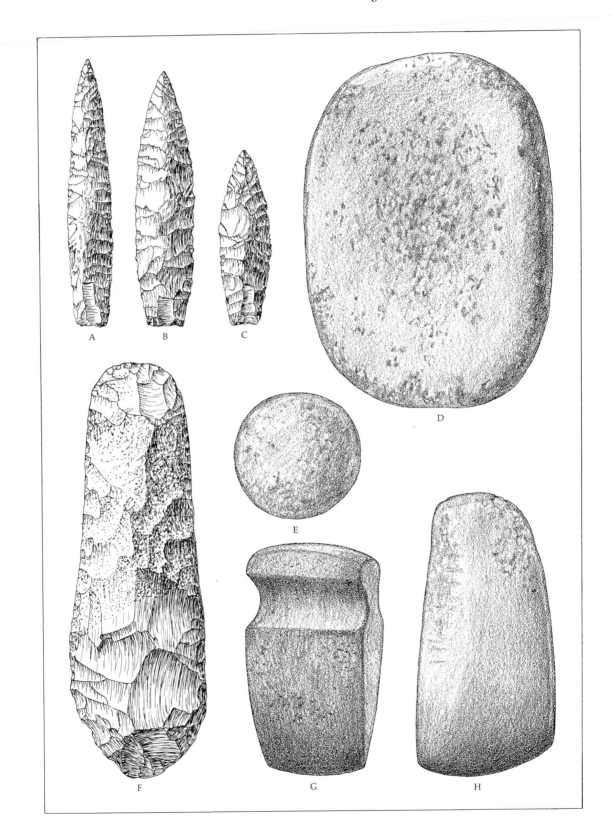

A

B

C

D

tools were Sedalia Lanceolate (Figure 8–13A) of which more than 200 specimens were found on the site. There were 31 examples of Etley Stemmed and 13 others that were similar to Etley Stemmed except that they lacked the prominent shoulders and barbs, 12 Stone Square Stemmed, 5 Smith Basal Notched, and a variety of other forms, including Langtry, Gary (Bell 1958: 28, 38), and corner notched. A single specimen of Afton Corner Notched, a serrated Graham Cave Notched, and a small triangular arrowhead may signify that the area around the site had been hunted upon by Indians in both earlier and later periods.

The most numerous items were hundreds of Clear Fork Gouges (Figure 8–15C–D) and Sedalia Diggers (Figure 8–15A–B). There were 73 drills made by reworking knives, many of which were Sedalia Lanceolate (Figure 8–13D), Stone Square Stemmed, and Smith Basal Notched (Figure 8–14C). A bannerstone, 2 three-quarter-grooved axes, 1 full-grooved ax, and 7 fragments of axes indicated that pecked- and ground-stone objects were being made. There were 33 pebble manos and 84 shaped manos. Choppers and hammerstones were very numerous. Four typical Nebo Hill Lanceolate came from the site, perhaps indicating contemporaneity of or a genetic relationship between the Nebo Hill complex and the Sedalia complex (Turner 1965).

Excavations have been made on several Sedalia complex sites through the auspices of the Hamilton Archaeological Field School, Lyman Archaeological Research Center, Department of Anthropology at the University of Missouri—Columbia, and the University of Pennsylvania under the direction of Kerry McGrath, who was using the information as the basis for her doctoral dissertation at the University of Pennsylvania. The Grimes site, where one of the excavations was conducted, supplied an assemblage of tools very similar to those reported for the Sedalia complex.

Northeast Prairie Region

An important site of the Sedalia complex and phase is the Geiger site (Figure 8–16), which lies in the Lower Missouri Valley II Locality (Keller 1961a). It was placed on the National Register of Historic Places because it was representative of the Sedalia complex. There were six definite black stains that delineated areas that were utilized; artifacts were concentrated in and around the stains (Figure 8–17).

A large collection had been gathered there by Judge S. P. Dalton and was available for study. A total of 3,636 artifacts was collected, 1,608 of which were Clear Fork Gouges and Sedalia Diggers and 521 were projectile point or knife forms. Etley Stemmed, Stone Square Stemmed, and notched varieties numbered 401, and 120 were Sedalia Lanceolate.

The excavation, 12 feet by 25 feet in one of the stained areas, was conducted in 1960 (Keller 1961a; 1961b) (Figure 8–17). No post holes or any other evidence of a house structure were produced. The only feature, on the extreme western edge of the black area, was an old pit 36 inches long, 30 inches wide, and 6½ inches deep, covered with slabs of limestone. The pit contained a secondary human burial, which consisted of a portion of a skull, a scapula fragment, an ulna, two humeri, two broken femora, three rib fragments, two pelvis fragments, and six vertebrae. There were no artifacts associated with the burial.

Keller (1961b) concluded that the stain represented an occupation area but was not able to determine its nature. Typical artifacts found in the excavation are shown in Figure 8–18. The Geiger assemblage was closely related to assemblages of other sites in Boone, Morgan, and Cooper counties.

A collection from the surface of the Pauling site in Howard County is typical of the Sedalia complex. The basic tools consist of large knives

---

Figure 8–13. Typical chipped-stone artifacts from the Sedalia complex (Mrs. Harry L. Collins Collection). Scale 7:9.
A, Sedalia Lanceolate; B, Stone Square Stemmed; C, Clear Fork Gouge; D, drill reworked from Sedalia Lanceolate.

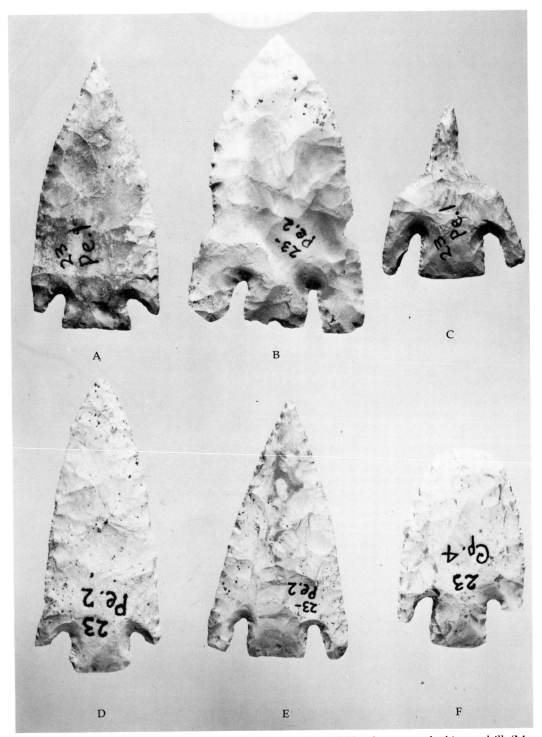

Figure 8–14.   Smith Basal Notched from the Sedalia complex. "C" has been reworked into a drill. (Mrs. Harry L. Collins Collection). Scale 3:4.

Figure 8–15.   Diggers and adzes from the Sedalia complex (Mrs. Harry L. Collins Collection). Scale 5:8.
A–B, Sedalia Diggers; C–D, Clear Fork Gouges.

Figure 8–16.   View of the Geiger site.

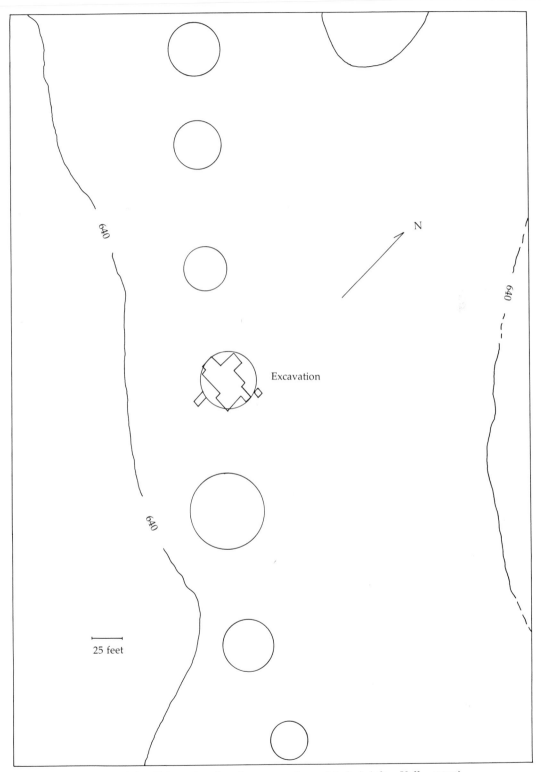

Figure 8–17.   Map of the Geiger site showing areas of use (circles) (after Keller 1951).

Figure 8–18. Artifacts from the excavations at the Geiger site. Scale 5:8.
A, Stone Square Stemmed; B, Etley Stemmed; C, Sedalia Lanceolate; D, drill made from Sedalia Lanceolate; E–F, Clear Fork Gouges; G–H, Sedalia Diggers.

Figure 8–19. Knives, daggers, or spear points from the Sedalia complex at the Pauling site (George Nichols Collection). Scale 3:4.

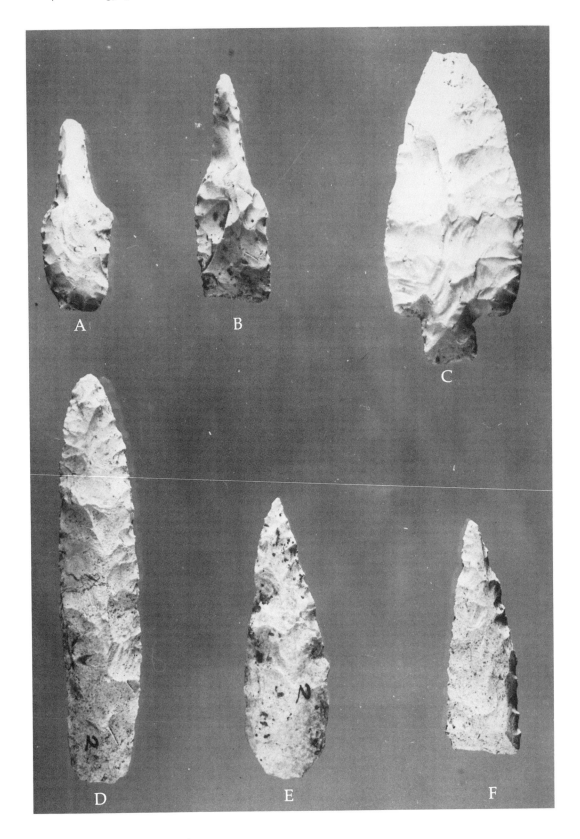

or daggers, drilling and cutting implements, digging and woodworking or pulping tools, and grinders (Figures 8–19 through 8–22). Site 23BO76 in Boone County also has been identified as Sedalia complex.

Klippel (1967; 1968; 1969) gave a very good review of the Late Archaic period in northeastern Missouri in his reports on the Booth site, and the following information is derived mainly from his description of the materials and their relationships to those of other sites. The Booth site is located along the south fork of the Salt River in the Cannon Reservoir area in Monroe County, Missouri, in the Salt Locality. The excavation of the site is the most extensive and intensive investigation of any single site from the Late Archaic period in Missouri.

A single group of people probably used the Booth site as a base of operations for collecting and processing vegetal materials. According to Klippel (1969) the site was frequented primarily during the summer, and there was no evidence that hunting was an important activity. The assemblage was made up wholly of stone materials, and the chipped items were most outstanding.

The diagnostic tool in the assemblage was Etley Stemmed, which made up 28 per cent of the artifacts. Other important items in the Booth assemblage were Stone Square Stemmed, Sedalia Lanceolate, drills or drill-like implements, Sedalia Diggers (Figure 8–23), Clear Fork Gouges, flakes with retouching, rubbed hematite, three-quarter-grooved axes, pitted anvilstones, manos (Figure 8–24), and metates.

The Burial Site 23LN11 in Lincoln County, Missouri, in the Cuivre Locality was reported on by Bacon and Miller (1957), but they did not discuss the placement of this specially used site in its relationship to other assemblages. The site consisted of a hilltop cemetery containing approximately 40 bundle burials and grave goods consisting of Etley Stemmed, Stone Square Stemmed, Red Ochre Lanceolate, dart points, Sedalia Lanceolate, and full- and three-quarter-

grooved axes (Figures 8–25 through 8–27). The associated artifacts were usually found beneath a bundle of bones that consisted primarily of long bones and the skull. Limestone rock slabs associated with the burials, sometimes separating them from other burials, were placed above them.

The Lincoln County site differed from others discussed previously because its use was only for the disposal of the dead and the ceremony associated with this activity. The fact that Etley Stemmed, Stone Square Stemmed, and Sedalia Lanceolate (Figures 8–25, 8–26) were found with the burials suggests a relationship to the Booth assemblage. Three dart points also found at the site were quite different (Figure 8–25F–H), but only one, a side-notched variety (Figure 8–25H), was associated with one of the burials. Two of the dart points were made of a different color stone and were not in association with the burials. Bacon and Miller (1957: 24) suggested that they were intrusive. Most of the chipped-stone artifacts associated with the burials were Red Ochre Lanceolate (Figures 8–25D–E; 8–26E–F).

It is proposed that the assemblage at the Cuivre River burial site is a ceremonial component of the Forager Tradition of the Late Archaic period in the Cuivre Locality.

A bannerstone from the Cuivre Locality should be related to the use of the area during the Late Archaic period along with engraved limestone plaques (Figure 8–28).

Another Cuivre ceremonial component is the Hatton mound (Henning 1962: 129–61), where burial offerings were a large specialized Etley Stemmed, Sedalialike lanceolate (Figure 8–29), drills, a gorget, hematite, galena, corner-notched projectile points, a snubbed-end flake scraper, choppers, chert-core hammerstones, manos, anvilstones, a calcite pendant, a beaver-incisor knife, antler tapping tools, antler flaking tools, a bone flesher, bone punches, bone awls, modified raccoon jaws, a tubular-bone bead, and fragments of copper. The burials of infants and adolescents in a rock and earth mound structure

Figure 8–20. Drilling and cutting implements from the Sedalia complex at the Pauling site (George Nichols Collection). Scale 3:4.
A–B, Drilling tools; C–F, cutting implements.

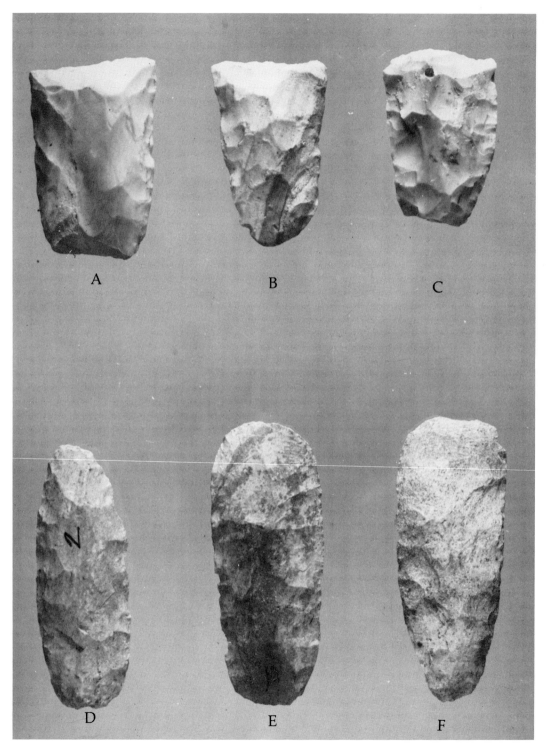

Figure 8–21. Digging and woodworking tools from the Sedalia complex at the Pauling site (George Nichols Collection). Scale 2:3.
A–C, Clear Fork Gouges; D–F, Sedalia Diggers.

Figure 8–22.   Shaped mano from the Sedalia complex at the Pauling site (George Nichols Collection). Scale 1:1.

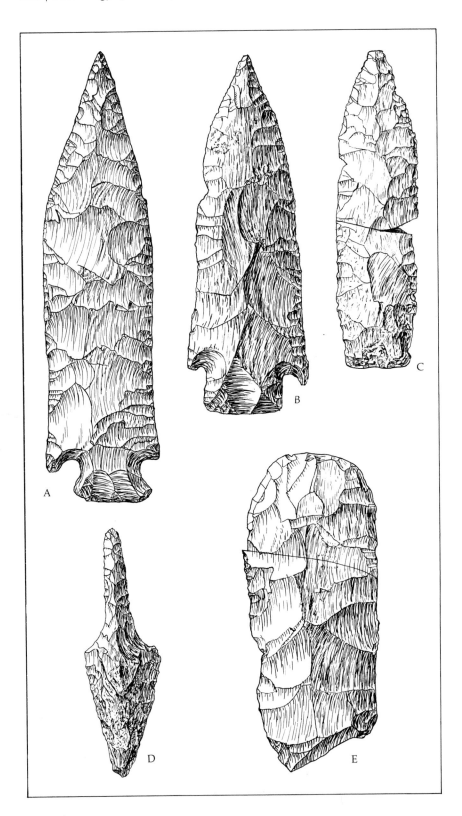

A

B

C

D

E

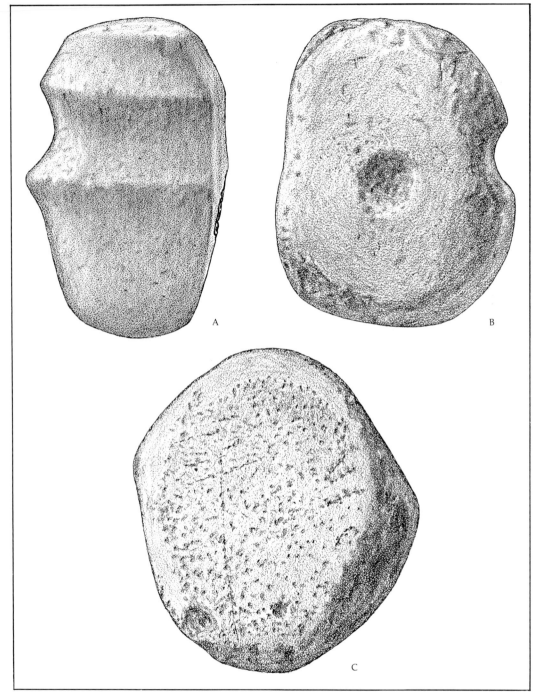

Figure 8–24. Tools from the Booth assemblage. Scale 7:9.
A, Three-quarter-grooved ax; B, pitted anvilstone; C, mano.

Figure 8–23. Typical chipped-stone tools from the Booth assemblage. Scale 4:5.
A, Etley Stemmed; B, Stone Square Stemmed; C, Sedalia Lanceolate; D, drill; E, Sedalia Digger.

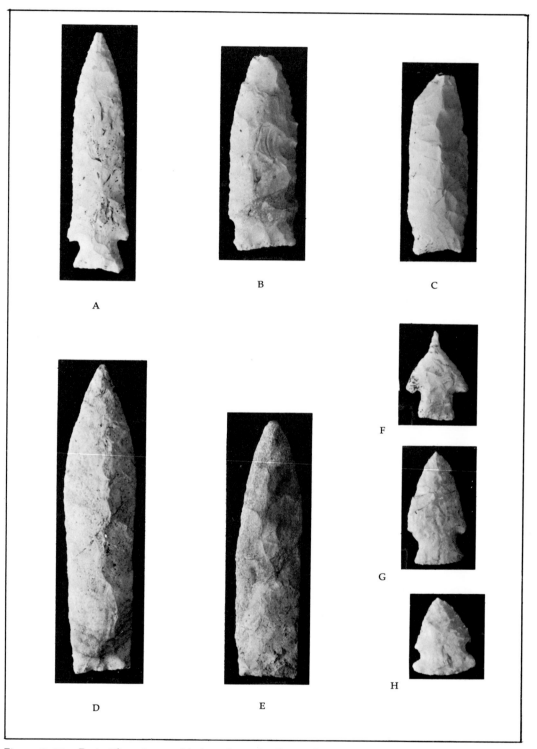

Figure 8–25. Projectile points and knives from the Cuivre River ceremonial component. Scale 1:2. A, Etley Stemmed; B–C, Stone Square Stemmed; D–E, Red Ochre Lanceolate; F–G, stemmed dart points; H, side-notched dart point.

were part of the component assemblage. The structure in which the burials were found was made up of chert cobbles and boulders, some weighing as much as 75 pounds. The burials had been placed in a shallow oval depression; they were flexed or bundled or consisted of piles of bones or scattered bone. Artifacts placed with the dead were in caches.

Red Ochre Lanceolate and Sedalialike lanceolate knives (Figure 8–30) have also been found on open campsites in the Northeast Prairie Region.

Southeast Riverine Region

Although bannerstones are found occasionally in most localities in Missouri, they tend to cluster in the Southeast Riverine Region and the Ozark Highland Region adjoining it. The various types of the ones that have been reported suggest that their form might have cultural or chronological-cultural significance. It is postulated that bannerstones are one of the markers of the Late Archaic period.

Two sites in the Bootheel Locality, Burkett and Weems, appear to have a nonpottery component that is characterized primarily by the large, thick, roughly flaked contracting-stemmed projectile points that have been called Burkett points (Chapman and Chapman 1964: 47). A similar type that is smaller continued to be used along with pottery in the same site. Clay balls, bannerstones, rectanguloid digging tools, trianguloid digging tools or axes, and reworked projectile point drills occurred as a part of the aggregate on the two sites. A Table Rock Stemmed projectile point was also present at Weems (Griffin and Spaulding 1951: 74; 1952: Figure 1A). Poverty Point clay balls were associated. Data from the two sites was not sufficient to name a Forager Tradition, Archaic period complex. A Late Archaic complex is no doubt in the region, but information is not sufficient to describe it or its manifestations with any certainty.

Regional Distribution of Evidences

The densest population in Missouri during the Late Archaic period appears to have been in the prairie regions of the central and northeastern sections and the riverine of the southeastern part of the state. The western regions may have had a very limited population, and the central Ozark Highland with its deep isolated valleys harbored Foragers who were still more dependent upon game than the groups who had fully adjusted to prairie and forest-edge foraging.

Southwest Drainage Region

Evidence of a complex similar to the James River complex in the White Locality is primarily found in the West and Southwest; hints of a similar complex appear as far as Texas (Crook and Harris 1952; Kelly 1947; Marshall 1963c; Ray 1934; 1938; 1948), where they may have derived from an earlier cultural base. There appears to be a discontinuous distribution of prairie–forest-edge adapted Foragers, for there is little evidence of them in the Ozark Highland Region. Perhaps this lack of evidence is due to the fact that few open campsites have been excavated there. The caves, which have received the most attention archaeologically, may not have been used by people of the Sedalia phase or James River complex. This seemed to be the case of the James River complex in the Southwest Drainage Region.

Western Prairie Region

The evidences of people in the region who were Foragers and which could possibly have been identified as from the Late Archaic period have been dated at a much later time (Calabrese, Pangborn, and Young 1968; Pangborn, Ward, and Wood 1967). Radiocarbon dates (Appendix I) indicate that the Foragers occupied the region as late as the Mississippi period. The reason that Late Archaic period sites have not been reported in the Western Prairie Region in Missouri may

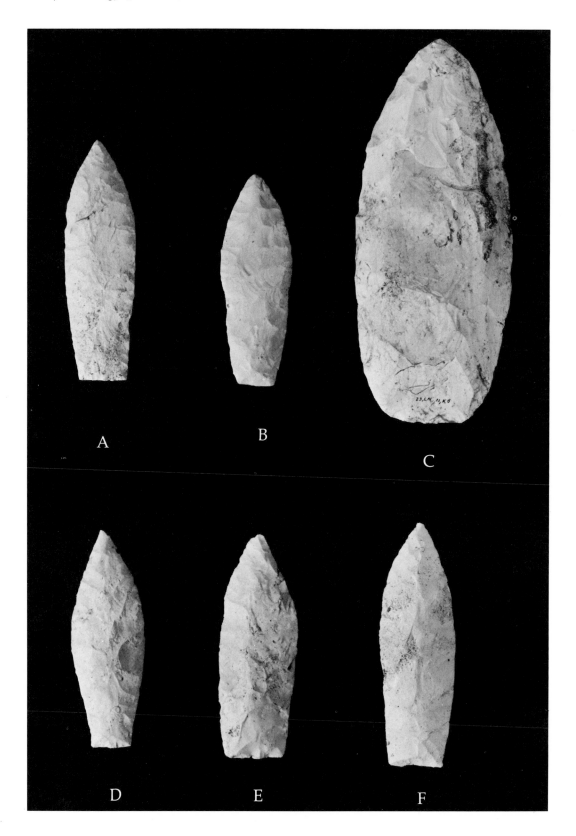

A

B

C

D

E

F

be due to the fact that they are deeply buried. Witty (1969) found Late Archaic Forager occupations, the Munkers Creek phase and another, in the Neosho River valley and the John Redmond Reservoir in Kansas. He had to dig 4–7 feet to reach the occupation levels. It is probable that similar early sites will be found in Missouri when more intensive archaeological investigations are made in terraces along the major streams.

Ozark Highland Region

There are evidences of use of the Ozarks by Foragers making distinctive Archaic period items in most localities but there has not been enough information to derive any complexes, components or aggregates. Late Archaic period artifacts were identified at Rodgers shelter in the Lower Osage Locality, in Tick Creek and Ramsey caves in the Gasconade Locality, and at Verkamp, Tonky West II and Stuesse shelters in the Meramec Locality. It is possible that the Middle Archaic period Foragers changed little but continued to live there through the Late Archaic period without much further adjustment to the region.

Northwest Prairie Region

The Sedalia complex centers in the Lamine Locality and is distributed to the east and north of that area in the Lower Missouri Valley II, Cuivre, and Salt localities. The complex appears to be closely related to the Nebo Hill aggregate in the Lower Missouri Valley I Locality, because Nebo Hill sites are primarily distributed in the Lower Missouri Valley I Locality in the Northwest Prairie Region (Shippee 1964: 24). To the west of the Missouri River, Wedel (1959) showed a few isolated projectile points or knives, but Strong (1935) reported no sites or materials from the Forager Tradition in the region.

Northeast Prairie Region

A secondary center of the Sedalia complex is in the upstream part of the Lower Missouri Valley II Locality. The complex is closely related to the Booth assemblage. Klippel (1968: 48–51)

identified the Booth assemblage as Late Archaic period and used Etley Stemmed as a diagnostic trait of the assemblage. In his comparative discussion, the Geiger site in the Lower Missouri Valley II Locality, the Etley site in Illinois, and other sites in Calhoun and Jersey counties, Illinois, in the Northeast Prairie Region were found to be very similar. The distribution of the assemblage was suggested on the basis of the occurrence of Etley Stemmed and Etleylike forms in St. Charles, Montgomery, Franklin, Lincoln, St. Louis, Osage, Pettis, Moniteau, and Monroe counties in Missouri, and Madison, Jersey, and Calhoun counties in Illinois. The assemblage is also found farther north in Grundy county and farther south in Iron county in Missouri. It overlaps with the Sedalia complex in both distribution and cultural content.

On the basis of Site 23LN11 in the Cuivre Locality and the Hatton site in the Salt Locality and their comparison with burial sites in the Titterington focus (Griffin 1968: 133), a distinct ceremonial complex of the Forager Tradition is proposed. The Cuivre River and Hatton ceremonial components appear to be related to the burial site at Marquette Park, Illinois (Titterington 1950: 20–22), where 21 Red Ochre Lanceolate were found with 2 burials. Another burial at the site, a multiple burial covered with limestone slabs, had with it 2 flint knives, 2 shell ornaments, 2 grooved axes, and a diorite ball.

The Etley site, Illinois (Titterington 1950: 22–24, Figures 2–4) was reported to consist of low mounds containing group burials; each group was made up of extended burials covered with red ochre and limestone slabs. Associated with the burials were 75 Red Ochre Lanceolate similar to those found at the Cuivre River ceremonial component, 13 Etley Stemmed, 25 grooved axes, 3 bannerstones, 3 copper celts, and a copper awl. There is a possibility that there could have been intrusive burials in the low mounds because no excavation data were presented. The Etley site has been included as a component of the Cuivre River ceremonial complex.

Figure 8–26. Chipped-stone artifacts from the Cuivre River ceremonial component. Scale 3:7. A–B, Sedalia Lanceolate; C, preform; D, Sedalia Lanceolate; E–F, Red Ochre Lanceolate.

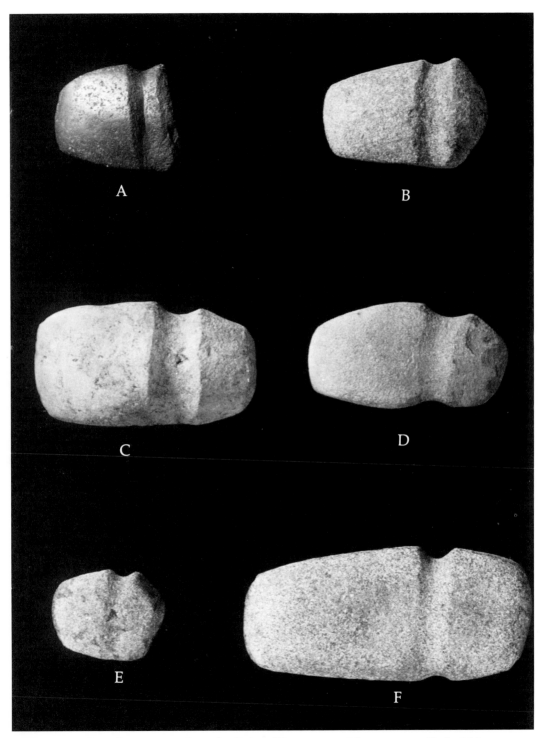

Figure 8–27.   Ground-stone axes from the Cuivre River ceremonial component. Scale 4:11.
A–C, Three-quarter-grooved axes; D, full-grooved axes; E, three-quarter-grooved ax; F, full-grooved
ax.

Figure 8–28. Possible Late Archaic period artifacts from the Cuivre Locality (Woolfolk and Taylor Collections). Scale 1:1.
A, Bannerstone; B–C, engraved limestone plaques.

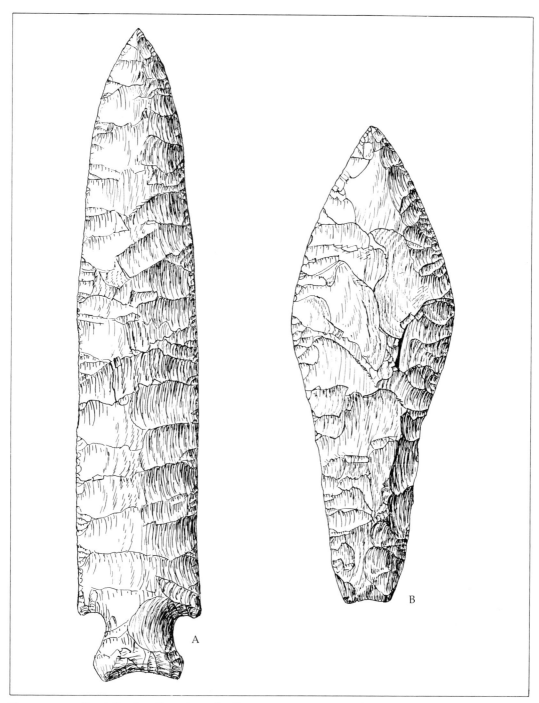

Figure 8–29.   Specialized artifacts from the Cuivre ceremonial component at Hatton Mound. Scale 5:6.
A, Variant of Etley Stemmed; B, Sedalialike lanceolate.

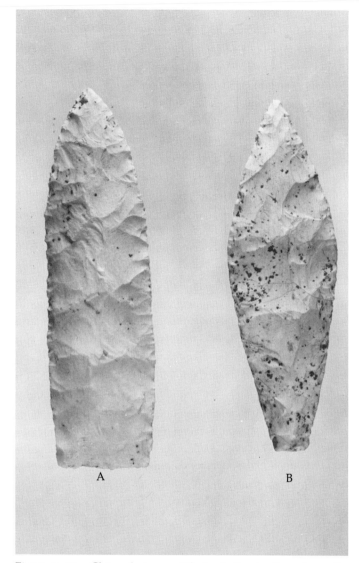

Figure 8–30. Chipped-stone artifacts similar to those from the Cuivre ceremonial components (J. A. Eichenberger Collection). Scale, A, 1:1; B 2:3.
A, Red Ochre Lanceolate; B, Sedalialike lanceolate.

The Gronefeld site near St. Charles, Missouri, covered an area 18 feet in diameter, and among the materials found there were 3 grooved axes, 49 chipped-stone forms, most of which were Red Ochre Lanceolate, and Etley Stemmed. Some of the artifacts could be related to the Cuivre River ceremonial complex. Along with these was a flare-bitted celt or spudlike object, a bow-tie bannerstone, a St. Charles Notched, and a Snyders Notched that had been reworked into a scraper. Just a few feet away from the burial were refuse pits containing grit-tempered and cord-impressed pottery of the Woodland period. It is suspected that some of the materials recovered in the burial area may also have been mixed with refuse from a Woodland period village and perhaps with an earlier component represented by the St. Charles Notched. It is possible that the grooved axes, Etley Stemmed, and Red Ochre Lanceolate were part of a ceremonial component related to the Cuivre River ceremonial complex.

Still another ceremonial component may be represented by the large side-notched Osceola form (Bell 1958: 68), rectangular gorgets, bow-tie and tabular bannerstones, stone beads, tubular pipe, plummets, and copper items in other burial sites in the St. Louis area (Titterington 1950).

The Sedalia complex and the Booth assemblage overlap and are similar enough to justify considering them as a unit. The term *Sedalia phase* is proposed to include the Sedalia complex and the Booth assemblage. It is further proposed that the Cuivre River ceremonial complex is an integral part of the Sedalia phase.

Horizon IV at the Koster site (Houart 1971: 48–49, Figure 10) contains a component which is described as representing one settlement type within a larger subsistence-settlement system. The component is tentatively placed within the Sedalia phase. Although there are several components in Illinois, there is no evidence that the Sedalia phase extended as far as the Wabash Valley (Winters 1967).

Southeast Riverine Region

The Forager Tradition and the Archaic period in the Southeast Riverine Region have been sadly neglected, partly because many of the Archaic period sites have been covered by later deposits. Perhaps the main reason has been the focus of attention on the spectacular later cultural developments in the area, such as the large Mississippian period townsites. In the Mississippi Valley Central Locality there was no separation of a Late Archaic complex accomplished by the excavations conducted by Adams (1941; 1949; 1953).

Potentially there is a Forager Tradition, Late Archaic period complex in the Bootheel Riverine Locality on the basis of surface collections. Sites of the Late Archaic period in the St. Francis Riverine Locality are being studied by the University of Michigan Powers phase project.

The Forager Tradition in the Late Archaic period offers a fertile field of research in southeastern Missouri and adjacent states.

Summary

Missouri holds a unique position in the Missouri–Mississippi Valley due to its central location in the North American Continent and the variety of physiographic regions that are encompassed within it or that border it. The major streams in central North America, the Missouri, Mississippi, and Ohio rivers, meet there. Broad physiographic areas, the Plains, Prairie Peninsula, woodlands, and southeastern alluvial lowlands, are adjacent or lap into Missouri. The Ozark Highland is a central store of minerals, clear-water springs and streams, and a variety of vegetation that could have been exploited by people who lived in adjacent physiographic provinces. The state was the crossroads where the overlapping of physiographic areas reached its greatest variety. It was a place where innovations in culture could develop through exposure to many different ecological niches and a place where new ideas could be exchanged through cultural contact.

Evidences are not conclusive but it is probable that America's earliest explorers during the Early Man period reached the lower Missouri–central Mississippi Valley, and by the Paleo-Indian period there was a concentration of Early Hunters near the junctions of the Missouri, Mississippi, and Ohio rivers, as evidenced by the numerous Clovis Fluted forms that have been found there. Settlement patterns were nomadic and seminomadic, and campsites were located primarily on the hilltops near the major stream valleys. Routes to the area were from the south following the major trench of the Mississippi River and perhaps secondarily from the Southwest across Texas, Oklahoma, and Kansas.

Little is known of the life of the Early Hunters because not one of their campsites containing undisturbed deposits has as yet been sufficiently excavated in Missouri. Only one site has yielded an aggregate of tools and debris from its surface and minimal excavation that aids in comparing Missouri manifestations with sites occupied by Early Hunters in other parts of eastern North America, and it may be representative of the end of the period. Distributions of fluted forms, Clovis Fluted and Folsom Fluted, have been used for broad interpretations of the distribution and settlement pattern of the Early Hunters during the Paleo-Indian period. Such interpretations are questionable, for fluted forms were still being manufactured at the beginning of the Dalton period, and it is not absolutely certain just when the manufacturing technique was discontinued. Fluting was probably replaced by basal thinning in the Dalton period.

In the Dalton and Early Archaic periods in Missouri there was a great variety in projectile point and knife forms which can be placed in three series that may be interpreted as technological traditions. These are lanceolate, stemmed, and notched.

It is probable, at the time when there was not much variety in the Plano complex projectile point and knife types used by the killers of big game in the Plains and southwestern United States, that a larger variety of forms was in use by people with diversified food-getting habits in the lower Missouri–central Mississippi Valley area. Perhaps the addition of large-bladed specialized cutting tools to the artifact inventory during the waning phase of the Paleo-

Indian period was one reason for this. A sequence of large-bladed cutting tools appears to be represented during the Dalton period at the Modoc shelter in Illinois (Deuel 1957; Fowler 1957; 1959a; 1959b; Fowler, Winters, and Parmalee 1956) and Rodgers shelter (Ahler 1971; McMillan 1971; Wood and McMillan 1969) in southwestern Missouri. It also appears that the contracting-stemmed point at Jakie shelter (Marshall and Chapman 1960b) and the Rice site (Bray 1956), Rice Contracting Stemmed, is contemporaneous with Agate Basin Lanceolate, and the same may be true at Rodgers shelter in the Western Prairie Region. Hardin Barbed occurred at the Walter site, an Early Hunter or Hunter–Forager Tradition site. Furthermore, along the main stem of the Mississippi River it is striking that, based on evidence available, the contracting stemmed form is predominant over all other projectile point and knife forms by Late Archaic time. It is characteristic of the Faulkner site in southern Illinois (MacNeish 1948) and it is the primary type of the Poverty Point phase (Ford and Webb 1956: 69). It is the earliest form found at Hidden Valley shelter (Adams 1941; Chapman 1948: 140–41) where it was given the name *Hidden Valley Stemmed.* It has been found in Modoc shelter, Illinois, in lower levels identified as Hidden Valley type and noted as an early form (Fowler 1959: 36–37). It appears that the contracting-stemmed form was a prominent shape throughout the Archaic period. It changed in size from the early large variety of Hidden Valley Stemmed to the late small varieties, Gary and Langtry (Baerreis, Freeman, and Wright 1958; Suhm, Krieger, and Jelks 1954).

Judging from the functional study by Ahler (1971) the stemmed and lanceolate forms were used in great part for cutting, slicing, sawing or splitting, rather than for specialized projectile points. It seems probable that the large bladed specimens were knives, whereas many of the smaller specimens with small blades were projectile points. The reduction of size in the Forager Tradition projectile points and knives from Early Archaic to Late Archaic periods may represent a change in function. Functional studies of series of the lanceolate, stemmed, and corner-notched

forms should confirm or invalidate the hypothesis.

It is difficult to show relationships of the Forager complexes, assemblages, and aggregates in the Archaic period to those described elsewhere. The Forager Tradition extends east along the tributaries of the Mississippi River to their headwaters, but relationships are general rather than specific. During the Early Archaic period the Forager Tradition in Missouri is comparable to some extent to the assemblages in Modoc shelter (Deuel 1957; Fowler 1959a; 1959b; Fowler, Winters, and Parmalee 1956). Another extension of the Early Archaic Forager Tradition appears to be into Arkansas and Oklahoma from the Southwest Drainage and Western Prairie regions (Baerreis 1951; Morse 1971; Wood 1962).

During the Middle and Late Archaic periods the Forager Tradition is represented by a number of aggregates, assemblages, complexes and phases in Missouri. These in turn are found in adjacent states where there is a continuation of the physiographic provinces.

Only an inkling of the life of the Hunter–Foragers of the Dalton period is available. The period was hypothetically a transition from Early Hunter to Forager Tradition. The cultural manifestations were theoretically a mixture of hunting and foraging subsistence patterns. Although the nomadic and seminomadic patterns of settlement continued in most regions during the period, the pattern in the Southeast Riverine Region may have evolved into a more stable form with the use of permanent base camps similar to those in Northeast Arkansas (Morse 1972; Morse and Goodyear 1973). Near the end of the Dalton period, probably because of a general change in the climate from cold and wet to milder temperatures and drier, the greatest emphasis of subsistence activities had begun to shift from hunting to gathering. Hunting of deer was still important in some regions, but methods were more efficient and a variety of smaller animals, such as squirrels and turtles, were hunted or trapped. Vegetal foods, seeds, nuts, and roots became a much more valued part of the diet of the people. Shellfish and fish may have been important fare. During the Archaic period the foraging subsistence base shifted in emphasis with climatic fluctuations and their effects on the plant and animal life in the various localities and regions in Missouri.

In general, during the Early Archaic period, subsistence activities were still more heavily weighted toward hunting than gathering. In the Middle Archaic period hunting was still important. There was a definite shift in favor of gathering plant foods by the beginning of the Late Archaic period. This generalization does not hold true for all of the physiographic regions of the state, as the Southwest Drainage, Ozark Highland, and Western Prairie regions retained a dominant hunting subsistence pattern throughout the Archaic period and continued into later periods. Although the Forager Tradition pattern was in general much the same, emphasis on different food procurement activities differed from one region to another.

The cultural materials tend to support the hypothesis that the effect of the drying out of the Plains reached the Foragers in the Northwest Prairie Region first. The late-surviving Plano complex of the Plains area to the west could have reached the prairies in the Early Archaic period. The Nebo Hill aggregate, which has elements of the Plainview, Angostura, Eden, and other types of Plano forms, seems to be the earliest of the prairie complexes in the Lower Missouri Valley I Locality. It may have begun some time in the Early Archaic, continued through Middle Archaic, and declined in the Late Archaic period. There are not as many digging tools and very few pulping planes or Clear Fork Gouges in the Nebo Hill aggregate. South and east of the Nebo Hill range and overlapping with it is the Sedalia phase made up of the Sedalia complex, the Booth assemblage, and the Cuivre ceremonial complex. The Sedalia phase could have derived from Nebo Hill or might represent a gradual movement eastward of prairie-adapted tool kits as the prairies continued to encroach on the woodlands in central and eastern Missouri. The adzes or pulping planes and digging tools were the predominant tools of the Sedalia phase rivaled only by the large daggerlike Sedalia Lanceolate, Etley Stemmed, and Stone Square Stemmed. Grinding

stones were also important items. These were tools adapted to foraging rather than hunting.

If the prairies were gradually moving eastward or the woodland retreating to the east, the culture adapted to prairie living could have moved east with the prairie. In turn the culture adapted to woodland might also have moved to the east, keeping within the bounds of woodland environment. The result would be that the woodland-adapted culture, in which the heat-treating technique was a step in the manufacture of chipped-stone tools in the Middle Archaic period, would not have been passed on to the prairie-adapted culture, which had a stone technology that did not include heat treating. The latter filled in the regions abandoned by the Middle Archaic Forager Tradition. The wetter period following the Late Archaic period then may have aided in reforestation, and those cultures in the eastern Woodland with cultural-genetic relationships to the Middle Archaic Foragers that included heat treating began to fill in the old areas in the Early Woodland period as they became forested and were abandoned by the prairie-adapted cultures, which in turn moved westward. The evidence for no heat treating in Early Archaic to heat treating in Middle Archaic, back to little or no heat treating in the Late Archaic and then again to heat treating in the Early Woodland, could thus be explained by cultures' differing in their stoneworking technology, moving in and out of the area in response to climatic changes. In any instance it is a hypothesis which can be tested by a study and comparison of stoneworking technologies in the local and regional sequences.

There was variety in adaptations in different regions. Hunting was important in some and unimportant in others. Vegetable resources had become very important to most Foragers toward the end of the Archaic period.

The greatest change occurred in the Late Archaic period in the prairie regions as demonstrated by the larger size of base camps, the great amount of stone that had been brought to them, and the specialized tools that were manufactured. The prairie Foragers consistently settled on ridges or hilltops. There was limited use of dart points, indicating that little time was devoted to hunting. For the most part, except in special hunting camps such as caves, there is little evidence of animal bones. Probably as a result of the deemphasis on hunting, there was little or no bone-working industry. Much stress was placed on ceremony in connection with the burial of the dead, as evidenced by specially constructed cemeteries, use of red ochre to cover the bones, and the inclusion in the graves of tools and ornaments made of exotic materials such as copper. According to Winters (1968) extensive trade networks may have developed during the period to replenish supplies of exotic materials.

The Archaic period had been one of experimentation in the use of numerous possibilities in the environment. It was a period of slow change and adaptation to local and regional environments. Experiments in utilizing plant foods had broadened the Foragers' diet. Perhaps observations were made that seed that had been buried in trash heaps produced new plants. Trials at planting seeds for ceremonial purposes and observations of plant life cycles must have prepared the way for the acceptance and utilization of cultivated plants when they were introduced to the area from the south in later periods. By the end of the Archaic period the Foragers had become adept at exploiting their local environment and were able to select the most desirable resources according to the group's preferences. Preference and specialization dominated their subsistence activities but did not prevent rescheduling of activities to use less desirable things in the environment in time of need.

Charts showing the chronological sequences of cultural developments in each region follow.

Chronological Sequence, Southwest Drainage Region

Cultural Evidence by Locality

Period	Date	Current–Eleven Point	White	Neosho
Historic				
Mississippi	A.D. 1700			
Woodland	A.D. 900			
Late Archaic	1000 B.C.	No data	James River complex	Smith Basal Notched, Afton Corner Notched from the surface of sites
Middle Archaic	3000 B.C.	No data	White River complex	Projectile or knife forms from the surface of sites and Big Sandy Notched from Orwood and Ash shelters
Early Archaic	5000 B.C.	Rice complex (?)	Rice complex	Scattered projectile points and knives of possible Early Archaic components
Dalton	7000 B.C.	Scattered Dalton Serrated	Scattered Dalton Serrated, possible mixture of Dalton occupations from Dalton and Early Archaic in some shelters	Scattered Dalton Serrated from the surface of a few sites
Paleo-Indian	8000 B.C.	Scattered Clovis Fluted	Scattered Clovis Fluted and Clovis Fluted from possible Paleo-Indian campsite on James River at mouth of Aunts Creek	One Folsom Fluted
Early Man	12,000 B.C. ?	No data		

Chronological Sequence, Western Prairie Region

Cultural Evidence by Locality

Period	Date	Upper Osage
Historic	A.D. 1700	
Mississippi		Nonceramic assemblages on Dryocopus and Flycatcher Village sites
	A.D. 900	
Woodland		
	1000 B.C.	
Late Archaic		Possible Forager component in Harrison shelter based on occurrence of Table Rock Stemmed and Afton Corner Notched points and in Cat Hollow shelter based on occurrence of Smith Basal Notched and Table Rock Stemmed, Munkers Creek phase, and John Redmond Reservoir manifestation, Kansas
	3000 B.C.	
Middle Archaic		Surface collections and tolls probably from the Middle Archaic in proper sequence in Brounlee and Woody shelters
	5000 B.C.	
Early Archaic		No data
	7000 B.C.	
Dalton		Possible use of Shelter 23BE108
	8000 B.C.	
Paleo-Indian		Only a few Clovis Fluted and Folsom Fluted
	12,000 B.C.	
Early Man	?	No data

Chronological Sequence, Ozark Highland Region

Cultural Evidence by Locality

Period	Date	Lower Osage	Gasconade	Meramec	Upper Black–St. Francis	Castor–Whitewater
Historic						
Mississippi	A.D. 1700					
Woodland	A.D. 900					
Late Archaic	1000 B.C.	Forager aggregate, Stratum 4, Rodgers shelter	Late Archaic at Tick Creek Cave probably includes a component that has Stone Square Stemmed, Afton Corner Notched, Table Rock Stemmed and Smith Basal Notched, bannerstones, and gorgets as distinctive items	Possible Late Archaic aggregate including Smith Basal Notched, Table Rock Stemmed, Agate Basin Lanceolate, Big Sandy Notched, and flake scrapers	No data	No data
Middle Archaic	3000 B.C.	Forager assemblage, Stratum 2, Rodgers shelter	Part of Tick Creek complex (?)	No data	No data	No data
Early Archaic	5000 B.C.	Upper part, Stratum 1, Rodgers shelter	Tick Creek "Complex"	Verkamp "Complex A"(?)	Questionable evidence Dalton Serrated and Rice Lanceolate	No data
Dalton	7000 B.C.	Earliest aggregate, Rodgers shelter, lower part of Stratum 1	Scattering of Dalton Serrated	Dalton Serrated present	Cache of Dalton Serrated	No data
Paleo-Indian	8000 B.C.	Earliest component, Rodgers shelter, Plainview point	No data	Clovis Fluted relatively numerous	No data	No data
Early Man	12,000 B.C. ?	Possible artifact associations with mastodon bones	No data	No data	No data	No data

Chronological Sequence, Northwest Prairie Region

Cultural Evidence by Locality

Period	Date	Lamine	Tarkio	Nodaway	Platte	Grand	Chariton	Lower Missouri Valley I
Historic	A.D. 1700							
Mississippi	A.D. 900							
Woodland	1000 B.C.							
Late Archaic		Sedalia phase	No data	No data	No data	No data	No data	Nebo Hill aggregate (?), Sedalia phase
Middle Archaic	3000 B.C. 5000 B.C.	No data	No data	No data	No data	No data	No data	Nebo Hill aggregate (?)
Early Archaic	7000 B.C.	No data	No data	No data	No data	No data	No data	Nebo Hill aggregate (?)
Dalton	8000 B.C.	Collateral flaked Planolike forms	No data	No data	No data	No data	No data	Planolike and Dalton Serrated
Paleo-Indian	12,000 B.C.	No data	No data	No data	No data	No data	No data	Several Clovis Fluted
Early Man	?	No data	Grundel mastodon	No data				Flake tool with Miami mastodon

Chronological Sequence, Northeast Prairie Region

Cultural Evidence by Locality

Period	Date	Lower Missouri Valley II	Greater St. Louis	Cuivre	Salt	Wyaconda–Fabius	Des Moines	Mississippi Valley North
Historic	A.D. 1700							
Mississippi	A.D. 900							
Woodland	1000 B.C.							
Late Archaic		Geiger assemblage of Sedalia complex, Sedalia phase; Gronefeld component, Cuivre ceremonial complex, Sedalia phase	No data	Cuivre component, Cuivre ceremonial complex, Sedalia phase	Booth assemblage and Hatton Mound ceremonial component of Cuivre complex of Sedalia phase	No data	No data	No data
Middle Archaic	3000 B.C.	Graham Cave, middle assemblage; Arnold Research Cave, Forager aggregate	No data	No data	Site 23MN290 Big Sandy Notched from surface of other sites	No data	No data	No data
Early Archaic	5000 B.C.	Arnold Research Cave, Early Forager assemblage; Dalton site assemblage; Graham Cave, Early Forager assemblage	No data	No data	No data	No data	No data	Hannibal "complex" (?)
Dalton	7000 B.C.	Graham Cave, Hunter–Forager component; Arnold Research Cave, Hunter–Forager component, Sims aggregate, Walter site aggregate	Dalton Serrated	No data	No data	No data	No data	Dalton Serrated
Paleo-Indian	8000 B.C.	Greatest concentration consists of Clovis Fluted, a few Folsom Fluted, Walter site aggregate		Clovis and Folsom Fluted present	Clovis Fluted present	Clovis Fluted present	No data	Several Clovis Fluted
Early Man	12,000 B.C. ?	No data						

Chronological Sequence, Southeast Riverine Region

Cultural Evidence by Locality

Period	Date	Mississippi Valley Central	St. Francis Riverine	Bootheel Riverine
Historic	A.D. 1700			
Mississippi	A.D. 900			
Woodland	1000 B.C.			
Late Archaic		bannerstones	bannerstones	Archaic components on Burkett and Weems sites
Middle Archaic	3000 B.C.	Hidden Valley Aggregate II; Layer 2, Bonacker shelter	Aggregate on Site 23S0138 (?)	Full-grooved axes and Big Sandy Notched
Early Archaic	5000 B.C.	Hidden Valley Aggregate I	Aggregate on Site 23S0136 containing Dalton Serrated and Hardin Barbed	No data
Dalton	7000 B.C.	Dalton Serrated and Graham Cave Fluted	Dalton Serrated	Dalton Serrated and Planolike form
Paleo-Indian	8000 B.C.	Several Clovis Fluted at Kimmswick site, possibly the earliest occupation Modoc shelter, Illinois	A few Clovis Fluted	A few Clovis Fluted
Early Man	12,000 B.C. ?	Possible artifact associations with mastodon bones at the Kimmswick site	No data	No data

Appendix I: Radiocarbon Dates

Only a few radiocarbon dates have been obtained on the early periods in Missouri, but there are enough from excavations to use as reliable estimates for establishing a chronological framework. The dates that have been recorded are listed here according to major time periods and by locality, region, radiocarbon laboratory number and the source of the information. All dates that were not originally reported as B.C. have been converted by subtracting 1950 from the before-present date; otherwise dates have not been adjusted unless the adjustment was done prior to the time they were reported. The name of the site and the reference to the source of the date are included as well as comments at the end of each group of dates.

Early Man Period

Lower Osage Locality, Ozark Highland Region

I-3922 Boney Spring, 14,630±220 B.C. (Buckley and Willis 1970: 90).

I-3535 4A Trolinger Bog, 18,550±450 B.C. (Buckley and Willis 1970: 89).

I-3536 4B Trolinger Bog, 15,300±600 B.C. (Buckley and Willis 1970: 89).

I-3537 4A-1 Trolinger Bog, 23,700±700 B.C. (Buckley and Willis 1970: 90).

I-3599 1A Trolinger Bog, 30,250±1900 B.C. (Buckley and Willis 1970: 90).

These samples probably have no association with the flakes and artifacts found in the bogs, but they are associated with mastodon (*Mammut*

americanum) and the possibility exists that some of the associated items were made by Hunter–Gatherer Tradition people.

Tarkio Locality, Northwest Prairie Region

I-1559 Grundel Mastodon site, 23,150±2200 B.C. (Buckley and Willis 1969: 77).

Mehl (1966) proposed that the mastodon had been butchered but no artifacts were found.

Paleo-Indian Period

Lower Osage Locality, Ozark Highland Region

ISGS-48 Rodgers shelter, 8530±650 B.C. (Coleman 1972: 154; McMillan 1971: 81).

M-2333 Rodgers shelter, 8250±330 B.C. (Crane and Griffin 1972a: 159).

Both of these dates range from the latter part of the Paleo-Indian period to the early part of the Dalton period. The cultural materials associated with the radiocarbon samples were not wholly distinctive of either the Early Hunter or the Hunter–Forager traditions. The majority appeared to be Hunter–Forager, but one point was fluted and another was a Plano form indicating that the occupation represented by the tool kits and the dates could be Paleo-Indian period and Early Hunter Tradition.

Mississippi Valley Central Locality, Southeast Riverine Region

C-907 Modoc shelter (Barbeau Creek rock shelter) Randolph County, Illinois, 8698±650 B.C. (Jelinek 1962: 457; Libby 1954: 736–37).

Dalton Period

Lower Missouri Valley II Locality, Northeast Prairie Region

M-130 Graham Cave, 7850±500 B.C. (Crane and Griffin 1956: 667; Chapman 1957: 47).

M-1889 Graham Cave, 7340±300 B.C. (Crane and Griffin 1968: 84).

M-1928 Graham Cave, 7530±400 B.C. (Crane and Griffin 1968: 85).

M-1497 Arnold Research Cave, 7180±300 B.C. (Crane and Griffin 1968: 69).

The earliest date, which ranges from 8350 to 7350 B.C., was recorded on material from the lowest level in Graham Cave. If the older date is taken, it could indicate that the cave was first occupied in the Paleo-Indian period. The character of the complex of artifacts from the earliest levels in both caves indicates that they are transitional between the Early Hunter and Forager traditions.

Mississippi Valley Central Locality, Southeast Riverine Region

C-908 Modoc shelter (Barbeau Creek rock shelter) Randolph County, Illinois, 7148±440 B.C. (Jelinek 1962: 457; Libby 1954: 736-37).

Fowler (1959a: 21) noted that the initial occupation of the shelter was primarily by a hunting people but that there were too few data for a definite analysis. Dalton Serrated, Graham Cave Notched, Hidden Valley Stemmed, what appears to be a Rice Lanceolate, snubbed-end flake scrapers, drills, choppers, and splinter bone awls were some of the items similar to those in the Dalton period in Missouri (Fowler 1959b: 258, Figures 1 and 2, table I). It was estimated that Zone I was occupied between 8000 and 6000 B.C.

Early Archaic Period

Lower Osage Locality, Central Ozark Highland Region

A-868A Rodgers shelter, 6150±300 B.C. (McMillan 1971: 81).

GaK-1170 Rodgers shelter, 6150±140 B.C. (McMillan 1971: 81).

M-1900 Rodgers shelter, 6080±300 B.C. (Crane and Griffin 1968: 84; McMillan 1971: 81).

These samples date the latter part of the Early Archaic period (Figure 4–8).

Lower Missouri Valley II Locality, Northeast Prairie Region

I-5217 Graham Cave, 5680±120 B.C. (Klippel 1971: 5).

I-5218 Graham Cave, 5660±140 B.C. (Klippel 1971: 65).

I-5219 Graham Cave, 5410±125 B.C. (Klippel 1971: 65).

I-5220 Graham Cave, 4850±120 B.C. (Klippel 1971: 65).

M-131 Graham Cave, 6880±500 B.C. (Crane and Griffin 1956: 666-67; Chapman 1957: 47).

M-132 Graham Cave, 5950±500 B.C. (Crane and Griffin 1956: 667; Chapman 1957: 47).

M-1495 Arnold Research Cave, 6170±350 B.C. (Crane and Griffin 1968: 69).

M-1496 Arnold Research Cave, 6240±400 B.C. (Crane and Griffin 1968: 69).

All dates are representative of the Early Archaic period occupation of the caves except I-5220, which was recorded at a lower depth than the others. Klippel says that this date must be 1,000 to 2,000 years later than it should be and must be incorrect. This is the period during which there was the most rapid deposition of wind blown soil in Graham Cave but we still do not know when it began (Klippel 1971: 66).

Mississippi Valley Central Locality, Southeast Riverine Region

C-903 Modoc shelter (Barbeau Creek rock shelter) Randolph County, Illinois. 6593±380 B.C. (Jelinek 1962: 457; Libby 1954: 736–37).

C-904 Modoc shelter (Barbeau Creek rock shelter) Randolph County, Illinois. 5847±900 B.C. (Jelinek 1962: 457; Libby 1954: 736–37).

Two other dates, (C-904 and C-905, Libby 1954: 736–37) have been considered unreliable by Fowler (1959a) and have not been included here. Hidden Valley Stemmed and Graham Cave

Notched were apparently important chipped stone artifacts in the zone estimated at 7000–5000 B.C. (Fowler 1959a: Table 5).

Middle Archaic Period

White Locality, Southwest Drainage Region

M-697, Jakie shelter, 5120±450 B.C. (Crane and Griffin 1960: 36–37).

M-698, Jakie shelter, 4330±400 B.C. (Crane and Griffin 1960: 36–37).

The Jakie shelter occupation from which the samples were obtained contained Forager Tradition Middle Archaic period artifacts from the White River complex.

Lower Osage Locality, Central Ozark Highland Region

ISGS-35, Rodgers shelter, 4350±590 B.C. (Coleman 1972: 153–54).

GaK-1171 Rodgers shelter 5060±160 B.C. (McMillan 1971: 81).

GaK-1172 Rodgers shelter 5540±170 B.C. (McMillan 1971: 81).

M-2281 Rodgers shelter, 3250±200 B.C. (Crane and Griffin 1972a: 159).

M-2332, Rodgers shelter, 3150±400 B.C. (Crane and Griffin 1972a: 159).

Rodgers shelter was occupied only sporadically during the period. This was perhaps due to the fact that it was not a desirable location at times when rapid deposition was taking place.

Lower Missouri Valley II Locality, Northeast Prairie Region

M-615, Arnold Research Cave, 4770±300 B.C. (Crane and Griffin 1960: 36).

M-616 Arnold Research Cave, 4230±300 B.C. and 3630±250 B.C. (Crane and Griffin 1960: 36).

M-617 Arnold Research Cave, 4550±300 B.C. (Crane and Griffin 1960: 36).

M-618A Arnold Research Cave, 4330±350 B.C. (Crane and Griffin 1960: 36).

Tool kits from this site that were used during the Early Archaic period apparently continued into the Middle Archaic period.

Mississippi Valley Central Locality, Southeast Riverine Region

C-899 Modoc shelter (Barbeau Creek rock shelter), Randolph County, Illinois 4002±235 B.C. (Jelinek 1962: 457; Libby 1954: 736–37).

C-900 Modoc shelter (Barbeau Creek rock shelter) Randolph County, Illinois. 3315±230 B.C. (Jelinek 1962: 457; Libby 1954: 736–37).

L-381-C Modoc rock shelter, Randolph County, Illinois, 5042±170 B.C. (Jelinek 1962: 457; Olson and Broecker 1959: 21).

Sample L-381-C comes from the 19–20 foot level in the shelter and should represent the beginning of the Middle Archaic period. Fowler (1959a) suggested that localized adaptation occurred during the early part of this period. Side-notched projectile points (Big Sandy Notched) predominated and a full-grooved ax was found at a depth of 19 feet, Zone II, interpreted to date about 5000 B.C. (Fowler 1959b: 262).

Late Archaic Period

Western Prairie Region (Kansas)

GaK-595 William Young Site 14MD304, 1, Morris County, Kansas, 1150 B.C.±400 (Kigoshi and Kobayashi 1966: 65).

GaK-596 William Young Site 14MD304, 2, Morris County, Kansas, 1450 B.C.±500 (Kigoshi and Kobayashi 1966: 65).

These dates are from the Munkers Creek phase at the William Young site (Witty 1969).

Lower Osage Locality, Central Ozark Highland Region

GXO-749, Blackwell Cave, 1150±80 B.C. (W.R. Wood 1970: Personal Communication).

Lamine Locality, Northwest Prairie Region

GaK-504 Helmerick shelter, Cooper County, 1260±90 B.C. (Kigoshi and Kobayashi 1966: 64).

These dates are possibly from the latter part of the Sedalia phase occupations.

Mississippi Valley Central Locality, Southeast Riverine Region

M-483 Modoc shelter, Randolph County, Illinois, 2763±300 B.C. (Crane and Griffin 1958: 1099; Jelinek 1962: 457).

M-484 Modoc shelter, Randolph County, Illinois, 3323±300 B.C. (Crane and Griffin 1958: 1099; Jelinek 1962: 457).

Fowler (1959b: 264; Fowler, Winters, and Parmalee 1956: 31) set the dates of Zone IV in Modoc shelter at 3325–2665 B.C. Fowler (1959a: 48) placed the occupation in the zone in a period of specialized adaptation, 3000–2000 B.C., which equates with the Late Archaic period.

Appendix II: Selected Types of Projectile Points and Knives from the Early Periods in Missouri

Although the functional terms *projectile point* and *knife* have been used throughout the book and in the title of this appendix, it is probable that they are misnomers in some instances. Only a few studies have been made to determine the function of the different forms and in one of them (Ahler 1971) the artifact shapes generally used as a major criterion in classification were not found to be necessarily indicative of their function. In view of these facts the use of the terms projectile point, point, and knife have been primarily to designate general types of forms rather than functional classes. Form has been substituted for them whenever possible.

The descriptions of the types have been compiled from both the published reports and unpublished manuscripts listed following each description. I have made some additions, deletions, and changes in the original descriptions. The format used is similar to that followed by Bell (1958; 1960a) in his *Guide to the Identification of Certain American Indian Projectile Points:*

Type Name: All names are binomial. A distinctive feature of shape has been added to type names, most of which have been proposed originally.

Derivation of Name: Most names have been derived from sites, towns, cities, counties, or archaeological cultures. A few have been applied on the basis of individual or landowner names.

Other Names or Similar Types: Occasionally several names have been proposed for types or for forms that have been identified as two or more types by others. The different names I have listed are not necessarily applied to forms that are exactly alike but to those that are similar or overlap.

Description: The form, flaking characteristics, and dimensions are described in most instances (Figure A-1). The measurements of various parts of the projectile point or knife are in centimeters or millimeters and have been rounded to the nearest half a unit.

Distribution: In this outline the main concern is the dispersion of the form in Missouri and nearby states. In some instances where there is good evidence more distant states have been included in the distribution.

Type Site: Usually the site listed is the one from which the type derived its name. Sometimes it is the site where the type was first identified with a period or a cultural tradition.

Age and Cultural Affiliation: The general period is listed for the time when the artifacts were used. Cultural tradition and subdivision are given if the information is available.

References: This list is the published or manuscript materials from which the data concerning the type were derived.

Illustrations: Figures in the text of this volume that illustrate examples of the type and the source of the accompanying illustration are noted here.

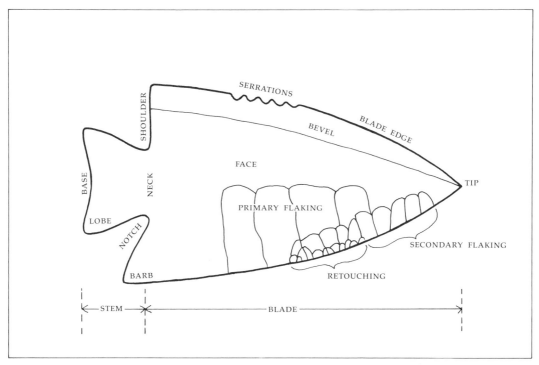

Figure A–1. Names of parts of projectile points and knives used in descriptions.

Afton Corner Notched

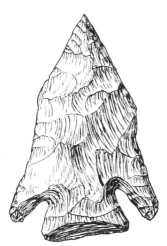

Figure A–2. Scale 1:1.

Derivation: It was named from specimens found in a spring near Afton, Oklahoma.

Other Names or Similar Types: Afton, Afton point.

Description: The type is a barbed corner-notched form with characteristic treatment of blade edges and a stem that flares to a convex or nearly straight base. The blade is typically divided into two sections; the part from the tip to the midsection is straight, incurvate, or excurvate. From the midsection to the barb it is usually incurvate. Large irregular flake scars are characteristic. Flakes were removed from both faces of the blade. The edges of the blade are evenly trimmed by removal of small flakes. Sixty per cent have angular edges or projections near the midpoint with concave blade edges from that point to the end of the barb. Forty per cent have straight to convex edges and lack the central protrusions. Length ranges from 4 cm to 10 cm and most examples are 5 cm–8.5 cm. Length is usually one and one-fourth to one and one-half the width but may be two times the width. Greatest width is at the shoulders or the barb tips and averages 3.5 cm. Barbs are small to prominent and are often pointed. Thickness is 5 mm to 8 mm. Notches are narrow and the stem is short in proportion to the blade length. Notches are usually at 45–60 degrees to the blade axis. The stem expands toward the base, which is convex or straight and often does not show secondary flaking.

Distribution: The type is found throughout Missouri and eastward to Ohio. It is also present in northeastern Oklahoma and northwestern Arkansas.

Type Site: Afton Spring, Ottawa County, Oklahoma.

Age and Cultural Distribution: Estimated dates are 3000 B.C.–A.D.1. The type is a trait in Blackwell Cave component B, the Holbert Bridge Mound in Missouri and Afton Spring, Oklahoma.

References: Bell 1958: 6, Plate 3; Bell and Hall 1953:7; Gregory and Towns 1966; Holmes 1903b; Wood 1961: 48–62, 88–90, Figures 13 and 15.

Illustrations: Figure 8–3. The specimen illustrated is from Jakie shelter, Missouri.

Agate Basin Lanceolate

Figure A–3.   Scale 1:1.

Derivation: It is named for Agate Basin, Colorado.

Other Names or Similar Types: Angostura, Guilford(?), Long, Oblique Yuma.

Description: It is a long, slender lanceolate form usually with a concave base, although occasionally the base may be straight or convex. Blade edges are convex with the widest part usually between the midpoint and the base. It narrows considerably toward the base. Primary flaking is relatively even and may be in part collateral producing flake scars that meet to form ribbon flaking across the blade. Fine secondary flake scars aid in producing the smooth appearance of many of the specimens. Length of the specimens vary from 5 cm to 13 cm, with a mean of 10 cm. Length is 2 to 4 times the width. The mean width is 3 cm. Thickness depends upon the quality of material used in the manufacture but is usually about 8mm. If the material was easily flaked, the cross section is lenticular and relatively thin in proportion to the width. Coe (1952) in describing Guilford, a similar form, noted that the width was two or three times that of the thickness and that the cross section was rounded and occasionally almost diamond shaped. The specimens from Missouri are much thinner. The edges near the base are usually ground to one-third or one-fourth of the total length. Heat treatment appears to have been part of the manufacturing technique of many of the specimens from Arnold Research Cave.

Distribution: In Missouri the type has been found in most parts of the state. The form is such a generalized one that it is difficult to determine the limits of its distribution throughout the United States. It is similar in many respects to Plano types in the high plains, as the name applied here suggests. Wormington and Forbis (1965: 20) noted that it was distributed from Alaska and Canada to Idaho and Wyoming. Luchterhand (1970) reported that it related typologically to forms west of the Illinois River valley, particularly in Nebraska, Wyoming, and Colorado. Its distribution may also be toward the Carolina Piedmont where the Guilford form appears to be comparable.

Type Site: Long site, Fall River County, South Dakota.

Age and Cultural Affiliation: It is estimated that in Missouri the type dates during the Middle Archaic period. It is a cutting tool of the Forager

Tradition. It is found in the Middle Archaic period components in Rice shelter, Rodgers shelter, and Arnold Research Cave. According to Luchterhand (1970: 10–11) the type dates much earlier in the west, 8000–6000 B.C., but Suhm and Jelks (1962) estimate the age from 6000–4000 B.C. Wormington and Forbis (1965: 70) gave the dates 8030 B.C. and 7400 B.C. for the form. It is the typical projectile point form of the Hot Springs focus, South Dakota.

References: Bell 1960a: 52, Plate 26; Cambron and Hulse 1965: A4; Coe 1952: 304; 1964: 43–44, Figures 35–36; Hughes 1949: 270–71; Luchterhand 1970: 10–11, 28–29; McMillan 1971: 222, Figure 45; Ritzenthaler 1967c: 19; Roberts 1943: 300; Shippee 1964; Suhm and Jelks 1962: 167, Plate 84; Suhm, Krieger, and Jelks 1954: 402, Plate 80; Wormington 1944: 25; 1957: 138-42.

Illustrations: Figures 5–17, 6–1, 6–2, 6–3, 6–4, 6–8, 6–9, 6–14. The specimen illustrated is from the Dalton site (S. P. Dalton Collection).

Big Sandy Notched

Figure A–4. Scale 1:1.

Derivation: It was named for the Big Sandy site, Tennessee.

Other Names or Similar Types: Graham Cave, Cache River, Raddatz Side-Notched, Rowan, White River Archaic, Black Sand Notched.

Description: It is a medium-sized, side-notched type with a concave base. Edges of the blade are usually convex. Length ranges from 4.5 cm to 9 cm with 6 cm the most typical. Length is usually two to three times the width. Width is generally 1 cm to 3.5 cm. The widest part is at the notches, either at the base or the shoulder. Thickness is 6 mm–8 mm. Heat treating was usually part of the process of manufacture.

Distribution: It is found in all regions in Missouri and is quite widespread over the Eastern United States from Wisconsin to Arkansas and Alabama eastward to the Appalachian Mountains.

Type Site: Big Sandy site, Henry County, Tennessee.

Age and Cultural Affiliations: Suggested dating of the type is 5000–500 B.C. The specimens in central and southwestern Missouri date primarily in the period 5000–3000 B.C., and those in eastern Missouri and Illinois date as late as 500 B.C. The type was manufactured in the Middle Archaic period in Graham Cave as a smaller and less precisely made version of Graham Cave Notched, which appears to be the progenitor. It continues throughout the Middle Archaic period and is the most distinctive type of the period in Missouri. It appears again in the Early Woodland period associated with the Early Woodland period, Black Sand phase, in Illinois. As the type was found in Hidden Valley shelter, Missouri, in a stratum above the Hidden Valley Stemmed type, its chronological position appears to be later. In the eastern part of the Missouri and western part of Illinois the type could have been Middle Archaic to Early Woodland period.

References: Cambron and Hulse 1965: A–11; Bell 1960: 8, Plate 4; Chapman and Chapman 1964: 37; Kneberg 1956: 25; Marshall 1958; 114–15, Figure 23; Perino 1971: 50, 88, Plates 25B, 38, 44F–I; Ritzenthaler 1967c: 24; Wittry 1959a: 44–46; 1959b: 177.

Illustrations: Figures 7–6, 7–14, 7–16, 7–17. The specimen illustrated is from Graham Cave, Missouri.

Clovis Fluted

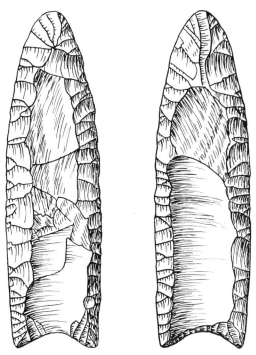

Figure A–5.   Scale 1:1.

Derivation: It is named for Clovis, New Mexico.

Other Names or Similar Types: Clovis, Clovis point, Fluted point, Folsomoid, Cumberland, Enterline, Enterline-Bull Brook, Eastern Fluted.

Description: It is usually a narrow, lanceolate shape with the broadest part near the midsection or toward the tip. Occasionally it is triangular with the broadest part at or near the base. The edges of the blade are usually convex but may be fairly straight. It ranges from 2.5 cm to 15 cm in length and averages 6.5 cm. Width is about 2–4 cm and is one-fourth to one-half the length. Thickness varies a great deal depending on the place of measurement and on how successful the individual manufacturer was in thinning the blade by fluting. It ranges from 3 mm to 10 mm. Flutes are most commonly produced by removal of multiple flakes and usually extend one-fourth to one-half the length from the base toward the tip.

One side generally has a longer flute than the other, and sometimes fluting is on one side only. In some instances single flakes were removed to produce the flutes. Bases are concave. Sides of the base and the concavity are usually smoothed by grinding.

Distribution: Clovis Fluted is widely distributed in Missouri, having been found in almost every area of the state where archaeological work has been conducted with any intensity. Greatest concentration is in the Lower Missouri Valley II and Greater St. Louis localities. It is widespread over North America. The heaviest concentration is in the central Missouri–Mississippi–Ohio river drainages.

Type Site: Blackwater Draw site, near Clovis, Curry County, New Mexico.

Age and Cultural Affiliation: It is generally considered that Clovis Fluted is one of the oldest projectile-point forms in North America. Most Clovis sites in the Southwest, Plains, and Eastern United States cultural areas have been radiocarbon dated between 9500 and 9000 B.C. Although it is generally thought to be the earliest type manufactured in Missouri, absolute evidence of its antiquity from excavations or associations with extinct animal forms has not been forthcoming, except at Rodgers shelter, where it is radiocarbon dated at 8580–8250 B.C. The type is associated with the Llano complex in the southwestern United States and Great Plains. In kill sites it is found with mammoth.

References: Bell 1958: 16–17; Bell and Hall 1953: 1; Cambron and Hulse 1965; Griffin 1952a; 1965; 1968; Haynes 1970; Irwin and Wormington 1970; Krieger 1947; McMillan 1971; Mason 1958; Ritchie 1961; Ritzenthaler 1967c; Roberts 1940; Sellards 1952; Suhm and Jelks 1962: 412; Suhm, Krieger, and Jelks 1954; Wormington 1957.

Illustrations: The variety in specimens from Missouri can be seen in Figures 3–1, 4–4, 4–9, 4–10, 4–14, 4–15, 4–16, 4–20, 4–21, 4–22, 4–23, 5–1. Typical examples from the western United States are shown in Figure 4–1. A series of Clovis Fluted from Missouri is shown in the accompanying Figure A–6. The specimen illustrated is from Missouri.

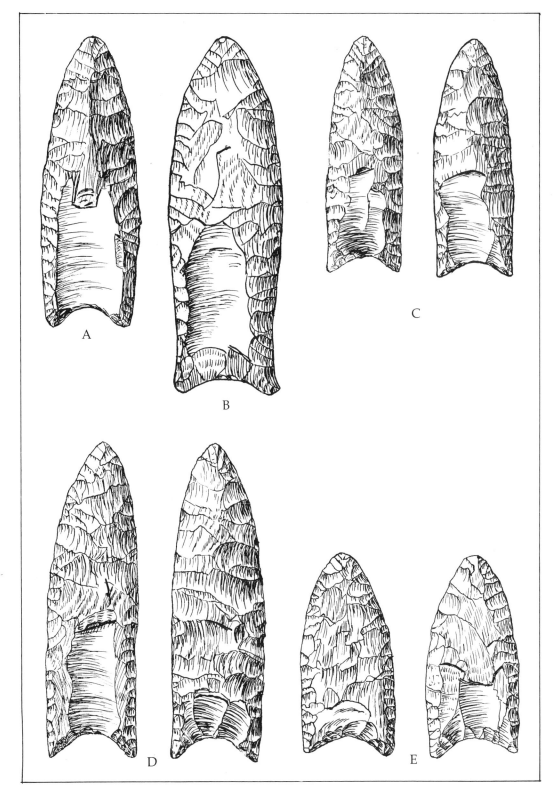

Figure A–6. Clovis Fluted from Missouri. Scale 1:1.

Dalton Serrated

Figure A–7. Scale 1:1.

Derivation: The form is named for Judge S. P. Dalton who discovered the site in a borrow pit on state highway property and supplied information on the materials he recovered from it.

Other Names or Similar Types: Dalton, Dalton point, Dalton-Meserve, Meserve-Dalton, Dalton Colbert, Dalton Greenbrier, Hardaway Dalton.

Description: Dalton Serrated is lanceolate or pentagonal in shape. The blade is essentially triangular. Edges of the blade are straight or slightly convex. Generally there are serrations on the blade edges, perhaps the result of resharpening the tool. The blade is often beveled by sharpening. Beveling may be steep or rather shallow. The length ranges from 4 cm to 17 cm. Most specimens are 5–7 cm. Width is 1.5 cm–3 cm. Proportions are 2 to 5 times as long as wide. Thickness is 5 mm–7 mm. Basal thinning is prominent and extends the same length as the grinding at the sides of the base. The base is usually the widest portion. It is relatively deeply concave with straight or slightly concave sides which are ground smooth.

Distribution: Dalton Serrated is found throughout much of the Eastern United States. It tends to concentrate in the Mississippi Valley, especially the central portion of the valley. It occurs throughout Missouri but is most numerous in the eastern half of the state.

Type site: Dalton site, near the mouth of the Osage River, Cole County, Missouri.

Age and Cultural Affiliation: Dates from 8500 to 6000 B.C. have been recorded for the type, and it is probable that it continued to be used as late as 5000 B.C. The form is characteristic of the Dalton and Early Archaic periods but appears in the Paleo-Indian period and may have lasted until the early part of the Middle Archaic period. It is the diagnostic type of the Hunter–Forager Tradition in the Dalton period. Dalton Serrated has been found *in situ* in the earliest levels of Graham Cave, Arnold Research Cave, and Rodgers shelter, and on numerous small sites on old land surfaces in the Mississippi alluvial valley of southeastern Missouri and Arkansas. In shape it resembles Meserve, which in turn appears to be a resharpening or reworking of the Plainview point. The two types, Dalton and Meserve, have been considered similar enough that the names have been used interchangeably. It is probable that they are of approximately the same time periods or at least overlap in time. However, they can be separated typologically because the Dalton has greater basal thinning and is usually serrated.

References: Bell 1958: 18–19; Bell and Hall 1953: 5; Cambron and Hulse 1965: A-28; Chapman 1948b: Figure 31, Number 9; 1957; Chapman and Chapman 1964: 36; Morse 1971; Scully 1951: 6; Shippee 1957a: 49–54.

Illustrations: Figures 4–11, 4–17, 4–18, 4–19, 4–20, 5–1, 5–3, 5–17, 5–18, 5–20, 5–21, 5–22, 5–25, 6–1, 6–6, 6–20. The large specimen illustrated is from Franklin County, Missouri, Richard S. Brownlee Collection, and the smaller specimen is from the Dalton site, S. P. Dalton Collection.

Etley Stemmed

Derivation: It is named for the Etley site, Illinois.

Other Names or Similar Types: Etley Barbed, Etley point, or Etley.

Description: It is a large, stemmed form with pronounced shoulders or barbs. The edges of the blade from the tip to the barb are usually excurvate-incurvate. Flake scars are flat, expanding, and massive. Secondary retouch scars are only at the margins of the blade and are inconsistent in size, shape, and distribution. Length ranges from 13 cm to 25 cm and the average is 17.5 cm. Proportions are approximately five times as long as wide. The greatest width is at the shoulder. Barbs are usually 7 mm–10 mm long and are rounded. They point diagonally downward from the blade. The stem is slightly flaring toward the base, which is straight or slightly convex. There is no heat treatment in the process of manufacture. It was probably used as a cutting tool or dagger.

Distribution: The type is found in the Northwest Prairie and Northeast Prairie regions in Missouri. It is also found where the Northeast Prairie Region extends into Illinois.

Type Site: Etley site, Calhoun County, Illinois.

Age and Cultural Affiliation: It is estimated to have occurred in the Late Archaic period. It is a diagnostic chipped-stone tool of the Booth assem-

Figure A–8.   Scale 1:1.

blage and the Cuivre River ceremonial complex (Titterington focus). It is one of the traits of the Sedalia phase.

References: Bell 1960a: 36, Plate 18; Klippel 1969: 7–11; Scully 1951: 2; Titterington 1950.

Illustrations: Figures 8–18, 8–23, 8–25. The specimen illustrated is from Howard County, Missouri, George W. Nichols Collection.

Folsom Fluted

Figure A–9. Scale 1:1.

Figure A–10. Scale 1:1.

Derivation: It was named for Folsom, New Mexico.

Other Names or Similar Types: Folsom, Folsom point, Folsomoid.

Description: In outline it is lanceolate shaped with the broadest part near the middle or close to the tip. Edges of the blade are convex to almost straight. Workmanship is distinguished by fine delicate chipping on the edges of the blade and tip. Length ranges from 2.5 cm to 13 cm but is usually 4 cm–6.5 cm. Widths range from 1.5 cm to 3 cm. Length is generally twice the width. It is characterized by flutes or grooves that extend along the faces of the blade from the base for most of the blade length. They are minimally three-fifths of the length. The typical cross-section of the point is bi-concave. It is thinned in the center and thick near blade edges. The edges around the base and along the blade for as much as one-third of the length of the blade are often smoothed by grinding.

Distribution: In Missouri the type is found in the Western Prairie and Northeast Prairie regions. It occurs mainly in the Southwest and Plains and less frequently in the Eastern United States cultural areas.

Type Site: Folsom site, Union County, New Mexico.

Age and Cultural Affiliation: The estimated date of Folsom Fluted is 9000–7000 B.C. It is presumed that it followed Clovis Fluted. It is one of the diagnostic forms of the Llano complex in the Southwest cultural area. Associations at kill sites are with *Bison taylori*. In Missouri the affiliation has not been established with any complex.

References: Bell 1960a: 26, Plate 13; Bell and Hall 1953: 2; Delling 1966; Krieger 1947; Roberts 1935; 1936; 1937; 1940; Stoltman and Workman 1969: 201-5, Figures 2, 5; Wormington 1957.

Illustrations: A typical western form is shown in Figure 4–1E. The large specimen illustrated is from the Marilyn Powell Delling Collection and the smaller is from the Robert Benson Collection. Both are from sites in Boone County, Missouri.

Graham Cave Fluted

Derivation: It is named for Graham Cave, Missouri.

Other Names or Similar Types: Lanceolate Type A.

Description: It is a long, narrow, triangular lanceolate form with a concave base. The shape of the blade, starting at the tip, is excurvate for one-fourth of the blade, then straight to the basal one-fourth which is incurvate. Flaking is carefully done, and the removal of small shallow flakes at the edges of the blade gives it a very smooth appearance. The length is 8 cm–11cm. The width is roughly one-third the length. The base is the widest portion. It is deeply concave. The lobes at the base flare slightly, and the base is ground in the concavity and along the sides equal to the length of the flutes or thinning flakes. The incurvate portion near the base is due in part to grinding of the sides of the base. It is not heat treated.

Distribution: Although the only places that Graham Cave Fluted have been found in excavations

Figure A–11.   Scale 1:1.

Graham Cave Notched

Figure A–12.   Scale 1:1.

are at Graham Cave and Arnold Research Cave, similar forms have been noted in private collections in the Northeast Prairie and Southeast Riverine regions of Missouri.

Type Site: Graham Cave, Montgomery County, Missouri.

Age and Cultural Affiliations: Radiocarbon dates of associated deposits are 7850–6880 B.C. The time during which the type was manufactured is estimated at approximately 8000–6000 B.C. The type is associated with the Hunter–Forager Tradition component, Dalton period, in Graham Cave, which is thought to have occurred at a time of change from the fluted tradition to lanceolate technological tradition.

References: Chapman 1952a: 88, Figure 8 A, F, J, N, O, 97; Chapman and Chapman 1964: 35; Klippel 1971: Figure 10C-H; Logan 1952: 27-31.

Illustrations: Figures 4–17, 5–8, 5–21. The specimen illustrated is from Graham Cave.

Derivation: It is named for Graham Cave, Missouri.

Other Names or Similar Types: Graham Cave, Graham Cave points, Kessel Side Notched, Osceola (?), Otter Creek points.

Description: It is a relatively long and narrow side notched form. Edges of the blade may be convex, relatively straight, or excurvate-incurvate from the tip to the shoulders. The length usually ranges between 8 cm and 15 cm. Width is 2 to 3 cm. It is usually 3 to 5 times as long as wide. Cross sections are thick and biconvex. Notches are U-shaped and at right angles to the blade axis. The edges below the notches are relatively straight sided, and occasionally are at a slight oblique angle to the central axis of the blade. Bases are always concave and usually deeply concave. The greatest width is at the base. Heat treating does not appear to be part of the stone working technology.

Distribution: Dispersion is in the Southwest Drainage, Ozark Highland, Northeast Prairie, and Southeast Riverine regions in Missouri and adjoining areas in Illinois.

Type Site: Graham Cave, Montgomery County, Missouri.

Age and Cultural Affiliation: The type is one of the markers of the Early Archaic period. Estimated dates are 8000–5000 B.C. It was found in early levels in Graham Cave, Arnold Research Cave, Rice shelter, and Rodgers shelter in Missouri, and was one of the types at the Godar site, Illinois, where it was probably associated with the early component. It was found in Zone I at Modoc shelter, Illinois, dated 8000–6000 B.C. (Deuel 1957: 2; Fowler 1959a: Table 5, Figure 14; 1959b: 258-62). A similar type, Kessell Side Notched, in the St. Albans site, West Virginia, was found on top of a hearth, radiocarbon dated at 7900±500 (Broyles 1966: 18).

References: Broyles 1966: 18; Chapman 1948b: 140, 142; 1952a: 87, 101; Logan 1952: 30, 32-33; McMillan 1971: Figure 46; Scully 1951: 8; Titterington 1950: Figure 1, Number 3.

Illustrations: Figures 6–1, 6–2, 6–3, 6–6, 6–14, 6–18. The specimen illustrated is from Graham Cave.

Hardin Barbed

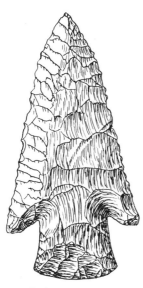

Figure A–13.   Scale 1:1.

Derivation: It is named for the town of Hardin, in the lower Illinois River valley, Calhoun County, Illinois.

Other Names or Similar Types: Hardin point, Hardin Stemmed, Hardin.

Description: It is a medium to large, stemmed form with small, sharp barbs. It has a long, slim triangular blade with straight or slightly convex edges. Workmanship is unusually fine with flat flake scars running from the blade edge to the midline. Blade edges were often evened with fine secondary chipping. Beveling of the blade is a common characteristic. The length varies from 5 cm to 13.5 cm and is normally 7.5 cm–8 cm. Width at the shoulders is 3 cm to 4.5 cm and is usually 3.5 cm. Thickness is 7 mm–11 mm and is generally 8.5 mm–9 mm. The cross section is flattened lenticular and thin. The stem flares toward the base, with the base concave, straight, or convex. Grinding is sometimes present along the sides of the stem and the base.

Distribution: The type is found most frequently near the junction of the Missouri and Mississippi rivers. It occurs in the Northwest and Northeast Prairie and Southeast Riverine regions in Missouri. Its distribution is primarily in the upper and central Mississippi alluvial valley, and east. It may extend as far south as Louisiana and as far east as the upper reaches of the Ohio River valley.

Type Site: Godar site, Calhoun County, Illinois.

Age and Cultural Affiliation: It is estimated to be Dalton to Early Archaic periods or 8000–5000 B.C. It is possible that it is derived from Scottsbluff I (Munson 1967; Wormington 1957).

References: Bell 1960a: 56, Plate 28; Logan 1952: Plate 6g; Luchterhand 1970: 9-11, 26-28, 59-60; Munson 1967; Redfield 1966: 53-57; Scully 1951: 31; Titterington 1950: Figure 2, Number 11.

Illustrations: Figures 4–11, 6–7, 6–16, 6–21. The specimen illustrated is from Franklin County, Missouri, Richard S. Brownlee Collection.

Hidden Valley Stemmed

Derivation: It is named for the Hidden Valley shelter in Missouri.

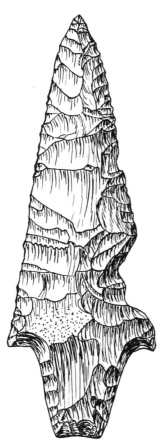

Figure A–14.   Scale 1:1.

Other Names or Similar Types: Hidden Valley point.

Description: It is a large contracting stemmed form with a roughly triangular blade. The blade edges are excurvate to straight. Flaking on the blade is usually carefully controlled and produces large flakes. The length ranges from 9 cm to 20 cm. The width at the shoulders is generally 3 cm–5 cm and the thickness is from 8mm to 10 mm. The stem contracts to the base with the edges even and in many instances with secondary flaking. The base is straight to slightly concave and is usually thinned with relatively long flakes removed from both faces. The edges of the stem and the base are sometimes smoothed by grinding. It was probably used as a cutting tool.

Distribution: The form occurs predominently in the Southeast Riverine Region. Its distribution in the rest of Missouri is not well known, but it is definitely present in the Ozark Highland Region.

Type Site: Hidden Valley shelter, Jefferson County, Missouri.

Age and Cultural Affiliation: It is possible that the type first occurred in the Dalton period and continued throughout the Early Archaic period. It is estimated that it was most popular in the Early Archaic period. It is similar to Rice Contracting Stemmed. It is one of the earliest types found in Hidden Valley shelter, and it is in the Early Archaic levels in Rodgers shelter, Missouri. It was reported to be associated with bannerstones in southeastern Missouri. It has been found in the early levels at Modoc shelter in Illinois, which yielded radiocarbon dates of 6593 B.C. and 5847 B.C. (Appendix I).

References: Adams 1941: Plate XB; Bell and Hall 1953: 5; Chapman 1948b: 140-42; Perino 1968: 18, Plate 9D, F; Scully 1951: 5.

Illustrations: Figures 6–2, 6–22. The specimen illustrated is from Hidden Valley shelter, Missouri.

Jakie Stemmed (Provisional)

Figure A–15.   Scale 1:1.

Derivation: It is named for Jakie shelter, Missouri.

Other Names or Similar Types: Fairland.

Description: In outline it is stemmed to corner-notched with a flaring base. The blade is symmetrical with excurvate to almost straight edges. It is from 5 cm to 10 cm long. The width at the shoulder is from 1.5 cm to 2.5 cm. Thickness is from 6 mm to 11 mm. The shoulders are often fairly pronounced or slightly barbed. The expanding stem may have a lobed appearance due to rounding of the corners of the base. Notches are moderate to large and the base is concave.

Distribution: Its range is primarily from central Missouri southeast into northeastern Oklahoma and perhaps as far as Texas.

Type Site: Jakie shelter, Barry County, Missouri.

Age and Cultural Affiliation: Estimated dates are 5000–3000 B.C. It is found in components of the Forager Tradition, Middle Archaic period, in Missouri. It is a companion of the Big Sandy Notched in Graham Cave, Jakie shelter, Rodgers shelter, and Rice site. In shape it tends to grade into the deeply concave-based Big Sandy Notched.

References: Bell 1960a: 92, Plate 46; Marshall 1960: 46–47; Suhm, Krieger, and Jelks 1954: 424, Plate 91; Suhm and Jelks 1962: 191, Plate 96.

Illustrations: Figures 7–6, 7–13, 7–14. The specimen illustrated is from Rodgers shelter, Missouri.

Nebo Hill Lanceolate

Derivation: It is named for the Nebo Hill site, Missouri.

Other Names or Similar Types: Nebo Hill, Nebo Hill point.

Description: It is a long, narrow lanceolate form. The broadest and thickest part is toward the tip, a little above the center in most specimens. Blade edges are predominantly excurvate but occasionally are straight. The flaking is usually irregular. Length is from 5 cm to 10 cm. Width is one-seventh to one-fourth the length. It is so thick that the cross section is often nearly diamond shaped or elliptical. The base is usually straight but may be slightly concave or convex. Often a single flake has been removed from one side of the base, but it is not really basal thinning and there is no grinding of the base or sides of the base.

Distribution: The distribution is basically in the Northwest Prairie Region but continues east into the Northeast Prairie Region in Missouri.

Type Site: Nebo Hill site, Clay County , Missouri.

Age and Cultural Affiliation: Estimated dates are 6000–2000 B.C. The Nebo Hill aggregate, with

Figure A–16.   Scale 1:1.

which it is associated, has been assumed to be Early Archaic to Late Archaic period, but no radiocarbon dating is available.

References: Bell and Hall 1953: 3; Chapman 1948b: 138, Figure 31, Numbers 14-19; Chapman and Chapman 1964: 29; Perino 1968: 60, Plate 30; Shippee 1948: 29–32; 1954: 5; 1957b: 42–46.

Illustrations: Figure 6–4, 8–12. The specimen illustrated is from the Nebo Hill site, Missouri.

Red Ochre Lanceolate

Derivation: It is named for the Red Ochre sites in the Greater St. Louis Locality.

Other Names or Similar Types: Red Ochre point, Red Ochre, Wadlow point.

Description: It is a medium to large lanceolate form with convex blade to straight blade edges. The sides of the blade below the midpoint are usually

relatively straight but may taper slightly. They never taper as abruptly as the Sedalia Lanceolate, Agate Basin Lanceolate, or Guilford Lanceolate types. The greatest width of the form is at the midpoint of the blade or forward of it at about two-thirds or three-fourths the length; rarely is it at the base. It is much broader and thicker than Sedalia Lanceolate and is more uniform in width from base to tip. It is usually three to four times as long as wide, and ranges in size from 8 cm to more than 25 cm in length. Width is usually from 4 cm to 7 cm. Thickness ranges from 11 mm to 19 mm. The base is usually straight but may be slightly concave or convex.

Distribution: It occurs in the Northeast Prairie Region of Missouri and Illinois. It has been found on the Cuivre River site, Lincoln County, Gronefeld site, St. Charles County in Missouri, and the Marquette Park site, Calhoun County, Illinois.

Type Site: Marquette Park site, Calhoun County, Illinois.

Age and Cultural Affiliation: It is estimated to date 3000–1000 B.C. in the Late Archaic period. It is associated with the Cuivre River ceremonial complex of the Sedalia phase of the Forager Tradition. It is a typical form of the Titterington focus.

References: Bacon and Miller 1957: 22-32; Cole and Deuel 1937; Perino 1968: 72, 98, Plates 36, 49; Scully 1951: 9; Titterington 1950: 2-8.

Illustrations: Figures 8–25, 8–26, 8–30. The specimen illustrated is from Site 23MN296, Monroe County, Missouri (a preform).

Rice Contracting Stemmed

Figure A–17.   Scale 1:1.

Figure A–18.   Scale 1:1.

Derivation: It is named for the Rice site, Missouri.

Other Names or Similar Types: Langtry(?).

Description: It is a medium-sized contracting stemmed form with pronounced shoulders but without barbs. Length ranges from 5 cm to 10 cm. The width, which is greatest at the shoulders, is 2.5 cm–4.5 cm. Thickness is 8 mm–10 mm. The stem usually contracts slightly toward the base, but its sides may be nearly straight. The base is usually concave but may be occasionally straight. It is thinned by the removal of two to five flakes from both faces. The edges of the stem and the base are smoothed. In general it is similar to Hidden Valley Stemmed but much thicker and not as well made. Also the Rice Contracting Stemmed is smaller, and the proportion of length to width is not as great as Hidden Valley Stemmed.

Distribution: The form is found in the Southwestern Drainage Region, Missouri, and southwest into northwestern Arkansas and northeastern Oklahoma. It also is present in the Ozark Highland Region of Missouri.

Type Site: Rice site, Stone County, Missouri.

Age and Cultural Affiliation: It is estimated to date from 7000 to 4000 B.C. It is associated with the Early Archaic period but may continue in the Middle Archaic period in the White Locality. The type occurred in the earliest levels at the Rice site and in Long Creek Site A. It is a trait of the White River complex.

References: Chapman 1956: 34–35, Figure 2B; Chapman and Chapman 1964: 28; Marshall 1958: 112–13.

Illustrations: Figures 6–1, 6–19. The specimen illustrated is from Jakie shelter, Missouri (resharpened).

Rice Lanceolate

Derivation: It is named for the Rice site, Missouri.

Other Names or Similar Types: Searcy.

Description: It is a medium-sized, lanceolate form with convex edges, and the widest part is at the midpoint or toward the base. The midportion of the blade is serrated, occasionally being serrated to the blade tip. Many specimens have the appearance of shallow beveling, probably due to

Figure A–19.   Scale 1:1.

resharpening. Length is 6 cm–7 cm. The width is 3 cm–3.5 cm. Thickness is from 5 mm to 12 mm. The basal one-fourth is often abruptly narrowed due to grinding of the edges. Specimens may thus have the appearance of being stemmed due to the slight broadening of the blade above the ground area. Grinding is lacking on some specimens. The base is concave, but never deeply concave. It is smoothed by grinding and is thinned by removal of one to three relatively long flakes from both faces.

Distribution: It has a discontinuous distribution, for it has been reported in the Northeast Prairie and Southwest Drainage regions in Missouri, in northwestern Arkansas, and in northeastern Oklahoma.

Type Site: Rice site, Stone County, Missouri.

Age and Cultural Affiliation: It is Early Archaic period, possibly continuing into the Middle Archaic period. It is associated with the earliest levels in the Rice site and at Jakie shelter. It is one of the major types from the Dalton site, Missouri. Perino (1968) noted that Searcy was younger than the Calf Creek points in Calf Creek Cave, Searcy County, Arkansas, and suggested a date of 5000–3000 B.C.

References: Bray 1956: 80–81; Chapman 1956: Figure 2c; Marshall 1958: 108–9, 171; Perino 1968: 84, Plate 42.

Illustrations: Figures 6–1, 6–2, 6–3, 6–8. The specimen illustrated is from Jakie shelter, Missouri.

Rice Lobed

Figure A–20.   Scale 1:1.

Derivation: It is named for the Rice site, Missouri.

Other Names or Similar Types: Schoonover point; Rice; Crawford Creek; Kirk Corner Notched (large variety).

Description: In outline it is corner notched with excurvate to straight blade edges, stem expanding toward the base and with lobed corners. In some instances it has incurvate blade edges due to resharpening. The blade edges are usually serrated and beveled with a distinctive type of flaking that is relatively pronounced. This characteristic may be due to resharpening the blade edges. Length varies from 4 cm to 12.5 cm. Greatest width is at the shoulder area and is approximately one-half the length. Thickness is from 5 mm to 7 mm. The shoulders are prominent. Barbs are small and usually are rounded. The stem is short in proportion to the blade and expands slightly toward the base. The base is somewhat thinned on both sides, but a distinctive feature is the rounded corners or lobes, which are prominent when the base is concave. Bases are straight to concave. The sides of the stem and the base are often deliberately smoothed by grinding.

Distribution: It is distributed throughout the Southwest Drainage, Ozark Highland, Northeast Prairie, and Southeast Riverine regions in Missouri. It ranges from northeastern Oklahoma to West Virginia.

Type Site: Rice site, Stone County, Missouri.

Age and Cultural Affiliation: Estimated dates are 7500–5000 B.C. It first appears in the Dalton period. It is typical of the Early Archaic period but lasts into the Middle Archaic in the Southwest Drainage Region. It is an important type in the White River complex in the White Locality in the Southwest Drainage Region and is an integral part of the Early Archaic component in Rodgers shelter in the Lower Osage Locality, Ozark Highland Region.

References: Bray 1956a: 128, 131; Broyles 1966: 20–21; Cambron and Hulse 1965: A-25; Chapman 1956: 34–35, 37; Chapman and Chapman 1964: 27; McMillan 1971; Perino 1968: 76, Plate 38; Schoonover 1960: 102–3.

Illustrations: Figures 6–1, 6–2, 6–3, 6–7, 6–14, 6–19, 7–7. The specimen illustrated is from the Rice site, Missouri.

St. Charles Notched

Derivation: It is named for St. Charles County, Missouri.

Other Names or Similar Types: Dovetail, Plevna, Thebes.

Description: It is corner notched with very narrow, finely made notches at the corners of an ovoid biface. It has a narrow blade that has straight or convex edges which are usually beveled. The mean length is 8 cm and varies between 4.5 to 9.5 cm occasionally reaching 15–18 cm. The width is 2.5 cm–5 cm. Maximum width is at the notches and is one-half to one-fourth the length. Thickness is 7 mm–10 mm. The notches are diagonal to the long axis. The base is strongly convex. It is thinned and is always ground.

Distribution: The type is found primarily in the Northeast Prairie and Southeast Riverine regions in Missouri. It extends eastward through Illinois and Indiana into Ohio and southeast through Tennessee to Alabama where a similar if not identical form is called the Plevna point.

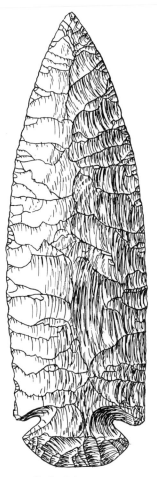

Figure A–21. Scale 1:1.

Type Site: Gronefeld site, St. Charles County, Missouri.

Age and Cultural Affiliation: It has been found in the early levels of Graham Cave, Arnold Research Cave, on the Dalton and Gronefeld sites in Missouri, and on the Godar site, Illinois. Scully (1951) assigned it to the Late Archaic and Early Woodland periods, but Bell (1960a) suggested that it lasted into the Middle Woodland period and perhaps ranged in date from 2000 B.C. to A.D. 1. Luchterhand (1970: 12) proposed that the type was made during the period 8050–6050 B.C. Cambron and Hulse (1962) suggested that it occurred prior to 3050 B.C. It is proposed here that it is representative of the Early Archaic period in Missouri. The Plevna points, according to Cambron and Hulse (1965), are probably ancestral to St. Charles Notched because they occurred more

than 5000 years ago. It is more likely that they are the same type and are contemporaneous.

References: Bell 1960a: 83, Plate 41; Cambron and Hulse 1965: A-72; Converse 1963: 112; Luchterhand 1970: 12, 31–32; Perino 1971: 96–97; Scully 1951: 4; Winters 1963.

Illustrations: Figures 6–7, 6–14, 6–15, 6–17. The specimen illustrated is from Franklin County, Richard S. Brownlee Collection.

Sedalia Lanceolate

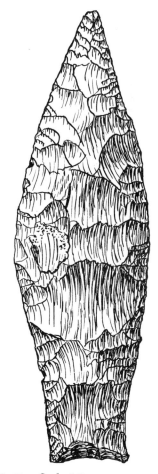

Figure A–22. Scale 1:1.

Derivation: It is named for the city of Sedalia, Missouri.

Other Names or Similar Types: Sedalia point.

Description: It is a relatively large lanceolate form with excurvate blade edges; the greatest width is toward the tip. Length varies from 8 cm to 18 cm. The blade is shaped by the removal of large primary flakes in most instances, but some exhibit secondary flaking. The width is approximately one-third to one-fifth the length. The blade is extremely long in proportion to width and tapers sharply to the base. Specimens are relatively thin and lenticular in cross section. The base may be straight, relatively concave, or less commonly, convex. Sometimes there is grinding or wear on the sides of the blade near the base.

Distribution: It is found primarily in the Northwest and Northeast prairie regions of Missouri, eastward into Illinois, and probably into Indiana and Ohio in the Prairie Peninsula.

Type Site: Site 23PE1, near Sedalia, Pettis County, Missouri.

Age and Cultural Affiliation: It is estimated to date from approximately 3000 to 1000 B.C. It is affiliated with the Sedalia complex, the Cuivre ceremonial component and Sedalia phase, which are judged to be Late Archaic. The form may have been derived from Nebo Hill Lanceolate.

References: Chapman 1948b: 139–40; Chapman and Chapman 1964: 39; Perino 1968: 86, Plate 43; Seelen 1961; Wormington 1957: 147.

Illustrations: Figures 8–13, 8–18, 8–19, 8–23, 8–26. The specimen illustrated is from the type site, near Sedalia, Missouri, from the Harry and Florence Collins Collection.

Smith Basal Notched

Derivation: It is named for the Smith site, Oklahoma.

Other Names or Similar Types: Marshall, Eva Basal Notched.

Description: It is a medium to large basal-notched form. Blade edges are usually convex but may be straight. Very large flake scars on the blade have been produced by percussion. Some specimens have been modified by retouching, producing small flake scars. Length ranges from approximately 6 cm to 15 cm. It is usually one and one-fourth to two times as long as wide. Greatest width is at the tip of the barbs. Barbs are prominent and may extend to a point almost even with

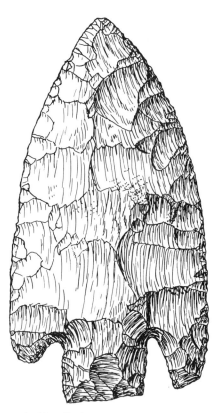

Figure A–23.   Scale 1:1.

the base. Thickness is 8 mm to 10 mm. The sides of the stem and the base are straight. The base of some specimens is slightly ground.

Distribution: It is found throughout Missouri. It also occurs in Arkansas, Oklahoma, and Texas.

Type Site: Smith site, Delaware County, Oklahoma.

Age and Cultural Affiliation: Estimated dates are 5000–1000 B.C. It is considered to be primarily Late Archaic period. It is the typical cutting tool of the James River complex of the Forager Tradition in the White Locality, Southwest Drainage Region, and occurs in the Late Archaic levels in Rodgers shelter, in the Lower Osage Locality, Ozark Highland Region.

References: Baerreis and Freeman 1960; Perino 1968: 90, Plate 45; Suhm and Jelks 1962: 211, Plate 106; Suhm, Krieger, and Jelks 1954: 444, Plate 101.

Illustrations: Figures 8–1, 8–2, 8–3, 8–9, 8–14. The

specimen illustrated is from the Richard S. Brownlee Collection.

Stone Square Stemmed

Figure A–24. Scale 1:1.

Derivation: It is named for Stone County, Missouri.

Other Names or Similar Types: Barry Square Stemmed, Archaic Stemmed points, Genesee and perhaps Benton and Johnson points.

Description: It is a medium to large stemmed form. The blade usually has straight edges for most of the length but sometimes they are convex. The widest part of the blade is at the shoulders. Length ranges from 5 cm to 13 cm and width from 2.5 cm to 3 cm. The proportion varies from 2 to 3½ times as long as wide. Thickness is 8 mm–12 mm. Cross section is biconvex or plano convex. Shoulders are pronounced and occasionally are barbed. A relatively broad stem with straight edges and straight base gives the impression that the stem is square. Bases may be slightly concave or convex. Sometimes the edges of the stem and the base are smoothed by grinding.

Distribution: It is found in the Southwest Drainage, Ozark Highland, and Northeast Prairie regions in Missouri, in northwestern Arkansas and in northeastern Oklahoma. It is considered that Benton and Johnson points are overlapping types. It is found in Ohio. The Genesee points in New York are very similar and date in the same period, so it is possible that the type extends from Oklahoma to New York.

Type Site: James River site, Stone County, Missouri.

Age and Cultural Affiliation: The type is estimated to date 5000–1000 B.C. It is associated with the White River complex of the Forager Tradition in the Middle Archaic period and with the Late Archaic James River complex and the Sedalia phase.

References: Bell 1960a: 6, Plate 3; Converse 1963: 104; Kneberg 1956: 25–26; Marshall 1958: 110–12, 118–20, Figures 22, 24; Perino 1968: 40, Plate 20; Ritchie 1961: 24–25.

Illustrations: Figures 8–1, 8–4, 8–5, 8–9, 8–13, 8–18, 8–23, 8–25. The specimen illustrated is from the Geiger site.

Table Rock Stemmed

Figure A–25. Scale 1:1.

Derivation: It is named for the Table Rock Reservoir, Missouri.

Other Names or Similar Types: Table Rock points, Bottleneck point.

Description: It is symmetrical, with the stem expanding slightly toward the base. The edges of the blade are even and finished with secondary flaking. The blade is usually convex and is relatively short in relation to the width. The length is usually from 4 cm to 8 cm, averaging 5 cm. Some very well-made specimens are much larger, as long as 18 cm, and have strongly convex blade edges. Shoulders are rounded and are never barbed or very prominent. Greatest width occurs at or above the shoulders. Width is from 1.5 cm to 3.5 cm. Thickness is from 4 mm to 8 mm. Grinding occurs along the edges of the base and on the base.

Distribution: It is present in small numbers in most localities of Missouri. It extends as far east as Ohio, and southwest into northeastern Oklahoma.

Type Site: Rice site, Stone County, Missouri.

Age and Cultural Affiliation: Estimated date is 3000–1000 B.C. Though originally considered to be Early or Middle Archaic (Chapman 1956:37), the type has been associated with aggregates from the Late Archaic period in the Table Rock Reservoir area, Missouri, and a Late Archaic context in Pohly rock shelter, Oklahoma.

References: Bray 1956a: 87; Chapman and Chapman 1964: 39; Converse 1963: 111; Marshall 1958; 117–18; 1960: 54, 169; Perino 1968: 96, Plate 48.

Illustrations: Figures 8–3, 8–4, 8–9. The specimen illustrated is from the Richard S. Brownlee Collection.

Bibliography

Abbott, C. C.
1881 *Primitive Industry*. Salem, Mass.
1888 "On the Antiquity of Man in the Valley of the Delaware." *Proceedings of the Boston Society of Natural History*, 23: 424–26.

Adams, L. M.
1950 "The Table Rock Basin in Barry County, Missouri." *Memoir, Missouri Archaeological Society*, No. 1: 1–63.
1958 "Archaeological Investigations of Southwestern Missouri." *The Missouri Archaeologist*, 20: 1–199.

Adams, R. M.
1941 "Archaeological Investigations in Jefferson County, Missouri 1939–1940." *Transactions of the Academy of Science of St. Louis*, 30 (5): 1–221.
1949 "Archaeological Investigations in Jefferson County, Missouri." *The Missouri Archaeologist*, 11 (3–4): 1–72.
1953 "The Kimmswick Bone Bed." *The Missouri Archaeologist*, 15 (4): 40–56.

Adams, R. M., and F. Magre
1939 "Archaeological Surface of Jefferson County, Missouri." *The Missouri Archaeologist*, 5 (2): 11–23.

Adams, R. M., F. Magre, and P. Munger
1941 "Archaeological Survey of St. Genevieve County, Missouri." *The Missouri Archaeologist*, 7 (1): 9–23.

Agogino, G. A.
1961 "A New Point Type for Hell Gap Valley, Eastern Wyoming." *American Antiquity*, 26 (4): 558–60.
1963 "The Paleo-Indian Relative Age and Cultural Sequence." *Great Plains Journal*, 3 (1): 17–24.
1968 "A Brief History of Early Man in the Western High Plains." *Eastern New Mexico University Contributions in Anthropology*, 1 (4): 1–5.

Agogino, G. A., and W. E. Frankforter
1960 "A Paleo-Indian Bison-Kill in Northwestern Iowa." *American Antiquity*, 25 (3): 414–15.

Agogino, G. A., and I. Rovner
1964 "Paleo-Indian Traditions: A Current Evaluation." *Archaeology*, 17: 237–43.

Agogino, G. A., I. Rovner, and C. Irwin-Williams
1964 "Early Man in the New World." *Science*, 143 (3612): 1350–52.

Ahler, S. A.
1971 "Projectile Point Form and Function at Rodgers Shelter, Missouri." *Missouri Archaeological Society Research Series*, No. 8: 1–201.

Alexander, H. L., Jr.
1963 "The Levi Site: A Paleo-Indian Campsite in Central Texas." *American Antiquity*, 28 (4): 510–28.

American Heritage
1966 *The American Heritage Pictorial Atlas of United States History*. New York.

Andrews, E.
1875 "Dr. Koch and the Missouri Mastodon." *American Journal of Science and Arts*, 110 (55): 32–34.

Anonymous
1878 "Discovery of a Mastodon Associated with Human Remains." *The American Antiquarian*, 1 (1): 54–55.
1965 "Science and the Citizen, 'Paleolithic Funeral.'" *Scientific American*, 212 (2): 53–54.

Antevs, E.
1935 "The Spread of Aboriginal Man to North America." *The Geographical Review*, 25 (2): 302–9.
1937 "Climate and Early Man in North America." In *Early Man*, eds. G. G. MacCurdy and J. C. Merriam, pp. 125–32. New York.

Atwood, W. W.
1940 *The Physiographic Provinces of North America*. Boston.

Aveleyra, L. A.
1956 "The Second Mammoth and Associated Artifacts at Santa Isabel Iztapan, Mexico."

American Antiquity, 22 (1): 12–28.
1964 "The Primitive Hunters." In *Handbook of Middle American Indians,* ed. R. C. West, 1: 384–412.

Aveleyra, L. A., and M. Maldunado-Koerdell
1953 "Association of Artifacts with Mammoth in the Valley of Mexico." *American Antiquity,* 18 (4): 332–40.

Babbitt, F. E.
1884a "Exhibition and Description of Some Paleolithic Quartz Implements from Central Minnesota." *Proceedings of the American Association for the Advancement of Science,* 33: 593–99.
1884b "Vestiges of Glacial Man in Minnesota." *American Naturalist,* 18 (6–7): 594–615, 697–708.

Bacon, W. S., and W. J. Miller
1957 "Notes on the Excavation of a Burial Area in Northeast Missouri." *The Missouri Archaeologist,* 19 (3): 19–34.

Baerreis, D. A.
1951 *The Preceramic Horizons of Northeastern Oklahoma.* Anthropological Papers, Museum of Anthropology, University of Michigan, No. 6.
1959 "The Archaic as Seen from the Ozark Region." *American Antiquity,* 24 (3): 270–75.

Baerreis, D. A., and J. E. Freeman
1960 *A Report on a Bluff Shelter in Northeastern Oklahoma (D1–47).* Archives in Archaeology, No. 1.

Baerreis, D. A., J. E. Freeman, and J. V. Wright
1958 "The Contracting Stem Projectile Point in Eastern Oklahoma." *Bulletin of the Oklahoma Anthropological Society,* 6: 61–82.

Bank, T. II
1962 "How Man Came to the New World." *Explorers Journal,* 40: 8–19.

Barbour, E. H., and C. B. Schultz
1932a "The Mounted Skeleton of Bison Occidentalis, and Associated Dart Points." *The Nebraska State Museum Bulletin,* 32 (1): 263–70.
1932b "The Scottsbluff Bison Quarry and its Artifacts." *The Nebraska State Museum Bulletin,* 32 (1): 283–86.
1936 "Paleontologic and Geologic Consideration of Early Man in Nebraska." *The Nebraska State Museum Bulletin,* 45 (1): 431–49.

Barth, F.
1950 "Ecologic Adaptation and Cultural Change in Archaeology." *American Antiquity,* 15 (4): 338–39.

Bayard, T.
1969 "Science, Theory and Reality in the 'New Archaeology.'" *American Antiquity,* 34 (4): 376–84.

Beals, R. L.
1957 "Father Acosta on the First Peopling of the New World." *American Antiquity,* 23 (2): 182–83.

Befu, H., and C. S. Chard
1960 "Preceramic Cultures in Japan." *American Anthropologist,* 62 (5): 815–49.

Bell, R. E.
1957 "Clear Fork Gouges Found in Oklahoma." *Bulletin of the Texas Archaeological Society,* 28: 285–88.
1958 *Guide to the Identification of Certain American Indian Projectile Points.* Special Bulletin of the Oklahoma Anthropological Society, No. 1.
1960a *Guide to the Identification of Certain American Indian Projectile Points.* Special Bulletin of the Oklahoma Anthropological Society, No. 2.
1960b "Evidence of a Fluted Point Tradition in Ecuador." *American Antiquity,* 26 (1): 102–6.

Bell, R. E., and D. A. Baerreis
1951 "A Survey of Oklahoma Archaeology." *Bulletin of the Texas Archaeological and Paleontological Society,* 22: 7–100.

Bell, R. E., and R. S. Hall
1953 "Selected Projectile Point Types of the United States." *Bulletin of the Oklahoma Anthropological Society,* 1: 1–16.

Bennett, J. W.
1945 *Archaeological Exploration in Jo Daviess County, Illinois.* Chicago.
1952 "The Prehistory of the Northern Mississippi Valley." In *Archaeology of Eastern United States,* ed. J. B. Griffin, pp. 108–23. Chicago.

Berry, B., J. E. Wrench, and C. Chapman
1940 "The Archaeology of Wayne County." *The Missouri Archaeologist,* 6 (1): 1–40.

Biggs, R. W., J. Stoutamire, and R. Vehik
1970 "The Walter Site—A Fluted Point Manifestation in North Central Missouri." *Memoir, Missouri Archaeological Society,* No. 8: 11–63.

Binford, L. R.
1962 "Archaeology as Anthropology." *American Antiquity,* 28 (2): 217–25.
1963 "A Proposed Attribute List for the Description and Classification of Projectile Points." *Anthropological Papers, Museum of Anthropology, University of Michigan,* No. 19: 193–221.

1965 "Archaeological Systematics and the Study of Cultural Process." *American Antiquity,* 31 (2): 203–10.

Binford, S. R., and L. R. Binford, eds.
1968 *New Perspectives in Archaeology.* Chicago.

Bird, J. B.
1946 "The Alacaluf." In *Handbook of South American Indians,* ed. J. H. Steward, Vol. I, pp. 55–80. Bureau of American Ethnology Bulletin, 145.
1965 "The Concept of a 'Pre-Projectile Point' Cultural Stage in Chile and Peru." *American Antiquity,* 31 (2): 262–70.

Birdsell, J. B.
1951 "The Problem of the Early Peopling of the Americas as Viewed from Asia." In *Papers on the Physical Anthropology of the American Indian,* ed. W. S. Laughlin, pp. 1–68. New York.
1957 "Some Population Problems Involving Pleistocene Man." *Cole Spring Harbor Symposia and Quantitative Biology,* 22: 47–69.

Bordaz, J.
1959 "Part I and II, 'First Tools of Mankind.'" *Natural History,* 68 (1): 36–51, 92–103.

Borden, C. E.
1960 *DjRi 3, An Early Site in the Frazer Canyon, British Columbia.* National Museum of Canada Bulletin, No. 162.
1961 "Frazer River Archaeological Project." *Anthropology Papers, National Museum of Canada,* 1: 1–6.
1962 "Review of Cressman, et al. Cultural Sequences at the Dalles, Oregon." *American Antiquity,* 27 (3): 437–38.
1968 "A Late Pleistocene Pebble Tool Industry of Southwestern British Columbia." *Eastern New Mexico University, Contributions in Anthropology,* 1 (4): 55–69.

Born, P. L., and C. H. Chapman
1972 "Ozark National Scenic Riverways, Alley Springs Archaeological Exploration." Report to National Park Service on Contract NPS–4970P20459, Midwest Research Center, Lincoln, Nebraska.

Branson, E. B.
1944 *The Geology of Missouri.* University of Missouri Studies, 19 (3).

Bray, R. T.
1956a "The Culture-Complexes and Sequence at the Rice Site (23SN200) Stone County, Missouri." *The Missouri Archaeologist,* 18 (1–2): 46–134.
1956b "Some Outstanding Finds from Table Rock Reservoir Area." *Missouri Archaeological Society Newsletter,* 99: 5–7.
1957 "Lander Shelter No. 1, 23SN189, Stone County, Missouri." *The Missouri Archaeologist,* 19 (1–2): 22–52.
1960 "Standlee Shelter I, 23BY386. Archaeological Investigations in the Table Rock Reservoir." Report to National Park Service on Contract 14–10–333–96, Midwest Research Center, Lincoln, Nebraska, pp. 485–532.
1962a "Comments on the Preceramic in Missouri." *Plains Anthropologist,* 8 (22): 231–37.
1962b "The Irvine Spring Site." *Missouri Archaeological Society Newsletter,* 157: 3–7.

Bridges, T.
1948 "The Canoe Indians of Tierra del Fuego." In *A Reader in General Anthropology,* ed. C. Coon, pp. 84–116. New York.

Broadhead, G. C.
1881 "The Mastodon." *Kansas City Review of Science and Industry,* 4 (9): 519–21.

Broeker, W. S.
1965 "Isotope Geochemistry and Pleistocene Climatic Record." In *The Quaternary of the United States,* eds. H. E. Wright, Jr., and D. G. Frey, pp. 737–53. Princeton.

Brown, A. H.
1963 "Sweden, Quiet Workshop of the World." *National Geographic Magazine,* 123 (4): 451–91.

Broyles, B. J.
1966 "Preliminary Report: The St. Albans Site (46Ka27), Kanawha County, West Virginia." *The West Virginia Archaeologist,* No. 19: 1–43.

Bryan, A. L.
1962 "Review of Cultural Sequence at the Dalles, Oregon: A Construction of Pacific Northwest Prehistory, by L. S. Cressman, et al." *Man,* 62: 108–9.
1964 "New Evidence Concerning Early Man in North America." *Man,* 64: 152–53.
1965 *Paleo-American Prehistory.* Occasional Papers of the Idaho State University Museum, No. 16.
1968 "Early Man in Western Canada: A Critical Review." *Eastern New Mexico University Contributions in Anthropology,* 1 (4): 70–77.
1969 "Early Man in America and the Late Pleistocene Chronology of Western Canada and Alaska." *Current Anthropology,* 10 (4): 339–65.

Bryan, K.
1939 "Stone Cultures Near Cerro Pedernal and Their Geological Antiquity." *Bulletin of the Texas Archaeological and Paleontological Society,* 11: 9–46.

Bryan K. and P. MacClintock
1938 "What is Implied by 'Disturbances' at the Site of Minnesota Man." *The Journal of Geology,* 46 (3): 279–92.

Bryson, R. A., D. A. Baerreis, and W. M. Wendland
1970 "The Character of Late-Glacial and Post-Glacial Climatic Changes." In *Pleistocene and Recent Environments of the Central Great Plains,* eds. W. Dort and J. K. Jones, pp. 53–74. Lawrence, Kansas.

Bryson, R. A., and W. M. Wendland
1967 "Tentative Climatic Patterns for some Late Glacial and Post-Glacial Episodes in Central North America." In *Life, Land, and Water,* ed. W. J. Mayer-Oakes, pp. 271–98. Winnepeg, Canada.

Buckley, J. D., and E. H. Willis
1969 "Isotopes Radiocarbon Measurements VII." *Radiocarbon,* 11 (1): 53–105.
1970 "Isotopes Radiocarbon Measurements VIII." *Radiocarbon,* 12 (1): 87–129.

Bushnell, G. H. S., and C. McBurney
1959 "New World Origins Seen from the Old World." *Antiquity,* 33 (130): 93–101.

Butler, B. R.
1961 *The Old Cordilleron Culture in the Pacific Northwest.* Occasional Papers of the Idaho State University Museum, No. 5.
1964 "A Recent Early Man Point Find in Southeastern Idaho." *Tebiwa,* 7 (1): 39–40.
1965 "A Report on Investigations of an Early Man Site near Lake Channel, Southern Idaho." *Tebiwa,* 8 (2): 1–20.

Butzer, K. W.
1971 *Environment and Archaeology: An Ecological Approach to Prehistory.* 2d ed. Chicago and New York.

Byers, D. S.
1954 "Bull-Brook—A Fluted Point Site in Ipswich, Massachusetts." *American Antiquity,* 19 (4): 343–51.
1955 "Additional Information on the Bull Brook Site, Massachusetts." *American Antiquity,* 20 (3): 274–76.
1956 "Ipswich, B.C." *Essex Institute Historical Collections:* 1–13.
1957 "The Bering Bridge—Some Speculations." *Ethnos,* 22 (1–2): 20–26.
1959 "Radiocarbon Dates for the Bull Brook Site, Massachusetts." *American Antiquity,* 24 (4): 427–29.
1965 "Saturday Morning Roundtable." *Proceedings of the 20th Southeast Archaeological Conference:* *Southeast Archaeological Conference Bulletin,* No. 2: 24–25.
1966a "The Debert Paleo-Indian Site: The Position of Debert with Respect to the Paleo-Indian Tradition." *Quaternaria,* 8: 33–47.
1966b "The Debert Paleo-Indian Site." *A Guide for Stop No. 11, Field Trip No. 4,* Geological Association of Canada—Mineralogical Association of Canada.
1969 "Debert and Delirium: Early Man in Nova Scotia." *Eastern States Archaeological Federation Bulletin,* 26–27:10.

Calabrese, F. A., R. E. Pangborn, and R. J. Young
1969 "Two Village Sites in Southwestern Missouri: A Lithic Analysis." *Missouri Archaeological Society Research Series,* No. 7.

Caldwell, J. R.
1954 "The Old Quartz Industry of Piedmont, Georgia, and South Carolina." *Southern Indian Studies,* 6: 37–39.
1958 "Trend and Tradition in the Prehistory of the Eastern United States." *American Anthropological Association Memoir, No. 88:* 1–87.

Cambron, J. W., and D. C. Hulse
1965 *Handbook of Alabama Archaeology Part I: Point Types.* University, Alabama.
1967 *Handbook of Alabama Archaeology Part II: Uniface Blade and Flake Tools.* Decatur, Alabama.

Campbell, J. M.
1961a "The Kogruk Complex of Anaktuvak Pass, Alaska." *Anthropologica,* 3: 3–20.
1961b "The Tuktu Complex of Anaktuvak Pass." *Anthropological Papers of the University of Alaska,* 9 (2): 61–80.
1963 "Ancient Alaska and Paleolithic Europe." *Anthropological Papers of the University of Alaska,* 10 (2): 29–49.

Carter, G. F.
1951 "Man in America: A Criticism of Scientific Thought." *Scientific Monthly,* 73 (5): 297–307.
1952 "Interglacial Artifacts from the San Diego Area." *Southwestern Journal of Anthropology,* 8 (4): 444–56.
1956 "Artifacts from the Glacial Gravels." *Ohio Archaeologist,* 6 (3): 82–84.
1957 *Pleistocene Man at San Diego.* Baltimore.
1958 "Archaeology in the Reno Area in Relation to Age of Man and the Culture Sequence in America." *Proceedings of the American Philosophical Society,* 102 (2): 174–92.
1959 "Pleistocene Man at San Diego: A Reply." *American Antiquity,* 23 (3): 319–20.

Central States Archaeological Society Journal
1967 14 (3): Figs. 51, 60.

1968 15 (2): Fig. 36.
1970 17 (4): Fig. 117.

Chamberlin, T. C.
1902 "The Geologic Relation of the Human Relics of Lansing, Kansas." *The Journal of Geology,* 10 (7): 745–77.

Chapman, C. H.
1935 "Stone Age Man of Crawford County." *Missouri Resources Museum Bulletin,* 16: 1–9.
1937 "Archaeological Survey of the Cuivre River Recreational Area." Report to National Park Service by student archaeologist on work conducted during the summer of 1937. University of Missouri—Columbia, American Archaeology Division, files.
1946 "A Preliminary Survey of Missouri Archaeology Part I: Historic Indian Tribes." *The Missouri Archaeologist,* 10 (1): 1–56.
1947 "A Preliminary Survey of Missouri Archaeology Part II: Middle Mississippi and Hopewellian Cultures." *The Missouri Archaeologist,* 10 (2): 57–94.
1948a "A Preliminary Survey of Missouri Archaeology Part III: Woodland Cultures and the Ozark Bluff Dwellers." *The Missouri Archaeologist,* 10 (3): 95–132.
1948b "A Preliminary Survey of Missouri Archaeology Part IV: Ancient Cultures and Sequence." *The Missouri Archaeologist,* 10 (4): 133–64.
1950 "Missouri Archaeology." In *Missouri, Its Resources, People, and Institutions,* ed. N. P. Gist, pp. 190–200. Columbia, Missouri.
1952a "Recent Excavations in Graham Cave." *Memoir, Missouri Archaeological Society,* No. 2: 87–101.
1952b "Culture Sequence in the Lower Missouri Valley." In *Archeology of Eastern United States,* ed. J. B. Griffin, pp. 139–51. Chicago.
1956 "A Resume of Table Rock Archaeological Investigations." *The Missouri Archaeologist,* 18 (1–2): 1–45.
1957 "Graham Cave." In *A Report of Progress: Archaeological Research by the University of Missouri,* A Special Publication of the Missouri Archaeological Society, pp. 47–49.
1960a "Archaeology." In *Appendix: A Proposal for Ozark Rivers National Monument,* pp. 29–42. Washington, D.C.
1960b "Vaughn II, 23SN204." C. H. Chapman and others. Archaeological Investigations in the Table Rock Reservoir. Report to National Park Service on Contract 14–10–333–96, Midwest Research Center, Lincoln, Nebraska, pp. 300–307.
1960c "The Crisp Site IV, 23BY430." C. H.

Chapman and others. Archaeological Investigations in the Table Rock Reservoir. Report to National Park Service on Contract 14–10–333–96, Midwest Research Center, Lincoln, Nebraska, pp. 319–22.
1960d "Summary and Conclusions." C. H. Chapman and others. Archaeological Investigations in the Table Rock Reservoir. Report to National Park Service on Contract 14–10–333–96, Midwest Research Center, Lincoln, Nebraska, pp. 1150–70.
1965a "The Gray Shelter, 23SR122, Revisited." C. H. Chapman and others. Preliminary Archaeological Investigations in the Kaysinger Bluff Reservoir Area. Report to National Park Service on Contracts 14–10–232–374 and 14–10–232–589, Midwest Research Center, Lincoln, Nebraska, pp. 449–80.
1965b "Carved Rock Shelter, 23SR127." C. H. Chapman and others. Preliminary Archaeological Investigations in the Kaysinger Bluff Reservoir Area. Report to National Park Service on Contracts 14–10–232–374 and 14–10–232–589, Midwest Research Center, Lincoln, Nebraska, pp. 409–12.
1965c "Cat Hollow Shelter, 23SR126." C. H. Chapman and others. Preliminary Archaeological Investigations in the Kaysinger Bluff Reservoir Area. Report to National Park Service on Contracts 14–10–232–374 and 14–10–232–589, Midwest Research Center, Lincoln, Nebraska, pp. 542–61.
1967a "Fluted Point Survey of Missouri: An Interim Report." *Missouri Archaeological Society Newsletter,* 215: 9–10.
1967b "Fluted Point Survey: Addenda." *Missouri Archaeological Society Newsletter,* 216: 6.
1972 "A Framework for Missouri Archaeology." *Missouri Archaeological Society Newsletter,* No. 264: 1–3.
1973 "Some Comments About the Distribution of Three Hundred Fluted Points in Missouri." *Missouri Archaeological Society Newsletter,* No. 275: 1–5.

Chapman, C. H., and R. T. Bray
1960 "Vaughn I, 23SN203." C. H. Chapman and others. Archaeological Investigations in the Table Rock Reservoir. Report to National Park Service on Contract 14–10–333–96, Midwest Research Center, Lincoln, Nebraska, pp. 268–99.

Chapman, C. H., and E. F. Chapman
1964 *Indians and Archaeology of Missouri.* Missouri Handbook No. 6. Columbia, Missouri.
1972 *Indians and Archaeology of Missouri.* Missouri Handbook No. 5. Columbia, Missouri.

Chapman, C. H., S. Denny, and R. B. McMillan
1964 "Report on the Archaeological Resources in the Bourbeuse River Valley and Lower Meramec Valley of the Meramec Basin Project Area, Missouri." Report to National Park Service on Purchase Order 32–NPS–293, Midwest Research Center, Lincoln, Nebraska, pp. 1–184.

Chapman, C. H., and D. R. Evans
1972 "Archaeological-Physiographic Regions and Localities of Missouri." *Missouri Archaeological Society Newsletter,* No. 263: 1–4.

Chapman, C. H., T. J. Maxwell, Jr., and E. Kozlovich
1951 "A Preliminary Archaeological Survey of the Table Rock Reservoir Area, Stone County, Missouri." *The Missouri Archaeologist,* 13 (2): 1–39.

Chapman, C. H., and R. Pangborn
1965 "The Brounlee Shelter, 23SR105." C. H. Chapman and others. Preliminary Archaeological Investigations in the Kaysinger Bluff Reservoir Area Part II. Report to National Park Service on Contracts 14–10–232–374 and 14–10–232–589, Midwest Research Center, Lincoln, Nebraska, pp. 415–48.

Chapman, C. H., and others
1960 "Archaeological Investigations in the Table Rock Reservoir, Missouri. Parts I-V." Report to National Park Service on Contract 14–10–333–96, Midwest Research Center, Lincoln, Nebraska, pp. 1–1179.
1962 "A Preliminary Investigation of the Stockton Reservoir Area." Report to National Park Service on Contract 14–10–232–537, Midwest Research Center, Lincoln, Nebraska, pp. 1–164.

Chard, C. S.
1958 " New World Migration Routes." *Anthropological Papers of the University of Alaska,* 7 (1): 23–26.
1959 "New World Origins, A Reappraisal." *Antiquity,* 33 (1): 44–49.
1960 "Routes to Bering Strait." *American Antiquity,* 26 (2): 283–85.
1963 "The Old World Roots: Review and Speculation." *Anthropological Papers of the University of Alaska,* 10 (2): 115–21.
1969 *Man in Prehistory.* St. Louis, Missouri.

Claypole, E. W.
1896 "Human Relics in the Drift of Ohio." *The American Geologist,* 18 (5): 302.

Cleland, C. E.
1965 "Barren Ground Caribou (*Rangifer arcticus*) from an Early Man Site in Southeastern Michigan." *American Antiquity,* 30 (3): 350–51.
1966 *The Prehistoric Animal Ecology and Ethnology of the Upper Great Lakes Region.* Anthropological Papers, Museum of Anthropology, University of Michigan No. 29.

Coe, J. L.
1952 "The Cultural Sequence of the Carolina Piedmont." In *Archeology of Eastern United States,* ed. J. B. Griffin, pp. 301–11. Chicago.
1964 "The Formative Cultures of the Carolina Piedmont." *Transactions of the American Philosophical Society,* 54 (5): 1–130.

Colbert, E. H.
1942 "The Association of Men with Extinct Mammals in the Western Hemisphere." *Proceedings of the Eighth Scientific Congress,* 2: 27.

Cole, F-C.
1946 "Neolithic Evidences of Old and New World Connections." *Journal of the Illinois State Archaeological Society,* 4 (2): 2–7, 30.

Cole, F-C., and T. Deuel
1937 *Rediscovering Illinois.* Chicago.

Cole, F-C., and others
1951 *Kincaid: A Prehistoric Illinois Metropolis.* Chicago.

Coleman, D. D.
1972 "Illinois State Geological Survey Radiocarbon Dates III." *Radiocarbon,* 14 (1): 149, 154.

Collier, J. E.
1953 *Geography of the Northern Ozark Border Region in Missouri.* Columbia, Missouri.
1955a "Geographic Regions of Missouri." *Annals of the Association of American Geographers,* 45 (4): 368–92.
1955b *Agricultural Atlas of Missouri.* Columbia, Missouri.
1959 *Geographic Areas of Missouri.* Parkville, Missouri.

Converse, R. N.
1963 "Ohio Flint Types." *Ohio Archaeologist,* 13 (4): 1–121.

Cooke, C. W.
1928 "The Stratigraphy and Age of the Pleistocene Deposits in Florida from which Human Bones have been Reported." *Journal of the Washington Academy of Science,* 18: 414–21.

Cooper, J. M.
1946 "The Yahgan." In *Handbook of South American Indians, the Marginal Tribes,* ed. J. H. Steward, Bureau of American Ethnology Bulletin, 143 (1): 81–106.

Cope, E. D.
1895 "The Antiquity of Man: North America." *American Naturalist,* 29 (342): 593–99.

Cotter, J. L.
1966 "Comments on Pre-Folsom Estimates of the Age of Man in America." *American Anthropologist,* 68 (1): 196–98.

Cozzens, A. B.
1939 "Analyzing and Mapping Natural Landscape Factors of the Ozark Province." *Transactions of the Academy of Science of St. Louis,* 30: 37–63.

Crabtree, D.
1969 "A Technological Description of Artifacts in Assemblage I, Wilson Butte Cave, Idaho." *Current Anthropology,* 10 (4): 366–67.

Crane, H. R., and J. B. Griffin
1956 "University of Michigan Radiocarbon Dates I." *Science,* 124 (3224): 664–72.
1958 "University of Michigan Radiocarbon Dates II." *Science,* 128 (3306): 1098–1105.
1960 "University of Michigan Radiocarbon Dates V." *Radiocarbon,* 2: 31–48.
1968 "University of Michigan Radiocarbon Dates XII." *Radiocarbon,* 10 (1): 61–114.
1972a "University of Michigan Radiocarbon Dates XIV." *Radiocarbon,* 14 (1): 155–94.
1972b "University of Michigan Radiocarbon Dates XV." *Radiocarbon,* 14 (1): 195–222.

Creager, J. S., and D. A. McManus
1967 "Geology of the Floor of Bering and Chukchi Seas—American Studies." In *The Bering Land Bridge,* ed. D. M. Hopkins, pp. 7–31. Stanford, California.

Cressman, L. S.
1946 "Early Man in Oregon: Stratigraphic Evidence." *Scientific Monthly,* 62 (1): 43–51.
1956 "Man in the New World." In *Man, Culture and Society,* ed. H. L. Shapiro, pp. 139–67. New York.
1960 "Cultural Sequences at the Dalles, Oregon, A Contribution to Pacific Northwest Prehistory." *Transactions of the American Philosophical Society,* 50 (10): 1–108.
1966 "Man in Association with Extinct Fauna in the Great Basin." *American Antiquity,* 31 (6): 866–67.

Cresson, H. T.
1890a "Early Man in the Delaware Valley." *Proceedings of the Boston Society of Natural History,* 24: 141–50.
1890b "Remarks Upon a Chipped Implement, Found in Modified Drift on the East Fork of the White River, Jackson County, Indiana." *Proceedings of the Boston Society of Natural History,* 24: 150–52.

Croneis, C.
1939 "Possible Evidence of Prehistoric Man in Southeastern Missouri." *Geological Society of America Bulletin,* 50 (12): Part 2.

Crook, W. W., Jr., and R. K. Harris
1952 "Trinity Aspect of the Archaic Horizon: The Carrollton and Elam Foci." *Bulletin of the Texas Archaeological and Paleontological Society,* 23: 7–38.
1957 "Hearths and Artifacts of Early Man near Lewisville, Texas, and Associated Faunal Materials." *Bulletin of the Texas Archeological Society,* 28: 7–97.
1958 "A Pleistocene Campsite near Lewisville, Texas." *American Antiquity,* 23 (3): 233–46.

Cruxent, J. M.
1962 "Phosphorus Content of Texas Street Hearths." *American Antiquity,* 28 (1): 90–91.

Cushing, E. J., and H. E. Wright, Jr.
1967 *Quaternary Paleoecology.* New Haven and London.

Daly, R. A.
1929 "Swinging Sealevel of the Ice Age." *Geological Society of America Bulletin,* 40 (12): 721–34.
1934 *The Changing World of the Ice Age.* New Haven.

Dana, J. D.
1875 "On Dr. Koch's Evidence with Regard to the Contemporaneity of Man and the Mastodon in Missouri." *American Journal of Science and Arts,* 109 (53): 335–45.

Daugherty, H. E.
1968 "Quaternary Climatology of North America with emphasis on the State of Illinois." In *The Quaternary of Illinois,* ed. R. E. Bergstrom, pp. 61–69. Urbana.

Daugherty, R.
1956a "Early Man in the Columbia-Intermontane Province." *Anthropology Papers, University of Utah Department of Anthropology,* 24: 1–123.
1956b "Archaeology of the Lind Coulee Site, Washington." *Proceedings of the American Philosophical Society,* 100 (3): 223–78.

Davis, B.
1965 "Phytogeography and Palynology of Northeastern United States." In *The Quaternary of the United States,* eds. H. E. Wright, Jr., and D. G. Frey, pp. 377–401. Princeton.

Davis, E. L., C. W. Brott, and D. L. Weide
1969 *The Western Lithic Co-Tradition.* San Diego Museum Papers No. 6.

Davis, E. M.
1962 *Archaeology of the Lime Creek Site in Southwestern Nebraska.* Special Publication of the University of Nebraska State Museum, No. 3.

Davis, S. N.
1955 "Pleistocene Geology of Platte County, Missouri." Ph.D. Dissertation, Geology Department, Yale University.

Deevy, E. S., Jr.
1949 "Biogeography of the Pleistocene." *Geological Society of America Bulletin,* 60 (9): 1315–1416.
1956 "The Human Crop." *Scientific American,* 194 (4): 105–12.
1960 "The Human Population." *Scientific American,* 203 (3): 194–205.

Dejarnette, D. I., E. B. Kurjack, and J. W. Cambron
1962 "Stanfield-Worley Bluff Shelter Excavations." *Journal of Alabama Archaeology,* 8 (1–2): 124.

Delling, D. R.
1963 "Site 23SL85." *Missouri Archaeological Society Newsletter,* 170: 3–7.

Delling, M. P.
1966 "A Folsom Point from Boone County, Missouri." *Plains Anthropologist,* 11 (3): 235.

Del Rio, H. A., H. Breuil, and R. P. L. Sierra
1911 *Les Cavernes de la Region Cantabrique (Espagne),* Monaco.

Deuel, T.
1957 "The Modoc Shelter." *Natural History,* 66 (8): 400–405.

Dice, L. R.
1943 *The Biotic Provinces of North America.* Ann Arbor.

Dickeson, M. W.
1846 "Report at Meeting of October 6, 1846." *Proceedings of the Academy of Natural Sciences of Philadelphia:* 106–7.

Dikov, N. N.
1968 "The Discovery of the Paleolithic in Kamchatka and the Problems of the Initial Occupation of America." *Arctic Anthropology,* 5 (1): 191–204.

Dillon, L. S.
1956 "Wisconsin Climate and Life in North America." *Science,* 123 (3188): 167–76.

Disser, E.
1965 "Some Early Points in the Disser Collection." *Missouri Archaeological Society Newsletter,* 188: 4–6.

Dorwin, J. T.
1966 "Fluted Points and Late Pleistocene Geochronology in Indiana." *Prehistory Research Series,* 4 (3): 141–87.

Driver, H. E.
1961 *Indians of North America.* Chicago.

Driver, H. E., and W. C. Massey
1957 "Comparative Studies of North American Indians." *Transactions of the American Philosophical Society,* 47 (2): 165–456.

Dunnell, R. C.
1971 *Systematics in Prehistory.* New York.

Durham, B.
1960 *Canoes and Kayaks of Western America.* Seattle.

Edwards, C. R.
1965 "Aboriginal Watercraft on the Pacific Coast of South America." *Ibero-Americana,* 47: 1–138.

Eichenberger, J. A.
1944 "Investigations of the Marion-Ralls Archaeological Society in Northeast Missouri." *The Missouri Archaeologist,* No. 19: 1–69.
1956 "The Hannibal Complex." *The Missouri Archaeologist,* 18 (4): 8–18.

Eiseley, L.
1945 "The Mastodon and Early Man in America." *Science,* 102 (2640): 108–10.
1946 "Man, Mastodons, and Myths." *Scientific Monthly,* 62 (5): 517–24.

Ekholm, G. F.
1955 "The New Orientation Toward Problems of Asiatic-American Relationships." In *New Interpretations of Aboriginal American Culture History,* pp. 95–109. Washington, D. C.

Emery, K. O., and R. L. Edwards
1966 "Archaeological Potential of the Atlantic Continental Shelf." *American Antiquity,* 31 (5): 733–37.

Epstein, J. F.
n.d. "The San Isidro Site, An Early Man Campsite in Nuevo Leon, Mexico." *Department of Anthropology, The University of Texas at Austin Anthropology Series,* No. 7: 1–148.

Falk, C. R.
1970 "The Application of a Factor Analysis in the Interpretation of Unmodified Vertebrate

Remains from an Archaeological Cave Deposit in Central Missouri." M.A. Thesis, Department of Anthropology, University of Missouri, Columbia.

Farmer, M. F.
1964 "The Arctic-North Atlantic as a Prehistoric Migration Route." *Anthropological Journal of Canada,* 2 (4): 2–4.

Fenneman, N. M.
1938 *Physiography of Eastern United States.* New York.

Fischel, H. E.
1941 "Supplementary Data on Early Man in America." *American Antiquity,* 6 (4): 346–48.

Fisher, R. G.
1935 *The Relation of North American Prehistory to Post-Glacial Climatic Fluctuations.* Monographs of the School of American Research, 3: 1–91.

Fitting, J.
1963 "Thickness and Fluting of Paleo-Indian Projectile Points." *American Antiquity,* 29 (1): 105–6.
1964 "Some Characteristics of Projectile Point Bases from the Holcombe Site, Macomb County, Michigan." *Papers of the Michigan Academy of Science, Arts and Letters,* 49 (2): 231–38.
1965 "Observations on Paleo-Indian Adaptive and Settlement Patterns." *The Michigan Archaeologist,* 11 (3): 103–9.
1968 "Environmental Potential and the Postglacial Readaptation in Eastern North America." *American Antiquity,* 33 (4): 441–45.

Fitting, J. E., J. de Visscher, and E. J. Wahla
1966 *The Paleo-Indian Occupation of the Holcombe Beach.* Anthropological Papers, Museum of Anthropology, University of Michigan, No. 27.

Flint, R. F.
1957 "Moving Picture of the Last Ice Age." *Natural History,* 46 (4): 188–89.
1963 "Status of the Pleistocene Wisconsin Stage in Central North America." *Science,* 139 (3553): 402–4.

Ford, J. A.
1954 "The Type Concept Revisited." *American Anthropologist,* 56 (1): 42–54.

Ford, J. A., and C. H. Webb
1956 *Poverty Point, A Late Archaic Site in Louisiana.* Anthropological Papers of the American Museum of Natural History, 46.

Ford, J. A., and G. R. Willey
1941 "An Interpretation of the Prehistory of the Eastern United States." *American Anthropologist,* 43 (3): 325–63.

Foster, J. W.
1881 *Prehistoric Races of the United States of America.* Chicago.

Fowke, G.
1922 *Archaeological Investigations.* Bureau of American Ethnology Bulletin, 76.
1928 "Archaeological Investigations—II." *44th Annual Report of the Bureau of American Ethnology,* 399-540.

Fowler, M. L.
1954 "Some Fluted Projectile Points from Illinois." *American Antiquity,* 20 (2): 170–71.
1957 "Archaic Projectile Point Styles 7,000–2,000 B.C. in the Central Mississippi Valley." *The Missouri Archaeologist,* 19 (1–2): 1–20.
1959a "Summary Report of Modoc Rock Shelter 1952, 1953, 1955, 1956." *Illinois State Museum Report of Investigations,* No. 8: 1–72.
1959b "Modoc Rock Shelter, An Early Archaic Site in Southern Illinois." *American Antiquity,* 24 (3): 257–70.

Fowler, M. L., H. Winters, and P. W. Parmalee
1956 "Modoc Rock Shelter Preliminary Report." *Illinois State Museum Report of Investigations,* No. 4: 1–58.

Frankforter, W. D.
1959 "A Pre-Ceramic Site in Western Iowa." *Journal of the Iowa Archaeological Society,* 8 (4): 47–72.

Frankforter, W. D., and G. A. Agogino
1959 "Archaic and Paleo-Indian Archaeological Discoveries in Western Iowa." *The Texas Journal of Science,* 11 (4): 482–91.

Franks, B. R.
1964 "Artifacts from St. John's Bayou, Missouri." *Missouri Archaeological Society Newsletter,* 182: 9–11.

Frye, J., H. B. Willman, and F. Black
1965 "Outline of Glacial Geology of Illinois and Wisconsin." In *The Quaternary of the United States,* eds. H. E. Wright, Jr., and D. G. Frey, pp. 43–61. Princeton.

Frye, J. C., H. B. Willman, M. Rubin, and F. Black
1968 *Definition of Wisconsin Stage: Contributions to Stratigraphy.* Geological Survey Bulletin, 1274-E.

Gerdes, H. H.
1956 "Artifacts from Franklin County." *Missouri Archaeological Society Newsletter,* 102: 9.
1965 "Some Aged Points from the New Haven, Missouri Vicinity." *Missouri Archaeological Society Newsletter,* 190: 6–7.

Giddings, J. L., Jr.
1954 "Early Man in the Arctic." *Scientific American,* 190 (6): 82–88.

Gidley, J. W.
1926a "Explorations of a Pleistocene Spring Deposit in Oklahoma." *Smithsonian Miscellaneous Collections,* 78 (1): 27–28.
1926b "Investigations of Evidences of Early Man at Melbourne and Vero, Florida." *Smithsonian Miscellaneous Collections,* 78 (1): 23–26.
1929 "Ancient Man in Florida: Further Investigations." *Bulletin of the Geological Society of America,* 40 (2): 491–501.
1930 "Investigations of Early Man in Florida." *Explorations and Fieldwork of the Smithsonian Institution in 1929,* 37–38.
1931 "Further Investigations of Evidence of Early Man in Florida." *Explorations and Fieldwork of the Smithsonian Institution in 1930,* 41–44.

Gidley, J. W., and F. B. Loomis
1926 "Fossil Man in Florida." *American Journal of Science,* 212 (69): 254–64.

Gilbert, B. M.
1972 "An Evaluation of Hypotheses Concerning the Earliest Peopling of the New World." *Missouri Archaeological Society Newsletter,* 259: 1–8.

Gilbert, C. K.
1889 "The Geological History of a Prehistoric Hearth found in Western New York." *American Anthropologist,* o.s., 2 (2): 173–74.

Goggin, J. M.
1950 "An Early Lithic Complex from Central Florida." *American Antiquity,* 16 (1): 46–49.

Graham, J. A., and R. F. Heizer
1967 "Man's Antiquity in North America: Views and Facts." *Quaternaria,* 9: 225–35.

Greenman, E. F.
1943 "An Early Industry on a Raised Beach Near Killarney, Ontario." *American Antiquity,* 8 (3): 260–65.
1948 "The Killarney Sequence and its Old World Connections." *Papers of the Michigan Academy of Science, Arts and Letters,* 32: 313–19.
1960 "The North Atlantic and Early Man in the New World." *The Michigan Archaeologist,* 6 (2): 19–39.
1963 "The Upper Paleolithic and the New World." *Current Anthropology,* 4 (1): 41–91.

Greenman, E. F., and G. M. Stanley
1943 "The Archaeology and Geology of the Two Early Sites Near Killarney, Ontario." *Papers of the Michigan Academy of Science, Arts and Letters,* 28: 505–30.

Gregory, J., and S. Towns
1966 "The Afton Point." *Central States Archaeological Journal,* 13 (3): 116–19.

Griffin, J. B.
1952a "Culture Periods in Eastern United States Archeology." In *Archeology of Eastern United States,* ed. J. B. Griffin, pp. 352–64. Chicago.
1952b "Radiocarbon Dates for the Eastern United States." In *Archeology of Eastern United States,* ed. J. B. Griffin, pp. 365–70. Chicago.
1955 "Observations on the Grooved Axe in North America." *Pennsylvania Archaeologist,* 25 (1): 32–44.
1961 "Some Correlations of Climate and Cultural Change in Eastern North American Prehistory." *Annals, New York Academy of Science,* 95: 710–17.
1964 "The Northeast Woodlands Area." In *Prehistoric Man in the New World,* eds. J. D. Jennings and E. Norbeck, pp. 223–58. Chicago.
1965 "Late Quaternary Prehistory in the Northeastern Woodlands." In *The Quaternary of the United States,* eds. H. E. Wright, Jr., and D. G. Frey, pp. 655–67. Princeton.
1966 "Some Prehistoric Connections between Siberia and America." In *New Roads to Yesterday,* ed. J. Caldwell, pp. 277–301. New York.
1967 "Eastern North American Archaeology: A Summary." *Science,* 156 (3772): 175–91.
1968 "Observation on Illinois Prehistory in Late Pleistocene and Early Recent Times." In *The Quaternary of Illinois,* ed. R. E. Bergstrom, pp. 123–37. Urbana.

Griffin, J. B. (ed.)
1952 *Archeology of Eastern United States.* Chicago.

Griffin, J. B., and A. C. Spaulding
1951 "The Central Mississippi Valley Archaeological Survey, Season 1950, A Preliminary Report." *Journal of the Illinois State Archaeological Society,* n.s., 1 (3): 74–84.
1952 "The Central Mississippi Valley Archaeological Survey, Season 1950, A Preliminary Report." *Prehistoric Pottery of Eastern United States,* 2–52: 1–7.

Grimm, R. E. (ed.)
1953 *Prehistoric Art.* St. Louis, Missouri.

Gross, H.
1951 "Mastodon, Mammoth and Man in America." *Bulletin of the Texas Archaeological and Paleontological Society,* 22: 101–31.

Gruhn, R. D.

1961 *The Archaeology of Wilson Butte Cave, South-Central Idaho.* Occasional Papers of the Idaho State College Museum, No. 6.

1965 "Two Early Radiocarbon Dates from the Lower Levels of Wilson Butte Cave, South-Central Idaho." *Tebiwa,* 8 (2): 57.

Guilday, J. E.

1967 "The Climatic Significance of the Hosterman's Pit Local Fauna, Centre County, Pennsylvania." *American Antiquity,* 32 (2): 231–32.

Guthe, A. K.

1966 "Tennessee's Paleo-Indian." *Tennessee Archaeologist,* 22 (2): 67–77.

Haag, W. G.

1962 "The Bering Strait Land Bridge." *Scientific American,* 206 (1): 112–23.

Hagsten, U.

1961 "Pleistocene Development of Vegetation and Climate in the Southern High Plains as Evidenced by Pollen Analysis." In *The Paleoecology of the Llano Estacado,* ed. F. W. Wendorf, pp. 51–91. Santa Fe.

Harrington, M. R.

1933 *Gypsum Cave, Nevada.* Southwest Museum Papers, No. 8.

Harrington, M. R., and R. D. Simpson

1961 *Tule Springs, Nevada, with Other Evidences of Pleistocene Man in North America.* Southwest Museum Papers, No. 18.

Haury, E. W.

1950 *The Stratigraphy and Archaeology of Ventana Cave, Arizona.* Tucson.

Haven, S. F.

1856 "Archaeology of the United States." *Smithsonian Contributions to Knowledge,* 8: 1–168.

Hay, O. P.

1918 "Further Consideration of Occurrence of Human Remains in the Pleistocene Deposits at Vero, Florida." *American Anthropologist,* 20 (1): 1–36.

Haynes, C. V., Jr.

1964 "Fluted Projectile Points: Their Age and Dispersion." *Science,* 145 (3639): 1408–13.

1966 "Elephant-Hunting in North America." *Scientific American,* 214 (6): 104–12.

1967 "Carbon-14 Dates and Early Man in the New World." In *Pleistocene Extinctions, the Search for a Cause,* eds. P. S. Martin and H. E. Wright, Jr., pp. 267–86. New Haven.

1969 "The Earliest Americans." *Science,* 166 (3906): 709–15.

1970 "Geochronology of Man in Mammoth Sites and Their Bearing on the Origin of the Llano Complex." In *Pleistocene and Recent Environments in the Central Great Plains,* eds. W. Dort, Jr., and J. K. Jones, Jr., pp. 77–92. Lawrence.

1971 "Time, Environment and Early Man." *Arctic Anthropology,* 8 (2): 3–14.

Haynes, C. V., Jr., and G. Agogino

1960 "Geological Significance of a New Radiocarbon Date from the Lindenmeier Site." *Proceedings of the Denver Museum of Natural History,* 9: 1–23.

Haynes, C. V., Jr., and E. T. Hemmings

1968 "Mammoth Bone Shaft Wrench from Murray Springs, Arizona." *Science,* 159 (3811): 186–87.

Haynes, H. W.

1889 "The Prehistoric Archaeology of North America." In *Narrative and Critical History of America, Vol. I,* ed. J. Winsor, pp. 329–68. Cambridge.

Heizer, R. F.

1948 *A Bibliography of Ancient Man in California.* Reports of the California Archaeological Survey, No. 2. Berkeley.

1958 "Radiocarbon Dates from California of Archaeological Interest." *Reports of the University of California Archaeological Survey,* No. 44, Part I: 1–16.

1964 "The Western Coast of North America." In *Prehistoric Man in the New World,* eds. J. D. Jennings and E. Norbeck, pp. 117–48. Chicago.

Heizer, R. F., and R. A. Brooks

1965 "Lewisville-Ancient Campsite or Wood Rat Houses?" *Southwestern Journal of Anthropology,* 2 (2): 155–65.

Heizer, R. F., and S. F. Cook

1952 "Flourine and Other Chemical Tests of Some North American Human and Fossil Bones." *American Journal of Physical Anthropology,* 10 (3): 289–304.

Heldman, D., and R. Wyatt

1959 A Preliminary Report on Research Cave, Callaway County, Missouri. University of Missouri—Columbia, American Archaeology Division, files.

Henning, A. E.

1966 "Fabrics and Related Materials from Arnold Research Cave." *The Missouri Archaeologist,* 28: 41–53, 92–107.

Henning, D. R.

1960a "Preliminary Archaeological Survey:

Joanna Reservoir." Report to National Park Service on Contract 14–10–232–370, Midwest Research Center, Lincoln, Nebraska, pp. 8–145.

1960b "An Archaic Hill-Top Site, 23SN562." C. H. Chapman and others. Archaeological Investigations in the Table Rock Reservoir, Part IV. Report to National Park Service on Contract 14–10–333–96, Midwest Research Center, Lincoln, Nebraska, pp. 795–813.

1961a "Archaeological Research in the Proposed Joanna Reservoir, Missouri." *The Missouri Archaeologist,* 23: 132–77.

1961b "Nebo Hill Revisited." *Missouri Archaeological Society Newsletter,* 154: 3–10.

1962 "Archaeological Investigations, Joanna Reservoir 1961." C. H. Chapman, D. P. Heldman, and D. R. Henning. Archaeological Investigations in the Joanna Reservoir Area, Missouri. Report to the National Park Service on Contract 14–10–232–401, Midwest Research Center, Lincoln, Nebraska, pp. 87–280.

Hester, J. J.
1966 "Origins of the Clovis Culture." *Congreso Internacional de Americanistas,* 36 (1): 129–42.

Hibben, F. C.
1937 "Association of Man with Pleistocene Mammals in the Sandia Mountains, New Mexico." *American Antiquity,* 2 (4): 260–65.

1941 "Evidences of Early Occupation in Sandia Cave, New Mexico, and Other Sites in the Sandia-Manzano Region." *Smithsonian Miscellaneous Collections,* 99 (23): 1–44, 15 plates.

1942 "Pleistocene Stratification in the Sandia Cave, New Mexico." *Proceedings of the Eighth American Scientific Congress, Vol. II Anthropological Science:* 45–49.

1943 "Discoveries in Sandia Cave and Early Horizons in the Southwest." *Proceedings of the American Philosophical Society,* 86 (2): 247–54.

1946 "The First Thirty-Eight Sandia Points." *American Antiquity,* 11 (4): 257–58.

1955 "Specimens from Sandia Cave and their Possible Significance." *Science,* 122 (3172): 688–89.

1957 "Radiocarbon Dates from Sandia Cave, Correction." *Science,* 125 (3241): 234–35.

Hodge, F. W. (ed.)
1912 *Handbook of American Indians North of Mexico.* 2 vols. Bureau of American Ethnology Bulletin, No. 30.

Holmes, W. H.
1886 "Ancient Pottery of the Mississippi Valley." *Fourth Annual Report of the Bureau of American Ethnology 1882–1883:* 361–436.

1890 "A Quarry Workshop of the Flaked-Stone Implement Makers in the District of Columbia." *American Anthropologist,* o.s., 3 (1): 1–26.

1893a "Vestiges of Early Man in Minnesota." *The American Geologist,* 11 (4): 219–40.

1893b "Traces of Glacial Man in Ohio." *The Journal of Geology,* 1 (2): 147–63.

1901 "Review of the Evidence Relating to Auriferous Gravel Man in California." *Smithsonian Institution Annual Report for 1899:* 419–72.

1903a "Aboriginal Pottery of the Eastern United States." *Twentieth Annual Report of the Bureau of American Ethnology 1898–1899:* 1–201.

1903b "Flint Implements and Fossil Remains from a Sulphur Spring at Afton, Indian Territory." *Report of the U.S. National Museum for 1901:* 233–52.

1910 "Nampa Image." In *Handbook of American Indians North of Mexico,* Vol. II, ed. F. W. Hodge, pp. 18–19. Bureau of American Ethnology Bulletin, No. 30.

1914 "Areas of American Culture Characterization Tentatively Outlined as an Aid in the Study of Antiquities." *American Anthropologist,* 16 (3): 413–46.

1919 *Handbook of Aboriginal American Antiquities.* Bureau of American Ethnology Bulletin, No. 60.

1925 "The Antiquity Phantom in American Archaeology." *Science,* 62 (1603): 256–58.

1928 "Pitfalls of the Paleolithic Theory in America." *International Congress of Americanists Rio de Janeiro, 1922,* 20 (2): 171–75.

Honea, K.
1965 *Early Man Projectile Points in the Southwest.* Santa Fe.

Hopkins, D. M.
1959 "Cenezoic History of the Bering Land Bridge." *Science,* 129 (3362): 1519–28.

Hopkins, D. M. (ed.)
1967 *The Bering Land Bridge.* Stanford.

Houart, G. L.
1971 *Koster: A Stratified Archaic Site in the Illinois Valley.* Illinois State Museum Reports of Investigations, No. 22.

Howard, E. B.
1935 "Evidence of Early Man in North America." *The Museum Journal, University Museum, University of Pennsylvania,* 24 (2–3): 61–171.

1936 "An Outline of the Problem of Man's Antiquity in North America." *American Anthropologist,* 38 (3): 394–413.

Howells, W. W.
1944 *Mankind So Far.* Garden City, New York.

Hrdlicka, A.
1903 "The Lansing Skeleton." *American Anthropologist,* 5 (2): 323–30.
1907 *Skeletal Remains Suggesting or Attributed to Early Man.* Bureau of American Ethnology, Bulletin 33.
1912 "Historical Notes." In "The Problem of Unity and Plurality and Probable Place of Origin of the American Aborigines," ed. J. W. Fewkes. *American Anthropologist,* 14 (1): 5–8.
1918 *Recent Discoveries Attributed to Early Man in America.* Bureau of American Ethnology Bulletin, No. 66.
1920 "The Newest Discovery of 'Ancient Man' in the United States." *American Journal of Physical Anthropology,* 3 (1): 187–93.
1925 "The Origin and Antiquity of the American Indians." *Smithsonian Institution Annual Report for 1923:* 481–94.
1928 "Man's Antiquity in America." *International Congress of Americanists Rio de Janeiro, 1922,* 20 (2): 57–61.
1932 "The Coming of Man from Asia in the Light of Recent Discoveries." *Proceedings of the American Philosophical Society,* 71 (7): 393–402.
1937a "The Minnesota 'Man.'" *American Journal of Physical Anthropology,* 22 (2): 175–99.
1937b "Early Man in America: What have the Bones to Say?" In *Early Man,* eds. G. C. MacCurdy and J. C. Merriam, pp. 93–104. London.
1942 "The Problem of Man's Antiquity in America." *Proceedings of the Eighth Scientific Congress of Anthropological Science,* 2: 53.

Hubbs, C. L.
1958 "General Conclusions." In *Zoogeography,* ed. C. L. Hubbs, pp. 469–77. Washington, D.C.

Hughes, J. T.
1949 "Investigations in Western South Dakota and Northeastern Wyoming." *American Antiquity,* 14 (4): 266–77.

Humphrey, R. L.
1966 "The Prehistory of the Utokok River Region, Arctic Alaska: Early Fluted Point Tradition with Old World Relationships." *Current Anthropology,* 7 (5): 586–88.

Hurley, W. M.
1965 "Archaeological Research in the Projected Kickapoo Reservoir, Vernon County, Wisconsin." *Wisconsin Archaeologist,* 46 (1): 1–113.

Hurt, W. R.
1953 "A Comparative Study of the Preceramic Occupation of North America." *American Antiquity,* 18 (3): 204–22.

Hyde, E. W.
1960 *Mid-Ohio Valley Paleo-Indian and Suggested Sequence of the Fluted Point Cultures.* West Virginia Archaeological Society Publication, No. 5.

Imbelloni, J.
1943 "The Peopling of America." *Acta Americana,* 1 (3): 309–30.

Irving, W. N.
1963 "Northwest North America and Central United States: A Review." *Anthropological Papers of the University of Alaska,* 10 (2): 63–67.
1971 "Recent Early Man in Research in the North." *Arctic Anthropology,* 8 (2): 68–82.

Irwin, H. T.
1971 "Developments in Early Man Studies in Western North America, 1960–1970." *Arctic Anthropology,* 8 (2): 42–67.

Irwin, H. T., and H. M. Wormington
1970 "Paleo-Indian Tool Types in the Great Plains." *American Antiquity,* 35 (1): 24–34.

Irwin-Williams, C.
1967 "Associations of Early Man with Horse, Camel, and Mastodon at Hueyatlaco, Valsequillo (Pueblo, Mexico)." In *Pleistocene Extinctions: The Search for a Cause,* eds. P. S. Martin and H. E. Wright, Jr., pp. 337–47. Proceedings of the VII Congress of the International Association for Quaternary Research, 6: 337–47. New Haven.
1968 "Archaeological Evidence on Early Man in Mexico." *Eastern New Mexico University Contributions in Anthropology,* 1 (4): 39–41.

Irwin-Williams, C., and H. J. Irwin
1966 *Excavations at Magic Mountain.* Proceedings of the Denver Museum of Natural History, No. 12.

Ivanova, I. K.
1968 "Comment on Valoch, Evolution of Paleolithic in Central and Eastern Europe." *Current Anthropology,* 9 (5): 375–76.

Ivanova, I. K., and A. P. Chernysh
1965 "The Paleolithic Site of Makarova V on the Middle Dniester." *Quaternaria,* 7: 197–217.

Jelinek, A. J.
1957 "Pleistocene Faunas of Early Man." *Papers of the Michigan Academy of Science, Arts, and Letters,* 42: 225–37.

1962 "An Index of Radiocarbon Dates Associated with Cultural Materials." *Current Anthropology,* 3 (5): 451–77.
1965 "The Upper Paleolithic Revolution and the Peopling of the New World." *The Michigan Archaeologist,* 11 (3–4): 85–88.
1971 "Early Man in the New World: A Technological Perspective." *Arctic Anthropology,* 8 (2): 15–21.

Jenks, A. E.
1936 *Pleistocene Man in Minnesota.* Minneapolis.
1937 *Minnesota's Browns Valley Man and Associated Burial Artifacts.* Memoirs of the American Anthropological Association, No. 49.
1938 "Minnesota Man: A Reply to a Review by Dr. Ales Hrdlicka." *American Anthropologist,* 40 (2): 328–36.

Jenks, A. E., and Mrs. H. H. Simpson
1941 "Beveled Artifacts in Florida of the Same Type as Artifacts Found Near Clovis, New Mexico." *American Antiquity,* 6 (4): 314–19.

Jenks, A. E., and L. A. Wilford
1938 "The Sauk Valley Skeleton." *Bulletin of the Texas Archaeological and Paleontological Society,* 10: 114–68.

Jennings, J. D.
1955 "Great Basin Prehistory: A Review." *American Antiquity,* 21 (1): 1–11.
1957 *Danger Cave.* Memoir of the Society for American Archaeology, No. 14.
1968 *Prehistory of North America.* St. Louis, Missouri.

Jennings, J. D., and E. Norbeck (eds.)
1964 *Prehistoric Man in the New World.* Chicago.

Johnson, F.
1951 "Early Man." *American Journal of Archaeology,* 55 (3): 264–65.

Johnson, L. H., III
1952 "Man and Elephants in America." *Scientific Monthly,* 75 (4): 215–21.

Josselyn, D. W.
1957 "Problems of Projectile Point Typology." *Journal of Alabama Archaeology,* 3 (2): 8–11.
1965a "The Lively Complex: Discussion of Some of the ABC's of this Technology." (Mimeo.). Birmingham, Alabama.
1965b "America's 'Crude Tools.'" *Tennessee Archaeologist,* 21 (2): 55–66.
1966 "Announcing Accepted American Pebble Tools, the Lively Complex of Alabama." *Anthropological Journal of Canada,* 4 (1): 24–31.

Kehoe, T. F.
1966a "The Distribution and Implication of Fluted Points in Saskatchewan." *American Antiquity,* 31 (4): 530–39.
1966b "The Small Side-Notch Point System of the Northern Plains." *American Antiquity,* 31 (6): 827–44.

Keller, C.
1961a "The Geiger Site." University of Missouri—Columbia, American Archaeology Division, files.
1961b "Preliminary Report on 23MU91, The Frank Geiger Site." *Missouri Archaeological Society Newsletter,* 151: 3–5.
1965 Preliminary Archaeological Reconnaissance and Testing. C. H. Chapman and others. Preliminary Archaeological Investigation in the Kaysinger Bluff Reservoir Area, Missouri. Report to National Park Service on Contracts 14–10–232–374 and 14–10–232–589, Midwest Research Center, Lincoln, Nebraska, pp. 171–220.

Kelley, J. C.
1947 "The Cultural Affiliations and Chronological Position of the Clear Fork Focus." *American Antiquity,* 13 (2): 97–109.

Kerby, M. L.
1964 "Climatic Succession in the Western Hemisphere from the Third Interglacial." *Quarterly Bulletin of the Archaeological Society of Virginia,* 19 (2): 26–35.
1965 "Earliest Migrations into North America: A Theoretical Outline of America's Origins." *Quarterly Bulletin of the Archaeological Society of Virginia,* 19 (3): 54–62.

Kidder, A. V., J. D. Jennings, and E. M. Shook
1946 *Excavations at Kaminaljuju, Guatemala.* Carnegie Institution of Washington, Publication 561.

Kigoshi, K., and H. Kobayashi
1966 "Gakushuin Natural Radiocarbon Measurements V." *Radiocarbon,* 8: 54–73.

King, D. B., E. V. Roberts, and R. K. Winters
1949 *Forest Resources and Industries of Missouri.* University of Missouri Agricultural Experiment Station Bulletin, No. 452.

King, T. F.
1971 "A Conflict of Values in American Archaeology." *American Antiquity,* 36 (3): 255–62.

Klippel, W. E.
1967 "Archaeological Research in the Cannon

Reservoir Area—1967." *Missouri Archaeological Society Newsletter,* 216: 8–10.

1968 "Archaeological Salvage in the Cannon Reservoir Area, Missouri: 1967." Report to National Park Service on Contract 14–10–2: 920–8 and Purchase Order 920–562, Midwest Research Center, Lincoln Nebraska, pp. 1–90, 14 plates.

1969 "The Booth Site: A Late Archaic Campsite." *Missouri Archaeological Society Research Series,* No. 6.

1970a "Prehistory and Environmental Change Along the Southern Border of the Prairie Peninsula During the Archaic Period." Ph.D. Dissertation, Department of Anthropology, University of Missouri—Columbia.

1970b "Preliminary Observations on Heat-Treated Chert from Late Archaic and Woodland Sites along the Southern Border of the Prairie Peninsula in Missouri." *Missouri Archaeological Society Newsletter,* 239: 1–7.

1971 *Graham Cave Revisited: A Reevaluation of its Cultural Position during the Archaic Period.* Memoir, Missouri Archaeological Society, No. 5.

Kneberg, M.
1956 "Some Important Projectile Point Types Found in the Tennessee Area." *Tennessee Archaeologist,* 12 (1): 17–28.

Knoblock, B. W.
1939 *Bannerstones of the North American Indian.* La Grange, Illinois.

Koch, A. K.
1839 "Remains of the Mastodon in Missouri." *American Journal of Science and Arts,* 37 (1): 191–92.

1841 *Description of the Missourium. . . .* London.

1843 *Description of the Missourium Theristocaulodon or Missouri Leviathan. . . .* Dublin.

1860 "Mastodon Remains in the State of Missouri, Together with Evidence of the Existence of Man Contemporaneously with the Mastodon." *Transactions of the Academy of Science of St. Louis,* 1: 61–64.

Kotani, Y.
1969 "Upper Pleistocene and Holocene Environmental Conditions in Japan." *Arctic Anthropology,* 5 (2): 133–58.

Krieger, A. D.
1947 "Certain Projectile Points of the Early American Hunters." *Bulletin of the Texas Archeological and Paleontological Society,* 18: 7–27.

1948 "Importance of the 'Gilmore Corridor' in Culture Contacts Between Middle America

and the Eastern United States." *Bulletin of the Texas Archeological and Paleontological Society,* 19: 155–78.

1953a "Basic Stages of Cultural Evolution." In *An Appraisal of Anthropology Today,* eds. S. Tax, and others, pp. 247–50. Chicago.

1953b "New World Culture History: Anglo America." In *Anthropology Today,* ed. A. L. Krocher, pp. 238–64. Chicago.

1954 "A Comment on 'Fluted Point Relationships.'" *American Antiquity,* 19 (3): 273–75.

1958 "Review of *Pleistocene Man at San Diego* by G. F. Carter." *American Anthropologist,* 60 (5): 974–78.

1962a "The Earliest Cultures in the Western United States." *American Antiquity,* 28 (2): 138–43.

1962b "Comment on Mason: Paleo-Indian in Eastern North America." *Current Anthropology,* 3 (3): 256–59.

1964 "Early Man in the New World." In *Prehistoric Man in the New World,* eds. J. D. Jennings and E. Norbeck, pp. 23–81. Chicago.

1965 "Reply to Bird." *American Antiquity,* 31 (2): 270–72.

Kroeber, A. L.
1939 *Cultural and Natural Areas of Native North America.* University of California Publications in American Archaeology and Ethnology, No. 38.

Krogman, W. M.
1941a "The Antiquity of Man and His Culture in the Americas." *Ciba Symposia,* 3 (1): 813–24.

1941b "Aboriginal Physical Types in the Western Hemisphere." *Ciba Symposia,* 3 (1): 804–12.

Kucera, C. L.
1961 *The Grasses of Missouri.* Columbia.

Kushner, G.
1970 "A Consideration of Some Processual Design for Archaeology as Anthropology." *American Antiquity,* 35 (2): 125–32.

Lancaster, J. B.
1968 "On the Evolution of Tool-Using Behavior." *American Anthropologist,* 70 (1): 56–66.

Lanning, E. P., and T. C. Patterson
1967 "Early Man in South America." *Scientific American,* 217 (5): 44–61.

Lee, R. B.
1968 "What Hunters do for a Living or, How to Make Out on Scarce Resources." In *Man the Hunter,* eds. R. B. Lee and I. Devore, pp. 30–48. Chicago.

Lee, T. E.
1953 "A Preliminary Report on the Sheguiandah Site, Manitoulin Island." *National Museum of Canada Bulletin,* 128: 58–67.
1955 "The Second Sheguiandah Expedition, Manitoulin Island, Ontario." *American Antiquity,* 21 (1): 63–71.
1956 "Position and Meaning of a Radiocarbon Sample from the Sheguiandah Site, Ontario." *American Antiquity,* 22 (1): 79.
1961 "The Question of Indian Origins." *The Science of Man,* 1: 159–67.
1968 "The Question of Indian Origins, Again." *Anthropological Journal of Canada,* 6 (4): 22–32.

Leidy, J.
1889 "Notice of Some Fossil Human Bones." *Transactions of the Wagner Free Institute of Science of Philadelphia,* 2: 9–12.

Leighton, M. M.
1960 "The Classification of the Wisconsin Glacial Stage of North-Central United States." *Journal of Geology,* 68: 529–52.

Leverett, F.
1893 "Supposed Glacial Man in Southwestern Ohio." *American Geologist,* 11 (3): 186–89.

Lewis, H. C.
1881 "The Antiquity and Origin of the Trenton Grave." In *Primitive Industry,* ed. C. C. Abott, pp. 521–51. Salem, Massachusetts.

Lewis, T. M. N., and M. K. Lewis
1961 *Eva, An Archaic Site.* Knoxville.

Libby, W. F.
1954 "Chicago Radiocarbon Dates V." *Science,* 120 (3123): 733–42.

Lindig, W.
1970 "On Evidence of Early Man in America." *Current Anthropology,* 11 (2): 168.

Little, E. L., Jr.
1971 *Atlas of United States Trees: Volume I Conifers and Important Hardwoods.* Washington, D.C.

Lively, M.
1965 "The Lively Complex: Preliminary Report on a Pebble Tool Complex in Alabama." (Mimeo.) Birmingham, Alabama.

Lively, M., and D. W. Josselyn
1965 *The Lively Complex Plates.* Guntersville, Alabama.

Logan, W. D.
1952 "Graham Cave: An Archaic Site in Montgomery County, Missouri." *Memoir, Missouri Archaeological Society,* No. 2: 1–86.

Long, R. J.
1953 "Glacial Drift Artifacts." *Ohio Archaeologist,* n.s., 3 (4): 24–26.

Loomis, F. B.
1924 "Artifacts Associated with the Remains of a Columbia Elephant at Melbourne, Florida." *American Journal of Science and Arts,* 208 (43): 503–8.

Luchterhand, K.
1970 "Early Archaic Projectile Points and Hunting Patterns in the Lower Illinois Valley." *Illinois State Museum Reports of Investigations,* No. 19.

McCary, B. C.
1951 "A Workshop Site of Early Man in Dinwiddie County, Virginia." *American Antiquity,* 17 (1): 9–17.
1954 "A Paleo-Indian Workshop Site in Dinwiddie County, Virginia." *Southern Indian Studies,* 6: 9–10.
1961 "Cores from the Williamson Site." *Quarterly Bulletin of the Archaeological Society of Virginia,* 16 (1): 7–9.

McCary, B. C., J. C. Smith, and C. E. Gilliam
1949 "A Folsom Workshop Site on the Williamson Farm, Dinwiddie County, Virginia." *Quarterly Bulletin of the Archaeological Society of Virginia,* 4 (2): 1–8.

MacClintock, P.
1937 "Pleistocene Glacial Stratigraphy of North America." In *Early Man,* eds. G. G. MacCurdy and J. C. Merriam, pp. 115–24. New York.

MacCurdy, G. G.
1917 "The Problem of Man's Antiquity at Vero, Florida." *American Anthropologist,* 19 (2): 152–261.

MacCurdy, G. G., and J. C. Merriam (eds.)
1937 *Early Man.* New York.

MacDonald, G. F.
1966 "The Technology and Settlement Patterns of a Paleo-Indian Site at Debert, Nova Scotia." *Quaternaria,* 8: 59–74.
1971 "A Review of Research on Paleo-Indian in Eastern North America, 1960–1970." *Arctic Anthropology,* 8 (2): 32–41.

McGee, W. J.
1889 "Paleolithic Man in America: His Antiquity and Environment." *Popular Science Monthly,* 34: 20–36.

MacGinitie, H. D.
1958 "Climate Since the Late Cretaceous." In

Zoogeography, ed. C. L. Hubbs, pp. 61–77. Washington, D.C.

MacGowan, K., and J. A. Hester, Jr.
1962 *Early Man in the New World.* Garden City, New York.

McKern, W. C.
1939 "The Midwestern Taxonomic Method as an Aid to Archaeological Study." *American Antiquity,* 4 (4): 301–13.

McKusick, M.
1964 *Men of Ancient Iowa.* Ames, Iowa.

McMillan, R. B.
n.d. "A Preliminary Report on (23PH21) Verkamp Shelter." University of Missouri—Columbia, American Archaeology Division, files.
1962 "The Essman Village Site (23CR263)." *Missouri Archaeological Society Newsletter,* 159: 3–7.
1963 "A Survey and Evaluation of the Archaeology of the Central Gasconade River Valley in Missouri." M.A. Thesis, Department of Anthropology, University of Missouri—Columbia.
1964 "Archaeological Reconnaissance in the Meramec Basin 1963–1964." C. H. Chapman, S. Denny, and R. B. McMillan. "Archaeological Resources in the Bourbeuse River Valley and Lower Meramec Valley of the Meramec Basin Project Area, Missouri." Report to National Park Service on Purchase Order 32-NPS-293, Midwest Research Center, Lincoln, Nebraska, pp. 41–184.
1965a "The Rodgers Shelter, 23BE125: A Preliminary Report." C. H. Chapman and others. Preliminary Archaeological Investigations in the Kaysinger Bluff Reservoir Area. Report to National Park Service on Contracts 14–10–232–374 and 14–10–232–589, Midwest Research Center, Lincoln, Nebraska, pp. 330–405.
1965b "Gasconade Prehistory." *The Missouri Archaeologist,* 27 (3–4): 1–114.
1965c "A Description of Artifacts from the Kaysinger Bluff Area Surface Survey." C. H. Chapman and others. Preliminary Archaeological Investigations in the Kaysinger Bluff Reservoir Area Part II. Report to National Park Service on Contracts 14–10–232–374 and 14–10–232–589, Midwest Research Center, Lincoln, Nebraska, pp. 223–63.
1965d "Archaeological Reconnaissance in the Proposed Hackleman Corner Reservoir, Missouri." Report to National Park Service on Purchase Order 32-NPS-418, Midwest Research Center, Lincoln, Nebraska, pp. 1–83.

1968 "Small Shelter Sites in and near the Stockton Reservoir, Missouri V: Summary and Comments." *Missouri Archaeological Society Newsletter,* 226: 6–11.
1970 "Early Canid Burial from the Western Ozark Highland." *Science,* 167 (3922): 1246–47.
1971 "Biophysical Change and Cultural Adaptation at Rodgers Shelter, Missouri." Ph.D. Dissertation, Department of Anthropology, University of Colorado, Boulder.

MacNeish, R. S.
1948 "The Pre-Pottery Faulkner Site of Southern Illinois." *American Antiquity,* 13 (3): 232–43.
1958 "Preliminary Archaeological Investigations in the Sierra de Tamanlipas, Mexico." *Transactions of the American Philosophical Society,* 48 (6): 1–203.
1959a "A Speculative Framework of Northern North America Prehistory as of April, 1959." *Anthropologica,* n.s., 1: 7–24.
1959b "Man out of Asia: As Seen from the Northwest Yukon." *Anthropological Papers of the University of Alaska,* 7 (2): 41–70.
1963 "The Early Peopling of the New World: As Seen from the Southwestern Yukon." *Anthropological Papers of the University of Alaska,* 10 (2): 93–106.
1964a "The Peopling of the New World as seen from Northwest America." *International Congress of Americanists, Mexico, 1962,* 35 (1): 121–32.
1964b "The Origins of the New World Civilization." *Scientific American,* 211 (5): 29–37.
1964c "Investigations in Southwest Yukon." *Papers of the Robert S. Peabody Foundation for Archaeology,* 6 (2): 201–488.

McQuigg, J. D.
1959 *Climates of the States: Missouri.* Washington, D.C.

Marshall, R. A.
1955 "Salvaged Sites in Greene County, Missouri." *The Missouri Archaeologist,* 17 (4): 7–30.
1956 "Lab Notes." *Missouri Archaeological Society Newsletter,* 102: 10–11.
1957a "Folsomoid Point from Jasper County." *Missouri Archaeological Society Newsletter,* 112: 11.
1957b "The Perkins Farm Site (23CR12)." *Missouri Archaeological Society Newsletter,* 114: 5; 115: 10.
1958 "The Use of Table Rock Reservoir Projectile Points in the Delineation of Cultural Complexes and Their Distribution." M. A. Thesis, Department of Anthropology, University of Missouri—Columbia.

1959 "The Verkamp Shelter, Phelps County, Missouri." University of Missouri— Columbia, American Archaeology Division, files.

1960 "Use of Table Rock Reservoir Projectile Points in the Delineation of Cultural Complexes and Their Distribution." C. H. Chapman and others. Archaeological Investigations in the Table Rock Reservoir Area, Missouri. Report to National Park Service on Contract 14–10–333–96, Midwest Research Center, Lincoln, Nebraska, pp. 5–172.

1963a "A Descriptive System for Projectile Points." *Missouri Archaeological Society Research Series,* No. 1.

1963b "Lander Shelter 2, 23SN245, Stone County, Missouri." *The Missouri Archaeologist,* 25: 109–34.

1963c "Archaeology of Jasper County, Missouri. The Ernest J. Palmer Collection." *Plains Anthropologist,* 8 (19): 1–26.

1965 "Archaeological Investigations in the Meramec Spring, St. James, Missouri Locality." University of Missouri and James Foundation Project. University of Missouri— Columbia, American Archaeology Division, files, pp. 1–283.

Marshall, R. A., and C. H. Chapman
1960a "The Rice Site, 23SN200, Revisited." C. H. Chapman and others. Archaeological Investigations in the Table Rock Reservoir Area, Missouri. Report to National Park Service on Contract 14–10–333–96, Midwest Research Center, Lincoln, Nebraska, pp. 988–1044.

1960b "Cultural Materials from Jakie Shelter, 23BY388." C. H. Chapman and others. Archaeological Investigations in the Table Rock Reservoir Area, Missouri. Report to National Park Service on Contract 14–10–333–96, Midwest Research Center, Lincoln, Nebraska, pp. 1131–49.

Martin, P. S.
1958 "Pleistocene Ecology and Biogeography of North America." In *Zoogeography,* ed. C. L. Hubbs, pp. 375–420. Washington, D.C.

Martin, P. S.
1967a "A Prehistoric Route to America." (Book Review.) *Science,* 158 (3805): 1168.

1967b "Pleistocene Overkill." *Natural History,* 76 (10): 32–38.

1971 "The Revolution in Archaeology." *American Antiquity,* 36 (1): 1–8.

Martin, P. S., G. I. Quimby, and D. Collier
1947 *Indians Before Columbus.* Chicago.

Martin, P. S., and H. E. Wright, Jr. (eds.)
1967 *Pleistocene Extinctions: The Search for a Cause.* Proceedings of the VII Congress of the International Association for Quaternary Research, 6. New Haven.

MASN (see *Missouri Archaeological Society Newsletter*)

Mason, C. I., and R. J. Mason
1961 "The Age of the Old Copper Culture." *The Wisconsin Archaeologist,* 42 (4): 143–55.

Mason, O. T.
1896 "Influence of Environment." *Annual Report of the Smithsonian Institution for 1895:* 639–65.

1912 "Environment." In *Handbook of American Indians North of Mexico,* ed. F. W. Hodge. Bureau of American Ethnology Bulletin, 30 (1): 427–30.

Mason, O. T., and M. S. Hill
1901 "Pointed Bark Conoes of the Kutenai and Amur." *Report of the U.S. National Museum for 1899,* pp. 523–27.

Mason, R. J.
1958 *Late Pleistocene Geochronology and the Paleo-Indian Penetration into the Lower Michigan Peninsula.* Anthropological Papers, Museum of Anthropology, University of Michigan, No. 11.

1959 "Indications of Paleo-Indian Occupation in the Delaware Valley." *Pennsylvania Archaeologist,* 29 (1): 1–17.

1960 "Early Man and the Age of the Champlain Sea." *The Journal of Geology,* 68 (4): 366–76.

1962 "The Paleo-Indian Tradition in Eastern North America." *Current Anthropology,* 3 (3): 227–46.

1963 "Two Late Paleo-Indian Complexes in Wisconsin." *Wisconsin Archaeologist,* 44 (4): 199–211.

Mather, J. R.
1954 "The Effect of Climate on New World Migration of Primitive Man." *Southwestern Journal of Anthropology,* 10 (3): 304–21.

Mattos, A.
1946 "Lagoa Santa Man." In *Handbook of South American Indians,* ed. J. H. Steward. Bureau of American Ethnology Bulletin, No. 143 (1): 399–400.

May, J.
1959 "Projectile Point from Montgomery County, Missouri." *Missouri Archaeological Society Newsletter,* 135: 11.

Mayer-Oakes, W. J.
1951 "Starved Rock Archaic, a Prepottery Horizon from Northern Illinois." *American Antiquity,* 16 (4): 313–24.

1959 "Relationships between Plains Early Hunters and Eastern Archaic." *Journal of the Washington Academy of Science,* 49 (5): 146–56.
1963 "Early Man in the Andes." *Scientific American,* 208 (5): 116–28.

Mayer-Oakes, W. J. (ed.)
1967 *Life, Land and Water.* Winnepeg, Canada.

Mehl, M. G.
1962 *Missouri's Ice Age Animals.* Rolla, Missouri.
1966 *The Grundel Mastodon.* Report on Investigations of the Missouri Geological Survey and Water Resources, No. 35.

Mehringer, P. J., Jr., J. E. King, and E. H. Lindsay
1970 "A Record of Wisconsin-Age Vegetation and Fauna from the Ozarks of Western Missouri." In *Pleistocene and Recent Environments in the Central Great Plains,* eds. W. Dort, Jr., and J. K. Jones, Jr., pp. 174–83. Lawrence, Kansas.

Mehringer, P. J., Jr., C. E. Schweger, W. R. Wood, and R. B. McMillan
1968 "Late-Pleistocene Boreal Forest in the Western Ozark Highlands." *Ecology,* 49 (3): 567–68.

Meighan, C. W.
1965 "Pacific Coast Archaeology." In *The Quaternary of the United States,* eds. H. E. Wright, Jr., and D. G. Frey, pp. 709–20. Princeton.

Meserve, F. G., and E. H. Barbour
1932 "Association of Arrow Point with Bison Occidentalis in Nebraska." *The Nebraska State Museum Bulletin,* 27 (1): 239–42.

Miller, J. P.
1958 "Problems of the Pleistocene in Cordilleran North America, as Related to Reconstruction of Environmental Changes that Affected Early Man." *University of Arizona Bulletin,* 28 (4): 19–50.

Miller, R. K.
1941 "McCain Site, Dubois County, Indiana." *Prehistory Research Series,* 2 (1): 1–60.

Missouri Archaeological Society Newsletter (*MASN*)
1948 "Folsom Points." 23:5.
1949 "Fluted Projectile Points: Collection of Paul V. Sellers, Lewistown." 29: 4.
1950 "Archaeological News." 41: 3.
1952a "Research Project." 56: 6.
1952b "Research Project." 57: 3.
1952c "Research Project." 59: 3.
1954 "Research Project." 80:3.
1956 "Cass County Points." 105: 4.
1957 "Artifacts from Lawrence County." 113: 9.

1958a "Artifacts from Cooper County, Missouri." 118: 6.
1958b "Early Artifacts from Missouri." 120: 2.
1958c "Projectile Points from Phelps County and Bull Shoals." 127: 3.
1959a "Early Points from Boone County, Missouri." 131: 7.
1959b "Bannerstone from Greene County, Missouri." 129: 8.
1959c "Dalton Point from California, Missouri." 129: 8.
1959d "Artifacts from Moniteau County." 130: 9–10.
1960a "Fragment of Bannerstone from Mississippi County, Missouri." 137: 2.
1960b "Eva Basal Notched—Marshall?" 144: 1–2.
1963 174: 7, c.
1965 "Some Artifacts from Gasconade County." 192: 4–5.
1966 199: 11.

Mitman, C. W.
1923 "Catalogue of the Watercraft Collection in the United States National Museum." *United States National Museum Bulletin,* 127: 81–292.

Mohr, C. E.
1964 "Exploring America Underground." *National Geographic Magazine,* 125 (6): 803–37.

Montagu, M. F. A.
1942 "The Earliest Account of the Association of Human Artifacts with Fossil Mammals in North America." *Science,* 95 (2467): 380–81.

Montagu, M. F. A., and C. B. Peterson
1944 "The Earliest Account of the Association of Human Artifacts with Fossil Mammals in North America." *Proceedings of the Philosophical Society,* 87 (5): 407–19.

Morlan, R. E.
1967 "The Preceramic Period of Hokkaido: An Outline." *Arctic Anthropology,* 4 (1): 164–220.

Morrison, W. M., and M. E. Tong, Jr.
1953 "The Seawright Site." *The Missouri Archaeologist,* 15 (4): 10–17.

Morse, D. F.
n.d. "Recent Indications of Dalton Settlement Pattern in Northeast Arkansas." *Arkansas Archaeological Survey.*
1969 "Introducing Northeastern Arkansas Prehistory." *The Arkansas Archaeologist,* 10 (1–3): 12–28.
1971 "The Hawkins Cache: A Significant Dalton Find in Northwest Arkansas." *The Arkansas Archaeologist,* 12 (1): 9–20.

1972 "Dalton Culture in Northeast Arkansas." *Florida Anthropologist,* 26: 23–38.

Morse, D. F., and A. C. Goodyear III
1973 "The Significance of the Dalton Adze in Northeast Arkansas." *Plains Anthropologist,* 18–62 (1–2): 316–22.

Mueller-Beck, H.
1966 "Paleohunters in America: Origins and Diffusion." *Science,* 152 (3726): 1191–1210.

Munson, P.
1967 "Hardin Barbed Projectile Points: Analysis of a Central Illinois Sample." *Central States Archaeological Journal,* 14 (1): 16–19.

Munson, P. J., and N. L. Downs
1968 "A Surface Collection of Plano and Paleo-Indian Projectile Points from Central Illinois." *The Missouri Archaeologist,* 30: 122–28.

Munson, P. J., and J. C. Frye
1965 "Artifacts from Deposits of Mid-Wisconsin Age in Illinois." *Science,* 150 (3704): 1722–23.

Neumann, G. K.
1952 "Archaeology and Race in the American Indian." In *Archeology of Eastern United States,* ed. J. B. Griffin, pp. 13–34. Chicago.

Nichols, G. W.
1970 "The Hinge Fracture Problem in Fluted Point Manufacture." *Memoir, Missouri Archaeological Society,* No. 8: 1–10.

Norris, S. E.
1953 "Is There a Case for Pleistocene Man in Ohio?" *Ohio Archaeologist,* n.s., 3 (2): 19–29.

Oakley, K. P.
1950 *Man the Toolmaker.* London.

Odum, E. P.
1971 *Fundamentals of Ecology,* 3d ed. Philadelphia.

Okladnikov, A. P.
1959 "Ancient Populations of Siberia and Its Cultures." *Russian Translation Series,* 1 (1): 67–68.
1961 "The Paleolithic of Trans-Baikal." *American Antiquity,* 26 (4): 886–97.
1964 "Paleolithic Remains in the Lena River Basin." *Arctic Institute of North America: Anthropology of the North: Translations from Russian Sources,* No. 5: 33–180.

Olson, E. A., and W. S. Broecker
1959 "Lamont Natural Radiocarbon Measurements V." *Radiocarbon,* 1: 1–28.

Orr, C.
1963 "Artifacts from a Multi-Occupation Site." *Missouri Archaeological Society Newsletter,* 176: 8–9.

Owen, L. A.
1909 "Another Paleolithic Implement and Possibly an Eolith From Northwestern Missouri." *Records of the Past,* 8: 108–11.

Pangborn, R. E., H. T. Ward, and W. R. Wood
1967 "Flycatcher Village: A Non-Pottery Site in the Stockton Reservoir, Missouri." *Archaeological Salvage Work in the Stockton Reservoir Area Southewestern Missouri:* 1–31.

Peabody, C., and W. K. Moorehead
1904 "The Exploration of Jacobs Cavern, McDonald County, Missouri." *Phillips Academy, Department of Archaeology, Bulletin 1:* 1–29, 10 plates.

Perino, G.
1968 "Guide to the Identification of Certain American Indian Projectile Points." *Special Bulletin of the Oklahoma Anthropological Society,* No. 3.
1971 "Guide to the Identification of Certain American Indian Projectile Points." *Special Bulletin of the Oklahoma Anthropological Society,* No. 4.

Potter, S.
1970 "Notes on Some Missouri Projectile Points and Knife Blades of the Early Big-Game Hunter Tradition." *Missouri Archaeological Society Newsletter,* No. 244: 1–5.

Powell, J. W.
1893 "Are there evidences of Man in the glacial gravels?" *Popular Science Monthly,* No. 43: 316–26.

Powell, M. J.
1962 "Archaeological Reconnaissance of the Proposed Stockton Reservoir Area." C. H. Chapman and others. A Preliminary Investigation of the Stockton Reservoir Area. Report to National Park Service on Contract 14–10–232–537, Midwest Research Center, Lincoln, Nebraska, pp. 1–68.

Proudfit, S. V.
1889 "Ancient Village Sites and Aboriginal Workshops in the District of Columbia." *American Anthropologist,* o.s., 2 (3): 241–46.

Prufer, O. H.
1960 "Early Man East of the Mississippi." Sonderdruck aus Festschrift für Lothar Zotz: Steinzeit fragen der Alten und Neuen Welt, *The Cleveland Museum of Natural History,* Cleveland, Ohio.

Prufer, O. H., and R. S. Baby
1963 *Paleo-Indians of Ohio.* Columbus, Ohio.

Putnam, F. W.
1888 "On a collection of Paleolithic implements

from America and Europe." *Proceedings of the Boston Society of Natural History,* 23: 421–24.

1890 "Summary Remarks." *Proceedings of the Boston Society of Natural History,* 24: 157–65.

1906 "Evidence of the Work of Man on Objects from Quaternary Caves in California." *American Anthropologist,* n.s., 8 (2): 229–35.

Quimby, G. I.
1956 "The Locus of the Natchez Pelvis Find." *American Antiquity,* 22 (1): 77–79.

1958 "Fluted Points and Geochronology of the Lake Michigan Basin." *American Antiquity,* 23 (3): 247–54.

1960 *Indian Life in the Upper Great Lakes, 11,000 B.C. to A.D. 1800.* Chicago.

Raiz, E.
1957 *Landforms of the United States.* (Map.) Cambridge.

Rau, C.
1873 "North American Stone Implements." *Annual Report of the Smithsonian Institution for 1872:* 395–408.

Ray, C. N.
1934 "Flint Cultures of Ancient Man in Texas." *Bulletin of the Texas Archaeological and Paleontological Society,* 6: 107–11.

1938 "The Clear Fork Culture Complex." *Bulletin of the Texas Archaeological and Paleontological Society,* 10: 193–207.

1941 "The Various Types of Clear Fork Gouges." *Bulletin of the Texas Archaeological and Paleontological Society,* 13: 152–62.

1948 "The Facts Concerning the Clear Fork Culture." *American Antiquity,* 13 (4): 320–22.

Redfield, A.
1966 "The Hardin Point, An Interim Analysis Report." *Bulletin of the Arkansas Archaeological Society,* 7 (3): 53–57.

Redfield, A., and J. H. Moselage
1970 "The Lace Place, a Dalton Project Site in the Western Lowland in Eastern Arkansas." *The Arkansas Archaeologist,* 11 (2): 21–44.

Reeves, C. C., Jr.
1965 "Pluvial Lakes and Pleistocene Climate in the Southern High Plains, Texas." *Great Plains Journal,* 5 (1): 44–50.

Richmond, G. M.
1965 "Glaciation of the Rocky Mountains." In *The Quaternary of the United States,* eds. H. E. Wright, Jr., and D. G. Frey, pp. 217–30. Princeton.

Ridley, F.
1960 "Transatlantic Contacts of Primitive Man: Eastern Canada and Northeastern Russia." *Pennsylvania Archaeologist,* 30 (2): 46–57.

Ritchie, W. A.
1957 "Traces of Early Man in the Northeast." *New York State Museum and Science Service Bulletin,* No. 358: 1–91.

1958 "The Paleo-Indian in the Northeast." *Massachusetts Archaeological Society Bulletin,* 19 (2): 21–22.

1961 "Typology and Nomenclature for New York Projectile Points." *New York State Museum and Science Service Bulletin,* 384: 1–119.

1965 *The Archaeology of New York State.* Garden City, New York.

Ritzenthaler, R. E.
1958 "Some Carbon 14 Dates for the Wisconsin Old Copper Culture." *The Wisconsin Archaeologist,* 39 (3): 173–74.

1966 "The Kouba Site: Paleo-Indians in Wisconsin." *The Wisconsin Archaeologist,* n.s., 47 (4): 171–87.

1967a "A Cache of Paleo-Indian Gravers from the Kouba Site." *The Wisconsin Archaeologist,* 48 (3): 261–62.

1967b "A Probable Paleo-Indian Site in Wisconsin." *American Antiquity,* 32 (2): 227–29.

1967c *A Guide to Wisconsin Indian Projectile Point Types.* Milwaukee Public Museum.

Ritzenthaler, R. E. (ed.)
1957 "The Old Copper Culture of Wisconsin." *The Wisconsin Archaeologist,* 38 (4): 186–328.

Ritzenthaler, R. E., and G. I. Quimby
1962 *The Red Ochre Culture of the Upper Great Lakes and Adjacent Areas.* Fieldiana: Anthropology, 36 (11).

Roberts, F. H. H., Jr.
1935 "A Folsom Complex: Preliminary Report on the Investigations at the Lindenmeier Site in Northern Colorado." *Smithsonian Miscellaneous Collections,* 94 (3): 1–35.

1936 "Additional Information on the Folsom Complex: Report on the Second Season's Investigations at the Lindenmeier Site in Northern Colorado." *Smithsonian Miscellaneous Collections,* 95 (10): 1–38.

1937 "The Folsom Problem in American Archaeology." In *Early Man,* eds. G. G. MacCurdy and J. C. Merriam, pp. 153–72. New York.

1940 "Developments in the Problem of the North American Paleo-Indian." *Smithsonian Miscellaneous Collections,* 100: 51–116.

1943 "Notes and News: A New Site." *American*

Antiquity, 8 (3): 300.
1951 "The Early Americans." *Scientific American,* 184 (2): 20–22.

Roberts, R. G.
1965 "Tick Creek Cave, An Archaic Site in the Gasconade River Valley of Missouri." *The Missouri Archaeologist,* 27 (2): 1–52.

Rogers, M. J.
1966 *Ancient Hunters of the Far West.* San Diego.

Rolingson, M. A.
1964 *Paleo-Indian Culture in Kentucky.* Lexington.

Rolingson, M. A., and D. W. Schwartz
1966 *Late Paleo-Indian and Early Archaic Manifestations in Western Kentucky.* Lexington.

Roosa, W. B.
1956 "The Lucy Site in Central New Mexico." *American Antiquity,* 21 (3): 310.
1965 "Some Great Lakes Fluted Point Types." *The Michigan Archaeologist,* 11 (3–4): 89–102.

Rouse, I.
1950 "Vero and Melbourne Man: A Cultural and Chronological Interpretation." *New York Academy of Science Transactions,* 12: 220–24.
1951 "A Survey of Indian River Archaeology, Florida." *Yale Publications in Anthropology,* No. 44: 1–263.
1952 "The Age of the Melbourne Interval." *Bulletin of the Texas Archeological and Paleontological Society,* 23: 293–99.
1960 *The Entry of Man into the West Indies.* Yale University Publications in Anthropology, No. 61.
1964 "The Caribbean Area." In *Prehistoric Man in the New World,* eds. J. D. Jennings and E. Norbeck, pp. 389–417. Chicago.

Rudenko, S. I.
1961 "The Ust-Kanskaia Paleolithic Cave Site." *American Antiquity,* 27 (2): 203–15.
1964 "The Culture of the Prehistoric Population of Kamchatka." *Arctic Institute of North America: Anthropology of the North: Translations from Russian Sources,* 5: 265–95.

Salisbury, R. D.
1893 "Man and the Glacial Period." *The American Geologist,* 11 (1): 13–20.

Sauer, C. O.
1920 *The Geography of the Ozark Highland of Missouri.* Chicago.
1944 "A Geographic Sketch of Early Man in America." *The Geographical Review,* 34 (4): 529–73.
1947 "Early Relations of Man to Plants." *The Geographical Review,* 37 (1): 1–25.

1957 "The End of the Ice Age and Its Witnesses." *The Geographical Review,* 47 (1): 29–43.

Schoonover, M.
1960 "The Schoonover Point—A New Type." *Ohio Archaeologist,* 10 (3): 102–3.

Schwartz, C. W., and E. R. Schwartz
1959 *The Wild Mammals of Missouri.* Columbia.

Schwartz, D. W.
1967 *Conceptions of Kentucky Prehistory.* Studies in Anthropology, 6. Lexington.

Scrivner, C. L., J. C. Baker, and B. J. Miller
1966 *Soils of Missouri.* Columbia.

Scully, E.
1951 "Some Central Mississippi Valley Projectile Point Types." (Mimeo.) Museum of Anthropology, University of Michigan.

Sears, P. B.
1948 "Forest Sequence and Climatic Change in Northeastern North America Since Early Wisconsin Time." *Ecology,* 29 (3): 326–33.

Seelen, R. M.
1961 "A Preliminary Report of the Sedalia Complex." *Missouri Archaeological Society Newsletter,* No. 153.

Sellards, E. H.
1916 "Human Remains and Associated Fossils from the Pleistocene of Florida." *Florida State Geological Survey Annual Report,* 8: 121–60.
1917 "Review of the Evidence on which the Human Remains Found at Vero are Referred to the Pleistocene." *Florida State Geological Survey Annual Report,* 9: 69–143.
1937 "The Vero Finds in the Light of Present Knowledge." In *Early Man,* eds., G. G. MacCurdy and J. C. Merriam, pp. 193–211. New York.
1940 "Pleistocene Artifacts and Associated Fossils from Bee County, Texas." *Geological Society of America Bulletin,* 51 (11): 1627–58.
1941 "Stone Images from Henderson County, Texas." *American Antiquity,* 7 (1): 29–38.
1947 "Early Man in America." *Geological Society of America Bulletin,* 58 (10): 955–78.
1952 *Early Man in America: A Study in Prehistory.* Austin, Texas.
1960 "Some Early Stone Artifact Developments in North America." *Southwestern Journal of Anthropology,* 16 (2): 160–73.

Sellards, E. H., G. L. Evans, G. Meade, and A. D. Krieger
1947 "Fossil Bison and Associated Artifacts from Plainview, Texas." *Geological Society of America Bulletin,* 58 (10): 927–54.

Sellers, P. V.
1956 "Fluted Points." *Central States Archaeological Journal,* 2 (3): 112–13.

Semenov, S. A.
1964 *Prehistoric Technology.* New York.

Sharrock, L. W., and others
1964 *1962 Excavations, Glen Canyon Area.* University of Utah Anthropological Papers, 77. Glen Canyon Series 25. Salt Lake City.

Shelford, V. E.
1963 *The Ecology of North America.* Urbana.

Shetrone, H. C.
1936 "The Folsom Phenomenon as Seen from Ohio." *Quarterly of the Ohio State Archaeological and Historical Society,* 45: 240–56.

Shimek, B.
1917 "The Loess and the Antiquity of Man." *Iowa Academy of Science Proceedings,* 24: 93–98.

Shippee, J. M.
1948 "Nebo Hill, A Lithic Complex in Western Missouri." *American Antiquity,* 14 (1): 29–32.
1950 "An Oblique Parallel Flaked Point from Missouri." *American Antiquity,* 16 (2): 164.
1953 "A Folsom Fluted Point from Marshall County, Kansas." *Plains Archaeological Conference Newsletter,* 5 (4): 54.
1954 "The Typical Nebo Hill Projectile Point." *Missouri Archaeological Society Newsletter,* No. 77: 5.
1955 "Cave Investigations." *Missouri Archaeological Society Newsletter,* 94: 2–4.
1957a "Research Cave Explorations." In *A Report of Progress: Archaeological Research by the University of Missouri 1955–1956,* pp. 49–56. A Special Publication of the Missouri Archaeological Society, Columbia.
1957b "The Diagnostic Point Type of the Nebo Hill Complex." *The Missouri Archaeologist,* 19 (3): 42–46.
1959 "Collateral Flaking on a Point Found Near Kansas City, Missouri." *Missouri Archaeological Society Newsletter,* 136: 11.
1961 "Comparison of Traits Between Sedalia and Nebo Hill Traits." *Missouri Archaeological Society Newsletter,* No. 154: 11.
1962 "Transriver Variations in Artifacts of Nebo Hill Complex Sites." *Missouri Archaeological Society Newsletter,* No. 162: 3–9.
1964 "Archaeological Remains in the Area of Kansas City: Paleo-Indians and the Archaic Period." *Missouri Archaeological Society Research Series,* No. 2: 1–42.
1966 "The Archaeology of Arnold-Research Cave, Callaway County, Missouri," *The Missouri Archaeologist,* 28: 1–107.

Shutler, R. J., Jr.
1968 "Tule Springs: Its Implications to Early Man Studies in North America." *Eastern New Mexico University, Contributions in Anthropology,* 1 (4): 19–26.

Shutler, R. J., Jr. (ed.)
1971 "Papers from a Symposium on Early Man in North America, New Developments: 1960–1970, held at the American Anthropological Association Meetings, San Diego, California, November 18–22, 1970." *Arctic Anthropology,* 8 (2): 1–2.

Silverberg, R.
1968 *Mound Builders of Ancient America.* Greenwich, Connecticut.

Simpson, G. G.
1943 "The Beginnings of Vertebrate Paleontology in North America." *Proceedings of the American Philosophical Society,* 86: 130–88.

Simpson, J. C.
1948 "Folsom-Like Points from Florida." *The Florida Anthropologist,* 1 (1–2): 11–15.

Smail, W.
1951a "Fluted Points from Missouri." *The Missouri Archaeologist,* 13 (1): 18–20.
1951b "Some Early Projectile Points from the St. Louis Area." *Journal of the Illinois State Archaeological Society,* n.s., 2 (1): 11–16.

Smith, A. G.
1953 "Waterworn Artifacts from Late Pleistocene Lake Beaches in Northern Ohio." *American Antiquity,* 19 (2): 156–57.
1954 "Waterworn Artifacts from Late Pleistocene Lake Beaches in Northern Ohio." *Ohio Archaeologist,* n.s., 4 (1): 30–33.

Smith, P. S.
1937 "Certain Relations Between Northwestern America and Northeastern Asia." In *Early Man,* eds. G. G. MacCurdy and J. C. Merriam, pp. 84–92. New York.

Soday, F. J.
1954 "The Quad Site, A Paleo-Indian Village in Northern Alabama." *Tennessee Archaeologist,* 10 (1): 1–20.

Solecki, R. S.
1951 "How Man Came to North America." *Scientific American,* 184 (1): 11–15.

Sollas, W. J.
1924 *Ancient Hunters.* New York, 3d revised ed.

Spencer, R. F., J. D. Jennings, and others.
1965 *The Native Americans.* New York.

Stalker, A. M.
1969 "Geology and Age of the Early Man Site at Taber, Alberta." *American Antiquity,* 34 (4): 425–28.

Stephenson, R. L.
1965 "Quaternary Occupation of the Plains." In *The Quaternary of the United States,* eds. H. E. Wright, Jr., and D. G. Frey, pp. 685–96. Princeton.

Steward, J. H.
1954 "Types of Types." *American Anthropologist,* 56 (1): 54–57.

Steward, J. H., and L. C. Faron
1959 *Native Peoples of South America.* New York.

Stewart, T. D.
1946 "A Reexamination of the Fossil Human Skeletal Remains from Melbourne, Florida, With Further Data on the Vero Skull." *Smithsonian Miscellaneous Collections,* 106 (10).
1951 "Antiquity of Man in America Demonstrated by the Fluorine Test." *Science,* 113 (2936): 391–92.
1960 "A Physical Anthropologist's View of the Peopling of the New World." *Southwestern Journal of Anthropology,* 16 (3): 259–73.

Steyermark, J. A.
1963 *Flora of Missouri.* Iowa City.

Stock, C.
1936 "The Succession of Mammalian Forms with the Period in which Human Remains are Known to Occur in America." *American Naturalist,* 70 (729): 324–31.

Stoltman, J. B., and K. Workman
1969 "A Preliminary Study of Wisconsin Fluted Points." *The Wisconsin Archaeologist,* 50 (4): 189–214.

Strong, W. D.
1935 "An Introduction to Nebraska Archaeology." *Smithsonian Miscellaneous Collections,* 93 (10).

Struever, S.
1968 "Problems, Methods and Organizations: A Disparity in the Growth of Archaeology." In *Anthropological Archaeology in the Americas, The Anthropological Society of Washington,* pp. 131–51. Washington, D.C.
1971 "Comments on Archaeological Data Requirements and Research Strategy." *American Antiquity,* 36 (1): 9–19.

Stubbs, F. L.
1950 "A Preliminary Report on the Mill Creek Area of Andrew County, Missouri." *The Missouri Archaeologist,* 12 (1): 1–48.

Stuckenrath, R., Jr.
1966 "The Debert Archaeological Project, Nova Scotia: Radio-Carbon Dating." *Quaternaria,* 8: 75–80.

Sudderth, W. E.
1965 "The Harrison Shelter, 23SR117." C. H. Chapman and others. Preliminary Archaeological Investigations in the Kaysinger Bluff Reservoir Area. Report to National Park Service on Contracts 14–10–232–374 and 14–10–232–589, Midwest Research Center, Lincoln, Nebraska, pp. 503–30.

Sudderth, W. E., and C. H. Chapman
1965 "The Woody Shelter, 23SR140." C. H. Chapman and others. Preliminary Archaeological Investigations in the Kaysinger Bluff Reservoir Area. Report to National Park Service on Contracts 14–10–232–374 and 14–10–232–589, Midwest Research Center, Lincoln, Nebraska, pp. 531–41.

Suhm, D. A., and E. B. Jelks (eds.)
1962 *Handbook of Texas Archeology: Type Descriptions.* Austin, Texas.

Suhm, D. A., A. D. Krieger, and E. B. Jelks
1954 "An Introductory Handbook of Texas Archaeology." *Bulletin of the Texas Archeological Society,* 25: 1–565.

Swanson, E. H., Jr.
1966 "Ecological Communities in Northwest Prehistory." *Quaternaria,* 8: 91–99.

Thomas, E. S.
1952 "The Orleton Farms Mastodon." *Ohio Journal of Science,* 52 (1): 1–5.

Thomas, W.
1898 "Prehistoric Art." *Report of the National Museum for 1896.* Washington, D.C.

Titterington, P.
1950 "Some Non-Pottery Sites in the St. Louis Area." *Illinois State Archaeological Society,* n.s., 1 (1): 19–31.

Tong, M. E.
1951a "The Tecumseh Site, Ozark County, Missouri." *The Missouri Archaeologist,* 13 (1): 21–26.
1951b "The Isom Corp Site, Ozark County, Missouri." *The Missouri Archaeologist,* 13 (1): 27–31.
1955 "An Archaic Manifestation at the Mouth of Hurricane Hollow, Ozark County, Missouri." *The Missouri Archaeologist,* 17 (4): 31–35.

Transeau, E. N.
1935 "The Prairie Peninsula." *Ecology,* 16 (3): 423–37.

Turner, R.
1965 "Green Ridge: A Late Archaic Site of the Sedalia Complex in West-Central Missouri." *Missouri Archaeological Society Research Series,* No. 3.

Tuttle, D.
1954 "A Dalton or Meserve Point from St. Louis County, Missouri." *Missouri Archaeological Society Newsletter,* 86: 7.

University of Missouri—Columbia. Archaeological Society of Missouri, files (UMC, ASM, files).

Upham, W.
1888 "The Recession of the Ice-Sheet in Minnesota in its Relation to the Gravel Deposits Analyzing the Quartz Implements Found by Miss Babbitt at Little Falls, Minn." *Proceedings of the Boston Society of Natural History,* 23: 436–49.
1893 "Man and the Glacial Period." *The American Geologist,* 11 (3): 189–91.

Upp, G.
1953 "Fifty Archaeological Sites in Central Missouri." *The Missouri Archaeologist,* 15 (3): 9–56.

Valoch, K.
1968 "Evolution of the Paleolithic in Central and Eastern Europe." *Current Anthropology,* 9 (5): 351–68.

Villiers, A.
1963 "Ships through the Ages: A Saga of the Sea." *National Geographic Magazine,* 123 (4): 494–545.

Walter, H. V., A. Cathoud, and A. Mattos
1937 "The Confins Man—A Contribution to the Study of Early Man in South America." In *Early Man,* eds. G. G. MacCurdy and J. C. Merriam, pp. 341–48. New York.

Watson, P. J., S. A. Leblanc, and C. L. Redman
1971 *Explanation in Archaeology.* New York and London.

Wayne, W. J.
1967 "Periglacial Features and Climatic Gradient in Illinois, Indiana and Western Ohio, East Central United States." In *Quaternary Paleoecology,* eds. E. J. Cushing and H. E. Wright, Jr., pp. 393–414. New Haven and London.

Webb, W. S.
1951 *The Parish Village Site, Site 45 Hopkins County, Kentucky.* University of Kentucky Reports in Anthropology, University of Kentucky, 3 (2).

Webb, W. S., and W. D. Funkhouser
1934 "The Occurrence of the Fossil Remains of Pleistocene Vertebrates in the Caves of Barren County, Kentucky." *Reports in Archaeology and Anthropology, the University of Kentucky,* 3: 39–65.

Wedel, W. R.
1943 *Archaeological Investigations in Platte and Clay Counties, Missouri.* United States National Museum Bulletin, 183.
1959 *An Introduction to Kansas Archaeology.* Bureau of American Ethnology Bulletin 174.
1964 "The Great Plains." In *Prehistoric Man in the New World,* eds. J. D. Jennings and E. Norbeck, pp. 193–220. Chicago.

Wendorf, F. E.
1961a "A General Introduction to the Ecology of the Llano Estacado." In *The Paleoecology of the Llano Estacado,* ed. F. E. Wendorf, pp. 12–31. Santa Fe.
1961b "An Interpretation of Late Pleistocene Environments of the Llano Estacado." In *The Paleoecology of the Llano Estacado,* ed. F. E. Wendorf, pp. 115–33. Santa Fe.
1961c "Appendix I: A Listing of Radiocarbon Dates." In *The Paleoecology of the Llano Estacado,* ed. F. E. Wendorf, pp. 134–36. Santa Fe.
1966 "Early Man in the New World: Problems of Migration." *The American Naturalist,* 100 (912): 253–70.

Wendorf, F., and J. J. Hester
1962 "Early Man's Utilization of the Great Plains Environment." *American Antiquity,* 28 (2): 159–71.

West, F. H.
1963 "Leaf-Shaped Points in the Western Arctic." *Anthropological Papers of the University of Alaska,* 10 (2): 51–71.

Weyer, E. M., Jr.
1964 "New World Lithic Typology Project: Part I." *American Antiquity,* 29 (4): 487–89.

Wheat, J. B.
1971 "Lifeways of Early Man in North America." *Arctic Anthropology,* 8 (2): 22–31.

Whitby, B.
1967 "The Beothucks and Other Primitive Peoples of Newfoundland: A Review." *Anthropological Journal of Canada,* 5 (4): 2–19.

Willey, G. R.
1966 *An Introduction to American Archaeology: Volume One, North and Middle America.* Englewood Cliffs, New Jersey.

Willey, G. R., and P. Phillips
1958 *Method and Theory in American Archaeology.* Chicago.

Williams, J. R.
1959 "Wayne County, Missouri: Prehistory." Paper for Anthropology, Problems Course 400. University of Missouri—Columbia, Archaeological Survey of Missouri, files.
1968 "Preliminary Evaluation of the Owls Bend Area in Shannon County, Missouri." A manuscript submitted to the Midwest Region, National Park Service, 1–23–68.

Williams, S.
1957 "The Island 35 Mastodon: Its Bearing on the Age of Archaic Cultures in the East." *American Antiquity,* 22 (4): 359–72.
1965 "The Paleo-Indian Era: Distribution of Finds." *Southeastern Archaeological Conference Bulletin,* No. 2.

Williams, S., and J. B. Stoltman
1965 "An Outline of Southeastern United States Prehistory with particular Emphasis on the Paleo-Indian Era." In *The Quaternary of the United States,* eds. H. E. Wright, Jr., and D. G. Frey, pp. 669–84. Princeton.

Williston, S. W.
1897 "Homo Sapiens in Pleistocene of Kansas." *Bulletin, Kansas University Geological Survey,* 2: 301.
1902 "A Fossil Man from Kansas." *Science,* 16 (396): 195–96.

Wilmsen, E. N.
1965 "An Outline of Early Man Studies in the United States." *American Antiquity,* 31 (2): 172–92.
1968a "Lithic Analysis in Paleoanthropology." *Science,* 161 (3845): 982–87.
1968b "Paleo-Indian Site Utilization." In *Anthropological Archaeology in the Americas, Anthropological Society of Washington, D.C.,* pp. 22–40. Brooklyn, New York.
1970 *Lithic Analysis and Cultural Inference: A Paleo-Indian Case.* Anthropological Papers of the University of Arizona, No. 16.

Wilson, M. T.
1895 "On the Presence of Fluorine as a Test for the Fossilization of Animal Bones." *The American Naturalist,* 29 (340): 301–17; 29 (341): 439–56; 29 (344): 719–25.

Wilson, T.
1895 "Paleolithic Man." *The American Naturalist,* 29 (342): 599–600.
1889 "The Paleolithic Period in the District of Columbia." *American Anthropologist,* o.s., 2 (3): 235–41.

Wilson, W. R.
1962 "23JA35, The Turner-Casey Site: A Nebo Complex site in Eastern Jackson County." *Missouri Archaeological Society Newsletter,* 161: 3–11.

Winchell, N. H.
1913 "A Consideration of the Paleoliths of Kansas. No. 1, The weathering of aboriginal stone Artifacts." *Minnesota Historical Society Collections,* 16 (pt. 1).

Winsor, J. (ed.)
1889 *Narrative and Critical History of North America, Vol. 1. Aboriginal America.* Cambridge.

Winters, H. D.
1962 "Distribution Patterns of Fluted Points in Southern Illinois." *Report No. 10 to Council for Illinois Archaeology.* (Mimeo.) Springfield.
1963 *An Archaeological Survey of the Wabash Valley in Illinois.* Illinois State Museum Reports of Investigations, No. 10.
1967 *An Archaeological Survey of the Wabash Valley in Illinois.* Illinois State Museum Report of Investigations, No. 10.
1968 "Value Systems and Trade Cycles of the Late Archaic in the Midwest." In *New Perspectives in Archaeology,* eds. S. R. Binford and L. R. Binford, pp. 175–222. Chicago.
1969 *The Riverton Culture.* Illinois State Museum Report of Investigations, No. 13.

Wislizenus, A.
1860 "Was Man Contemporaneous with the Mastodon?" *Transactions of the Academy of Science of St. Louis,* 1: 168–71.

Wissler, C.
1938 *The American Indian.* New York.

Witthoft, J.
1952 "A Paleo-Indian Site in Eastern Pennsylvania: An Early Hunting Culture." *Proceedings of the American Philosophical Society,* 96 (4): 464–95.
1954 "A Note on Fluted Point Relationships." *American Antiquity,* 19 (3): 271–73.
1957a "The Art of Flint Chipping: The Human Factor: Flint Technology." *Ohio Archaeologist,* 7 (1): 17–20, 35.
1957b "The Art of Flint Chipping." *Ohio Archaeologist,* 7 (2): 42–46.
1957c "The Art of Flint Chipping: Bladelets and Microblades." *Ohio Archaeologist,* 7 (3): 80–88, 92.

Wittry, W. L.
1959a "The Raddatz Rockshelter, SK5, Wisconsin." *The Wisconsin Archeologist*, 40 (2): 33–82.
1959b "Archeology Studies of Four Wisconsin Rockshelters." *The Wisconsin Archeologist*, 40 (4): 137–267.
1965 "The Institute digs a Mastodon." *Cranbrook Institute of Science Newsletter*, 35 (2): 14–19.

Wittry, W. L., and R. E. Ritzenthaler
1956 "The Old Copper Complex: An Archaic Manifestation in Wisconsin." *American Antiquity*, 21 (3): 244–54.

Witty, T. A., Jr.
1969 "Notes on Flint Hills Archaeology." *Kansas Anthropological Association Newsletter*, 14 (8).

Wood, W. R.
1957 "Five Projectile Points from Western Missouri." *Missouri Archaeological Society Newsletter*, 116: 10–11.
1961 "The Pomme de Terre Reservoir in Western Missouri Prehistory." *The Missouri Archaeologist*, 23: 1–131.
1963 "Breckenridge Shelter—3CR2 An Archeological Chronicle in the Beaver Reservoir Area." *Arkansas Archeology*, 1962: 67–96.

Wood, W. R., and R. B. McMillan
1967 "Recent Investigations at Rodgers Shelter, Missouri." *Archeology*, 20 (1): 52–55.
1969 "Archaeology and Paleontology of the Western Ozark Highlands." A final report to the National Science Foundation.

Wood, W. R., and R. E. Pangborn
1968a "Small Shelter Sites in and near the Stockton Reservoir I: Mache Hollow Shelter, 23CE–111." *Missouri Archaeological Society Newsletter*, 221: 8–12.
1968b "Small Shelter Sites in and near the Stockton Reservoir, Missouri III: Toler Cave, 23DA–207." *Missouri Archaeological Society Newsletter*, 222: 2–10.

Woodall, J. N.
1972 *An Introduction to Modern Archaeology.* Cambridge, Mass.

Wormington, H. M.
1944 *Ancient Man in North America.* Denver.
1957 *Ancient Man in North America.* 3d ed., revised. Denver, Colorado.
1962 "A Survey of Early American Prehistory." *American Scientist*, 50 (1): 230–42.
1964a "Problems Relating to Paleolithic Flaking Techniques in the New World." *International Congress of Americanists, Mexico 1962*, 35 (1): 9–10.

1964b "The Problem of the Presence and Dating in America of Flaking Techniques Similar to the Paleolithic in the Old World." *The Minnesota Archaeologist*, 26 (4): 133–43.
1964c "Supplementary Comments on Tule Springs." *The Minnesota Archaeologist*, 26 (4): 145.
1971 "Comments on Early Man in North America, 1960–1970." *Arctic Anthropology*, 8 (2): 83–91.

Wormington, H. M., and R. G. Forbis
1965 "An Introduction to the Archaeology of Alberta, Canada." *Proceedings Denver Museum of Natural History*, Number 11: 1–207.

Wrench, J. E., B. Berry, and C. Chapman
1940 "The Archaeology of Wayne County." *The Missouri Archaeologist*, 6 (1): 1–40.

Wright, G. F.
1888 "On the Age of the Ohio Gravel Beds." *Proceedings of the Boston Society of Natural History*, 23: 427–36.
1890 "The Age of the Philadelphia Red Gravels." *Proceedings of the Boston Society of Natural History*, 24: 152–57.
1892 *Man and the Glacial Period.* New York.
1893 "Evidences of Glacial Man in Ohio." *Popular Science Monthly*, 43 (1): 29–39.
1895 "New Evidence of Glacial Man in Ohio." *American Naturalist*, 29 (346): 951–53.
1912 *Origin and Antiquity of Man.* Oberlin, Ohio.

Wright, H. E., Jr.
1968 "History of the Prairie Peninsula." In *The Quaternary of Illinois*, ed. R. E. Bergstrom, pp. 78–88. Urbana.
1970 "Vegetational History of the Central Plains." In *Pleistocene and Recent Environments of the Central Great Plains*, eds. W. Dort, Jr., and J. K. Jones, pp. 157–72. Lawrence, Kansas.

Wright, H. E., Jr., and D. G. Frey (eds.)
1965 *The Quaternary of the United States.* Princeton.

Wright, H. E., Jr., and R. V. Ruhe
1965 "Glaciation of Minnesota and Iowa." In *The Quaternary of the United States*, eds. H. E. Wright, Jr., and D. G. Frey, pp. 29–41. Princeton, New Jersey.

Yarnell, R. A.
1964 *Aboriginal Relationships between Culture and Plant Life in the Upper Great Lakes Region.* Anthropological Papers, Museum of Anthropology, University of Michigan, No. 23.

Zimmerman, E.
1955 "A Cache of Early Blades." *Missouri Archaeological Society Newsletter*, 91: 9.
1957 "Artifacts from St. Francois County." *Missouri Archaeological Society Newsletter*, 113: 3.

Index

Pages indicating figures are in italics, those denoting charts are in parentheses.